AF600106

SPACE AND SELF IN EARLY MODERN EUROPEAN CULTURES

SPACE AND SELF IN EARLY MODERN EUROPEAN CULTURES

Edited by
David Warren Sabean and
Malina Stefanovska

Published by the University of Toronto Press in association with the UCLA Center for Seventeenth- and Eighteenth-Century Studies and the William Andrews Clark Memorial Library

www.utppublishing.com

ISBN 978-1-4426-4394-9

Library and Archives Canada Cataloguing in Publication

Space and self in early modern European cultures / edited by David Warren Sabean and Malina Stefanovska.

(UCLA Clark Memorial Library series)
Includes bibliographical references and index.
ISBN 978-1-4426-4394-9

1. Self – Europe – History – 17th century. 2. Self – Europe – History – 18th century. 3. Space – Social aspects – Europe – History – 17th century. 4. Space – Social aspects – Europe – History – 18th century. 5. Self in literature. 6. Self in art. I. Sabean, David Warren II. Stefanovska, Malina III. Series: UCLA Clark Memorial Library series

BF697.S67 2012 155.2'09409032 C2012-901622-5

This book has been published with the help of a grant from the UCLA Center for Seventeenth- and Eighteenth-Century Studies.

University of Toronto Press acknowledges the financial assistance to its publishing program of the Canada Council for the Arts and the Ontario Arts Council.

Canada Council for the Arts Conseil des Arts du Canada

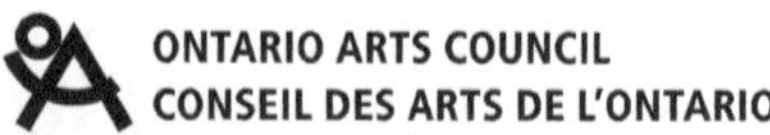

University of Toronto Press acknowledges the financial support of the Government of Canada through the Canada Book Fund for its publishing activities.

To
Peter Hanns Reill

Contents

PART III: NEW DIMENSIONS: INTERSTICES AND INTENSITIES

Figures

Acknowledgments

We would like to thank the UCLA Center for Seventeenth- and Eighteenth-Century Studies and the William Andrews Clark Memorial Library for generous help in organizing, in 2007–8, 'Spaces of the Self,' the series of conferences that provided the basis for this book. We are grateful to all the participants whose scholarly contributions and animated discussions contributed to our topic. Our conferences could not have materialized without the expertise of Center staff Candis Snoddy, Suzanne Tatian, Alistair Thorne, Elizabeth Landaw, Camie Howard-Rock, and Mark Pokorski; or of Clark librarians Bruce Whiteman, Nina Schneider, Carol Sommer, and Rebecca Fenning, with their assistant, Scott Jacobs. Our book would not have been possible without the critical and meticulous editing done by Ellen Wilson, the contribution of the University of Toronto Press acquisitions editor Richard Ratzlaff, and the work of copyeditor John St James. Finally, both conferences and book are greatly indebted to Center/Clark director Peter Reill and assistant director Patrick Coleman, whom we thank heartily.

Our gratitude goes in particular to Peter Reill, who has devoted twenty years of his academic career to serving as the director of both the Center and the Clark. During his tenure, Peter has considerably expanded the reach and broadened the nature and scope of their academic and public programs, and has truly transformed the library, and with it UCLA, as a destination for scholars and students of early modern European history and literature. Without his unflinching encouragement and support this book would not have been possible.

The topic of this book, space and self, has naturally invited visual as well as verbal explorations, and for this we are especially indebted to the following institutions, which have graciously supplied us with images of items in their holdings and licenses for their reproduction in our volume: Bayerische Staatsbibliothek München; Bridgeman Art Library; British Library; Collection Rijksmuseum, Amsterdam; Gemäldegalerie and Kupferstichkabinett, Staatliche Museen zu Berlin/Jörg P. Anders, both through bpk; National Gallery, Prague; Niedersächsische Staats- und Universitätsbibliothek Göttingen; Research Library, The Getty Research Institute, Los Angeles; Special Collections, University of Amsterdam; Special Collections, Young Research Library, University of California, Los Angeles; The Huntington Library, San Marino, California; The Newberry Library, Chicago; The Reeves Center, Washington and Lee University, Lexington, Virginia; The Trustees of the British Museum; and Universitäts- und Landesbibliothek Darmstadt.

David Warren Sabean
Malina Stefanovska
Los Angeles, California, December 2010

SPACE AND SELF IN EARLY MODERN EUROPEAN CULTURES

Introduction

DAVID WARREN SABEAN AND MALINA STEFANOVSKA

The World that I regard is my selfe.

Sir Thomas Browne[1]

Le silence éternel de ces espaces infinis m'effraie.

Blaise Pascal[2]

The notion of the self has been a central focus of inquiries in philosophy, psychology, literary studies, and many other disciplines.[3] Those historians who have chronicled its transformations have tended to develop teleological narratives leading towards greater reflexivity, psychological depth, and consistency of personality. Indeed, 'selfhood' seems to imply integrity, self-sufficiency, introspectiveness, and autonomy, characteristics of 'modernity' and, in many versions of the story, of the Western world.[4] Yet, although 'pre-*modern*,' and 'early *modern*' have been fitted into this genealogy, with the 'long' seventeenth century marking the crucial transition to the new (inevitably 'bourgeois') selfhood, we suggest that there have been at all times multiple tracks and alternative possibilities for forming identities, marking personhood, experiencing life as concrete, singular individuals, or constructing subjectivities. The very ambiguity of the word 'subject' points to its two opposite origins – subjection and autonomy – while the absence (or recent coining) of the term 'self' in a number of national languages, testifies to its historical and cultural origins and limitations.[5]

The chapters in this volume are meant to be exploratory. They demonstrate the complex and varied possibilities for being selves in the early modern period. Collectively they hardly add up to a narrative of origins and trajectories, although they situate the issues within the rise of new institutions, perceptual apparatuses, technologies, political operations, and theatres of activity. They cover a wide range of geographical and conceptual domains and quite diverse artefacts, from images to texts, instruments, words, sculptures, and maps. Each of them investigates the reciprocal implications of space and self in specific historical manifestations. In general, they operate within three broad areas, indicated, though not circumscribed, by the triadic structure of the book: places and their *habituses*, embodied selves as they are plotted in and through space, and their reciprocal interpenetration, or their common borders.

The first concerns the way in which individual existence is concretely embedded in spaces constituted by rules and practices, defined as private or social, as sites of contemplation or expression, of inclusion and exclusion, of subjection and of mediation between self and others.[6] These locales have to be understood in their historical specificity: the Renaissance scholarly study, a print club in eighteenth-century London, the stage of Richelieu's political theatre, or the disoriented, goalless pilgrimage of a Protestant refugee. They operate within certain fundamental differentiations, such as the ontological opposition between sacred and secular. Thus, courts and salons provided grounds for 'self-fashioning' profoundly different from convents, chapels, and religious retreats. Perhaps even more difficult to grasp is the pendular movement between these two realms – the public ceremony and the solitude of the 'desert' – by the same individuals.[7] The contributions to this book illustrate in multiple ways how space and place play a fundamental role in producing the self, framing it, situating it, and giving it concrete expression.[8]

But one must not imagine a series of static sites between which early modern people might wander: space itself came to be reconfigured in this period. One needs to put alongside each other the activities of cartographers, land surveyors, military engineers, church builders, and architects, of religious exiles, explorers, and merchants, and of theologians, philosophers, and playwrights. This was an age bent on exploring or redesigning interiority, parsing dreams, or exploring the rhetorical possibilities of nature, the age when perspective was fully incorporated in the visual arts, landscape painting became a genre of its own, and garden art patterned itself after geometry. Thus, it was difficult to reconfigure a home, draw a map, or build a chapel without touching on the personal relationship to time, the sacred, or the path of life.

Both space and self, as ideas and as lived experience, were consequently in flux. The world that 'just happened upon a new one,' as Montaigne put it, was still adjusting to its new shape and positioning in a vastly expanded universe. And that could lead to frightening disorientation. This period saw no less than the 'destruction of the Cosmos,' the disappearance of the world as a finite, closed, and hierarchically ordered whole, and its replacement by an infinite universe bound together by physical laws.[9] The novel idea of a 'vacuum' could be extraordinarily unsettling. And science, to destabilizing effect, offered at once a new prospect of the vastness of nature and of the infinitesimal smallness of its elements.[10] Individual identities were forever altered by physical travels, explorations, and displacements: from religious exiles and armies criss-crossing Europe, to Jesuit missionaries working their way into China, new expanses were traversed by itinerants and, through their innumerable reports, mapped onto the European imagination.

Yet even as old physical and conceptual boundaries melted away, both space and self were increasingly harnessed, measured, and charted, as testified by the great cartographers of the age, the first ethnographers, and the newly popular landscape designers and painters. The political and religious vicissitudes of the emerging nation states articulated with these developments, and it is not by accident that the new art of the land surveyor or the army engineer, promoted by kings and states, would become a favoured metaphoric realm for the enterprise of studying the self or that the age abounded in 'political anatomies' analysing the kingdom in terms of the human body. For within the self, no less than within the realm of the state, spatial extension was charted and theorized, penetrating early modern subjectivity as it served to describe it. Indeed, 'inwardness,' the trait by which selfhood came to be characterized in the modern era, is as much a spatial as a psychological term.[11] The soul was described as having 'hidden folds' and 'inner recesses,' and individuals were commonly instructed to 'retreat into their selves' or to access their 'inner sanctum.' The author of the thinking subject, Descartes, actually deemed that the human soul was located in the pineal gland, a precise physical spot of the brain. Materially and spiritually, individuals were moving in new spaces and being transformed, if not created, by them.

The discussions in the various chapters here explore in turn physical sites (studio, *cabinet*), spatial representations (maps, oral descriptions), and rhetorical tropes (poetic topoi). They connect cityscapes of London with Chinese gardens, discuss landscape engravings, analyse paintings and sculptures. Some read religious texts, or moral philosophy, others quote preachers' letters, allegorical plays, or poetry. Certain contributions highlight spaces of sociability, others dwell on the implications of poetic solitude, symbolic retreats, or physical and spiritual interiority. They explore individual, domestic, and public spaces like the stage and the club. And, as they examine exterior surroundings and architectural forms, they also move to uncover interior depths and expanses in the body or mind – dreams, gaps, and multiple temporalities.

They thus open up, each in its manner, the second broad area of our inquiry, the embodiment of the self. Many of the contributions follow bodies on their itineraries or consider them in their very spatiality, exteriors with complex and multifaceted relationships to interior space. Are the passions housed in the body or in the soul? Can the body be considered a plane of desire? Is it constructed as a unified locus, and does it promote or inhibit the coalescence of the self into a whole? Is it the foundation for a 'plot,' a trajectory, a storyline, and can its coordinates indeed be plotted? Why did geometrical accounting for bodies produce such anxiety at the outset of the early modern? These and other questions track the multiple paths of bodies in space. Even the experience of exile for sixteenth-century religious migrants, or the practice of self-denial in seventeenth-century Puritan discourses, which located the self in a hostile world, suggested specific modalities of boundedness or depth.

Yet, real bodies and physical spaces must be parsed for their entanglement with the self only with a keen awareness that both space and self are discursive categories and operate within complex social and symbolic relations. The space and its user's identity are interdependent, and everyone connected to the scholar (or artist) is set off against his/her studio and delineated through its boundaries. Nature can be as much a rhetorical *topos* aimed at asserting certain aristocratic values as a lived environment. A mechanistic celestial model provides a specific paradigm for social conflicts, while the belief that time is predetermined by God sanctifies the spatial trajectories of mankind. The physical plane intersects with the conceptual, the discursive, or the spiritual.

A third direction suggested by many of the contributions follows just these dimensions: surfaces, interstices, and crossings. The threshold to a study could mediate or define a particular *persona*. The theatrical stage could be mobilized in a project of subjection. Natural settings could offer a field of self-projection. The self could be experienced as invaded, expropriated, or displaced. Skin could be understood as permeable to outward or inward flows, introspection modelled on the spying out of an unfamiliar area by a foreign observer or military reconnaissance. The acknowledged borderlines of the person were modified in fits and starts, and ever new permutations and contours of being ensued. The European aesthetic modelled on linearity, confronting an Asian aesthetic of spatial depth, could provoke a new appreciation of what lies between or, indeed, fails to exist between opposites. And novel readings of ancient objects could subject surfaces to an intensive gaze able to dissolve them and provoke a spatial and mental disorientation.

The first part of the book focuses on concrete habitats such as the studio, the coffee house, the club, the stage, and the countryside. Contributors take up issues of domesticity and solitude, absorption and companionship, thinking and sociability, within which early modern scholars and artists managed and represented their daily existence. The work space – whether study or *cabinet*, studio, back-shop or *arrière-boutique* – defined the identity of its dweller and provided the concrete expression of *habitus*. It represented at the same time container, a metonym for the self, and a real physical and material site that contributes to situating, even constructing, the individual within a social or domestic universe. Such a space assists in exploring the physical or rhetorical loci of sociability and the social relations, among them non-conformity, subjection, or shared ethos, that play out within its walls.

Focusing on the companions represented alongside Renaissance scholars in their study, Gadi Algazi interprets the former as mediating instances between the scholar's *vita solitaria* and controlled dependence on others, two facets that were being renegotiated with the spread of silent reading and cursive writing, both of which required greater concentration. He argues that a silent companion, such as a dog, could represent productive solitude, while family members crowding the alchemist's study would stand for disarray.

This articulation between sociability and art is taken up by David Packwood in an analysis of Poussin's self-portraits which questions the current interpretations of the artist as a philosopher, and shows that the artist's production – including that of the self-as-artist – intersects with his domestic economy. Reading subtle testamentary and familial themes in Poussin's celebrated self-portrait in his studio, he argues that the painter, as well as his model, Montaigne, should be viewed as a socially grounded man of affairs.

The relation between study and *habitus* is further explored by Ann Vila, who presents the *cabinet* of Enlightenment *philosophes* as a space badly in need of medical and moral regulation, because of the exhaustion and mental stress caused by intellectual labour. Medical treatises and other portrayals of scholars at work demonstrate that the cultural image of the 'learned' was shaped by the site of their scholarly work, which thus functions both as metonym for the user and as a physical enclosure directly affecting his health.

David Shields in turn probes the relationship between selfhood and sociability in an eighteenth-century London print club, the Witenagamot, which regularly gathered in a Grub Street coffee house to read printed books and pamphlets and discuss news of the day. Unlike most other clubs of the period, this historical precursor to the fictional Pickwick Club thrived on non-conformity, and thus helped replace 'character' as an organizing concept of personhood with that of 'personality,' with associations to eccentricity and genius rather than normalcy and common sense.

Focusing on the theatrical stage – crucial for identity formation in early modern culture – Déborah Blocker takes up the relationship between subjection and subjectivity in the dramas of 'pageantry' commissioned by Richelieu, Louis XIII's prime minister, for the French court, with the goal of extolling submission to the state. In interpreting Richelieu's efforts as an experiment in fashioning subjects through drama, she argues that subjection to a higher authority determines early modern subjectivity more than reflexivity or self-awareness.

Basing himself of Saint-Amant's poetry, Michael Taormina opens up the issue of self-fashioning onto the broader realms of nature and its underlying rhetorical commonplaces. The French baroque poet fashioned for himself a (fictional) noble ethos by projecting onto nature the poetic *topoi* of freedom, leisure, and independence. Taormina shows not only how Saint-Amant constructs a self-portrait which 'performs nobility' through themes of elevation, repose, spontaneity, and vitality, but also how the natural world functions as a utopian space for the poet's self-discovery.

The second part of the book turns from inhabited or imagined spaces to the problematic 'spatialization' and permeability of embodied selves. In the philosophical and theological works here examined, personal differences could be accounted for by different bodies rather than different minds or souls. External impact and touch could be understood as the motivating vectors of human action. The self could be modelled as a space of invasion and colonization, or as a body following unknown paths in fractured landscapes. Dreams provided concrete interpretive systems offering biographic coherence. The new cartographers, surveyors, and engineers opened perspectives from outside the embodied self and new coordinates to locate and understand it.

The 'modern' concept of the 'inner self' – now commonly associated with depth psychology, individuality, and authenticity – is questioned by Robert Dimit's close readings of British and French medical texts and of Descartes. Showing that in Descartes's *Treatise on the Passions of the Soul* individuation, and the past itself, were encoded in the body, Dimit argues that the individuation we associate today with an authentic inner self was attributed in the seventeenth century to external factors – divine grace and the body – rather than to the individual's soul or reason.

Erec Koch takes up the peculiar conflation of the individual self with the socio-political order established by the seventeenth-century French moral philosopher, Nicole who developed his moral theory by projecting Descartes's mechanistic physics onto the socio-political order of his times. Nicole used the concept of physical collision or impact to create an analogy between the processes that shape the material universe and those that drive human behaviour, particularly the passions and individual actions in the body politic. In a detailed comparison with Hobbes, Koch highlights the crucial role of a spatial, mechanical model in Nicole's attempt to naturalize the socio-political order and the individual's position within it.

The articulation between inwardness, space, and writing is further probed by Frédéric Gabriel, who studies the constitution of the self as a rhetorical and theological space in Puritan texts that extol the practice of self-denial. A theoretical model of a stable self as a primary reference for reflexivity is used to set off the Puritan understanding of the self, not as a mark of individuation, but as a 'screen' between man and his salvation. Defined negatively by the Puritans, the self is to be examined and denied by the individual in imitation of Christ. However, paradoxically, as Gabriel argues, self-denial is also a sort of sublimated self-seeking which enables the Christian to discover a new, sacred, internal space that makes him a member of the divine and that is marked by images of exile, invasion, and uprooting.

At the beginning of the modern era, cartographers, land surveyors, and engineers considerably complicated the relationship between subjectivity and space, and the reaction for many observers was extreme disorientation. Measuring and representing exterior spaces seemed to invite a dangerous exploration of the self. At least that was true for Dürer, Montaigne, and Descartes. And, in another respect, the mass experience of exile, together with its wandering along unmarked paths, prompted Calvin to reshape his configuration of personhood. Such experiences called for new metaphors and allegorical representations and had defining implications for notions of the sacred. Space, in turn, impinged upon time; landscapes, dreamscapes, and symbolic itineraries became conflated.

The role played by religious exiles and their itineraries in certain early modern Protestant views on space and subjectivity is speculated upon by Lee Palmer Wandel, who juxtaposes Mercator's cartography and Calvin's letters, highlighting the manner in which they viewed the road to follow in exile. From these sources Palmer Wandel draws material that highlights the constitutive effects on the self of a road learned by word of mouth, not seen in cartographic representation. She argues that exile produced a particular, abstract sense of self as a solitary soul set on an open-ended path without evident course or perceivable end, a path laid out by God, but which could be delineated only in the trusting steps of the wayfarer. Her exploration teases out important connections between the Calvinists' inner experience of exile and a new geometrical representation of external, abstract space.

The spatialization of the self is further pursued by Andreas Bähr through an investigation of the spatio-temporal structure of divinatory dreams and of the specific early modern understanding of time, space, and self evidenced by their narratives. In the late Renaissance universe of resemblances between microcosm and macrocosm, and of correspondences between providential time and divine eternity, dreams were viewed as mediators that could reveal the dreamer's future or even bring it about. The efficacy of the dream depended on the assumption that the divine cosmos was spatially closed, containing all that was happening in time, with future events all already present in it. Here space was regarded as a container rather than a category of perception. In examining *De vita propria* by Jerome Cardan, Bähr elucidates its author's understanding of entering the future and making it happen. He thus historicizes notions of space and time, and demonstrates how their cosmic, providential concepts informed early modern consciousness.

The correlation sketched out between the early modern subject and cartography is further set in relief by Christopher Wild in his study of German baroque iconography and poetry. Discussing the cartographic motif in baroque poetry and common iconographic representations of melancholic characters as geometers or land-surveyors, Wild highlights the historical confluence of melancholy with the 'geometrical gaze' created by measuring space. He underlines the transposition of time into figures of spatial simultaneity where chronological progression is expressed in spatial terms and history merges into the scene of events. In a gesture which characterizes both the infinitesimal method and topographical practice, the melancholic gaze makes time enter space as the figure of a ruin that haunts the melancholic subject. But, Wild argues, the geometer's gaze also has an opposite, liberating effect, creating distance between the observer and the object being observed. The spiritual freedom of the early modern melancholic subject thus also enables him to travel through time and space by viewing abstract maps, although this 'view from above' (from God's perspective) comes with a price, the melancholic experiencing of his mortality.

In a subtle reading of the interplay between textual and cartographic mapping in Montaigne and Descartes, Tom Conley further probes the mapping of the early modern subject by two of its seminal thinkers. He demonstrates that the metaphorical undertow of the *Essays* and the *Discourse on Method* was informed by early modern topography and cartography, as practised by the first ethnographers of the new world, as well as by the 'royal engineers' charged with mapping national territory and designing its defence. In revealing that the discourses of the self are grounded in novel practices of topographical investigation, Conley also brings to light their emergence from within a broader context of conflict, war, and colonization.

The third and closing section of the book further weaves together spatiality and selfhood in early modern iconographic and textual representations by importing conceptual categories extraneous to early modern Europe – on the one hand, 'the interstitial,' and on the other, the 'intensive' character of space. These concepts, transposed from their distant geographical or theoretical origins, serve to interrogate the very notion of the self as it has been viewed by early modern European culture.

Challenging a distinctly Western understanding of space and time, Robert Batchelor develops the Mandarin concept of *jian*, or 'the interstitial,' as a conceptual tool for opening up notions of space and self, as they were transposed from eighteenth-century Beijing to London by the Vincentian priest Matteo Ripa, a landscape engraver, cartographer, and mathematician, who speculated on space and left a unique annotated map of China. *Jian*, defined as 'a state of betweenness,' or 'an interstice or interval in time and space,' aptly renders the process of translating and transposing heterogeneous material techniques and conceptual frameworks. The mixture of Western etching and the Chinese technique of 'boundary painting' marks engravings of the royal gardens of the Kangxi emperor by Ripa, but also English porcelain plates inspired by the fashion of 'chinoiseries.' Bringing into contact jarring antinomies and destabilizing distinct traditions with different relationships to space, Batchelor's reading uncovers an alternative relationship between self and space that informed early modern European culture.

A final venture into the conceptual constitution of the self is undertaken by Jean-Philippe Antoine, who rereads Winckelmann's celebrated descriptions of the famous Elgin marbles, opposing current views that the eighteenth-century critic projects an inner self onto the sculptures in order to create an empathetic reaction in the reader. A different construct of body and space underlies the comparisons of the sculpted surfaces with an ocean swell or a mountainous terrain. Antoine terms this interplay of surfaces and deep forces 'intensive space,' in opposition to the 'extensive' or measurable space of sculptors (and topographers), and he defines it as a field of coexistence of varying intensities. Such a understanding of space, he argues, enables Winckelmann to represent the actual stillness of a sculpture as movement, but one that is impersonal, inorganic, and not embraceable by a unified gaze. Winckelman's images evoke aggregates of slowly moving forces, and a body independent from aesthetic prescriptions, to which Antoine applies the term 'body without organs,' after a concept that Deleuze and Guattari borrowed from Artaud. Defined by fragmentation, by refusal to participate in physical exchanges with the outside world, and by an absolute turn inward, the concept is perfectly embodied by the celebrated Belvedere torso, a fragmented ruin that Winckelman's description turns into a 'glorious body,' autonomous and engaged in no other exchange but with gods. Winckelmann's stance, Antoine convincingly argues, can be viewed as a defence against new demands placed on the early modern self, and it foreshadows Artaud's modern refusal to consider the body as a productive organism and the individual self as an entity to be enlisted in production, war, and consumption.

NOTES

1 Sir Thomas Browne, *Religio Medici* (1643), quoted in Helen Wilcox, '"The Birth Day of My Selfe": John Donne, Martha Moulsworth and the Emergence of Individual Identity,' in A.J. Piesse, ed., *Sixteenth-Century Identities* (Manchester, 2000), 157.

2 'The eternal silence of these infinite spaces frightens me.' Blaise Pascal, *Pensées*, ed. P. Sellier (Paris, 1999), no. 233.

3 As summed up by Wolfram R. Keller, *Selves and Nations: The Troy Story from Sicily to England in the Middle Ages* (Heidelberg, 2008), 19: 'Selfhood in its various guises of identity, individuality, the subject, and subjectivity has received much attention in the last couple of decades . . . The flood of publications on the subject cannot be surveyed anymore.' See, among others, Dror Wahrman, *The Making of the Modern Self: Identity and Culture in Eighteenth-Century England* (New Haven, 2004); Patrick Coleman, Jayne Lewis, and Jill Kowalik, *Representations of the Self from the Renaissance to Romanticism* (Cambridge, 2000); Jerrold Seigel, *The Idea of the Self: Thought and Experience in Western Europe since the Seventeenth Century* (Cambridge, 2005); Jan Goldstein, *The Post-Revolutionary Self: Politics and Psyche in France, 1750–1850* (Cambridge, MA, 2005).

4 See Charles Taylor's seminal *Sources of the Self: The Making of the Modern Identity* (Cambridge, 1989).

5 See M. James and C. Crabbe, eds, *From Soul to Self* (London and New York, 1999). In the chapter 'Body, Soul and Intellect in Aquinas,' Anthony Kenny argues that the misconceived notion of the 'self' originates in 'a grammatical error,' namely, in allowing the space which differentiates 'my self' from 'myself' to 'generate the illusion of a mysterious metaphysical entity distinct from, but obscurely linked to, the human being who is talking' (40). See also Gabriele Jancke and Claudia Ulbrich, eds, *Vom Individuum zur Person: Neue Konzepte im Spannungsfeld von Autobiographietheorie und Selbstzeugnisforschung*, Jahrbuch für Frauen- und Geschlechterforschung 10 (Göttingen, 2005).

6 Useful places to start thinking about the self in concrete spaces are Henri Lefebvre, *The Production of Space*, trans. Donald Nicholson-Smith (Oxford, 1991) and Gaston Bachelard, *The Poetics of Space: The Classic Look at How We Experience Intimate Places*, trans. Maria Jolas, foreword John R. Stilgoe (Boston, 1969).

7 For exterior spaces see Bernard Beugnot, *Le discours de la retraite au XVIIe siècle: Loin du monde et du bruit* (Paris, 1996). For interior spaces see Nicholas Paige, *Being Interior: Autobiography and the Contradiction of Modernity in Seventeenth-Century France* (Philadelphia, 2000).

8 Notions of space and social space have been extensively studied by, among others, Michel Foucault, Pierre Bourdieu, Henri Lefebvre, Michel de Certeau, David Harvey, and Marc Augé. In *Space and Place: The Perspective of Experience* (Minneapolis, 1977), a prominent thinker on the subject, the geographer Yi-Fu Tuan, distinguishes between space and place as follows: space, a more abstract concept, is created by movement and lies more open, suggesting the future and inviting action. Place, by contrast, is 'enclosed and

humanized space' (6). Through human experience and its expression, 'what begins as undifferentiated space becomes place as we get to know it better and endow it with value.' Although we find his distinction useful, we feel that for our purpose the more abstract 'space' – at times used interchangeably with place or site – is more appropriate.

9 Alexandre Koyré, *From the Closed World to the Infinite Universe* (Baltimore and London, 1968), 2. Koyré notes, for instance, that Descartes did not accept the notion of vacuum, and that the new concept of homogeneous empty space entailed an equivalent understanding of time. For the relation of self to 'homogeneous empty time' see also Taylor, *Sources of the Self*, 288.

10 Hence, Pascal's fragment, quoted above, or fragment no. 249, which gives the following definition of the human being: 'Un néant à l'égard de l'infini, un tout à l'égard du néant, un milieu entre rien et tout, . . . également incapable de voir le néant d'où il est tiré et l'infini, où il est englouti' (A nothing in regards to infinity, a whole in regards to nothingness, a middle ground between nothing and everything, . . . equally incapable of seeing the nothingness from which he came and the infinity which engulfs him).

11 Taylor, *Sources of the Self*, 28, emphasizes the link of the human psyche with spatial orientation.

PART I

HABITAT AND HABITUS

chapter one

At the Study: Notes on the Production of the Scholarly Self

GADI ALGAZI

Wagner: Es ist ein pudelnärrisch Thier.
Du stehest still, er wartet auf;
Du sprichst ihn an, er strebt an dir hinauf;
Verliere was, er wird es bringen,
Nach deinem Stock ins Wasser springen.
Faust: Du hast wohl recht, ich finde nicht die Spur
Von einem Geist, und alles ist Dressur.
Wagner: Dem Hunde, wenn er gut gezogen,
Wird selbst ein weiser Mann gewogen.
Ja, deine Gunst verdient er ganz und gar
Er, der Studenten trefflicher Scolar.

Goethe, *Faust*, part 1, 1.1167–78[1]

In that famous passage insisting that scholarship is utterly incompatible with family life, Heloise – or rather, Abelard, claiming to quote Heloise – described the predicament of lovers of wisdom seeking to concentrate on their thoughts and to avoid babies' cries and nurses' lullabies. Was this utterly impossible? Heloise continues: 'The rich can do so, you will say, for their palaces and large mansions have places of abode [or perhaps, recesses: *deversoria*]; their wealth does not feel the expenses, nor are they crucified by daily cares. But the condition of philosophers, I would say, is not the same as that of the rich, and those who are concerned with wealth or involved in worldly matters would not be free to attend to the claims [or devote themselves to the offices] of religion or philosophy.'[2]

It seems as if the *deversoria* invoked in Abelard's *History of My Calamities* (written around 1133) prefigure *ex negativo* what was to become the study, an architectural innovation of the later Middle Ages.[3] Yet accepting this new form of demarcating space within households was a matter not only of economic means, but of making room for engagement in private study, of negotiating a *social* arrangement. About a hundred and forty years later, however, even a pope's palace did not yet include a private chamber for study. This is what the scholar-turned-pope, John XXI, was to discover when he ascended the throne of St Peter in 1276. Unlike several popes of the thirteenth century, Petrus Juliani (also known as 'Petrus Hispanus,' born between 1210 and 1220) was neither a lawyer nor a theologian, but a learned physician.[4] He was a transitional pope, elected to defer the struggle between the rival factions. The few descriptions we have emphasize his ignorance in matters of governance and timidity in political affairs, even his embarrassing clumsiness; he was *studiosus*, endowed with *industria*, someone who delighted in the sciences rather than in practical matters, indeed, one whose *habitus* was *doctissimus* – a scholar *mal placé*.[5]

Petrus Juliani was intent on continuing his studies in the papal palace in Viterbo. He had a special room built for himself. In the chronicles it is sometimes called a new chamber (*camera nova*) or cubicle (*cubiculum*) for study, constructed adjacent to the rear part of the palace, probably an improvised tower-shaped structure added on top of an existing one.[6] On the night of 14 May 1277, after only six months in office, while he was alone in his improvised study, the roof collapsed over him; he was fatally injured and died six days later. His detractors did not fail to explain that he had died while writing a wicked and heretical book.[7] What else could a scholar do late at night, all by himself?

Taking this incident as a possible point of departure, one can spin a straightforward story of the formation of the scholar's study and its gradual diffusion.[8] From rare and precious evidence on papal palaces in Avignon and Viterbo, or perhaps even earlier, through incidental mentions in humanists' correspondence, to references in prefaces to learned treatises and dry inventories of scholars' belongings, one can track the spread of the *studiolo* from high-ranking scholars to Renaissance artists with intellectual ambitions, to humble teachers and country pastors, as well as its evolution from a prestige object to a common element of middle-class housing arrangements.[9] By the late sixteenth century, a study would not be considered an extraordinary privilege but an essential part of scholars' homes, even humble ones. In the protocols of visitations conducted in rural Protestant parishes, not only pastors but deacons and schoolteachers were expected to have their own *Studierstüblein* to read, write, and 'find refuge from their wife and children.' One pastor in Dubro (Saxony, south-east of Wittenberg) was clever enough to first ask the church inspectors in 1555 for a study and then – as he also needed to replace his barn, destroyed by fire – to request that parishioners be ordered to build it on top of a new barn.[10] Among Jewish rabbis, some set aside 'rooms of learning' in their domiciles as early as the fifteenth century. By 1630, not only major rabbis, but even minor Jewish scholars, such as Asher Levi of Reichshofen (Alsace), contemplated constructing a study. In his new house, wrote Levi in a diary entry, he introduced three innovations: a private bathroom, an oven, and a 'little chamber' in which to learn and pray regularly and to store his books.[11]

Whereas early sources do not have a proper name for the new room, it gradually acquired a proper designation: *studiolo, museum, studorium,* and eventually a host of vernacular names.[12] If semantic codification is one indicator of the growing cultural recognition of this new division of domestic space, changing iconography is another. Whereas scholars of the central Middle Ages were depicted primarily as teachers talking to students, or occasionally as authors dictating to a scribe, in the fifteenth and sixteenth centuries they were increasingly represented seated in their studies, alone. There even seems to be an identifiable prototype, Francesco Petrarca's portrait of himself in his study, which is also an innovation in terms of the visual representation of interiors, for Petrarca is not positioned within an imagined structure, a generic space, but encased in an individualized, particular room whose proportions, as Wolfgang Liebenwein has pointed out, almost coincide with those of the person it contains (figure 1.1).[13] Note that this successful image was capable of accommodating female scholars too: one only had to replace the codified image of the scholar in his study with that of a woman, as in the case of the illustrations to Christine de Pizan's works (figure 1.2).[14] The mind may have had no sex, but it certainly had a gender, for the widow Christine, seated alone in her study, as she described herself, assumed the role of the scholar vis-à-vis her mother, who was expected to take care of her daily needs – that is, to become the ambivalently coded 'wife' in this family household. The basic structure, a gendered division of labour which underpinned that of domestic space, hence survived the uncommon constellation in which a woman inhabited the position of a humanist scholar living 'solitary and abstracted from the world.'[15]

The diffusion of the study is closely related to changes in the techniques of cultural production, first and foremost to the spread of silent reading in the later Middle Ages and the development of the cursive

Figure 1.1 Portrait of the author in his study, with his dog. Francesco Petrarca, *De viris illustribus*, Universitäts- und Landesbibliothek Darmstadt, Hs 101, fol. 1v. Photograph courtesy of the Universitäts- und Landesbibliothek Darmstadt.

Figure 1.2 Miniature of the author, at her desk, accompanied by her dog. Christine de Pizan, 'Collected Works' (1407). Photograph © The British Library Board [Image 067363, Ms. Harley 4431, fol. 4].

script, which enabled a new synchronization of head and hand, of the flow of thoughts and the movements of the hand in the act of writing.[16] Taken together, these changes made silence a precondition of intellectual labour among bookish scholars and brought forward an image of individual authorship which devalued scribal assistance and persisting forms of tacit collaboration. Securing silence and managing attention, however, became crucial challenges as scholars gradually moved out of the artificial communities – monasteries, colleges, and canonries – which had sheltered them, into family households, where they had to accommodate themselves within the crowded, initially undifferentiated spaces typical of pre-modern housing.[17] I am inclined to see the study (together with the bathroom, perhaps) as a nucleus of privacy in the context of the emergence of scholars' family households in northern Europe between 1400 and 1630. From that point of view, the study would be one major form of securing cherished solitude within the shared spaces of family quarters; regulating physical access would be complemented by the erection of invisible walls around scholars, by their learning to manage attention and to cultivate concentration and forms of forgetfulness.[18]

There are some serious difficulties, however, with this sort of story. It is hazardous to assume that a given physical division or an architectural element would have stable and uniform social functions across historical periods, among different groups, and in changing everyday contexts. This general issue is especially relevant during the early phases of the differentiation process, in which very few spaces were expected to have specialized functions and 'the study' itself had floating designations suggesting multiple uses. A clear genealogy may be misleading, as other lines of tradition also led to the creation of secluded spaces within domestic units. One thinks of *camera Regis,* the less accessible nucleus of a public court: for kings, princes, prelates, and those who sought to imitate them, privacy was one of the *insignia* of power, and differential access a tangible measure of social hierarchy. No less relevant, and far more difficult to distinguish from scholars' studies, would be merchants' private chambers, where their papers, account books, and letters could be found – perhaps not their primary work space, as with domestic scholars, but certainly an important pole complementary to their heavily socialized forms of conducting their business. Finally, the diffusion of the study by itself provides only very imperfect clues on lived divisions of domestic social space. A study could be a pure object of social representation, an effective marker of social identity, while playing a minor role in everyday life; it could serve a range of functions – both a place of seclusion and the preferred site of particular forms of sociability.[19] It could function as an impermeable shield encasing scholars, but also as a sentient boundary mediating between self and others.[20] It is significant, to take up again the example of Christine de Pizan, that she not only depicted herself as a secluded scholar in her *celle* or *estude* at the opening of *The City of Ladies,* but also departed significantly from accepted literary conventions by describing herself as interrupted by her mother, who came to tell her daughter, absorbed in reading, that it was time for supper, reminding her of the bodily needs scholars could reliably forget. And indeed, it is only by chance, through some incidental mention, that we occasionally realize who else could actually be in a scholar's sixteenth-century study, as when Philipp Melanchthon (1497–1560) casually refers to his daughters (or perhaps granddaughters) playing in his study while he was working – the very same study in which he is reputed to have locked himself up in order to avoid his wife.[21]

Scholars were not necessarily alone in their studies. Attention has repeatedly been drawn to Petrarca's servants accompanying him in his hours of solitude, or to Erasmus's long series of amanuenses – the predecessors of the later 'invisible technician.'[22] Images of solitary thought and individual, self-sufficient cultural production are easy, perhaps too easy, to debunk. But then we would miss their crucial role in the production of the self as a complex articulation of representations, material divisions, and social arrangements. Recognizing that studying in solitude was a fragile social construct tells us very little about how it was maintained and how it occasionally became a lived experience. On that subject, I can offer two remarks, each making a whole set of questions relevant:

(1) Scholars were of course not constantly all by themselves in their studies; the real social privilege they claimed consisted in legitimately avoiding the company of others when they wished to – and summoning them when needed. What really mattered was regulating access and controlling social intercourse. This is a question of power and social position, not of a presumed right to privacy. Literary and visual images of solitary scholars were not meant to suggest that they consistently *were* alone but rather that they were *entitled* to be so, and that this was a distinctive element of their way of life. In that respect, oscillations between guarding solitude and celebrating hospitality and scholarly sociability seem contradictory only when viewed normatively, in relation to codified ideals of *vita solitaria* and scholarly *otium*; in fact, these were complementary aspects of the same *habitus* and of the privileged position claimed for academic selves, privileging their own needs and work rhythms over competing social obligations and the daily needs of intimate others.[23] The study could turn from a physical division of domestic space to a social institution, as its boundaries won recognition and it became enmeshed in practices of dividing time, attention, and interaction. This raises a series of questions: was it legitimate

for scholars to have a snack at their desks instead of joining others at the table, ignoring the requirement of sociability? Could wives enter their closet freely? Were children tolerated, and if so, when? And since doors and locks were in themselves not enough, who would guard the threshold of a study and regulate access?

(2) Constructing scholarly solitude did not involve only – or necessarily – regulating *actual* access.[24] No less crucial was making *others* disappear from view, by ignoring their presence through forms of *solitudo imaginaria* and self-absorption, or by advancing representations of the scholarly self which made significant others insignificant. Here, constructing the invisibility of wives and children should not be confused with the prevalent tendency to ignore servants' presence in a wide variety of social and literary contexts, for family members stood for legitimate interdependence, mutual obligations, and intimate claims. If scholars' social reproduction heavily depended on marriage alliances and a reliable domestic division of labour, if by founding family households they joined the secular trend of the later Middle Ages when family units and interdependent 'working couples' became the cornerstone of the social formation, then constructing scholarly solitude was indeed a complicated task, one not necessarily shared by merchants and bishops, kings or aristocrats, who cultivated conspicuous forms of privacy.[25] Unlike an artisan's *bottega*, a king's *camera*, a bishop's private chapel, or a merchant's secret room, the scholar's study was taking shape along with the whole social figuration – the scholarly family – in which it was embedded; both were in this sense equally new.[26] The emergence of the scholar's study is an aspect of the production of a specific social self, one that imagines itself and requires to be recognized by others as autonomous and self-sufficient, while deepening its intimate dependence on the working of family households. This suggests that at stake in representations of the self-sufficient scholar was also the image of scholarly work and the ensuing entitlements, an image which downplays, if not utterly conceals, forms of interdependence and collaboration. Can we appraise concretely the social specificity of scholars' images? How can we use historical documents to get a sense not only of the imperceptible presence of others in a scholar's study, but also of the process of making them invisible?

Although these questions can primarily be tackled through case studies of particular scholars' households, I shall try a different path here, using visual representations of scholars in their studies as my guiding thread, invoking more detailed examples, not in order to claim they are representative, but rather to exemplify the spectrum of possibilities and to identify underlying forces. Having accumulated hundreds of such images, some of which have benefited from insightful interpretations by art historians but most of them run-of-the-mill visual representations, I would like to explore some of the possibilities they offer for clarifying these issues.

The first and most simple observation to be made is that scholars are uniformly depicted alone in their studies. This remains quite consistent between 1400 and the second half of the seventeenth century. A trickle of images of scholars with their wives or children in the study, encountered late in the seventeenth century, turns into a rather steady flow in the eighteenth century, but even then this remains far from the dominant model.[27] This seems to correlate broadly with the historical development of viable models for scholarly family life, marriage alliances, modes of socialization, and a domestic division of labour. Marriage was not an obvious choice for scholars in the first half of the sixteenth century; hesitations and insecurities were still characteristic of the second half. Reliable, endogamous marriage markets, established sets of expectations, and daily routines seem to be in place by the seventeenth century.[28]

This model of representation is rather distinctive. Setting aside for a moment images of scholars in their study and considering portraits more generally, those of scholars seem to diverge from models of *Bürgerlichkeit* taking shape in the very same period: wealthy merchants and urban patricians occasionally represented themselves with their wives in diptychs or double portraits, showcasing important marriage alliances; humanists seem to be under-represented in such portraits, whereas Protestant reformers – otherwise sharing humanists' cultural preferences and central aspects of their social identity – conform in this respect more closely with the preference for *Ehepaarbildnisse*.[29] Major artists, often aspiring for recognition as scholars of sorts, adopted various elements of their social posture, sometimes going so far as to drive their assistants out of their ateliers, allegedly in order to think and concentrate properly.[30] In the ostentatious rejection of marriage, scholarly attitudes could easily converge with prominent artists' cultivation of the image of the 'dissolute artist'; some painters may indeed have paid tribute to the misogamist tradition by portraying the woes of family life, as in Marcus Gheeraerts the Elder's drawing *The Family of the Unhappy Painter*.[31] Still, unlike bookish scholars, and rather like well-off artisans, artists did represent themselves occasionally with their wives and children.[32] One even encounters a painter portraying himself working in the company of his family; this was certainly not meant to represent everyday reality, but to convey the family's centrality to his professional identity and an explicit recognition of its role.[33] Humanists, for their part, although occasionally ordering diptychs of themselves and their wives, were distinctive in articulating the importance of male bonding among scholars – a tradition going back to medieval doctors' group portraits – in images of humanist friendship and patronage, as in Quentin Matsys's famous double portrait of Desiderius Erasmus and Peter Giles.[34]

Series are good to think with if they do not serve to efface exceptions but turn our attention to their potential heuristic value. One such exception is Bernhard Strigel's portrait (1520) of the physician and humanist poet Johannes Cuspinian with his family. This, however, is primarily a courtier's portrait, in which Cuspinian, having become a confidential councillor to the emperor and permanent curator of the University of Vienna, celebrated his social ascendancy. Cuspinian is not portrayed here in his role as a scholar but as the emperor's confidential adviser; he commissioned the painting as a companion piece to a portrait of the emperor's family, and the resulting diptych celebrates their alliance.[35] Consider another case, that of Johannes Neudörfer (1497–1563), who had himself portrayed with a pupil sometimes identified as his son.[36] Neudörfer was an expert calligrapher and teacher of the art of calculation (*Schreib- und Rechenmeister*); although insisting on the intellectual status of his craft, by having himself portrayed transmitting his knowledge (he eventually founded a dynasty of sorts) he positioned himself closer to the conventions governing the visual representation of skilled artisans, for which family reproduction represented indeed the primary mode of passing on their social position and skills.[37] The earliest image I have come across that seems to depict a scholar with his wife in a study is a painting (ca. 1640) by Karel Škréta (1610–74), now in the National Gallery in Prague (figure 1.3), yet it is not at all clear that the man depicted is indeed a mathematician, as a later title suggests; earlier catalogues described him simply as a man who holds a drawing pen in one hand and a plan in the other. It has recently been argued that the man portrayed is actually Samuel Globic of Bučina (ca. 1618–98), the first land surveyor in the Bohemian lands.[38] Globic's trajectory bears striking parallels with that of Neudörfer: as a highly skilled land surveyor, Globic learned his craft working as an apprentice with his predecessor, and his son became a painter himself. At the same time, his library bears witness

Figure 1.3 A scholar, depicted with his wife. Karel Škréta, *Portrait of an Unknown Man – so-called 'Mathematician' with his Wife* (ca. 1640), oil on canvas, National Gallery, Prague (Inv. no. O21). Photograph © National Gallery in Prague 2011.

to his scholarly pretensions, and he was eventually ennobled after participating in the defence of Prague against the Swedes. This is not a common portrait of an academic, but a document of a remarkable social career.

There is, however, another exception to the rule that recurs more regularly. In several depictions of humanists' studies and portraits there is indeed someone at their side – almost invariably a dog. It is the only living creature that is depicted quite conventionally as sharing with scholars the same space while they work (cats are a different story).[39] Patrik Reutersward has pointed to its importance in the iconography of the scholar in the study.[40] The prototype can be found in Petrarca's portrait; a closer look reveals a dog sleeping in his study (see figure 1.1 again). The sleeping dog is retained in the fresco of the Sala virorum illustrium in Padua, and in some manuscript illustrations.[41] A little dog is also not missing from several of Christine de Pizan's portraits (see figure 1.2 again).[42] It occurs again in Carpaccio's justly famous depiction of the Vision of St Augustine in the Scuola di San Giorgio degli Schiavoni in Venice (1502). Dürer's scholarly *St. Jerome in His Study* has both a lion – one of St Jerome's traditional attributes, alluding to the lion whose injury he had cured – and a sleeping dog to keep him company in his study.[43] It is tempting to construct a line of descent leading from the saint's lion, through humanists' dogs, to the poodle barking in the opening scene of Goethe's *Faust*.[44]

A sleeping dog in a scholar's study is not restricted to idealized images; the Basel edition of Jacob Locher's (1471–1528) Latin version of Sebastian Brant's *Ship of Fools* has one to illustrate the chapter on the uselessness of books (figure 1.4).[45] The model became established enough to shape the fictive depiction of an ancient scholar; the illustration to the 1552 German edition of Flavius Josephus's *Jewish War* portrays the Jewish-Roman author in the posture of a Renaissance humanist, with some weapons thrown in to allude to his military skills as a former officer, and a dog quietly sleeping in his study (figure 1.5).[46] The extent to which dogs came to be considered essential for a scholar's portrait can be gauged from the fact that although Thomas More is not said by Erasmus to have owned a dog and Holbein the Younger's preparatory sketch for the portrait of his family household included no dog, later versions added two, one of them sleeping.[47]

A dog – in most instances slumbering – was no doubt part of the standard iconography of the scholar in his study in the fifteenth and sixteenth centuries. It was evidently a symbolical dog – its most obvious ancestor being St Jerome's lion – transformed as humanists recast the

Figure 1.4 A scholar, in his study, with his dog. *Sebastian Brant, Stvltifera navis mortalium, in qva fatvi affetvs, mores, conatvs, atqve stvdia, quibus vita haec nostra . . . Olim à clariss. viro d. Sebastiano Brant juriconsult . . . & per Iacobvm Locher Sueuum Latinitati donatus* (Basiliae [1572]), 1. Photograph courtesy of Department of Special Collections, Charles E. Young Research Library, UCLA [License LA11FEB173].

figure of St Jerome and turned him into their patron.[48] Dogs were polyvalent symbols; in other contexts, they could stand for faith and loyalty; here they are said to have stood for devotion to study, perseverance, and sagacity.[49] But there were real dogs as well, and some of them were also portrayed. Petrarca himself had one dog in Vaucluse, and later another, left to him by his friend Matteo Longo. Bernardino Corio (1459–1519) had himself depicted, in the frontispiece of his book *Mediolanensis patria historia* (Milan, 1503), working in his study, his dog Apathes at his feet.[50] So did Conrad Celtis (1459–1508), who instructed Albrecht Dürer to include his dog Lachne on the front page of his book *Quatuor libri amorum.* As befits a humanist dog, it was given a name with a classical pedigree standing for its owner's cultural pretensions: Lachne was one of Actaeon's dogs in Ovid's *Metamorphoses,* a copy of which can indeed be seen on Celtis's desk in the woodcut.[51] Still, it was a flesh-and-blood dog, to which Celtis is said to have been deeply attached. He also composed a short Latin poem celebrating Abbot Trithemius's (1462–1515) dog, who was trained to obey certain commands given in Greek.[52] Willibald Pirkheimer (1470–1530) and Cornelius Agrippa (1486–1535) also owned dogs – and Dürer himself, a skilled artisan among humanists who

Figure 1.5 Flavius Josephus, imagined as a Renaissance humanist. Flavius Josephus, Jüdische *Chronik. Von grossmechtiger Erhöhung des Judenthumbs Königreich und Fürstenthumb* . . . (Franckfort am Meyn: Chr. Egenolff, 1552), SUB Goettingen, Shelf mark 4 AUCT GR V, 2238. Photograph reproduced by permission from the Niedersächsische Staats- und Universitätsbibliothek Göttingen.

gradually adopted many elements of their social posture, ended up buying one too, around 1495. For Christoph Scheurl (1481–1542), Sixtus Tucher's nephew and Celtis's disciple, Dürer prepared in 1512 a coat of arms with a slumbering dog in the foreground.[53] The learned physician from Ulm, Wolfgang Reichart (1486–1547), composed in 1523 a Latin poem for his son, congratulating him on completing his baccalaureate in the name of the house dogs and cats, the horse, and the house *genius.*[54] Jacob Locher (1471–1528) went even further, including a dedication to his favourite female dog, Scaramella, in his polemical attack on scholasticism of 1506. In the woodcut, Scaramella watches over Locher's book so that it is not gnawed by mice or set to fire by fools (figure 1.6).[55]

Figure 1.6 Jacob Locher's dog, Scaramella, protector of books against fools and mice. Jacob Locher, *Continentur. In hoc opusculo a Jacobo Locher Philomuso facili Syntaxi concinnato. Vitiosa sterilis Mule, ad musam: roscida lepiditate predictam, Comparatio* (Nurnberge: Veissenburger, 1506), Bayerische Staatsbibliothek München, Res/4 Germ.g.197 g#Beibd.2, fol. 131v [Image 00062]. Photograph reproduced by permission from the Bayerische Staatsbibliothek München.

A Greek inscription hovers over the text; Locher addresses his dog in German, but Scaramella describes herself in Latin verse, but this, claims Locher, is his translation because her favourite language was Greek.[56] His learned jests perhaps echo Leon Battista Alberti's (1404–72) panegyric for his learned dog, versed in the seven liberal arts, brave, and no doubt quite talented.[57]

Dogs are referred to in such displays of erudition within dense textual networks of classical allusions. It is their close association which enabled humanists to describe themselves through their dogs, offering us occasionally an ironical portrait of their own cultural pretensions. There was nothing ironical, however, in the fresco commissioned by Tycho Brahe for his observatory at Uraniborg. Tycho provided an illustration of the mural with detailed explanations in his *Astronomiae instauratae mechanica* (1598). It shows himself, his instruments, laboratory, and assistants, and next to the number 12, his dog: 'one of my hounds is lying at my feet. This dog was exceptionally faithful and sagacious and is shown in shape and size much as he was in life, a symbol not only of his noble race but also of sagacity and fidelity.' Noble, sage, and faithful, Tycho's dog played an important role in the self-image Tycho was seeking to project.

What were dogs, real and imagined, doing in humanists' studies? They were mostly sleeping. Was it because scholars are quite dull people, or rather because studying – at least among bookish scholars not engaged in experimentation and operating instruments – was, by definition, a quiet, almost invisible activity? Humanists' dogs were not aristocrats' hounds (Tycho Brahe and Guillaume Budé stand out here), but mostly small pet dogs, rather like those held by ladies and churchmen in contemporary paintings; they seem closest to those portrayed in court scenes, and mark their owners as members of non-warring sectors of the social elite.[58] But dogs in scenes of court life are usually portrayed jumping, wagging their tails, sitting in their lady's lap; by contrast, when humanists' dogs are not listening attentively and watching their master, they are, invariably, sleeping soundly in his study. They are not the logical dogs discussed by Karl Josef Höltgen, hounds tracing the tracks of truth.[59] Rather, they are a visible icon of the silence reigning in the studio, of its peace and quiet – essential preconditions for bookish scholarship, reading, excerpting, thinking, and writing.[60] When awake, standing attentively, watching their master, they assume a function not unlike that of scribes in medieval visual representations of learned authors: imperfect witnesses to inaudible thoughts.

The dog in the study also seems to articulate a specific model of scholarly solitude: not simply the wish to be alone, to avoid others' company, but to have company at will without entangling oneself in a web of reciprocal obligations. To have a more concrete sense of the type of relationship they stood for, I would like to look more closely into some texts by Petrarca, given his crucial role in the shaping of the image of the humanist in his study.

Petrarca, author of the influential *De vita solitaria* (written between 1346 and 1371), which shaped ideals of scholarly solitude among humanists, described his self-sufficiency in his secluded refuge at Vaucluse in these words: 'I have someone to serve me, someone to keep me company, and someone to carry me – that is, servants, a dog, and a horse.'[61] And again: 'My steward is my servant; and my companions are myself and my dog, the faithful animal.'[62] In both formulations, the dog is mentioned as his primary companion. Both dog and servants stand for an intimate and unacknowledged presence, for a profoundly asymmetric relationship which allows the scholar to regulate social intercourse. Petrarca is well aware of the risks of solitude, especially for those prone to melancholy.[63] He needs friends, but only when he summons them, not when they threaten to disturb his musing on their own. He insists that he may invite them as he pleases, according to his own needs, and ignore them at will; with dogs and servants this type of relationship is assumed as given. The dog in a humanist's study is never portrayed as demanding attention of his master, playing, or barking, a source of immediate needs: his silent sleep nicely complements the scholar's self-absorption.[64] The same would apply for Faust's poodle: he is welcome, Faust tells him, but only as 'a silent guest.'[65] It is hence not merely silence that is invoked by repeated representations of sleeping dogs and accounts of humanists' special relationship with their dogs, but *otium*, a form of leisure required for scholarly work – a specific structure of social relations coded as 'solitude.'

The function which Petrarca attributes to his dog – keeping company without requiring attention – seems fairly generalizable; the further functions his first dog is said to have assumed are not, but they provide insight into the tensions involved in this mode of producing the solitary self. Cardinal Giovanni Colonna gave Petrarca the noble white dog he himself had received as a present from the king of Spain. In his letter to Colonna, Petrarca describes how 'brought down from high to low estate,' the dog gradually forgot 'the luxuries he left behind' and accepted the frugal freedom of Petrarca's country dwelling: 'He likes my food, / My life of leisure, my relief from cares.'[66] Accompanying his master in the fields, his collar reminds the dog of his high descent, and he is proud of it: 'Reminded thus / That you [Colonna] were once his master, he grows proud, / And ready to defy all lesser folk.' Indeed, 'the villagers / Who once had brought their importunities / So often to my threshold, come no more, / For fear of him.' No doubt, Petrarca recognizes himself in his dog: a being that prefers simple food, solitude, and freedom from obligations to court life; that combines frugality and self-sufficiency with aristocratic self-esteem. Even the dog's courtly taste in picking his prey, which makes itself felt once in a while, reflects Petrarca's ambivalent attitude to his solitary life, singing its praises incessantly while being attracted to public recognition and glory.

Petrarca's dog is more than his reflection; he also assumes functions essential for his particular way of life. He protects Petrarca's cherished spots during his walks: 'He stops, holding the path, with his great body / Blocking the entrance; and if anyone / Should come, he barks to let me know, / And then, unless I tell him to be still, / He dashes to defend me.' The threshold guardian regulating access to Petrarca's open-air study recognizes his friends but drives away the peasants from Petrarca's door:

'Peasants who used to come to me to ask / About the knots of the law, about their rights, / About their households, or a daughter's marriage / (As if I were another Appius / Or an Acilius), and thus disturb / The peace of the Muses, turn away in fear / When he is lying there, across the path. / So now they deal with their own perplexities, / Leaving me to myself, to live my life / As I long to live it.' This amounts to clearly disregarding his gentlemanly obligations; elsewhere, Petrarca mentions with pride how neighbours used to come to consult his grandfather on 'household matters, business affairs, contracts, and the marriage of their children.'[67] And as if this were not enough, Petrarca's dog is also depicted as helping him to get his day in order: unrestrained by collective routines and common divisions of the day, scholars are in need of special forms of self-discipline if they wish to turn leisure into scholarly *otium*, a special form of labour. If Petrarca slept too long, his dog would scratch his door and wake him up gently for his day's work.[68]

If Heloise's imagined secluded place prefigures the later study, Petrarca's literary dog foreshadows the tasks later relegated to scholars' wives, and later still, to their secretaries: first, to serve as a magnifying mirror, reflecting and enhancing a scholar's fragile self-image of grandeur; second, to act as a gatekeeper and mediator, controlling accessibility and selecting preferred forms of sociability; and third, to support gently the scholar lacking in self-discipline. I do not claim that Petrarca's dog was actually capable of all these formidable tasks; rather, that through his dog Petrarca was able to articulate the vaguely admitted needs and contradictions engendered by this particular way of life.

Switching back from the analysis of particular texts to the series of images, I want to point out a last and hitherto neglected exception, which I shall consider very briefly. There is in fact one sort of scholar quite regularly depicted in a crowded and noisy study, surrounded by apprentices, helpers, servants, and occasionally by a wife and children. Throughout the sixteenth century and well beyond, alchemists – and actually 'bad scholars' of every sort who are hence labelled 'alchemists' – are portrayed in this way (figure 1.7).[69]

Alchemists, almost by definition, mixed the kitchen and the study – the two sharply separated yet mutually interdependent poles of scholars' family households. This serves to remind us that the model of carefully separated domains, of silence and *otium* in the secluded study, and of highly gendered division between scholars and their wives, was primarily related to the traditions of bookish scholarship. Functioning laboratories (and perhaps observatories as well) would not necessarily conform

Figure 1.7 The alchemist, also a scholar. *Der Alchimist*, copperplate engraving, 1558, by an unknown artist after a drawing by Pieter Brueghel the Elder (Philip Galle), Kupferstichkabinett, Staatliche Museen zu Berlin, Inventory no. 45-1964. Photograph © bpk / Kupferstichkabinett, SMB / Jörg P. Anders [00045336].

to these divisions between head and hand, contemplation and sense perception, books and cauldrons, scholars and household members.[70] Alchemists' laboratories shared a lot with the world of artisans; experimental households could give rise to new forms of recognized cooperation within family households, and alchemists are often portrayed in crowded, shared, and often untidy spaces (figure 1.8).[71]

Yet alchemists, too, were often seeking to create closeted work spaces and to control actual access to their laboratories. The same would hold true, *mutatis mutandis*, for experimentalists. Deborah Harkness has provided us with a fine-grained analysis of the ways Jane and John Dee coped with the inherent contradictions involved in the mediation between household obligations and the practice of natural philosophy.[72] In fact, unorthodox scholars were not necessarily breaking down social divisions of domestic space and creating shared workplaces within family households. The quest for honorability and the need to withdraw from the public eye, occasionally even to cultivate secrecy, made them insist on a clear separation of spheres.

Still, scholars gone astray, and particularly those engaging in illicit forms of knowledge, were portrayed as confounding cultural categories and mixing separate domains in domestic settings, even when in practice those engaged in observation, manipulation, and experimentation, much like bookish humanists, were at pains to uphold such boundaries and renegotiate the terms under which they could be crossed. Depicting studies crowded with wives and children was no less interested than representing solitary scholars: it was a recurrent admonishment, propagated through images of failure, to maintain proper order; crying children entering the study stand for the breakdown of a family household, impoverished by vain experiments and excessive devotion to learning.[73] In that respect, derisive images of 'the alchemist' belonged to the same class as caricatures of scholars so excessively immersed in their books that they ignored what was happening in front of them. They taught how to be a proper scholar, what to avoid, how to recognize one, and how to pretend to be one.

Images of scholars so intent on their work that they lost sight of their surroundings had of course a long history, but they acquired new relevance as early modern households became the primary site of scholarship. Establishing a study was but one aspect of a scholar's attempt to become inaccessible, invisible at will; this meant making significant others invisible, unnoticeable. A successfully functioning family household would make the work essential for maintaining a scholarly self

Figure 1.8 The alchemist's crowded working space. Ioan. Collaert, *Distillatio*, plate 7, in Jan van der Straet, *Nova reperta* [Antwerp: Ioan. Galle excudit Antuerpiae, 1600], The Huntington Library, Catalogue no. RB 761925. This item is reproduced by permission of The Huntington Library, San Marino, California.

inconspicuous, ignorable; by the same token, complete immersion in learning could also endanger that self's position as head of household, a position requiring constant attention. Visual images of scholars in their study were obviously neither reflections of actual practices nor pure ideology. They were part of a cultural toolkit for conducting, or for adequately recognizing, a specific form of life. Some of them served as condensed articulations of the social contradictions and the constitutive ambivalences inherent therein. It was not always easy to make out whether a scholar was absorbed in reading or daydreaming in front of an open book. Solitude had its risks – both to one's household and to the economy of one's soul. Such images were, hence, the reverse side of the scholarly cultivation of high concentration, or, in Petrarca's words, of the attempt 'to forget those things which are behind, and to reach forth unto those things which lie ahead of me – and to shut my eyes to those things which now are present.'[74]

As a social institution, walls and doors and bookshelves alone did not make a study. The actual boundary constitutive of a scholarly self consisted of other persons; this boundary itself was not merely a protective shield, but a mediating instance consisting of people and things, and charged with regulating intercourse. Similarly, textual and visual images of the scholar in his study often functioned as ambivalent mediations between scholars and their social surroundings – occasionally depicting them as ridiculous and queer, but also providing them with a culturally well-established shield behind which they could enjoy some freedom from common conventions and obligations.

NOTES

1 '*Wagner*: Tis the absurdest, drollest beast. / Stand still, and you will see him wait; / Address him, and he gambols straight; / If something's lost, he'll quickly bring it, – / Your cane, if in the stream you fling it. *Faust*: No doubt you're right: no trace of mind, I own, / Is in the beast: I see but drill, alone. / *Wagner*: The dog, when he's well educated, / Is by the wisest tolerated. / Yes, he deserves your favor thoroughly, – / The clever scholar of the students, he!' Translation from Goethe, *Faust*, trans. Bayard Taylor (New York, 1908). See notes 44 and 65 below.

2 'Id, inquies, divites possunt, quorum palatia vel domus amplae deversoria habent, quorum opulentia non sentit expensas nec cotidianis sollicitudinibus cruciatur. Sed non est, inquam, haec condicio philosophorum quae divitum,

nec qui opibus student vel saecularibus implicantur curis, divinis seu philosophicis vacabunt officiis' (Abelard, *Historia calamitatum*); from J.T. Muckle, ed., 'Abelard's Letter of Consolation to a Friend (*Historia calamitatum*),' *Mediaeval Studies* 12 (1950), 187. I have modified the English translation by Betty Radice, *The Letters of Abelard and Heloise* (Harmondsworth, 1974); cf. also Dag Nikolaus Hasse, ed., *Abaelards 'Historia calamitatum': Text, Übersetzung, literaturwissenschaftliche Modellanalysen* (Berlin and New York, 2002).

3 Note that in Radice's translation, the houses of the rich are said to 'provide privacy,' privacy being a concept notably missing from the text; also, both Radice and Hasse narrow down the semantic range of the verb *vacare* – dedicating oneself, freeing oneself, or having the leisure for the claims (or perhaps even the offices) of religion or philosophy – to having no *time* to engage in them.

4 See Richard Stapper, *Johannes XXI: Eine Monographie* (Münster, 1898). For a recent reconstruction of this pope's earlier trajectory, see Iona McCleery, 'Opportunities for Teaching and Studying Medicine in Medieval Portugal before the Foundation of the University of Lisbon (1290),' *Dynamis: Acta Hispanica ad Medicinae Scientiarumque Historiam Illustrandam* 20 (2000), 305–29. The significant body of writings attributed in the past to 'Petrus Hispanus,' who became Pope John XXI, has dwindled radically as their authorship has been questioned; for a recent contribution, see Angel d'Ors, 'Petrus Hispanus O.P., Auctor Summularum (II), Further Documents and Problems,' *Vivarium* 39, 2 (2001), 209–54.

5 'Hic magnus Magister in scientiis plus delectabatur quam omnibus reliquis in negotiis': Ricobaldo of Ferrara, *Historia Romanorum*, in L.A. Muratori, ed., *Rerum italicarum scriptores*, vol. 9, cap. 72, col. 181; 'Hic doctissimus est habitus, sed ignoratione rerum gerendarum plus detrimenti quam honoris pontificatui attulit. Multa enim stolide et leniter gessit, in uno tamen commendatione dignus quod adolescentes litterarum studiosos inopes maxime beneficiis ecclesiasticis et pecunia iuvit. In verbis promptus erat, in rebus agendis timidus et ineptus'; quoted from a fifteenth-century anonymous *Lives of the Popes* by L.M. De Rijk, 'Biographical Introduction' to *Tractatus: Called Afterwards Summule logicales*, by Peter of Spain (Assen, 1972), xli.

6 Maria Terese Gigliozzi, *I palazzi del papa. Architectura e ideologia: Il Duecento* (Rome, 2003), 124–25, with plan, 112; Gary M. Radke, *Viterbo: Profile of a Thirteenth-Century Papal Palace* (Cambridge, 1996), 49–50, 237, 340nn13–14.

7 Horace K. Mann and Johannes Hollensteiner, *Lives of the Popes in the Middle Ages* (London, 1932), 16:55.

8 See esp. Wolfgang Liebenwein, *Studiolo: Die Entstehung eines Raumtyps und seine Entwicklung bis um 1600* (Berlin, 1977); Dora Thornton, *The Scholar*

in His Study: Ownership and Experience in Renaissance Italy (New Haven and London, 1997); Diana Webb, *Privacy and Solitude in the Middle Ages* (London, 2007), esp. 157–72; Ugo Rozzo, *Lo studiolo nella silografia italiana, 1479–1558* (Udine, 1998).

9 Radke, *Viterbo*, 81–6.

10 '. . . der pfarrer hat gebeten, dieweil er kein stüblein hab, darinnern er besonder seines studirens warten könt, auch noch wol ein stall bedürfte, das ihm ein stall von 5 gebünden und darauf ein studir stüblein gebauet werde an die stete der verbranten pfarn'; Visitation in Dubro, 1555, repr. in Karl Pallas, ed., *Die Registraturen der Kirchenvisitationen im ehemals sächsischen Kurkreise, Abteilung 2, Teil 3: Die Ephorien Prettin und Herzberg* (Halle, 1908), 573–4; twenty years later, the parishioners had still failed to build either the study or the stable [*Stall*] (ibid., 575).

11 Moïse Ginsburger, ed., *Die Memoiren des Ascher Levy aus Reichshofen im Elsaß, 1598–1635* (Berlin, 1913), 32. See Debra Kaplan, 'The Self in Social Context: Asher ha-Levi of Reichshofen's *Sefer Zikhronot*,' *Jewish Quarterly Review* 97, 2 (2007), 210–36.

12 Marcin Fabianski, 'Musaea in Written Sources of the Fifteenth to Eighteenth Centuries,' *Opuscula Musealia* 4 (1990), 7–40.

13 Liebenwein, *Studiolo*, 53–5; Theodor E. Mommsen, 'Petrarch and the Decoration of the Sala Virorum Illustrium in Padua,' *Art Bulletin* 34 (1952), 108–9, reproduced in Liebenwein, *Studiolo*, fig. 17; Mommsen, 'Petrarch,' fig. 5; see Joseph B. Trapp, 'The Iconography of Petrarch in the Age of Humanism,' in *Studies of Petrarch and His Influence* (London, 2003), 1–117. On Tomaso da Modena's nearly contemporaneous series of frescoes of Dominican scholars, see Robert Gibbs, *Tomaso da Modena: Painting in Emilia and the March of Treviso, 1340–80* (Cambridge, 1989), 50–87.

14 See Lucie Schaefer, 'Die Illustrationen zu den Handschriften der Christine de Pizan,' *Marburger Jahrbuch für Kunstwissenschaft* 10 (1937), 119–208; from early fifteenth-century Paris, see the illumination depicting Amalthea in a Boccaccio manuscript, Ms. fr. 12420, fol. 36, Bibliothèque nationale, Paris, reproduced in Charles D. Cuttler, *Northern Painting: From Pucelle to Bruegel* (New York, 1968), fig. 48; on the medieval tradition, see Katrin Graf, *Bildnisse schreibender Frauen im Mittelalter. 9. bis Anfang 13. Jahrhundert* (Basel, 2002).

15 'sollitaire et soubtraitte du monde': Christine de Pizan, *La cité des dames*, in Maureen Curnow, 'The *Livre de la Cité des Dames* of Christine de Pisan: A Critical Edition,' unpublished PhD diss., Vanderbilt University, 1975, 628; Jacqueline Cerquiglini, 'L'étrangère,' *Revue des Langues Romanes* 92 (1988), 239–53; V.A. Kolve, 'The Annunciation to Christine: Authorial

Empowerment in *The Book of the City of Ladies*,' in Brendan Cassidy, ed., *Iconography at the Crossroads* (Princeton, NJ, 1993), 172–96; Susan Groag Bell, 'Christine de Pizan in Her Study,' *Cahiers de recherches médiévales: Études christiniennes*, published online 10 June 2008 at http://crm.revues.org/index3212.html; Gadi Algazi, 'Scholars in Households: Refiguring the Learned Habitus, 1480–1550,' *Science in Context* 16, 1–2 (2003), 26–7.

16 Paul Saenger, 'Silent Reading: Its Impact on Late Medieval Script and Society,' *Viator* 13 (1982), 367–414; Saenger, 'Books of Hours and the Reading Habits of the Later Middle Ages,' *Scrittura e civiltà* 9 (1985), 239–69. On late medieval monastic traditions of reading, see Jessica Brantley, *Reading in the Wilderness: Private Devotion and Public Performance in Late Medieval England* (Chicago, 2007); Sönke Lorenz, Oliver Auge, and Robert Zagolla, eds, *Bücher, Bibliotheken und Schriftkultur der Kartäuser: Festgabe zum 65. Geburtstag von Edward Potkowski* (Stuttgart, 2002).

17 For an instructive survey, see John Schofield and A.G. Vince, *Medieval Towns: The Archaeology of British Towns in Their European Setting*, 2nd ed. (London and New York, 2003), 79–120; see also John Schofield, *Medieval London Houses* (New Haven and London, 1994), 81; Jaap van der Veen, 'Eenvoudig en stil: studeerkamers in zeventiende-eeuwse woningen, voornamelijk te Amsterdam, Deventer en Leiden,' *Nederlands kunsthistorisch jaarboek* 51 (2000), 136–71.

18 The period 1400–1630 is the time frame of my research project, of which this text is a part; some provisional findings presented in previous papers are occasionally referred to in the following. On learned forgetfulness, see Algazi, 'Gelehrte Zerstreutheit und gelernte Vergesslichkeit: Bemerkungen zu ihrer Rolle in der Formierung des Gelehrtenhabitus,' in Peter von Moos, ed., *Le faux pas* (Cologne, Weimar, and Vienna, 2001), 235–50.

19 See esp. Paula Findlen, *Possessing Nature: Museums, Collecting, and Scientific Culture in Early Modern Italy* (Berkeley, 1996); Findlen, 'Masculine Prerogatives: Gender, Space, and Knowledge in the Early Modern Museum,' in Peter Gallison and Emily Thompson, eds, *The Architecture of Science* (Cambridge, MA, 1999), 29–57.

20 On boundaries and several of the topics discussed below, see Steven Shapin's path-breaking study 'The House of Experiment in Seventeenth-Century England,' *Isis* 79 (1988), 373–404. For Shapin's seventeenth-century experimentalists, mediating the results of experiments conducted within laboratories and creating chains of trust stretching across their sites of knowledge production were both crucial issues; fifteenth- and sixteenth-century humanists, and bookish scholars in general, discussed here, were not confronted to a similar extent with this problem.

21 Stefan Rhein, 'Katharina Melanchthon, geb. Krapp: Ein Wittenberger Frauenschicksal der Reformationszeit,' in Stefan Oehmig, ed., *700 Jahre Wittenberg: Stadt – Universität – Reformation* (Weimar, 1995), 501–18; Algazi, 'Scholars in Households,' 27–8.

22 Franz Bierlaire, *La familia d'Érasme: Contribution à l'histoire de l'humanisme* (Paris, 1968); for a grand scale *familia*, organized as a rationalized aristocratic household, see John Robert Christianson, *On Tycho's Island: Tycho Brahe and His Assistants, 1570–1601* (Cambridge, 2000). See also Steven Shapin, 'The Invisible Technician,' *American Scientist* 77 (1989), 554–63; Shapin, '"The Mind Is Its Own Place": Science and Solitude in Seventeenth-Century England,' *Science in Context* 4 (1990), 191–218.

23 For a supporting case study, see Algazi, 'Food for Thought: Hieronymus Wolf Grapples with the Scholarly Habitus,' in Rudolf Dekker, ed., *Egodocuments in History: Autobiographical Writing in Its Social Context since the Middle Ages* (Hilversum, 2002), 21–44. This is where I disagree with characterizations of scholars' habitus in terms of philosophical asceticism.

24 This would remain a difficult task; even a Charles Darwin had to be ill to avoid the obligations of middle-class sociability in Victorian England. The Irish poet William Allingham (1824–89) noted that Darwin 'has his meals at his own times, sees people or not as he chooses, [and] has invalid's privileges in full, a great help to a studious man.' Quoted in Ralph Colp, Jr, *To Be Invalid: The Illness of Charles Darwin* (Chicago, 1977), 87; see also Janet Browne, 'I Could Have Retched All Night: Charles Darwin and His Body,' in Christopher Lawrence and Steven Shapin, eds, *Science Incarnate: Historical Embodiments of Natural Knowledge* (Chicago, 1998), 240–87, esp. 248–9.

25 Heide Wunder, *He Is the Sun, She Is the Moon: Women in Early Modern Germany* (Cambridge, 1998); Wunder, 'Überlegungen zum Wandel der Geschlechterbeziehungen im 15. und 16. Jahrhundert aus sozialgeschichtlicher Sicht,' in Heide Wunder and Christina Vanja, eds, *Wandel der Geschlechterbeziehungen zu Beginn der Neuzeit* (Frankfurt am Main, 1991), 12–26.

26 The designations are fluctuating and are used here for clarity's sake. See, for bishops, Maureen C. Miller, *The Bishop's Palace: Architecture and Authority in Medieval Italy* (Ithaca, NY, 2000); for kings, Richard Firth Green, *Poets and Princepleasers: Literature and the English Court in the Late Middle Ages* (Toronto, 1980), 38–70; for merchants, Jaume Aurell, 'Merchants' Attitudes to Work in Barcelona of the Later Middle Ages: Organisation of Working Space, Distribution of Time and Scope of Investments,' *Journal of Medieval History* 27, no. 3 (2001), 197–218; for artisans, Diane Shaw, 'The Construction of the Private in Medieval London,' *Journal of Medieval and Early Modern Studies* 26 (1996), 447–66; Linda Bauer, 'From Bottega to Studio,' *Renaissance Studies*

22 (2008), 642–49; and, more generally, Philippe Braunstein, 'Toward Intimacy: The Fourteenth and Fifteenth Centuries,' in Georges Duby, ed., *A History of Private Life*, vol. 2, *Revelations of the Medieval World* (Cambridge, MA, 1988), 535–630.

27 David Smith argues that Rembrandt's *The Shipbuilder and His Wife* (1633) played a pivotal role in shaping the topic of 'The Interrupted Husband' and offers an analysis of Abraham van den Tempel, *Portrait of a Scholar and His Wife* (Budapest, Szépmüvészeti Muzeum) and of Gonzales Coques, *Portrait of a Scholar and His Wife* (Leipzig, Museum der Bildenden Künste); David R. Smith, *Masks of Wedlock: Seventeenth-Century Dutch Marriage Portraiture* (Ann Arbor, 1982), 126–37. For the eighteenth century, see especially Hildegard Westhoff-Krummacher, *Als die Frauen noch sanft und engelsgleich waren: Die Sicht der Frau in der Zeit der Aufklärung und des Biedermeier*, catalogue of the exhibition at the Westfälisches Landesmuseum für Kunst und Kulturgeschichte, 19 November 1995 to 11 February 1996 (Münster, 1995), e.g., Willem Josef Laquy, *Family Portrait* (ca. 1790), oil painting (fig. 12); Ferdinand Georg Waldmüller, *Cartographer with His Wife* (1824), oil painting (fig. 16).

28 For a short sketch, see Algazi, 'Eine gelernte Lebensweise: Figurationen des Gelehrtenlebens zwischen Mittelalter und Früher Neuzeit,' *Berichte zur Wissenschaftsgeschichte* 30, 2 (2007), 107–18. Susanne Skowronek observes a passage around 1600 from individualized portraits to serial images of scholars, to be collected, reproduced, and displayed, documenting their collective claims; Susanne Skowronek, *Autorenbilder: Wort und Bild in den Porträtkupferstichen von Dichtern und Schriftstellern des Barock* (Würzburg, 2000), 75–6.

29 On marriage alliances and kinship networks within Augsburg's merchant elite and particularly on wives' roles, see Mark Häberlein, *Brüder, Freunde und Betrüger: Soziale Beziehungen, Normen und Konflikte in der Augsburger Kaufmannschaft um die Mitte des 16. Jahrhunderts* (Berlin, 1998), esp. 360–92. On the tradition of married couples' portraits, see in general Berthold Hinz, 'Studien zur Geschichte des Ehepaarbildnisses,' *Marburger Jahrbuch für Kunstwissenschaft* 19 (1974), 139–218.

30 Rudolf Wittkower and Margot Wittkower, *Born under Saturn: The Character and Conduct of Artists: A Documentary History from Antiquity to the French Revolution* (New York, 1969 [1963]); Gunter Schweikhart, 'Künstler als Gelehrte: Selbstdarstellungen in der Malerei des 16. Jahrhunderts,' in Ulrich Rehm and Nicole Birnfeld, eds, *Die Kunst der Renaissance: Ausgewählte Schriften* (Cologne, 2001), 229–38; Michael Wayne Cole and Mary Pardo, 'Origins of the Studio,' in Michael Cole and Mary Pardo, eds, *Inventions of the Studio, Renaissance to Romanticism* (Chapel Hill, NC, 2005), 1–35; and the perceptive comments by Beth Holman, 'Review: *Inventions of the Studio,*' *Art Bulletin* 88, 3 (2006), 601–5.

31 *The Family of the Unhappy Painter*, or *The Worries of the Painter* (1577), drawing, Cabinet des dessins, Bibliothèque nationale, Paris; Edward Hodnett, *Marcus Gheeraerts the Elder of Bruges, London, and Antwerp* (Utrecht, 1971), 63–4; see also Adam Elsheimer, *The Despaired Painter*, drawing, ca. 1600, reproduced in John Walsh, *Jan Steen: The Drawing Lesson* (Malibu, CA: J. Paul Getty Museum, 1996), fig. 33; Werner Sumowski, 'The Artist in Despair: A New Drawing by Adam Elsheimer,' *Master Drawings* 33 (1995), 152–6.

32 Anja K. Ševčik, 'Familie und Künstlertum im Spiegel des Selbstporträts,' in *Tobias Pock: Vlastní podobizna s rodinou* (Prague, 1997), 22–32.

33 See Gabriele Hofner-Kulenkamp, *Das Bild des Künstlers mit Familie: Porträts des 16. und 17. Jahrhunderts* (Bochum, 2002), 71–8 and passim.

34 Lorne Campbell, Margaret M. Phillips, H.S. Herbruggen, Joseph M. Trapp, 'Quentin Matsys, Erasmus, Pieter Giles and Thomas More,' *Burlington Magazine* 120 (1978), 716–25; Kurt Löcher, 'Humanistenbildnisse – Reformatorenbildnisse: Unterschiede und Gemeinsamkeiten,' in Hartmut Boockmann et al., eds, *Literatur, Musik und Kunst im Übergang vom Mittelalter zur Neuzeit* (Göttingen, 1995), 359–60. On the changing uses of humanists' portraits, see esp. Dieter Mertens, 'Oberrheinische Humanisten im Bild: Zum Gelehrtenbildnis um 1500,' in Konrad Krimm and Herwig John, eds, *Bild und Geschichte: Studien zur politischen Ikonographie. Festschrift für Hansmartin Schwarzmaier* (Sigmaringen, 1997), 221–48. For group portraits, see Andrea von Hülsen-Esch, 'Gelehrte in Gruppen, oder: Das "Gruppenportrait vor der Erfindung" des Gruppenportaits,' in Martin Brüchsel, ed., *Das Porträt vor der Erfindung des Porträts* (Mainz, 2003), 173–89; von Hülsen-Esch, *Gelehrte im Bild: Repräsentation, Darstellung und Wahrnehmung einer sozialen Gruppe im Mittelalter* (Göttingen, 2006).

35 Bernhard Strigel, *Portrait of the Cuspinian Family* (1520), oil painting, private collection; Hans Georg Thümmel, 'Bernhard Strigels Diptychon für Cuspinian,' *Jahrbuch der kunsthistorischen Sammlungen in Wien* 76 (1980), 96–110; Pamela Sheingorn, 'Appropriating the Holy Kinship: Gender and Family History,' in Carol Neel, ed., *Medieval Families: Perspectives on Marriage, Household, and Children* (Toronto, 2004), 291. Compare with Lucas Cranach the Elder's earlier diptych (1502) of Cuspinian and his first wife, Anna Putsch, in which he is portrayed as a courtier but surrounded by learned allusions; in Dieter Koepplin, *Cranachs Ehebildnis des Johannes Cuspinian von 1502: Seine christlich-humanistische Bedeutung*, Phil.-Hist. diss.,University of Basel, 1973. On Cuspinian's career, see Nancy G. Siraisi, *History, Medicine, and the Traditions of Renaissance Learning* (Ann Arbor, 2008), 198–206.

36 Nicolas Neufchâtel, *Portrait of Johann Neudörfer and a Pupil* (1561), Germanisches Nationalmuseum, Nuremberg. The attentive pupil is assumed to

be Johann the Younger (1543–81), who succeeded his father as a calligrapher; but neither the inscription nor the contemporary description of the piece lends explicit support to this assumption. See Oliver Linke and Christine Sauer, *Zierlich schreiben: Der Schreibmeister Johann Neudörffer d. Ä. und seine Nachfolger in Nürnberg* (Munich, 2007), 18–21 (with a portrait of Neudörfer and his wife).

37 An important exception I have come across is a wood relief showing the humanist physician and historian Georg Tannstetter (1482–1535) with his son Christian, now at the Abbey of Melk, Austria; reproduced in Franz Graf-Stuhlhofer, *Humanismus zwischen Hof und Universität: Georg Tannstetter (Collimitius) und sein wissenschaftliches Umfeld im Wien des frühen 16. Jahrhunderts* (Vienna, 1996), fig. 3.

38 Karel Škréta, *Portrait of an Unknown Man – So-Called 'Mathematician' with His Wife* (ca. 1640), oil painting, Inv. no. O21, National Gallery, Prague; Michal Šronek, 'Karel Škréta, Samuel Globic of Bučína et infelicissima quadratura circuli,' *Bulletin of the National Gallery in Prague* 9 (1999), 20–32, esp. 21–3 and 30n17.

39 See note 64 below.

40 See Patrik Reutersward, 'The Dog in the Humanist's Study,' *Konsthistorisk Tidskrift* 50, 2 (1981), 53–69, following some early hints by Karl-August Wirth, 'Die kolorierten Federzeichnungen im Cod. 2975 der Österreichischen Nationalbibliothek: Ein Beitrag zur Ikonographie der Artes Liberales im 15. Jahrhundert,' *Anzeiger des Germanischen Nationalmuseums* (1979), 72–80, and complemented by Reutersward, 'Three Cats in a Humanistic Context (To Say Nothing of the Peacock, the Partridge, and a Dog),' *Konsthistorisk Tidskrift* 61, 4 (1992), 137–44; Karl Josef Höltgen, 'Clever Dogs and Nimble Spaniels: On the Iconography of Logic, Invention, and Imagination,' *Explorations in Renaissance Culture* 24 (1998), 1–36; Jan Papy, 'Lipsius and His Dogs: Humanist Tradition, Iconography and Rubens's *Four Philosophers*,' *Journal of the Warburg and Courtauld Institutes* 62 (1999), 167–98.

41 See, for instance, Francesco Antonio del Chierico, Ms. 905, fol. 1v, Bibliotheca Trivulziana, Milan, reproduced in Trapp, 'Iconography of Petrarch,' 64.

42 For three examples of portraits of Christine de Pizan, see Ms. Harley 4431, fol. 4, British Museum, London; Ms. fr. 835, fol. 1, Bibliothèque nationale, Paris; and Cod. Gall. 11, fol. 2, Bayerische Staatsbibliothek, Munich; for all three, see Schaefer, 'Illustrationen,' figs. 2, 54, and 158, respectively.

43 Erwin Panofsky, *Albrecht Dürer* (London and Princeton, 1943; rev. ed., 1948), 1:154–6; see also Lucas Cranach the Elder's version, *Cardinal Albrecht of*

Brandenburg as St. Jerome in His Study (1525), mixed media on limewood, Hessisches Landesmuseum Darmstadt.

44 Goethe, *Faust*, pt. 1, ll. 1167–78; the poodle would soon be transformed into a travelling scholar, the guise assumed by Mephistopheles; a tradition about Faust being accompanied by a dog occasionally assuming the form of a servant was transmitted by the sixteenth-century Protestant preacher Johann Gast.

45 Jakob Locher, *Stultifera navis mortalium. Olim a Sebastiano Brant Germanicis rhythmis conscriptus et per Iacobum Locher Latinitati donatus. Nunc vero rev.* (Basel, 1572), 1.

46 Flavius Josephus, *Jüdische Chronic. Von großmechtiger erhöhung des Judenthumbs Königreich und Fürstenthumb* (Frankfurt am Main, 1552), title woodcut; see also Ovid in his study in a 1522 Venetian edition of the *Metamorphoses*, reproduced in Liebenwein, *Studiolo*, fig. 33; the introduction to book 5 of Hieronymus Brunschwig, *Liber de arte distillandi de compositis* (Strassburg, 1512), fol. 283r, depicts both the author and a dog sleeping in the study – the tired author seeking rest after completing the fourth book of his *opus*.

47 Compare Hans Holbein the Younger's sketch of More's family (ca. 1527), Kupferstichkabinett, Öffentliche Kunstsammlung, Basel, with Rowland Lockey's painting, done after Holbein (1593), Nostell Priory, West Yorkshire. See Lesley B. Lewis, *The Thomas More Family Group Portraits after Holbein* (Leominster, 1998). I owe this observation to Richard Marius, *Thomas More: A Biography* (New York, 1984), 230, who may have mistaken More's critique of hunting in *Utopia* (bk. 2) for a general dislike of dogs. Similarly, early testimonies about Isaac Newton insist that 'he kept neither Dog nor Cat in his Chamber,' but traditions woven around his person insist on attributing to him a dog, Diamond: Gale E. Christianson, *In the Presence of the Creator: Isaac Newton and His Times* (New York, 1984), 305; Derek Gjertsen, *The Newton Handbook* (London, 1986), 177–8.

48 Eugene F. Rice, Jr, *Saint Jerome in the Renaissance* (Baltimore, 1985); Christiane Wiebel, *Askese und Endlichkeitsdemut in der italienischen Renaissance: Ikonologische Studien zum Bild des heiligen Hieronymus* (Weinheim, 1988); Hubert Locher, *Domenico Ghirlandaio, Hieronymus im Gehäuse: Malerkonkurrenz und Gelehrtenstreit* (Frankfurt am Main, 1999).

49 Reuterswärd, 'The Dog,' 55.

50 Reproduced in Thornton, *The Scholar in His Study*, fig. 196.

51 Reproduced in Claudia Wiener et al., eds, *Amor als Topograph: 500 Jahre* Amores *des Conrad Celtis. Ein Manifest des deutschen Humanismus* (Schweinfurt, 2002), 29. On Celtis's ambitious integration of text and image, see Peter Luh, *Die unvollendete Werkausgabe des Conrad Celtis und ihre Holzschnitte:*

Kaiser Maximilian gewidmet (Frankfurt am Main and New York, 2001), 123–55; Arwed Arnulf, 'Dürers Buchprojekte von 1511: Andachtsbücher für Humanisten,' *Marburger Jahrbuch für Kunstwissenschaft* 31 (2004), 161–5.

52 Noel L. Brann, *The Abbot Trithemius (1462–1516): The Renaissance of Monastic Humanism* (Leiden, 1981), 243.

53 Albrecht Dürer, *Das Wappen der Scheurl und Tucher* (1512), woodcut; reproduced in *Das Zeitalter Albrecht Dürers: Die Kunst der Graphik. Werke aus dem Besitz der Albertina* (Vienna, 1964), fig. 98.

54 Walther Ludwig, ed., *Vater und Sohn im 16. Jahrhundert: Der Briefwechsel des Wolfgang Reichart, genannt Rychardus, mit seinem Sohn Zeno (1520–1543)* (Hildesheim, 1999), no. 66, 150–3; on the literary tradition, see Papy, 'Lipsius and His Dogs,' 167–98.

55 Jacob Locher, 'Continentur in hoc opusculo a Jacobo Locher Philomuso facili Syntaxi concinnato. Vitiosa sterilis Mule, ad musam: roscida lepiditate predictam, Comparatio' (Nuremberg, 1506), fol. 131r–1v; available at 'Digitisation of the Printed Books of the 16th Century Published in the German-Language Area,' http://daten.digitale-sammlungen.de/~db/bsb00006122/images/.

56 On German humanists using Latin to talk to their servants or dogs, see Emile V. Telle, *L'Erasmianus sive Ciceronianus d'Étienne Dolet* (Geneva, 1974), 349–50.

57 Alberti, 'Canis,' in Cecil Grayson, *Studi su Leon Battista Alberti*, ed. Paola Claut (Florence, 1998), 363–72.

58 Cf. Simon Teuscher, 'Hunde am Fürstenhof: Köter und 'edler Wind' als medien sozialer Beziehungen vom 14. bis 16. Jahrhundert,' *Historische Anthropologie* 6, 3 (1998), 347–69; compare with illuminations of huntsmen and their dogs, in Gaston Phébus's *Livre de chasse*, reproduced in Wilhelm Schlag, ed., *The Hunting Book of Gaston Phébus: Manuscrit français 616, Paris, Bibliothèque nationale* (London, 1998). On later uses of dogs among German students and academics, see Barbara Krug-Richter, 'Hund und Student: Eine akademische Mentalitätsgeschichte (18.–20. Jh.),' *Jahrbuch für Universitätsgeschichte* 10 (2007), 77–104, and fig.4 (depicting a sleeping dog in a rich student's home).

59 Höltgen, 'Clever Dogs.'

60 The emblem for silence in several editions of Andrea Alciato's *Emblemata* is a scholar in his study; see, for instance, *Emblemata* (Lyon, 1550), 17; *Emblematum liber* (Augsburg, 1534) [without pagination]; *Liber emblematum . . . Kunstbuch* (Frankfurt am Main, 1567), fol. 21r.

61 'habeo . . . qui michi serviat, qui me sotiet, qui me vehat, quo tegar, ubi iaceam, ubi spatier, quo delecter'; Petrarca, *Ep. fam.* XVI.3; I am following

here Bernardo's English translation: Francesco Petrarca, *Letters on Familiar Matters: Rerum familiarium libri IX–XVI*, trans. Aldo S. Bernardo (Baltimore, 1982), 296. For the notion of scholarly solitude, see esp. Francesco Petrarca, *De vita solitaria: Kritische Textausgabe und ideengeschichtlicher Kommentar*, ed. Karl A.E. Enenkel (Leiden, 1990); Peter von Moos, 'Petrarcas Einsamkeiten,' in Aleida Assmann and Jan Assmann, eds, *Einsamkeit* (Munich, 2000), 213–37.

62 'Villicus est servus; michi sum comes ipse canisque, / Fidum animal'; Petrarca, *Ep. met.* 1.6; English trans. in Ernest Hatch Wilkins, ed. and trans., *Petrarch at Vaucluse: Letters in Verse and Prose* (Chicago, 1958), 9 (trans. modified).

63 Petrarca, *Ep. fam.* 16.7.

64 We don't know, of course, whether scholars possessed more dogs than cats or what they actually did in their studies, but cats seem not to have assumed the symbolic role assigned to dogs in scholars' images; note the instructive difference between the kitten asking for an author's attention and the sleeping dog by his side in Andreas Herneisen's portrait of Hans Sachs with the Painter (1576), Herzog August Bibliothek, Wolfenbüttel, reprinted and discussed in Reuterswärd, 'Three Cats,' 141–2. See also Joseph B. Trapp, 'Petrarch's Inkstand and His Cat,' in Renzo S. Crivelli and Luigi Sampietro, eds, *Il passaggiere italiano: Saggi sulle letterature di lingua inglese in onore di Sergio Rossi* (Rome, 1994), 23–40.

65 'If I must share my chamber with thee, / Poodle, stop that howling, prithee! / Cease to bark and bellow! Such a noisy, disturbing fellow / I'll no longer suffer near me. / One of us, dost hear me! / Must leave, I fear me. / No longer guest-right I bestow; / The door is open, art free to go' (Soll ich mit dir das Zimmer theilen, / Pudel, so laß das Heulen, / So laß das Bellen! / Solch einen störenden Gesellen / Mag ich nicht in der Nähe leiden. / Einer von uns beyden / Muß die Zelle meiden. / Ungern heb ich das Gastrecht auf, / Die Thür' ist offen, hast freyen Lauf), Goethe, *Faust*, trans. Taylor, 1:1238–47.

66 Petrarca, *Ep. met.* 3.5, in Wilkins, *Petrarch in Vaucluse*, 63–8.

67 Petrarca, *Ep. fam.* 6.3. Petrarca explicitly compares his grandfather to the Roman patrician Appius Claudius Caecus – the role he rejects in describing how his dog keeps away the peasants asking for his advice.

68 Cf. *Ep. fam.* 15.3 for his daily routine, and the efforts to combat sleepiness.

69 Discussions of the visual image of the scholar in this period usually exclude them, because when using visual evidence we tend to adopt the formal classifications of art history, in which such representations are subsumed under a different heading – as specimen of depictions of 'the alchemist,'

not of 'the scholar.' The most famous example, which may have shaped the genre, is Pieter Bruegel the Elder's *Alchemist* (1558), ink on paper, Kupferstichkabinett, Staatliche Museen zu Berlin; see Jacques van Lennep, 'L'Alchimiste: Origine et développement d'un thème de la peinture du dix-septième siècle,' *Revue Belge d'archéologie et d'histoire d'art* 35 (1966), 149–68.

70 See the depiction of Hevelius and his wife using their brass sextant in Johannes Hevelius, *Machina coelestis pars prior* (Gdansk, 1673), reproduced in J.A. Bennett, *The Divided Circle: A History of Instruments for Astronomy, Navigation and Surveying* (Oxford, 1987), fig. 61; but notice the difference with the image of Hevelius seated alone in his study by Daniel Schultz (1677), Gdansk Library of the Polish Academy of Science. Hevelius was quite conscious about making his young wife's role in observation explicit; see Alan Cook, 'Johann and Elizabeth Hevelius, Astronomers of Danzig,' *Endeavour* 241, 1 (2000), 8–12, quote on 10. He was a wealthy brewer; the division of scientific work in his household is placed by Londa Schiebinger in the context of the craft tradition: see Schiebinger, *The Mind Has No Sex? Women in the Origins of Modern Science* (Cambridge, MA, 1989), 66–101, esp. 81–2; Monika Mommertz, 'Schattenökonomie der Wissenschaft: Geschlechterordnung und Arbeitssysteme in der Astronomie der Berliner Akademie der Wissenschaften im 18. Jahrhundert,' in Theresa Wobbe, ed., *Frauen in Akademie und Wissenschaft: Arbeitsorte und Forschungspraktiken 1700–2000* (Berlin, 2002), 31–62; Alix Cooper, 'Homes and Households,' in Katharine Park and Lorraine Daston, eds, *The Cambridge History of Science*, vol. 3: *Early Modern Science* (Cambridge, 2006), 235; cf. Christianson, *Tycho's Island*, 68, for Tycho's sister, Sophie Brahe, helping him with observations.

71 Owen Hannaway, 'Laboratory Design and the Aim of Science: Andreas Libavius versus Tycho Brahe,' *Isis* 77 (1986), 586–610, esp. 600–2; William R. Newman, 'Alchemical Symbolism and Concealment: The Chemical House of Libavius,' in Galison and Thompson, eds, *The Architecture of Science*, 59–77; Deborah E. Harkness, 'Managing an Experimental Household: The Dees of Mortlake and the Practice of Natural Philosophy,' *Isis* 88 (1997), 247–62; Tara Nummedal, 'Alchemical Reproduction and the Career of Anna Maria Zieglerin,' *Ambix* 49 (2001), 56–68; Pamela H. Smith, *The Body of the Artisan: Art and Experience in the Scientific Revolution* (Chicago, 2004).

72 Harkness, 'Managing an Experimental Household'; Tara E. Nummedal, *Alchemy and Authority in the Holy Roman Empire* (Chicago, 2007), esp. 119–46.

73 Dürer's famous engraving *The Temptation of the Idler (or The Doctor's Dream)* could belong here, if we adopt an interpretation close to Panofsky's: Erwin Panofsky, 'Zwei Dürerprobleme (der sogenannte "Traum des Doktors" und die sogenannten "Vier Apostel"),' *Münchner Jahrbuch der Bildenden Kunst* n.s.

8 (1931), 1–48; see Jan Steen, *The Scholar at the Desk* (1665–70), oil painting, National Gallery, Prague, reproduced in Sabine Schulze, ed., *Leselust: Niederländische Malerei von Rembrandt bis Vermeer* (Stuttgart, 1993), fig. 76 (note the alembic on the scholar's desk); cf. the different versions of The *Alchemist* by Thomas Wijck (1616–77) in the Rijksmuseum Amsterdam, the Chemical Heritage Foundation's Collections, Philadelphia, the Hermitage Museum, St Petersburg, the Fitzwilliam Museum, Cambridge, and the Museum für Kunst and Kulturgeschichte, Dortmund, as well as Richard Brakeburgh's *Alchemist,* also at the Chemical Heritage Foundation's Collections, Philadelphia, discussed in Lloyd DeWitt and Laurence M. Principe, 'Alchemy and Its Images in the Eddlemann and Fisher Collections at the Chemical Heritage Foundation,' in Jacob Wamberg, ed., *Art and Alchemy* (Copenhagen, 2006), 221–47; Eva-Maria Hanebutt-Benz, *Die Kunst des Lesens: Lesemöbel und Leseverhalten vom Mittelalter bis zur Gegenwart* (Frankfurt am Main, 1985), fig. 81; Gerlinde Lütke Notarp, *Von Heiterkeit, Zorn, Schwermut und Lethargie: Studien zur Ikonographie der vier Temperamente in der niederländischen Serien- und Genregraphik des 16. und 17. Jahrhunderts* (Münster, 1998), 217–33.

74 'quamque me in ea que ante sunt cum Apostolo extendens, et preterita oblivisci nitor et presentia non videre': Petrarca, *Ep. fam.* 7.4, in Wilkins, ed. and trans., *Petrarch in Vaucluse,* 62 (trans. here modified). The formulation alludes to Paul's Epistle to the Philippians 3:13, but Petrarca may have adopted it from Augustine, *Confessions* 9.29.39.

chapter two

From *Pictor Philosophus to Homo Oeconomicus*: Renegotiating Social Space in Poussin's Self-Portrait of 1649–1650

DAVID PACKWOOD

Social space did not really become visible in Nicolas Poussin until the early nineteenth century, when a number of his artistic admirers saw fit to give the painter a life in pictures.[1] Some artists inserted aspects of the world outside the artist's studio into their studies of the painter. One of them, Léon Benouville, working within a realist frame of reference in 1856, retrieved this lost social dimension by showing Poussin watching ordinary people such as washerwomen, who supposedly provided inspiration for such classically conceived works as the *Saving of Moses*.[2] The figure of Poussin in this painting is clearly based on the Louvre self-portrait of 1649–50 (hereafter *Self-Portrait I*, figure 2.1), yet it is unframed from his self-portrait, with the result that he is no longer a prisoner of his studio.[3] Not every nineteenth-century artist, however, sought to move Poussin from studio to scenes of everyday life. In the 1830s, François Marius Granet ignored the commonplace by keeping the painter in his studio, where one might say he has remained ever since, despite attempts to free him.[4] The treatment of Poussin here marks the idea of retreat into the space of work, a trope telling us more about Granet's own melancholic tendencies than about his subject's personality.[5] More significantly, Granet's construction of this social space as predominantly artistic should alert us to the fact that despite the emergence of the domestic private sphere in the eighteenth century and the appearance of the social in later interpretations of Poussin's life, his workshop continued to be regarded as separate from his family and the domestic sphere.[6] The result of this retreat to the interior is that the artist's studio has become a non-social space and *Self-Portrait I* has been turned into a mechanism for producing theories

Figure 2.1 Nicolas Poussin (1594–1665), *Portrait of the Artist*, 1650, oil on canvas, Louvre, Paris, France. Photograph © Giraudon / The Bridgeman Art Library International [XIR 62289].

about art, this despite the fact that Poussin actually positions himself within both *social* and artistic space.

Granet's antisocial take on *Self-Portrait I* raises issues about the precise meaning of social space in that work. When such space is mentioned in discussions of Poussin's art, generally the allusion is to the space of humanism occupied by the artist's patrons and friends, and more specifically, the space of friendship as described by Montaigne, whose ideas have long been connected with *Self-Portrait I.*[7] These readings ignore Poussin's family, implying that his workshop operation was rigidly separated from his domestic situation. It is the investigation into how the domestic economy overlaps with the space of male friendship that I call the 'renegotiation of social space.'

This form of renegotiation bears directly on the other major issue raised in Granet's work, the nature of the relation of domestic space to high art. One view is that non-participation in the domestic space is a necessary condition of access to high art, because the space surrounding the painter's easel contrasts with the space of the house itself; artistic authority breaks down once it enters into a recognizable domestic domain. *Self-Portrait I* raises similar questions about the nature of the artistic and the domestic. It is difficult to determine whether the large rectangular structure at the rear of the studio is a large canvas, a group of different sized canvases stacked up against a door, or just a door leading out of the studio. According to a recent analysis, we are looking at a group of canvases, with the furthest reversed.[8] One must ask a question not posed by Revel: is this mysterious oblong a canvas or a door? If a door – something that cannot be ruled out – then it leads unproblematically from the studio into non-artistic space, assuming we accept the claim that workspace and the rest of the house were kept rigidly separate. If not a door but rather a canvas, then the image might indicate that Poussin is trying to place a barrier between his artistic practice and his family, although this is not the only possible interpretation. Here I explore yet another alternative – the door/canvas as a mediating figure, a motif that alerts us to the problem of how artistic production and the domestic economy intersect within the space of the studio. Invariably, when Poussin's studio is discussed, his immediate family hardly seems to warrant attention because his workspace is perceived as an abstraction, a site that mediates the formal and the theoretical – a space for structuring seeing rather than a space in which the biographical subject is seen. Thus, Oskar Bätschmann stresses the abstract rather than the real in *Self-Portrait I*: the 'row of paintings' in his view representing the 'decrease of visibility' despite the strong possibility that, as previously stated, the last of these could actually be a door leading to the rest of Poussin's house, through which his family may well have entered to view his work.[9]

As Donatella Sparti has pointed out, there may not have been a physical division between the space of painting and the domestic sphere in Poussin's house. According to inventories of the artist's possessions, canvases, brushes, palettes, easels, plaster casts, and antique busts were dispersed throughout the house, not just in his studio.[10] It seems extremely probable that Poussin's working tools would have coexisted harmoniously with domestic objects in current use in his house, a fact suggesting that the mundane and the artistic overlapped in this dwelling. This is significant, since the sinking of artistic objects of invention down to the level of daily routine destabilizes the polarity between the sphere of high art and the domestic economy. Rather than possessing the status of artistic implements, artefacts like brushes and palettes are humbled, now mere domestic objects rather than exclusively aids to artistic invention.

Poussin's implements are usually seen as metonymic of the studio rather than the domestic sphere, but as Sparti's research on the artist's house demonstrates, he saw his artistic tools as part of the ebb and flow of material, domestic life. To give just one example: in his final testament of 1665, Poussin left his niece Barbara, who lived with her uncle in his final years, his working tools as well as money.[11] Such implements and artefacts as appear in *Self-Portrait I*, in Sparti's view, reflect a modus vivendi et operandi: they link Poussin not only with the art of painting but also with the life of the house itself; these painterly attributes would have lived harmoniously with domestic routine.[12]

By concentrating on Poussin's economic and material existence, we move further away from the abstraction of the *pictor-philosophus* towards the socially grounded *homo oeconomicus*. Seen as the complete antithesis of Rembrandt, the *pictor vulgaris* or shop-soiled painter who spills paint on his clothes, Poussin remains the *pictor doctus*, the abstract theoretical mind unencumbered by the distractions of a messy, painterly body.[13] Although useful, these oppositional terms mask the complexities behind representations of the painter and the studio in the early modern period. Abstraction in seventeenth-century studios need not necessarily mean the disappearance of the social sphere or the economic life of the painter. Thus, the so-called pictor vulgaris, Rembrandt, painted himself (figure 2.2) before a wall containing two abstract symbols of painting: two arcs signifying Apelles, the exemplar of draughtsmanship. Here the *ingenium* or natural ability of the pictor vulgaris is conjoined with the *studium* and *ars* of the pictor doctus, unsettling the opposition between the two types of painter.

Relating art theory to the domestic sphere, mathematical and theoretical symbols supposedly separate from the family reappear in Rembrandt's *Self-Portrait*, this time in an unmistakably domestic scene. An earlier etching, not reproduced here, had shown Rembrandt seated in front of his wife, Saskia, as he was delineating a circle and a rectangle, and had suggested an explicit connection between art theory and the family, namely, the idea that draughtsmanship was the father of art. It has been claimed that this image shows not a domestic scene but rather the importance of marriage to the painter and his art. Leaving that issue aside, if Rembrandt can link the idea of marriage with such abstract symbolism, then one could speculate that artistic theory in *Self-Portrait I* should be viewed in a similar way.

In a biographical study, Jacques Thuillier cautiously suggested that the beautiful woman embraced by a pair of hands in a canvas at the

Figure 2.2 Rembrandt Harmensz. van Rijn (1606–69), *Self-Portrait*, ca. 1665, oil on canvas, The Iveagh Bequest, Kenwood House, London, UK. Photograph © English Heritage Photo Library / The Bridgeman Art Library International [EHT 369202].

back of Poussin's studio in *Self-Portrait I* represents the painter's wife, Anne-Marie.[14] This reading is traditionally rejected in the literature on the artist. Instead, the canonical interpretation is that this figure held warmly by male hands, possibly Poussin's own, emblematizes 'friendship and the love of painting.'[15] Part of the problem here is that the conspicuous absence of Anne-Marie in the studio space portrayed in *Self-Portrait I* encourages the assumption that the mysterious female figure is Poussin's muse rather than his wife. *Pittura* therefore displaces spouse.[16] This separation of art and the family in *Self-Portrait I* has been exacerbated by the use of Montaigne's essays as a filter through which *Self-Portrait I* is viewed. In the essay 'De l'affection des pères aux enfants,' the writer wonders if it would be better to produce children through intercourse with the muses rather than through his own wife.[17] As Poussin produced no children, non-biological generation dovetails with the absence of the family within his art: marriage to Anne-Marie produces love, but the biological potential of that love is neutralized and displaced into the sphere of art. The only 'children' Poussin produces are his paintings, and images of infants within the paintings allude to the artist's childless condition.[18]

In a similar vein, Montaigne's essay on fathers and children as used by Svetlana Alpers explains Rembrandt's misogynistic attitude towards his family; he never represented himself with his wife or children, therefore echoing Montaigne's 'misogynist desire' to form a child by the muses rather than his wife.[19] For Alpers, because Rembrandt decided to rent warehouse space away from the oversized house in Amsterdam inhabited by his family, his misogyny replicates Montaigne's.[20] Rembrandt's separation of family from workspace may imply such an attitude, but Poussin's situation was very different. His studio was actually part of his Roman house, perhaps even a small room, an assumption which would support my idea that the large oblong at the back of *Self-Portrait I* is a group of canvases stacked against the door: in other words, in Poussin's real studio, as opposed to the one imagined by Granet, space would have been limited. But as Poussin's working environment was in a building housing Anne-Marie, her parents Jacques Dughet and Dorothea Scaruffa, as well as their immediate family, can domesticity be confidently separated from artistic production? Poussin's canvases may lack the realist appeal of Rembrandt, where recognizable members of the latter's family appear as models, but it is hard to square the image of the silent, uninterrupted painter in *Self-Portrait I* with the one of a small house bursting with relatives and their offspring. In order to reconcile this problem, it is necessary to reconsider Montaigne's ideas on solitude and sociability, which have promoted the view that Poussin kept work and the family away from each other.

Montaigne scholars claim that the essayist's library, which he called his *arrière-boutique* or 'back-shop,' was a space of reflection. Montaigne himself had used the idea that a room must be reserved at the back of the shop for oneself as a metaphor for the detachment of self from the travails of the world.[21] A similar definition of the arrière-boutique appears close to Montaigne's own time in the *Tresor de la langue française* by Jean Nicot, published in 1606. In defining the term, Nicot says that merchants reserve their best goods for the back of the shop, which functions also metaphorically as a space where the true self is shown rather than the one revealed in the presence of people.[22] Although it is clear from Nicot's text that the metaphorical aspects of arrière-boutique relate specifically to the legal profession, the concept applies to a variety of occupations and social roles later in the century. In late seventeenth-century France, the arrière-boutique was seen as the equivalent of a study or comptoir, a place of reflection and refuge for the merchant, artist, or even baroque politician.[23] In her book on space and meaning in seventeenth-century Dutch art, Martha Hollander connects Montaigne's arrière-boutique with architectural design in the whole of Europe. Hollander sees the essayist's concept as coexistent with an emerging self-consciousness, a 'sense of the personal' defined in a space separate from the larger community, but fixed in the home.[24] Montaigne scholars generally consider the arrière-boutique in Hollander's terms, namely, as an architectural metaphor conveying space at the back of the mind to which the troubled soul can retreat from the domestic sphere and mundane matters.[25] Yet for Hollander, Montaigne's arrière-boutique is remarkable precisely because it uses a domestic image: a room in a household to suggest a space of solitude.

In a study that is even more germane to the themes discussed in this essay, George Hoffmann has re-evaluated the image of Montaigne as an 'intellectual recluse' concealed from sight in his back-shop. Bucking scholarly trend, Hoffmann has placed Montaigne in a commercial situation: a 'noisy shop,' where the writer conducted his business with constant interruptions.[26] Rather than understanding his subject as a solitary humanist philosopher in retreat in his arrière-boutique, Hoffmann reconstructs Montaigne as an industrious merchant, multitasking and actively engaging with all around him – a model that invites us to re-evaluate the contiguity of the public professional and the private intellectual in the early modern period.

Hoffmann's reconstruction of Montaigne is important because it has implications for our construal of the image of Poussin in his studio, especially given the prevailing view that this painter used Montaigne's ideas to construct an identity within *Self-Portrait I*.[27] The *Death of Eudamidas* of 1648 does seem to have been inspired by Montaigne's essay on friendship, and certain sentiments and phrases in his correspondence seem to have been derived from reading the French author. But the nearest Poussin comes to the concept of the arrière-boutique is in a letter of 1647, to Paul Fréart de Chantelou, the owner of *Self-Portrait I*. Here, Poussin uses the phrase 'petit coin' or 'little corner' to describe a vantage point from which historical events are observed. This is an idea taken from the theatre, since Poussin compares himself to a spectator watching the 'comedy' of history from safety: 'It is a great pleasure to live in a century in which such great events take place, provided that one can take shelter in some little corner and watch the play in comfort.'[28] A stoic gloss has been applied to this idea of spectatorship, with Blunt promoting the idea of Poussin as philosopher surveying the play of history with detachment.[29] Moreover, stoic observation has become associated with *Self-Portrait I*, seen as the visual correlative of letters in which Poussin expresses such 'stoic' sentiments to Chantelou. The painter supposedly looks out from his petit coin, the camera obscura of his Roman studio, towards his epistolary friend who is enduring political troubles at the hand of Mazarin in distant and dangerous France.[30]

Apart from the vexed question of whether Poussin was a 'stoic,' there is also the issue of whether these comments should be divorced from his economic life.[31] When Poussin announces to Chantelou that men have nothing and everything is on loan, he is not necessarily adopting a stoic pose but hinting at his financial state and his own domestic situation.[32] Sparti has even seen the comment about holding things on loan as implying that Poussin never purchased his own house, a misunderstanding arising, significantly, from an inaccurate modern reading of Poussin's testament by Jouanny, the editor of his correspondence, who was influenced by a nineteenth-century source that stated that Poussin bought the house with Anne-Marie's dowry.[33] A valuable lesson here is that the concept of material self-interest can open up perspectives on the study of kinship relations; early modern anthropological and sociological studies demonstrate that family and friendship networks overlapped.[34] Admittedly, this is pure conjecture, but it may be possible to see in the 'friendship' within *Self-Portrait I* not only the ethos of male client networks but also the financial and social dynamics of the painter's own family.

Within the paradigm of friendship, the space that Poussin occupies in *Self-Portrait I* becomes a male one, constructed with the aid of Montaigne, whose essays fostered the creation of such a male-dominated space. For Blunt, Poussin's workshop shown in *Self-Portrait I* was this space of friendship, occupied only by the artist and his male clients who arrived in numbers guaranteed to 'keep him [Poussin] occupied for the rest of his life.'[35] The studio as an area is detached from normal routine and the domestic sphere – a purely male preserve. This is bringing us back to the idea of the studio space as one of male generativity in which the discourse reproduced excludes the family, the familial thus failing to coexist with the production of art. Yet, as Hollander points out, this kind of 'Montaignean' male discourse conducted within the workshop is inseparable from the domestic sphere. She states that there was no stark separation of family from workspace in seventeenth-century Dutch homes. The evidence is that many men in cities like Amsterdam worked at home as agents, a fact reflected in architectural design: business and residence were contained in a single home with a section of the building used as an area of commerce.[36] According to Hollander, in the *koopmanshuis*, or merchant's house, business and dwelling were harmonized, a trend visible in Dutch paintings of working families.[37] However, images of what she calls 'family cooperation' could be deceptive, because the retreat to the back-shop was coming into existence in the seventeenth century. She shows that the theme of solitude in writing and art is the masculine version of the idea of women's conscientious and dutiful domestic tasks like sewing or reading letters, present in courtly poetry and depictions of the home.[38] Such tasks were instrumental in the construction of distinct personalities, whose identities became associated with specific rooms in houses such as the comptoir or the painter's studio.

With these insights in mind, we need to ask a question about the studio shown in *Self-Portrait I.* Was it a room associated with a specific identity or function, or a multi-occupational space where painting was practised along with other activities like the writing of letters, testaments, and other business documents? Certainly the painting itself, which depicts Poussin holding an object shaped like a document or manuscript, enclosed in a beribboned case, supports the latter interpretation. And, as we have already seen, Poussin's testament is indivisible from the material life of his studio, since he bequeathed his painting implements to members of his family. It is likely that Poussin did not reserve his studio for painting alone, but also wrote or perhaps dictated business documents such as wills and contracts, probably to his brother-in-law, co-worker, and 'bras droit,' Jean Dughet.[39] Jean not only engraved Poussin's paintings but also acted in a secretarial capacity, performing such acts as copying paper manuscripts in the presence of notaries.[40] There may also be a link between notarial culture and Poussin's own artistic practice: in the *Testament of Eudamidas*, a painting commissioned by a man whose will was holographic, Poussin made the decision to include a notary whose writing hand represents the *manus publica*, the hand of the public rather than the hand of a man writing a will in private, the *scripta privata*.[41]

To surmount the problem of how testamentary ideas overlap with the studio, it is helpful to turn to the earlier self-portrait of 1648, painted for another client, Jean Pointel (hereafter *Self-Portrait II*). In this painting (figure 2.3) death, represented by a sculptural tomb (the tomb inscription can be seen at the top of the image), exists side by side with painting in life, the latter embodied in the figure of Poussin holding a chalk holder and book. Comparing Poussin's depiction of himself before a

Figure 2.3 Nicolas Poussin, *Self-Portrait*, 1648, Gemäldegalerie, Staatliche Museen zu Berlin. Inventory no. 1488. Photograph © Bpk / Gemäldegalerie SMB / Jörg P. Anders [22.971].

sepulchre with Leonardo da Vinci's representation of himself embossed on a tomb, Bätschmann concluded that Poussin must still be symbolically alive in *Self-Portrait II*; unlike Leonardo, depicted in profile and situated next to a completed inscription, Poussin 'stood next to a slab that had not yet finished telling his story.'[42] Poussin's inscription is incomplete, meaning that it was not yet time to write his epitaph since he was still living. However, the written inscription on the tomb in *Self-Portrait II* can be seen not only as an epitaph but also as a testament, a document written to be read before an audience, but only after its author has died. Poussin could have fashioned this image with such an audience in mind rather than, as Bätschmann has maintained, with the idea of trying to convey a meditation on the ephemerality of the painter's art and its poetics by depicting the difference between the transience of paintings and the permanence of sculptures.[43]

Traditional readings maintain that the overlapping of painting and writing in *Self-Portraits I* and *II* signifies the pictor-philosophus who uses his pen to write down his observations on art for future generations rather than his written legal testament.[44] Louis Marin was the first scholar to forge links between Poussin's book, drawing pen, and artistic testament in a semiotic analysis of *Self-Portraits I* and *II*. Noting an inconsistency in *Self-Portrait II*, namely that, despite holding a draughtsman's pencil in his right hand, in the left Poussin is holding not a corresponding sheet of drawing paper but rather a book, Marin said that this suggested a 'deeper analogy': the pencil, the draughtsman's tool, resembled a quill for writing, and the book was like a painting.[45] By collapsing painting and writing into each other, Marin was seeking to make connections between the two forms of representation, supposedly contained in the book. He saw the book as both treatise and testament: Poussin's projected treatise on art, the literary counterpoint to the artistic ideas embedded in *Self-Portrait I*, and the written artistic testament that Poussin planned to leave to posterity.

This interpretation of testament within *Self-Portraits I* and *II* depends, again, upon the polarity between the pictor-doctus and the pictor-vulgaris, an opposition that has been shown to be unstable. Another example of the opposition at work is present in Richard Verdi's 1994 catalogue, which describes a physically declining Poussin turning away from the paintbrush in order to pick up his pen and write down his observations on art, unlike the elderly Rembrandt remaining at his easel.[46] In conjuring up this vignette, Verdi relies heavily on the pictor-doctus/pictor-vulgaris opposition: Poussin, the learned artist in his old age, calmly and methodically writing his theory of art, his artistic testament, is contrasted with Rembrandt, the pictor vulgaris, impulsively and energetically painting to the very end without thought for any kind of artistic closing statement. This is a questionable scenario, since Poussin's orderly approach to his actual artistic testament was severely compromised by his debilitating illness, which made writing of any kind almost impossible.

It is odd that Verdi, in considering those observations, which he clearly regards as Poussin's self-inscribed 'eulogy' for his art, overlooked the theme of testament within *Self-Portraits I* and *II*. In the same catalogue, he wondered what kind of self-image Poussin would have produced had he been commissioned to paint *Self-Portrait I* in the 1660s, and he contrasted the scarcity of self-images in Poussin's work with their abundance in the work of artists such as Rembrandt and Van Dyck. However, Verdi failed to consider the possibility that, had the imagined self-portrait actually been executed in the 1660s, it might well have contained iconography similar to that in *Self-Portraits I* and *II*.[47] And he similarly failed to see that Poussin's artistic testament might better be connected with the book in the second of the extant self-portraits than with the written observations.

It may be impossible to resolve the question of the presence of artistic testament in Poussin's late observations, but evidence certainly exists to suggest that the artist's contemporaries confidently related the idea of such a testament to *Self-Portraits I* and *II* in the 1640s. One artist, Jean Pesne, in an engraving after *Self-Portrait II*, even added the words DE LVMINE ET COLORE to the spine of the depicted book, in order to suggest that it was the treatise that Poussin was planning to write on his theory of art.[48] As Poussin holds this 'treatise' before a tomb, the logical conclusion is that Pesne saw it as an artistic testament to be contemplated after the painter's death.

Despite the problems with Verdi's interpretation of Poussin's 1665 observations, his conjecture is useful to the themes in this essay because he considers how legal testament intertwines with the notion of artistic legacy. Poussin may have put down his brushes in order to write, or more likely, due to his infirmity, to dictate his final thoughts to Jean Dughet, his right-hand man; but he also attended to his legal testament, settling disputes about his will with relatives in Normandy who had contested it after Anne-Marie's death in 1664. Poussin was familiar with notaries, and, as already stated, the *Testament of Eudamidas* may indicate his knowledge of seventeenth-century Roman notarial culture. Rembrandt, by contrast, driven by some compulsive need to paint, remained at his easel, eventually dying intestate in 1669.[49] In contrast to Rembrandt, who ignored patrons and notaries, Poussin showed his careful attention to testamentary affairs when he asked Chantelou, the owner of *Self-Portrait I* and the recipient of his letters, to administer his final will, the terms of which stipulated caring for the artist's poor relatives in Normandy.[50] This reading runs counter to the view that *Self-Portrait I* shows Poussin's determination to efface all signs of his early career, including his humble origins in distant Les Andelys.[51] It maintains that Poussin epitomizes the aspirational painter intent on rising from poverty to wealth, a figure within a 'modern tradition of bourgeois success.'[52] Under this sign, of social class, the word *Andelyensis* on the large canvas seems strange, since most arrivistes expunge all trace of their origins. Yet, *Andelyensis* surely demonstrates that Poussin remembered his original family in Les Andelys, recalled by this painted/written word. Instead of Roman cosmopolitanism and some abstract notion of 'Frenchness' (Poussin did not write 'Gallus'), the inscription could be seen in terms of a testamentary structure: the painted and written sign evoking the official notarial record of wills designed to care for both the Roman and French branches of Poussin's family from 1642 onwards.[53] As stated previously, analogies are often made between the paintings and the letters that Poussin sent to his French friends. Surely such analogies can also accommodate the idea of testament, since Poussin's letters to his friends allude to his will, which is being managed by the very people who possess his paintings and, in the case of Chantelou, the owner of *Self-Portrait I*, read his letters.

If one foregrounds the domestic and the legal within the web of relationships and obligations encompassed within *Self-Portrait I*, it becomes possible to narrow the gap between family and workspace in Poussin's paintings. At stake is the much-needed project in Poussin studies of a social history of the art, whose crux is the problem of reconciling the figure of the ideal painter with daily life. As pointed out at the start of this essay, social space only became visible in Poussin when nineteenth-century artists with realist tendencies interpreted his life in their paintings – Granet even representing the seventeenth-century master on his deathbed in a room containing a version of *Self-Portrait I*.[54] Poussin's everyday life was claimed by nineteenth-century artists, but the homo oeconomicus evoked in this essay was a product of seventeenth-century Rome. Much in the same spirit as Hoffmann clothing Montaigne in the costume of the merchant, I have tried to portray Poussin with something of the air and concerns of the northern mercantile artist, a man aware of notarial culture, as the *Testament of Eudamidas* confirms, and at odds with the rarefied pictor-philosophus hiding in his quiet corner in Rome.[55] Such a re-visioning of Poussin opens up his art to the social dimension, which despite being invisible in the paintings, must be present as historical fact.

NOTES

1 Richard Verdi, 'Poussin's Life in Nineteenth-Century Pictures,' *The Burlington Magazine* 3 (1969): 741–50.

2 For a reproduction of Benouville's painting, see Henry Keazor, *Poussin* (Cologne, 2007), 94.

3 On the concept of unframing, see David Carrier, *Poussin's Paintings: A Study in Art-Historical Methodology* (University Park, PA, 1993), 26–9.

4 For Granet's depiction of Poussin in his studio, see Verdi, 'Poussin's Life,' 749.

5 Marc Gottlieb, 'Creation and Death in the Romantic Studio,' in Michael Cole and Mary Pardo, eds, *Inventions of the Studio: Renaissance to Romanticism* (Chapel Hill, NC, 2005), 147–85.

6 On the public sphere, see Jürgen Habermas, *The Structural Transformation of the Public Sphere*, trans. Thomas Burger (Cambridge, MA, 1989).

7 Elizabeth Cropper and Charles Dempsey, *Nicolas Poussin: Friendship and the Love of Painting* (Princeton, 1996), 177–96.

8 Emmanuel Revel, *L'autoportrait de Nicolas Poussin* (Paris, 1997), 56.

9 Oskar Bätschmann, *Nicolas Poussin: Dialectics of Painting* (London, 1990), 51.

10 Donatella Sparti, 'La maison de Nicolas Poussin,' in *Nicolas Poussin (1594–1665)*, Actes du colloque organisé au Musée du Louvre par le Service culturel, 19–21 October 1994, 2 vols. (Paris, 1996), 1:52; hereafter this collection is cited as *Nicolas Poussin*, Actes du colloque.

11 For this section of Poussin's last testament, see Sparti, 'La maison,' 58: 'à Barbara . . . il laisse tous les meubles, ustensiles et instruments que ledit testateur possédera dans sa maison au moment de sa mort, y compris toutes les pièces d'or, d'argent et les deniers qui y seront jusqu'à concurrence de la somme de vingt écus romains et cela quant aux deniers comptants.'

12 Sparti, 'La maison,' 54.

13 On the *pictor vulgaris* see H. Perry Chapman, *Rembrandt's Self-Portraits: A Study in Seventeenth-Century Identity* (Princeton, 1990), 97. For timely remarks about the lack of attention paid to Poussin's body, see Philip Sohm, *The Artist Grows Old: The Aging of Art and Artists in Italy 1500–1800* (London and New Haven, 2007), 66.

14 Jacques Thuillier, *Nicolas Poussin* (Paris, 1988), 134.

15 G.P. Bellori, *Le vite de' pittori, scultori, e architetti moderni*, ed. E. Borea (Turin, 1976), 455. For significant discussions resulting from Bellori's interpretation, see G. Kaufmann, *Poussin-Studien* (Berlin, 1960), 82–98; M. Winner, 'Poussin's Selbstbildnis im Louvre als Kuntstheoretische Allegorie,' *Römisches Jahrbuch für Kunstgeschichte* 20 (1983): 417–39; Cropper and Dempsey, *Nicolas Poussin*, 182; Bätschmann, *Nicolas Poussin*, 47–9.

16 For a discussion of this in the northern context, see Ivan Gaskell, *Vermeer's Wager: Speculations on Art History, Theory and Museums* (London, 2000), 73. Gaskell links the iconography of art/marriage in the north with seventeenth-century French art theory.

17 Montaigne, *Essais,* ed. André Tournon, 3 vols. (Paris, 1998), 2:116.

18 First suggested by Howard Hibbard in *Poussin: The Holy Family on the Steps* (London, 1974), 42, this theme was also adopted by Richard Verdi in his exhibition catalogue *Nicolas Poussin: 1554–1665* (London, 1995), 37.

19 Svetlana Alpers, *Rembrandt's Enterprise: The Studio and the Market* (Chicago, 1988), 30.

20 Ibid., 67.

21 Montaigne, Essais, 1:392: 'Il se faut réserver une arrière-boutique toute notre.'

22 Jean Nicot, *Tresor de la langue française* (Paris, 1606), 47: 'Et parce que les marchants tiennent communement leur meilleure marchandise aux arrière-boutiques.'

23 For example, it appears in the political machinations of the Cardinal de Retz. See Malina Stefanovska, *La politique du cardinal de Retz: Passions et factions* (Rennes, 2008), 84, 133.

24 Martha Hollander, *An Entrance for the Eyes: Space and Meaning in Seventeenth-Century Dutch Art* (Berkeley and Los Angeles, 2002), 179.

25 Ibid., 178.

26 George Hoffmann, *Montaigne's Career* (Oxford, 1998), 24.

27 Cropper and Dempsey, *Nicolas Poussin,* 17. These authors see Montaigne as a model for Poussin within a project of self-representation.

28 Nicolas Poussin, *Lettres et propos sur l'art,* ed. Anthony Blunt (Paris, 1964), 135: 'C'est un grand plaisir de vivre en un siècle là où il se passe de si grandes choses, pourvu que l'on puisse se mettre à couvert en quelque petit coin pour pouvoir voir la comédie à son aise.'

29 Anthony Blunt saw echoes of this idea in Montaigne and Guillaume du Vair. See Blunt's *Nicolas Poussin* (1967; London, 1995), 169.

30 For the camera obscura in relation to the secluded, politically safe space, see Malina Stefanovska, 'Strolling through the Galleries, Hiding in a Cabinet: Clio at the French Absolutist Court,' *The Eighteenth Century: Theory and Interpretation* 35, 3 (1994), 275. On how *Self-Portrait I* fits into the French political context, see Todd Olson, *Poussin and France: Painting, Humanism, and the Politics of Style* (New Haven and London, 2002), 71–4. On the link between the self-portraits and the epistolary relationship between Poussin and Chantelou, see Marc Fumaroli, *L'école du silence: Le sentiment des images au XVIIe siècle* (Paris, 1994), 53–147. See also Cropper and Dempsey, *Nicolas Poussin,* 185–8.

31 For the problem of Poussin as a 'stoic,' see David Packwood, 'Theological and Philosophical Themes in Poussin's Art,' PhD diss., Birmingham University, 2005, 145–82.

32 Malcolm Bull, 'Poussin's Snakes,' in Richard Kendall, ed., *Cézanne and Poussin: A Symposium* (Sheffield, 1993), 35.

33 Sparti, 'La maison,' 63n18. It was E. Gander who in 1860 claimed that Poussin had used Anne-Marie's dowry to purchase his house, but this seems unlikely, as he bequeathed to his family just what was in the house at his death.

34 Peter Laslett and Richard Wall, eds, *Household and Family in Past Time* (Cambridge, 1972); Jack Goody, Joan Thirsk, and E.P. Thompson, eds, *Family and Inheritance: Rural Society in Western Europe 1200–1800* (Cambridge, 1976); Hans Medick and David Warren Sabean, eds, *Interest and Emotion: Essays on the Study of Family and Kinship* (Cambridge, 1984).

35 Blunt, *Nicolas Poussin,* 171.

36 Hollander, *An Entrance for Eyes,* 202.

37 Ibid., 180.

38 Ibid., 178–9.

39 Sparti, 'La maison,' 57.

40 Ibid., 59n80.

41 On notaries in the seventeenth century, see Laurie Nussdorfer, *Brokers of Public Trust: Notaries in Early Modern Rome* (Baltimore, 2009); Julie Hardwick, *The Practice of Patriarchy: Gender and the Politics of Household Authority in Early Modern France* (University Park, PA, 1998).

42 Bätschmann, *Nicolas Poussin,* 47.

43 Ibid.

44 For an exception to the rule see Olson's discussion of the *Testament of Eudamidas* in *Poussin and France,* 163–81, although Olson does not relate the concept of testament to Poussin's own will.

45 Louis Marin, *Sublime Poussin,* trans. Catherine Porter (Stanford, 1999), 194.

46 Verdi, *Nicolas Poussin,* 40.

47 Ibid., 272.

48 Pesne's engraving of *Self-Portrait II* is reproduced in Oskar Bätschmann, *Nicolas Poussin: Dialectics of Painting* (Chicago, 1999), 46. A similar inscription was recently removed from *Self-Portrait II* because it was a later addition: see Verdi, *Nicolas Poussin,* 270. Verdi believed that the Berlin inscription replaced an original one by Poussin himself. See also Thomas Puttfarken, 'Poussin's Thoughts on Painting,' in *Commemorating Poussin: Reception and Interpretation of the Artist* (Cambridge, 1999), 53–75.

49 On Rembrandt's financial condition, see David Packwood, 'Rembrandt, Art and Money,' *Art History* 31 (2008), 270–4.

50 Poussin, *Lettres*, 161.

51 David Carrier, untitled review essay of selected Poussin volumes, *The Art Bulletin*, September 1998, 571.

52 Malcolm Bull, 'A Dance to the Music of Space,' *Art History* 12 (1989), 517. Bull uses this phrase to describe Thuillier's biographical study. See also Carrier, *Poussin's Paintings*, 37–40.

53 On Poussin's wills, see Olivier Michel, 'La fortune matérielle de Poussin,' in *Nicolas Poussin*, Actes du colloque, 1:27–44.

54 For a reproduction of this, see Gottlieb, 'Creation and Death,' 159.

55 Hoffmann, *Montaigne's Career*, 1.

chapter three

The Scholar at Work: Habitus and the Identity of the 'Learned' in Eighteenth-Century France

ANNE C. VILA

Seen from a bird's-eye view, the Republic of Letters in eighteenth-century France might look like a very gregarious place: *salons*, academies, and *cafés* abounded; the *Encyclopédie* championed the values of collective intellectual endeavour; and the new-style *philosophe* was commonly portrayed as a convivial person who enlivened polite society with a gracious combination of urbanity, reason, and civic-mindedness.[1] This vision of the 'enlightened' man or woman of learning, seamlessly integrated into the elite social world, was widely circulated, but it was far from being universally accepted. Quite the contrary: many of the period's moralists, pedagogues, physicians, and literary writers grounded scholarly identity not in circles of intellectual sociability, but rather in the solitary or semi-solitary spaces in which bona fide *savants* pursued their mental work.

Study was, indeed, defined as work in eighteenth-century France – an activity held to rival hard manual labour in its effects on the human machine. Although they did not entirely eschew the older, humanist topos that associated intellectual endeavour with *otium*, or philosophical leisure, Enlightenment-era commentators tended both to glorify and to bemoan the labour that went into the process.[2] The view of study as difficult, health-sapping work was embraced by a variety of authors, from the growing number of physicians who took up the pen to warn the public about the medical risks of mental application, to prominent literary writers who used it either for polemical reasons or as part of their self-image. Rousseau famously declared that library work (*le travail de cabinet*) makes men delicate, weak of temperament, and effeminate; whereas Voltaire's voluminous correspondence is filled with references to the ardent, illness-inducing stints of writing he undertook in the confines of his private apartment or bedchamber.[3] The perceived dangers of study permeated debates about the health of the French Republic of Letters in both a metaphoric and a literal sense, inspiring worries about the scholar as a type, and about the *place* in which intellectual work was conducted, most particularly, the scholarly study (*cabinet*).[4]

This chapter explores selected portrayals of scholars at work in eighteenth-century France, with an eye to determining how the cultural image and personal identity of the 'learned' were shaped by the interior spaces in which they carried out their mental labours. Although Enlightenment-era scholars continued the Renaissance tradition of investing pride and affection in the rooms in which they read, wrote, or meditated, they had to contend with a growing number of exhortations to get out of their studies for the sake of their health and the good of society.[5] For various reasons, the study was perceived as a space in need of regulation, medical and moral. It was also a space of ideological conflict, featured both in stage satires against the 'philosophic' movement and in pro-Enlightenment tributes to the delights of study, to the wonders of the creative process, and to the upstanding private qualities of the great minds of the day.[6]

In other words, although the study often carried pejorative, sometimes pathological connotations in the culture wars of eighteenth-century France, it remained a preferred location for real and fictional scholars alike. As constructed in the period's imaginative literature, it provided not just a site of retreat from the demands and distractions of social life, but also an ideal setting for reflections on everything from art, to nature, to the nature of the self. Here, too, the study functioned not just as a metonymic substitute for the scholar as thinking subject, but as a physical space whose contours acted, either sympathetically or antagonistically, on the physical and moral being who inhabited it.

The Scholarly Workplace and Its Inhabitants

From the stage to the medical treatise, no single room more frequently framed the work of a real or putative scholar in eighteenth-century France than his or her study. The French word *cabinet* could, of course, also denote a piece of furniture or serve as shorthand for secret courtly intrigues.[7] However, the term's principal meaning, according to the 1762 *Dictionnaire de l'Académie française*, was as a place of retreat for work, private conversation, the storage of papers, or the display of books, paintings, and other precious objects.[8] Interestingly, this definition is followed promptly by a reference to its principal inhabitant: 'The name *homme de cabinet* refers to a man who loves study.'[9] At mid-century, therefore, the intellectual-as-homme de cabinet was a recognized species, his identity closely intertwined with the place in which he undertook his favourite activity.

The very existence of the title *homme de cabinet* signalled a social group much larger than the study-loving individual, a group designated by the term *gens de lettres* (men of letters). Roughly speaking, the latter expression denoted learned people of all varieties: literary authors of both sexes, natural philosophers, antiquarians, the new-style intellectual known as the philosophe, and even (as Voltaire emphasized in his *Encyclopédie* article 'Gens de lettres') people who simply thought a lot without ever putting pen to paper.[10] Although diverse in composition, this group had clear, distinguishing traits, including the tendency to set itself apart from the unscholarly in spatial terms as well as in temperament and habits. In many ways, the group habitus of eighteenth-century intellectuals was based on the model that emerged when fifteenth-century northern European scholars first moved their dwelling places from university or monastic settings into urban family units: like its earlier incarnations, the eighteenth-century French *cabinet* functioned, to quote Gadi Algazi, as a 'shield for a scholar's vulnerable self'; and the period's self-described learned people continued both to yearn for solitude (and sometimes the clerical celibacy of yore) and to view as irksome disturbances the rooms and people located outside the study's walls.[11]

Those traits are neatly illustrated by the philosophe character Ariste, of Philippe-Néricault Destouches's hit comedy *Le philosophe marié, ou, Le mari honteux de l'être* [The Married Philosophe, or, The Husband Ashamed of So-Being] (1727). Act 1 of the play begins with Ariste surrounded by his books, pens, mathematical instruments, and globe, exulting in the solitary pleasures of his study until he remembers that a very different existence awaits him in the next room:

> My retreat is my Louvre, and I command here like a king.
> But it is only here that I exercise supreme power;
> Outside of my study, I am no longer the same
> In the other apartment, I am always annoyed
> Here, I am a bachelor; there, I am married.[12]

By replaying three or four times the scene of Ariste's dismay at seeing the various women in his household enter his sanctum (including the lovely Mélite whom he has married secretly), Destouches's comedy attests to the currency of the long-established scholarly topos of disdain for family life, for the 'fair' sex, and for non-scholarly social obligations.[13] That attitude was not limited to male scholars: Mme du Châtelet also displayed it at Cirey and at the court of Sceaux, where she and Voltaire worked so incessantly and kept such odd hours that they offended their more sociable companions. As the exasperated Baronne de Staal (Mme de Staal-Delaunay, protégée of the Duchesse du Maine, who held court at Sceaux) complained in a letter to the Marquise du Deffand, the great thinkers were like 'two spectres, with an odour of embalmed corpses that they seemed to have brought from their tombs . . . Our ghosts don't show themselves during the day; they appeared yesterday at ten at night, and I don't think we'll see them any earlier today. One is busy describing great events, the other commenting Newton. They want neither to gamble nor to go for a stroll: they are, indeed, two non-values in a society where their erudite writings have no pertinence.'[14]

More often than not, however, the topos of scholarly detachment from non-scholarly activities was reserved for male denizens of the eighteenth-century Republic of Letters. It was codified both in pedagogical works and in the scholar-specific hygiene manuals that became popular after 1750. For example, in his treatise *L'homme de lettres* (1764), the antiquarian and Hebrew professor Jean-Jacques Garnier urged his students to confine themselves as much as possible to their libraries and avoid everything that could distract them from their studies – including the tumult of worldly life, social visits, gambling, dissipation, and even passing romantic involvement. The true man of letters, Garnier declared, was devoted exclusively to the cultivation of the mind: 'His life is a continuous meditation, and retreat is his element.'[15] At the same time, Garnier warned his young readers to pay proper attention to the conditions in which they performed their studies: the best personal library, he emphasized, was not the 'most beautiful' but the 'most commodious'; and men of letters had to take care of their health and avoid overstuffing themselves with book-reading.[16]

Exhortations of this sort echoed the discourse that was directed at scholars by contemporary physicians who, although belonging themselves to the intelligentsia, nonetheless worried greatly over the debilitating effects of social and intellectual refinement.[17] To some degree, the medical community's mixed attitude towards the ills of scholarship reflected differences in personal ideology among the physicians who weighed in on the subject. Doctors who sympathized with the

Enlightenment movement tended to glamorize the ailing scholar persona, whereas more conservative physicians generally dismissed the expansion of learnedness as a misguided fad and saw few true geniuses among those who got swept up in it. Some historians have attributed the mid-to-late eighteenth-century upsurge in writings on intellectual pathologies to the influence of Jean-Jacques Rousseau, particularly his famous denunciations of book learning in the *Discours sur les sciences et les arts* (1749) and the *Discours sur les origines de l'inégalité parmi les hommes.*[18] One does, indeed, hear echoes of Rousseau (and occasionally direct citations of him) in works like Samuel-Auguste-André-David Tissot's *De la santé des gens de lettres* (Of the Health of Men of Lettres) (1768) and Hugues Maret's *Mémoire dans lequel on cherche à déterminer quelle influence les moeurs des François ont sur leur santé* (Memoir Seeking to Determine What Influence the Mores of the French Have on Their Health) (1772). However, although a broad strand of Rousseauism ran through medical portrayals of the sickly scholar – as it did in the specialized literature on female vapours that proliferated at the same time – it was neither consistent, nor consistently favourable to Rousseau. Moreover, physicians who wrote on intellectual pathologies were just as apt to cite ancient or Renaissance authors (like Celsus and Ficino) as the celebrated 'Jean-Jacques,' suggesting that even the most Rousseauistic among them were motivated by reasons that went beyond the desire to lend credence to his anti-worldly moral philosophy.

Eighteenth-century interest in the intellectual as patient was closely connected to the expansion of hygiene as a distinct branch of medicine. This was the period when hygiene first came to be regarded as an important part of the medical curriculum, when self-help manuals on the art of conserving health were published in abundance, and when French physicians began to write on diseases specific to certain professions.[19] Clearly, a blend of optimism and entrepreneurialism underpinned the emerging medical effort to identify and treat the health problems of learned people.[20] There was more involved in this effort, however, than the simple expansion of occupational medicine: the medical community's alarm over the perceived bodily dangers of mental application was more intense and personal than their concerns over the work-related disorders of other 'at-risk' groups (like hatters, spinners, or goldsmiths).[21] After all, doctors who treated genteel patients were themselves men of letters: even if they did not publish actively, they were regarded as members of the Republic of Letters through their academic affiliations, their membership in medical and philosophical societies, their correspondence, and the fashionable circles they frequented.[22] Moreover, physicians not only played a fundamental role in the cultivated society of eighteenth-century France, they also took part in the campaign to bathe great thinkers in an aura of heroism via glowing testimonials and eulogies.[23] Thus, when physicians published books warning about the dangers of mental work, they were also writing (in part, at least) about themselves.

The scholarly study was a central feature in those warnings: in the most famous and frequently reprinted French-language contribution to this genre, *De la santé des gens de lettres,* Tissot chastised men of letters for sitting huddled over their books for hours on end, failing to refresh the stale, hot air of their studies, and neglecting to leave them even to eat, drink, or answer the call of nature.[24] Gabriel Grégoire Lafont-Gouzi expanded on this sort of anti-study medical diatribe forty-five years later: he blamed not just the bad air and elevation of urban living quarters but also their excessively comfortable furnishings for the head colds, nervous illnesses, and (according to Lafont-Gouzi's strange causal logic) moral degeneracy characteristic of *gens de cabinet.*[25] Lafont-Gouzi's condemnation of luxurious interior decoration brings to mind Diderot's semi-facetious account of how his own study was transformed from 'the edifying little room of the Philosopher' into a 'scandalously' upwardly mobile space by his sumptuous new scarlet dressing gown, which, from the moment he began wearing it to work in his studio, demanded so many improvements on the room's furnishings that he feared his natural qualities of sensitivity, affability, and frankness might be changed as well.[26]

According to these various portraits of the scholar in his study, the room itself had transformative powers: it could both destroy the health of its frail inhabitant and reshape his moral character in 'unnatural' ways. These depictions of the scholar's workplace thus confirm the idea (recently advanced by various cultural historians) that the self in the age of sensibility was an entity shaped as much from without as from within.[27] To extend that idea, the self of the intellectual toiling in his study was formed not just by the inward-directed experiences of reading and meditation, but also by its placement in, and exposures to, the physical and social worlds. With the rise of the image of the scholar as an impression-vulnerable, acutely sensitive type, it was no longer enough to configure the study in ways that shielded the scholar from the demands and distractions of domestic life. Now, the scholar's workplace also had to adhere to the prescriptions of medical and moral hygiene, both to protect scholars from the dangerous, potentially debilitating effects of the study environment and to ensure that they remained fit to partake in family life and the larger social realm.

Thinking as Work

In the minds of those concerned about the potentially damaging effects of the scholarly workplace, attention had to be paid not just to the place but also to the *work* done there. The progressive revalorization of scholarship that occurred in eighteenth-century France brought mental work into greater proximity with manual work – both through the metaphors of pain and exhaustion which apologists of intellectual activity borrowed from the language of physical labour, and through the emerging perception that the intellectual and the farmhand were equally useful and necessary to the healthy functioning of the state.[28] According to the profession-specific tradition of writing about health which was popularized at the very beginning of the century by Bernardino Ramazzini's *Treatise of the Diseases of Tradesmen*, intellectuals were just as susceptible as manual labourers to the bodily fatigue and dysfunction brought on by carrying out their chosen professions.[29] What mattered, from this perspective, was not the social standing of the worker or even the particular nature of his or her work; rather, it was the disruptive effect of that work on the organism.

One consequence of this concern over study as work was increased anxiety over the working habits of scholars. As Vladimir Janković has emphasized, the sensibility-inspired conception of the human being as a 'reactive' organism, acutely vulnerable to its physical and social surroundings, had a profound effect on eighteenth-century disease theory: first, it reoriented the medical quest for the causes of illness towards the outside environment, creating (among other things) an almost obsessive concern with air quality; and second, it tapped into the larger cultural idea that contemporary European society was itself pathogenic, both because of the overstimulating social conditions it created and because of the unhealthy living climate of modern European cities.[30] These developments fed the perceived need for expanded medical supervision over the interior climates frequented by those who possessed the most refined sensibilities, most particularly, Europe's scholars.

Yet doctors also paid increasing attention to the act of study itself, painting it in terms of threats that came as much from within the individual as from without. That sense of threat was inscribed in the very term which eighteenth-century writers typically used to characterize serious thinking: 'la contention d'esprit,' or mental exertion. Interestingly, the application of the term 'contention' to mental activity was a fairly recent phenomenon: *contention* had originally denoted battle or dispute.[31] By mid-century, however, this was the default meaning of the term – as is illustrated by Denis Diderot's short entry on the subject in the *Encyclopédie*:

> CONTENTION [EXERTION], s. f. (*Gramm. & Métaph.*): Long, strong, and painful application of the mind to some object of meditation. *Exertion* supposes difficulty, importance on the part of the subject matter, and persistence and fatigue on the part of the philosophe. There are things that one can understand only through *exertion* . . . There is only a difference of degree between *exertion* and application. *Exertion* is distinguished from meditation by the ideas of persistence, duration, and fatigue, which *exertion* supposes, and meditation does not. *Exertion* is the result of reiterated efforts.[32]

No flesh-and-blood adversary is present in the battle described here: the struggle is solitary and internal, directed solely at an object of meditation. This brief portrait of the philosophe engaged in intense mental application emphasizes both the necessity of *contention* for grasping difficult ideas and the fatigue brought on by the effort. And fatigue, as Diderot underscored in his *Encyclopédie* article on that subject, was the inevitable effect of any 'considerable effort' – whether the part at work was the body or the mind.[33]

This image of men of letters as exhausted by incessant mental exertion was circulated in a variety of contexts, including academic *éloges* and conduct books.[34] It was (predictably) vigorously promoted in the period's medical literature: in a treatise directed largely at medical students, Marin-Jacques-Clair Robert maintained that major mental exertion triggered body-shaking spasms in the entire organism.[35] As Robert described it, the 'extraordinary' work involved in mental labour fell largely upon the nerves, which underwent enormous tension when a thinker engaged in serious meditation.[36] The medical popularizer Vandermonde also tied mental work to overexertion of the nerve system in the long section of the *Dictionnaire portatif de santé* (Portable Dictionary of Health, 1759) which he devoted to the professional illnesses of scholars: 'Men of Letters typically err through an excess opposite to that committed by manual workers: they have their minds continuously strained and occupied, which taxes the nerves and makes the functions languish, the stomach lazy, and digestion slow.'[37] By ardently pursuing his studies in response to the insidiously flattering pleasure of discovering truths, the man of letters strained his nerves beyond their natural capacity and harmed their 'spirits,' either by corrupting them or draining them away from their normal channels. When a scholar overindulged in study, the damage done was all too apparent: Vandermonde cited, as proof, the heaviness and weakness which scholars commonly felt when they had worked too much, as well as their reddened, inflamed faces.[38]

Enlightenment-era physicians often compared overstudy with indulgence in other, more carnal sorts of passions (although they did not generally see scholars as inclined to self-gratification of anything but their brains). The fashionable Parisian doctor Anne-Charles Lorry interspersed his discussion of the special dietary needs of men of letters with cautions about the havoc they wrought upon their bodies by engaging too regularly in the absorbing, 'ecstatic' pleasures of the mind.[39] Tissot, more pointedly, contended that scholars were 'like lovers who fly off the handle when one dares to say that the object of their passion has defects; moreover, they almost all have the sort of fixity in their ideas that is created by study.'[40]

The urge to procure the pleasures of thinking – also commonly characterized as the 'passion for arts and sciences,' the 'ardour' of study, or 'literary intemperance' – was thus clearly an underlying culprit in the etiology of the diseases to which scholars were deemed vulnerable during the Enlightenment and the decades that followed it. As the Swiss physician Johann Georg Zimmermann put it, 'The desire to acquire enlightenment, or to make use of the knowledge which one has acquired can easily be ranked among the passions, because it is so strong in some people that it absorbs almost all their other passions.'[41] Although Zimmermann expressed admiration for those whose consuming passion was study, he cautioned that this mode of pleasure was appreciated by precious few in society at large – and that 'a man taken with this sort of *volupté* does not enjoy it unadulterated for long, if he indulges in it without discretion.'[42] Those who applied their minds too ardently to study were, he argued, at risk of succumbing to numerous ailments, including digestive disorders, debilitating headaches, weakened nerves, hypochondria, loss of sight and hearing, and profound melancholy.[43]

All those dangers combined in the dramatic tableau which Paul-Victor de Sèze painted to describe the cascade of dire physiological events that unfolded when a scholar undertook the task of thinking:

> At the moment when a man fixes all of his attention on the object of his research, his brain swells: its fibres stretch and attract a greater portion of the body's general activity, such that the humours are carried to the brain in greater abundance. However, the action of the brain does not suffice on its own: it must be reinforced by a strong tension in the phrenic centre,

> in the intestines and all the viscera of the lower abdomen. One can see, when a person has meditated a long while, that the diaphragm, stretched and hampered in its movements, impedes freedom of respiration and even suspends it, such that the person is forced to sigh from time to time. The constriction of the epigastrum and of the entire intestinal canal supposes an effort that can be made only at the expense of the exterior organ [the skin], which remains inactive. In fact, a man plunged in mental work does not see, even though he has his eyes open; his senses are inactive; only the head and the epigastrum are in action.[44]

According to this scenario, the brain 'swelling' brought on by mental labour muted the scholar's sensibility to his surroundings, to the point of shutting down his sense organs. If, de Sèze continued, the scholar had the intestinal fortitude necessary to counterbalance the swelling and tension his brain was experiencing, then he could emerge relatively unscathed from the almost catatonic absorption in which he had been plunged.[45] If, however, his viscera were weak, his brain's intense action would wreak havoc there, causing the abdominal organs also to compress, first by thickening and then by slowing down their functions.[46] In an intriguing twist – due, perhaps, to the fact that de Sèze designed this tableau partly to discourage his female readers from even attempting study – he went on to compare the brain's disruptive effects in the scholarly body to those created by the uterus in the female body, which was held to wreak its revenge for 'unnatural,' worldly living by causing hysteria (a close cousin during this period to the stomach-based malady called hypochondria).[47]

The intense, exhausting, mental effort which physicians attributed to the cerebralist did, of course, coexist in the period's medical imagery with excessive sedentariness, a condition best cured by exercise, including manual labour (*le travail des mains*).[48] Yet scholarly sedentariness per se seemed to worry doctors less than the frailty to which intellectuals were vulnerable. Medical anxiety over lack of exercise was, moreover, somewhat less pronounced among French doctors discussing intellectual pathologies than among their British counterparts; and those who did worry about the health effects of sedentariness often targeted vaporous ladies and other worldly sorts more than they did scholars.[49] It may be that, in the eyes of physicians, the French man of letters partook of the frenetic qualities which Montesquieu had famously attributed to his countrymen in *Les lettres persanes* (1721), where he mocked French presumptions to have reached one of the summits of human achievement by maintaining a social pace that (as his character Rica described it) was so overactive as to approach the superhuman.[50]

Judging from Voltaire's astounding rate of literary production – not to mention the ambitious scope of the *Encyclopédie* project – the eighteenth-century French Republic of Letters did, indeed, seem to operate at an exhausting pace. The medical perspective on thinking as labour was thus in keeping with the self-image of Enlightenment intellectuals as heroically active in mind, if not always in body. It also suited the period's tendency to blur existing distinctions among the types of cerebralists who were included under the broad umbrella term *gens de lettres*: if they were all to be understood first and foremost as mental workers, then it was unnecessary to delve deeply into the particular nature of their mental work.

Early nineteenth-century French physicians would move away from the levelling effect of the 'thinking as work' medical paradigm by introducing new ways of ranking intellectuals: pioneering alienists like Philippe Pinel, for example, classified thinkers according to their susceptibility to certain sorts of mental illness, declaring scientists and mathematicians to be largely exempt from imagination-induced diseases such as mania.[51] These doctors would, however, continue to endorse two strands of medical thought that were related to this conceptual scheme: first, the idea that cerebral work had deleterious effects, not just on the brain, but also on the abdominal region; and second, the notion that sustained mental application drastically altered the body's overall sensibility, making scholars both more susceptible to bad conditions in their physical milieu or workspace and (paradoxically, perhaps) strangely oblivious to their surroundings while in the heat of their passionate labours.

In Defence of the *Cabinet*: The Irresistible Charms of Intellectual Absorption

Several non-medical writers of eighteenth-century France also launched rhetorical campaigns to coax scholars out of the study and into more sociable climes; this was particularly evident among those connected to the group known as the philosophes. Voltaire, for example, deemed contemporary men of letters superior to their predecessors because 'the spirit of the century has made most of them as well-suited for society [*le monde*] as for the study [*cabinet*]'; and he repeatedly rebuked poets, philosophers, historians, and political leaders who passed judgment on humanity from the confines of their studies.[52] In their writings on the new theatrical genre known as the *drame*, Diderot and Mercier likewise enjoined playwrights to get out of their studies and observe real-life people in society.[53] At the same time, however, all three of these writers frequently celebrated the solitary pleasures that could be found only in that confined space – or, for the itinerant Voltaire, anywhere he set up a work station.[54] They also set different standards for intellectuals whom they viewed as ill suited for any setting *other* than their studies, like Newton (for Voltaire) or Leibniz (for Diderot).[55]

Leibniz – or, more properly speaking, Leibniz as seen through the eyes of Diderot – is an interesting case with which to conclude. Drawing on Fontenelle's curious biographical portrait of Leibniz as a solitary (an image that, as Dinah Ribard underscores, glosses over the very active, worldly existence which Leibniz led as a courtly diplomat), Diderot depicted Leibniz as a 'deep thinker,' a man so wrapped up in cogitation that his being in the world simply didn't matter.[56] Although his evocations of Leibniz were merely anecdotal – much like the brief, equally fanciful portraits of d'Alembert as absorbed geometer – they nonetheless serve as a benign, disease-free counter-narrative to the alarmist image of mental absorption circulated by Diderot's medical contemporaries.

Diderot was hardly a solitary himself: he situated his most expansive scenes of personal philosophizing in social settings (see *Le neveu de Rameau*) or in the open air (see *Les entretiens sur le fils naturel*, the 'promenade Vernet' section of *Les salons*). At the same time, however, he was fascinated by the asocial nature of creative geniuses, whom he viewed as people too absorbed in their thoughts to pay much heed to family, physical setting, or other material concerns. That fascination is amply apparent in the brief portrait of Leibniz which he sketched in *Réfutation d'Helvétius* (1775):

> When Leibniz holed himself up, at the age of twenty, and spent thirty years in his dressing gown, plunged in the depths of geometry or lost in the shadows of metaphysics, he gave no more thought to obtaining a position, sleeping with a woman, or filling an old chest with gold, than if he'd been at death's door. He was a reflecting machine, like a weaving loom or a machine for making stockings; he was a being who took pleasure in meditating; he was a sage or a madman, whichever you like, who placed infinite importance on the approval of his peers, who loved the sound of [intellectual] praise like a miser loves the sound of a coin.[57]

Diderot's attitude here oscillates between half-serious alarm over the oblivious, mechanical quality of the thinker and admiration for the single-minded pleasure which Leibniz seemed to take in thoughtful reverie. So absolute was that pleasure, Diderot imagined, that if someone had broken down Leibniz's door and entered his study 'with pistol in hand,' saying 'your money, or your discovery of the calculus,' Leibniz would have handed over the key to his safe with a smile.[58] Diderot often expressed this sort of perplexed fondness for figures like Leibniz: in *Le rêve de d'Alembert*, he gently poked fun at the geometer d'Alembert for spending two-thirds of his life dreaming with his eyes open; and in the *Salon de 1767*, he characterized geniuses as 'poetic beings' who were sublime when labouring in isolation over an idea or a work of art, but mad – or, at least, utterly inept – the minute they stepped out in public.[59]

Thus, as Diderot described them, cerebralists of the highest order were a species apart: when they were absorbed in meditation, their conscious selves became impervious both to their surroundings and to the conventional expectations of civil society. Such brilliant individuals were, he maintained, simply too exceptional in temperament and constitution to be judged by the criteria applied to the rest of humanity. They existed in such a different mental space that they strolled through their physical and social environments spectre-like – lost in thought, and guided not by their wills but by the mechanical habits of their bodies. For scholars such as these, the workplace was any place; and the world outside the study had little significance, beyond the glory that it might bestow upon them.

NOTES

1 Many historians have emphasized the importance of sociability among eighteenth-century French intellectuals and their aspiration to full membership in 'polite' culture. See, among other studies, Dena Goodman, *The Republic of Letters: A Cultural History of the French Enlightenment* (Ithaca, 1994); Daniel Gordon, *Citizens without Sovereignty: Equality and Sociability in French Thought, 1670–1789* (Princeton,1994); Emmanuel Bury, *Littérature et politesse: L'invention de l'honnête homme* (Paris, 1996); and Gregory S. Brown, *A Field of Honor: Writers, Court Culture and Public Theater in French Literary Life from Racine to the Revolution* (New York, 2002).

2 On the Renaissance topos of idleness, see Virginia Krause, *Idle Pursuits: Literature and Oisiveté in the French Renaissance* (Newark, 2003). Anson Rabinbach locates the disappearance of idleness and the accompanying shift to an association of work with fatigue in the nineteenth century; see Rabinbach, *The Human Motor: Energy, Fatigue, and the Origins of Modernity* (New York, 1990), 1–44. Rabinbach does not, however, focus specifically on mental work, an

area in which fatigue-based concepts already seem established in the eighteenth century.

3 'Le goût des lettres, de la philosophie et des beaux-arts amollit les corps et les ames. Le travail de cabinet rend les hommes délicats, affoiblit leur tempérament, et l'ame garde difficilement sa vigueur quand le corps a perdu la sienne. L'étude use la machine, épuise les esprits, détruit la force, énerve le courage' (The taste for letters, philosophy, and the fine arts softens bodies and minds. Library work makes men delicate, weakens their temperament, and the mind is hard pressed to retain its vigour when the body has lost it own. Study wears out the machine, exhausts the spirits, destroys strength, weakens courage). For this passage, see Jean-Jacques Rousseau, 'Préface à *Narcisse ou l'Amant de lui-même* [Preface to 'Narcissus or the Self-Lover'] (1752), in Rousseau, *Oeuvres complètes,* 5 vols. (Paris, 1964), 2:966, my translation. Unless otherwise indicated, all translations are my own.

Voltaire also linked intensity of mental application to bodily frailty – albeit in personal, rather than polemical, terms. See, for example, the letter he wrote to Stanislas Leszczynski, king of Poland, as part of a campaign to get the king's steward, Alliot, to serve Voltaire his meals in his room at Lunéville: 'Elle [His Majesty] sait que je suis très malade, et que de travaux continuels me retiennent dans mon appartement, autant que mes souffrances' (His Majesty knows that I am quite ill, and that continuous labours keep me in my apartment, as much as my ailments do). The quotation is from Voltaire to Stanislas Leszczynski, 29 August 1749, Letter 3451, in *Voltaire's Correspondence,* ed. Theodore Besterman, 107 vols. (Geneva, 1953–65), 17:149.

4 On the studious life as a perceived medical problem elsewhere in eighteenth-century Europe, see John Mullan, *Sentiment and Sociability: The Language of Feeling in the Eighteenth Century* (Oxford, 1988), 201–40; Anita Guerrini, *Obesity and Depression in the Enlightenment: The Life and Times of George Cheyne* (Norman, OK, 2000), 119–25; and Susan Meld Shell, 'Kant's Hypochondria,' in *Embodiment of Reason: Kant on Spirit, Generation, and Community* (Chicago, 1996), 264–305. For the sake of non-francophone readers, I have generally replaced the French term *cabinet* with 'study' or, in some places, 'library.'

5 See Dora Thornton, *The Scholar in His Study: Ownership and Experience in Renaissance Italy* (New Haven and London, 1997). See also Peter Thornton, *Seventeenth-Century Interior Decoration in England, France, and Holland* (New Haven, 1978), esp. chap. 12, 'Specific Rooms and Their Decoration.'

6 Anti-philosophical satires set in or around a scholarly study include Teisserenc, *La femme philosophe* [The Woman Philosopher] (1759) and Jean-Jacques Rutledge, *Le bureau d'esprit* [The Office of Wit] (1777). As Elena Russo notes, Louis-Sébastien Mercier was particularly active in using theatre for

pro-philosophical purposes, including the composition of plays that showcased great thinkers and writers in their *cabinets* and other domestic settings; Russo, *Styles of Enlightenment: Taste, Politics, and Authorship in Eighteenth-Century France* (Baltimore, 2007), 194–213. Jean-Claude Bonnet also discusses the use of plays to fuel the eighteenth-century fervour for intellectual heroes; see *Naissance du Panthéon: Essai sur le culte des grands hommes* (Paris, 1998).

7 On the multiple denotations of the related term *bureau* (a room, as well as a piece of furniture), and the meanings invested in the sort of desk known as a *secrétaire*, see Dena Goodman, 'The Secrétaire and the Integration of the Eighteenth-Century Self,' in Dena Goodman and Kathryn Norberg, eds, *Furnishing the Eighteenth Century: What Furniture Can Tell Us about the European and American Past* (New York and London, 2007), 183–203.

8 'Lieu de retraite pour travailler, ou converser en particulier, ou pour serrer des papiers, des livres, pour mettre des tableaux, ou quelqu'autre chose de précieux'; *Dictionnaire de L'Académie française*, 4th ed. (1762), 229; accessed via ARTFL (http://colet.uchicago.edu); hereafter *D.A.F.*

9 'On appelle *Homme de cabinet*, Un homme qui aime l'étude'; 'Cabinet,' *D.A.F.* (1762), 229. The term *homme de cabinet* evolved in intriguing ways. In Jean-François Féraud's *Dictionnaire critique de la langue française* (Marseille, 1787–8), one finds a greater emphasis on repose and books: '*Homme de cabinet*, qui aime le repôs et les livres' (*Cabinet* man [Man of (the) study], who loves repose and books). By contrast, in 1835, the term – and the place – was associated with professional obligations: '*Homme de cabinet*, Homme que sa profession oblige à travailler dans le cabinet' (*Cabinet* man: man whose profession obliges him to work in a study or bureau or office); see *Dictionnaire de L'Académie française*, 6th ed. (1832–5); also accessed via ARTFL; subsequent citations to the *Dictionnaire* are to the ARTFL online edition.

10 'Il y a beaucoup de gens de lettres qui ne sont point auteurs, et ce sont probablement les plus heureux; ils sont à l'abri des dégoûts que la profession d'auteur entraîne quelquefois, des querelles que la rivalité fait naître, des animosités de parti, et des faux jugements; ils sont plus unis entre eux; ils jouissent plus de la société; ils sont juges, et les autres sont jugés' (There are many men of letters who are not authors, and they are probably the happiest; they are shielded from the weariness that the writerly profession sometimes brings, from the quarrels that rivalry engenders, from partisan animosities, and false judgments; they have more solidarity among themselves, and take greater pleasure in society; they are the judges and the others are judged). For this passage, see Voltaire, 'Gens de lettres,' in Diderot and d'Alembert, eds, *Encyclopédie ou dictionnaire raisonné des sciences, des arts*

et des métiers, 18 vols., here 7:599 (accessed via ARTFL); cited hereafter as *Encyclopédie*.

11 Gadi Algazi, 'Scholars in Households: Refiguring the Learned Habitus, 1480–1550,' *Science in Context* 16, 1–2 (2003), 26. Lorraine Daston emphasizes that many Enlightenment intellectuals vociferously defended the precept of distance from society: 'This was an ideology of distance, both metaphorical and literal, from all human ties'; Daston, 'Enlightenment Fears, Fears of Enlightenment,' in Keith M. Baker and Peter H. Reill, eds, *What's Left of Enlightenment? A Post-Modern Question* (Stanford, 2001), 121.

On nostalgia for scholarly celibacy in eighteenth-century France, see Éric Walter, 'Le complexe d'Abélard ou le célibat des gens de lettres,' *Dix-huitième siècle* 12 (1980), 127–52; and Jean M. Goulemot and Daniel Oster, *Gens de lettres, écrivains et bohèmes: L'imaginaire littéraire, 1630–1900* (Paris, 1992), esp. 77–84. Many participants in the Enlightenment Republic of Letters maintained that high-level intellectual activity was incompatible with marriage or even sexuality; as Madame Geoffrin put it, 'nos savants ne se marient point'; cited in Elisabeth Badinter, *Les passions intellectuelles*, vol. 1, *Désirs de gloire, 1735–1751* (Paris, 1999), 29.

12 'Ma retraite est mon Louvre, et j'y commande en roi. / Mais je n'use qu'ici de mon pouvoir suprême; / Hors de mon cabinet je ne suis plus le même / Dans l'autre appartement, toujours contrarié: / Ici, je suis garçon, là, je suis marié'; Philippe-Néricault Destouches, *Le philosophe marié, ou le mari honteux de l'être*, in *Oeuvres dramatiques de N. Destouches* (Paris, 1822), 2:374.

13 We should note, however, that *Le philosophe marié* culminates with the transformation of its *philosophe* protagonist into a proper, well-socialized spouse. For a fuller reading of that play, see Vila, '*Faux savants, femmes philosophes*, and *philosophes amoureux*: Foibles of the Philosophe on the Eighteenth-Century French Stage,' *Studies on Eighteenth-Century Culture* 35 (Spring 2006), 213–32.

14 'Madame du Châtelet et Voltaire . . . parurent comme deux spectres, avec une odeur de corps embaumés qu'ils semblaient avoir apportée de leurs tombeaux . . . Nos deux revenants ne se montrent point le jour; ils apparurent hier à dix heures du soir; je ne pense pas qu'on les voie guère plutôt aujourd'hui; l'un est à décrire de hauts faits, l'autre à commenter Newton. Ils ne veulent ni jouer ni se promener: ce sont bien des non-valeurs dans une société où leurs doctes écrits ne sont d'aucun rapport'; letter of 15 March 1747, in *Vie privée de Voltaire et de Mme du Châtelet pendant un séjour à Cirey; par l'auteur des Lettres péruviennes, suivies de cinquantes lettres inédites, en vers et en prose, de Voltaire* [*The Private Life of Voltaire and Mme du Châtelet during a Stay at Cirey; by the Author of the Peruvian Letters, Followed by Fifty Unpublished*

Letters, in Verse and Prose, by Voltaire] (Paris, 1820), 283, 286. Although attributed only to Mme de Graffigny, this volume includes letters by various other authors, including Mme de Staal [Staal-Delaunay]. The court of Sceaux, scene of the episode related by Mme de Staal, was the 'oppositional' court established by the Duc du Maine (illegitimate son of Louis XIV and Mme de Montespan) and his culture-loving wife, the Duchesse du Maine. On the visit which Voltaire and du Châtelet made there, see André Maurois's biography 'Voltaire,' in *Dictionnaire des lettres françaises XVIIIe siècle* (Paris, 1960), 2:648.

In an earlier part of this epistolary anthology, Mme de Graffigny painted a similar picture of life at Cirey in 1739. She described the long nights which du Châtelet spent working, glued to her *secrétaire*; Graffigny, letter 21, in *Vie privée de Voltaire*, 276–77. See, in contrast, Voltaire's posthumous depiction of du Châtelet as the consummate socialite, in Voltaire, 'Éloge historique de Madame la Marquise du Châtelet' (1752), in *Oeuvres complètes de Voltaire*, 52 vols. (Paris, 1877–85), 23:515–21. On the double bind confronting women intellectuals in eighteenth-century France, see Vila, '"Ambiguous Beings": Marginality, Melancholy, and the Femme Savante,' in Sarah Knott and Barbara Taylor, eds, *Women, Gender and Enlightenment* (Basingstroke, 2005), 53–69.

15 'Sa vie est une méditation continuelle, et la retraite est son élément'; Jean-Jacques Garnier, *L'homme de lettres* (Paris, 1764), 112. On Garnier, see Rémy G. Saisselin, *The Literary Enterprise in Eighteenth-Century France* (Detroit, 1979), 135–40; and Roger Chartier, 'L'homme de lettres,' in Michel Vovelle, ed., *L'homme des lumières* (Paris, 1996), 159–209, esp. 189–91.

16 Garnier, *L'homme de lettres*, 111–12.

17 Daniel Roche emphasizes that eighteenth-century French physicians frequented high society and contributed actively to the genre of academic eulogy, which bathed great thinkers in an aura of posthumous heroism; see his chapter 'Médecins et lumières au XVIIIe siècle,' in *Les républicains des lettres: Gens de culture et lumières au XVIIIe siècle* (Paris, 1988), 308–30.

18 See, for example, Chartier, 'L'homme de lettres,' 197. The influence of Rousseau was, in fact, less pronounced among physicians writing on study-induced ailments than among those concerned with the 'vapours.' On the use of Rousseauistic themes among these authors, see Elizabeth A. Williams, *A Cultural History of Medical Vitalism in Enlightenment Montpellier* (Aldershot, 2003), 147, 154, and 223–4. See also Sean Quinlan, *The Great Nation in Decline: Sex, Modernity and Health Crises in Revolutionary France c. 1750–1850* (Aldershot, 2007), esp. chap. 1.

19 See Laurence Brockliss and Colin Jones, *The Medical World of Early Modern France* (Oxford, 1997), 441–79; and William Coleman, 'Health and Hygiene

in the *Encyclopédie*: A Medical Doctrine for the Bourgeoisie,' *Journal of the History of Medicine* 29 (1974), 399–421.

20 Among other things, this sort of medical publication fed the market for France's mineral waters, frequently prescribed as a remedy for study-induced digestive and nervous disorders. I discuss aspects of the eighteenth-century fad for hydrotherapy in Vila, 'The Body in Crisis: Vitalism, Hydrotherapy, and Medical Discourse in the *Encyclopédie*,' *SVEC* 2002:5, 247–64.

21 On the hygienic advice that was directed at those groups, see Lindsay Wilson, *Women and Medicine in the French Enlightenment* (Baltimore, 1993), 141–8.

22 For example, the famous Swiss physician Théodore Tronchin wrote little beyond letters but was nonetheless very prominent as a practitioner and peer to members of the French and Swiss social elite; see Henri Tronchin, *Théodore Tronchin: Un médecin du XVIIIe siècle* (Paris, 1906). On the ways in which Parisian physicians exploited their high-society connections, see Paul Delaunay, *Le monde médical parisien au dix-huitième siècle* (Paris, 1905); and Elizabeth A. Williams, 'Hysteria and the Court Physician,' *Eighteenth-Century Studies* 32, 2 (2002), 247–55.

23 See Roche, *Les républicains des lettres*, 308–30. On the eulogistic strand of the 'cult' of great thinkers, see also Bonnet, *Naissance du Panthéon*; David A. Bell, *The Cult of the Nation: Inventing Nationalism, 1680–1800* (Cambridge, MA, 2001), 107–39; and Dinah Ribard, *Raconter, vivre, penser: Histoires de philosophes, 1650–1766* (Paris, 2003)

24 Samuel-Auguste-André-David Tissot, *De la santé des gens de lettres* ([1768]; Geneva, 1981), 82, 88, 93. Tissot was particularly concerned about the bad air of the study: 'L'air enfermé que les hommes, qui ne vivent qu'avec leurs livres, respirent continuellement est une cinquième cause, à laquelle on ne fait généralement pas assez d'attention, qui contribue beaucoup à aggraver leurs maux' (88–9) (The closed air continually breathed by men who live only with their books is a fifth cause, one to which we don't generally pay sufficient attention, that contributes to aggravating their ills). He maintained that, because a typical scholar's study was rarely aired out, the air inside was 'épais, vaporeux, sans élasticité' (thick, vaporous, lacking in elasticity) – thus heating up the body and hampering perspiration.

25 Gabriel Grégoire Lafont-Gouzi, *Coup d'oeil sur la dégénération qui s'est opérée dans le tempérament des hommes* [A Glance at the Degeneration That Has Occurred in the Temperament of Men] (Paris, 1811), 22.

26 Denis Diderot, *Regrets sur ma vieille robe de chambre, ou Avis à ceux qui ont plus de goût que de fortune* (1772) [Regrets on Parting with My Old Dressing Gown, or, A Warning to Those with More Taste than Money], in *Oeuvres complètes* (Paris, 1975–), 18:56–7. Diderot remarks that when he walks into

his study wearing 'la somptueuse écarlate' (sumptuously robed in scarlet), he feels himself and the room to be transformed. As the embodiment of his newly acquired luxury, the dressing gown threatens both his 'natural' state and his old sense of harmony with the space of his study: 'Non, mon ami, non: je ne suis point corrompu. Ma porte s'ouvre toujours au besoin qui s'adresse à moi; il me trouve la même affabilité. Je l'écoute, je le conseille, je le secours, je le plains. Mon âme ne s'est point endurcie; la tête ne s'est point relevée. Mon dos est bon et rond, comme ci-devant. C'est le même ton de franchise; c'est la même sensibilité. Mon luxe est de fraîche date et le poison n'a point encore agi. Mais avec le temps, qui sait ce qui peut arriver?' (No, my friends, and again no; I am not yet corrupted. My door is still open to anyone in need who turns to me for help, and he will find me as generous as ever. I will listen to his tale of woe, give him advice if he wants it, help him if I can, and in any event show my sympathy for him in his misfortune. My heart hasn't grown any harder; my head hasn't swelled; and my nose isn't any higher in the air than it used to be. I still walk with an amiable stoop, just as in times past. My speech is still without affectation; I am still easily moved to laughter or tears. My luxurious mode of life is still new to me and its poison has not yet had time to take effect. But who can tell what the passage of time may bring?); English from Denis Diderot, *Rameau's Nephew and Other Works*, trans. Jacques Barzun and Ralph H. Bowen (Indianapolis, New York, Kansas City, 1964), 313–14.

Useful studies of Diderot's *Regrets* include Orest Ranum, 'Les refuges de l'intimité,' in Philippe Ariès and Georges Duby, eds, *Histoire de la vie privée*, vol. 3, *De la renaissance aux lumières* (Paris, 1985–87), 234; Jane B. McLelland, 'Changing His Image: Diderot, Vernet, and the Old Dressing Gown,' in *Diderot Studies* 22 (1988), 129–41; Christie V. McDonald, 'Robe,' *Stanford French Review* 7, 2–3 (1984), 167–74; and Samuel Sadaune, 'L'ouverture excentrique du Salon de 1769, ou portrait du philosophe en robe de chambre,' *Recherches sur Diderot et sur l'Encyclopédie* 35 (Oct. 2003), 7–23.

27 Valuable contributions to the history of the eighteenth-century self include Barbara Duden, *The Woman beneath the Skin: A Doctor's Patients in Eighteenth-Century Germany* (Cambridge, MA, 1991); Dror Wahrman, *The Making of the Modern Self: Identity and Culture in Eighteenth-Century England* (New Haven, 2004); Sarah Knott, 'Sensibility and the American War for Independence,' *American Historical Review* 109, 1 (2004), 19–40; and Jan Goldstein, *The Post-Revolutionary Self: Politics and Psyche in France, 1750–1850* (Cambridge, MA, and London, 2005).

28 Roche, *Les républicains des lettres*, 233–41. In his *Dictionnaire de la conservation de l'homme* (1799), Louis-Charles-Henri Macquart explicitly compared the

intellectual and the labourer in terms of social utility: 'Les savants, les gens de lettres, sont, après les laboureurs, les personnages les plus utiles à la société' (After farmhands, scholars and *gens de lettres* are the most useful people to society). This passage is quoted in Alexandre Wenger, *La fibre littéraire: Le discours médical sur la lecture au XVIIIe siècle* (Geneva, 2007), 196. Wenger does an incisive analysis of the pathologies attributed to reading (scholarly and otherwise) by eighteenth-century physicians, including their attention to details of posture and aeration; see esp. chap. 5.

29 Bernardino Ramazzini, *Treatise of the Diseases of Tradesmen* (Latin, 1700; English trans. London, 1705), 246–74.

30 Vladimir Janković, *Confronting the Climate: British Airs and the Making of Environmental Medicine* (New York, 2010). See chap. 1, 'Exposed and Vulnerable.'

31 The 1762 *Dictionnaire de l'Académie française*, 382, describes *contention* as referring primarily to a debate or dispute involving two parties; but it also mentions the intellectual meaning that was ascribed to the term: 'On dit, *Contention d'esprit*, pour dire, Grande, extrême application d'esprit. *Il travaille à cela, il s'y applique avec grande contention d'esprit. La contention d'esprit altère sa santé*' (People say *mental exertion* to refer to great, extreme application of the mind. *He is working on that, he is applying himself with great mental exertion. Mental exertion is altering his health).* The term often appeared in the medical discussions of mental work: see, for example, the chapter title 'De la trop grande contention d'esprit, considérée comme cause éloignée des maladies' [On Excessive Mental Exertion, Considered as an Indirect Cause of Illness], in Johann Georg Zimmermann, *Traité de l'expérience en général, et en particulier dans l'art de guérir* ([Zürich, 1763; French trans., 1774]; Paris, 1855), 477–88.

32 'Application longue, forte, & pénible de l'esprit à quelque objet de méditation. La *contention* suppose de la difficulté, & même de l'importance de la part de la matiere, & de l'opiniâtreté & de la fatigue de la part du philosophe. Il y a des choses qu'on ne saisit que par la *contention* . . . Il n'y a entre la *contention* & l'application, de différence que du plus au moins; entre la *contention* & la méditation, que les idées d'opiniâtreté, de durée, & de fatigue, que la *contention* suppose, & que la méditation ne suppose pas. La *contention* est une suite d'efforts réitérés'; *Encyclopédie*, 4:111–12.

33 'C'est l'effet d'un travail considérable. Il se dit du corps & de l'esprit, & il se prend quelquefois pour le travail même: on dit indifféremment les travaux & les fatigues de la guerre; cependant l'un est la cause, & l'autre l'effet. Il faut encore remarquer que dans l'exemple que nous venons d'apporter, le mot travaux peut avoir deux acceptions, l'une relative à la personne, & l'autre à l'ouvrage' (It is the effect of a considerable effort. It is said about

the body and the mind, and it is sometimes used to refer to the work itself: people say both the work and the fatigue of war; yet one is the cause, and the other the effect. We must also point out that in the example we just gave, the word 'work' can have two meanings, one relative to the person, and the other to the piece of work). See 'Fatigue,' *Encyclopédie*, 6:429.

34 As the Parisian polygraph Jean André Perreau put it in his *Instruction du peuple* (1786), 'Il est vrai qu'il n'y a que le peuple qui se livre aux travaux du corps mais il est d'autres travaux qui, sans paraître aussi fatigants, le sont peut-être plus. Quel est donc ce genre de travail? Le travail de l'esprit, celui des affaires. Quand le corps bien portant d'ailleurs a été bien fatigué par le long travail du jour, quelques heures de repos suffisent pour le rétablir, mais souvent le travail de l'esprit empêche de jouir de ce repos: c'est ce qui fait que les gens de cabinet, les gens chargés de beaucoup d'affaires ont rarement une santé aussi bonne que celles des gens du peuple, et que souvent ils regarderaient comme un très grand bien de pouvoir se livrer aux travaux du corps' (It is true that only the common people undertake physical work, but there are other sorts of work that may not seem so tiring but may be even more. What, then, is this sort of work? It is the work of the mind, the work of business. Moreover, when the healthy body has been tired by the day's long work, a few hours of rest suffice to restore it, but often mental work prevents a person from enjoying this rest: that is why the health of those who spend their time in studies, people heavily engaged in business, is rarely as good as that of common people, and why they would often welcome the chance to be able to undertake physical labour). This passage is cited in Roche, *Les républicains des lettres*, 226.

35 'Je ne crois pas qu'on puisse nier l'existence d'un spasme général dans les grandes contentions d'esprit, il est designé par le mot seul de contention, car elle suppose un travail extraordinaire. Ces sortes de travaux sont un ralliement de toutes les forces mises en action, et dirigées vers les organes, dont le jeu est nécessaire aux opérations que l'on médite' (I do not think that anyone can deny the existence of a general spasm during major mental exertions: this is indicated by the very word 'exertion,' because it supposes an extraordinary effort. These sorts of labours entail a rallying of all the [body's] activated forces, which are directed towards the organs whose functioning is necessary for the operations being meditated). See Marin-Jacques-Clair Robert, *Traité des principaux objets de la médecine* (Paris, 1766), 51.

36 'Qui dit une contention d'esprit, dit une tension excessive du genre nerveux; je dis plus, l'abbattement qui succede aux grandes méditations, annonce bien qu'il s'est fait un emploi d'action considérable' (Whoever speaks of mental exertion implies an excessive tension in the nervous system; I'd

go so far as to say that the exhaustion which follows intense meditations is a clear sign that a considerable action has taken place); see Robert, *Traité*, 51.

37 'Les Gens de Lettres pechent ordinairement par un excès opposé à ceux qui travaillent du corps: ils ont l'esprit continuellement tendu et occupé; ce qui tend tous les nerfs, rend les fonctions languissantes, l'estomac paresseux, la digestion lente'; Charles Auguste Vandermonde, *Dictionnaire portatif de santé*, new ed. (Paris, 1760), 2:80–1.

38 Ibid., 2:81.

39 'Si vous considérez l'extérieur d'un homme entièrement appliqué à son objet, vous le verrez dans une espèce d'extase. Il ne voit, n'entend, ne respire qu'à peine. Si vous prenez son pouls, vous le trouverez égal, développé, mais lent. Les évacuations se suspendent; il ne transpire, n'urine point. Les évacuations reparoissent, quand le travail est fini. Cette distraction des sens est aussi la suspension des fonctions; on oublie la nécessité de la réparation de la machine, elle est aussi moins nécessaire. Tout le mouvement est dans l'Ame; il y en a moins dans le corps. On rapporte que l'Algébriste Viette [Viète] fut trois jours sans manger, trois nuits de suite sans dormir, pendant qu'il cherchoit à reconnoître un chiffre que le Cardinal de Richelieu vouloit découvrir. On ne peut comparer l'état produit dans la machine par le travail et l'application, qu'aux effets du chagrin et de la crainte, dans lesquels l'esprit de même occupé d'un objet, ne peut se distraire par aucun autre' (If you look at the face of a man who is completely applied to his object [of study], you will see him in a sort of ecstasy. He barely sees, hears, or breathes. If you take his pulse, you'll find it even, well-developed, but slow. His evacuations are suspended; he barely perspires or urinates. The evacuations resume when the work is done. This distraction of the senses is equivalent to a suspension of the [organic] functions: one forgets the necessity of repairing the machine, which is also less necessary. All movement is in the Soul; there is less in the body. It has been reported that the algebraist Viette went three days without eating, and three nights in a row without sleeping, while he was trying to recognize a cipher that Cardinal Richelieu wanted to uncover. The state produced in the body by work and application can be compared only to the effects of chagrin and fear, in which the mind, likewise occupied by an object, can be distracted by no other). I have consulted Anne-Charles Lorry, *Essai sur l'usage des alimens, pour servir de commentaire aux livres diététiques d'Hippocrate* (Paris, 1757), 2:234; the first edition was published as *Essai sur les alimens, pour servir de commentaire aux livres diététiques d'Hippocrate* (Paris, 1754).

40 'La première difficulté qu'on a à vaincre avec les Gens de Lettres quand il s'agit de leur santé, c'est de les faire convenir de leurs torts; ils sont comme

les amants qui s'emportent quand on ose leur dire que l'objet de leur passion a des défauts; d'ailleurs ils ont presque tous cette espèce de fixité dans leurs idées que donne l'étude'; Tissot, *De la santé*, 122. Tissot, also the author of a well-known treatise on onanism, saw a close relation between overzealous scholars and masturbators; see Vila, *Enlightenment and Pathology: Sensibility in the Literature and Medicine of Eighteenth-Century France* (Baltimore, 1998), 100–7 and 'The Scholar's Body: Health, Sexuality, and the Ambiguous Pleasures of Thinking in Eighteenth-Century France,' in Angelica Goodden, ed., *The Eighteenth-Century Body: Art, History, Literature, Medicine* (Oxford, 2002), 115–34.

41 'L'envie d'acquérir des lumières, ou de faire usage des connaissances que l'on a acquises peut sans difficulté se ranger parmi les passions, puisqu'elle est si forte dans quelques personnes, qu'elle y absorbe presque toutes les autres passions'; Zimmermann, *Traité de l'expérience*, 477.

42 'Mais un homme épris de cette volupté ne la goûte pas long-temps pure, s'il s'y livre sans discrétion'; Zimmermann, *Traité de l'expérience*, 478.

43 Ibid., 478–83.

44 'Au moment où l'homme fixe toute son attention sur l'objet de ses recherches, le cerveau se gonfle, ses fibres se tendent, attirent une portion de l'action générale, les humeurs s'y portent en plus grande abondance; mais l'action du cerveau ne suffit pas; elle doit être aidée d'une forte tension du centre phrénique, des intestins et de tous les visceres du bas-ventre. On s'aperçoit, quand on a médité longtemps, que le diaphragme tendu et s'abaissant moins facilement, s'oppose à la liberté de la respiration, la gêne, la suspend, et qu'on est de temps en temps forcé de soupirer; le serrement de l'épigastre et de tout le canal intestinal, suppose un effort qui ne peut se faire qu'aux dépens de l'organe extérieur qui n'agit pas; et en effet, un homme plongé dans le travail, ne voit point, quoiqu'il ait les yeux ouverts, ses sens sont inactifs; la tête seule et l'épigastre sont en action'; Paul-Victor de Sèze, *Recherches physiologiques et philosophiques sur la sensibilité* [Physiological and Philosophical Studies on Sensibility] (Paris, 1786), 226–7. The 'exterior organ' mentioned here generally designated the skin in contemporary medical language: the skin was seen as both a primary site of interface between the body and the outside world, and the third centre (after the brain and abdomen) in the triadic conception of the animal economy popular among the vitalist physicians of the Montpellier school, with whom de Sèze was associated. See Elizabeth A. Williams, *The Physical and the Moral: Anthropology, Physiology and Philosophical Medicine in France, 1750–1850* (Cambridge, 1994), 38–9, 43–4, 51, 59.

45 This scenario bears a striking resemblance to the muting of sensibility described by English physician William Corp in the chapter 'Of Intention or Study' in his *Essay on the Changes Produced in the Body by Operations of the Mind*: 'The first and most apparent change is in Sensibility. Those who have been engaged in literary pursuits will, I believe, easily recollect incidents which have arisen during Study, sufficiently to convince themselves that their Sensibility must have been at that time considerably diminished: for example, it not unfrequently happens that a studious man continues in his room many hours in pursuing a train of thought, without knowing that his fire has gone out, or feeling the least inconvenience from such a circumstance . . . The senses, indeed, are sometimes so impaired by a close and elaborate attention, that even considerable noises pass unnoticed, and those objects which we *seem* particularly to observe, make no impression on us . . . This wholly depends on the intensity of our application; for as soon as that is diminished, we become more sensible, and when the Mind withdraws from those objects which so fully engaged it, our perception of every impression is as distinct and perfect as usual'; William Corp, *An Essay on the Changes Produced in the Body by Operations of the Mind* (London, 1791), 28–9; Corp's emphasis.

46 De Sèze, *Recherches physiologiques*, 228.

47 'L'action du cerveau sera comme celle de la matrice, en jettant tous les autres organes dans la langueur, en amenant le désaccord de leur jeu' (The action of the brain will be like that of the uterus, casting all the other organs into languor and upsetting their functions); ibid.

48 See, for example, the medical article 'Oisiveté,' in the *Encyclopédie*: 'Le travail est le remede à tous les maux qu'entraîne avec elle l'*oisiveté*. De-là vient que le célebre Loke [*sic*] ordonne d'exercer beaucoup la jeunesse, & de l'accoutumer dès l'âge le plus tendre au travail; cette méthode seroit plus utile, & il arriveroit que les gens de lettres s'adonneroient aux différens exercices du corps, ce qui les rendroit plus sains & plus robustes. L'amour du travail des mains & sa continuité donne aux gens de la campagne cette vigueur qui ne se trouve point dans les villes, & qui résiste à toutes les maladies dont nous avons parlé. Les médecins devroient donc insister sur la nécessité de changer l'éducation journaliere; ils contribueroient en cela à la conservation de la santé' (Work is the remedy for all the ills brought on by idleness. That is why the famous Locke recommended that young people be given ample exercise and get accustomed to work from an early age; this method would be more useful, and scholars would end up engaging in different physical exercises, which would make them healthier and more robust. The love of manual work and its continuity give country dwellers a

vigour that is not found in cities, and which resists all the diseases we have discussed. Doctors should thus insist on changing day-to-day education; by doing so, they would contribute to the conservation of health); *Encyclopédie*, 11:446.

49 On the therapeutic powers which eighteenth-century British novelists and physicians attributed to exercise, see Carol Houlihan Flynn, 'Running Out of Matter: The Body Exercised in Eighteenth-Century Fiction,' in G.S. Rousseau, ed., *The Languages of Psyche: Mind and Body in Enlightenment Thought* (Berkeley and Los Angeles, 1990), 147–85. On exercise as a remedy for scholarly spleen, see esp. 156.

50 Charles-Louis de Secondat de Montesquieu, letter 87, *Les lettres persanes*, in *Oeuvres complètes* (Paris, 1949), 1:261. Montesquieu gave a more charitable portrait of his countrymen in letter 90 (265–6), where he described Frenchmen as passionate seekers of glory, whether on the battlefield or in a field of intellectual endeavour.

51 Pinel identified several 'versificateurs extasiés de leurs productions' (versifiers enraptured by their productions) among the patients at the Bicêtre asylum, but reported finding not a single naturalist, physicist, chemist, or geometer; Philippe Pinel, *Traité médico-philosophique sur l'aliénation mentale, ou la manie* (1800), 11, cited in Juan Rigoli, *Lire le délire: Aliénisme, rhétorique et littérature en France au XIXe siècle* (Paris, 2001), 434.

52 'L'esprit du siècle les a rendus pour la plupart aussi propres pour le monde que pour le cabinet; et c'est en quoi ils sont fort supérieurs à ceux des siècles précedents'; Voltaire, 'Gens de lettres,' in *Encyclopédie*, 7:599. See the similar argument made in the *Encyclopédie* entry 'Philosophe.' For various versions of that text, see Herbert Dieckmann, '*Le philosophe': Texts and Interpretations* (St Louis, 1948).

A search on Voltaire électronique (http://www.lib.uchicago.edu/efts/VOLTAIRE/) yields 225 occurrences of *cabinet*, many of which (as in chap. 7 of *Micromégas*) criticize kings and princes who wage war solely from their study. Voltaire's most common rebuke for a political leader applies to the sort who passes decrees 'sans sortir de son cabinet' or 'du fond de son cabinet' (without leaving his study, or, from the depths of his study). He made the same criticism of dramatic poets in the 'Seconde lettre au même M. Falkener,' which served as preface to *Zaïre*: 'Un poète, du fond de son cabinet, ne peut peindre des moeurs qu'il n'a point vues; il aura plutôt fait cent odes et cent épîtres, qu'une scène où il faut faire parler la nature' (A poet, from the depths of his library, cannot paint mores he has not observed; he is more likely to produce a hundred odes and a hundred epistles than a scene in which one must express the voice of nature); see *Oeuvres complètes de Voltaire / Complete Works of Voltaire*, ed. Ulla Kölving et al. (Geneva, 1968–),

8:415. Note, however, that Voltaire praised Newton for having discovered a measurement of the earth without leaving his study; Voltaire [1736], *Éléments de la philosophie de Newton*, in *Oeuvres complètes de Voltaire*, 15:695.

53 As Mercier saw it, rather than engaging with the contemporary social world, the typical playwright was content to imitate established models: 'L'écrivain, moins audacieux qu'esclave, n'a gueres vu que son cabinet, au lieu de la société' (Rather than society, the writer, less audacious than slavish, mostly has seen his study); from Louis-Sébastien Mercier, *Du théâtre, ou, Nouvel essai sur l'art dramatique* ([Amsterdam, 1773]; Geneva, 1970), v. He made a similar reproach to moralists who misunderstood the edifying potential of sensibility: 'Plusieurs moralistes, qui croient que la rudesse est vertu et que l'ennui est méritoire, ont si mal raisonné dans la froide solitude de leur cloître ou de leur cabinet, qu'ils ont dit qu'en rendant le coeur sensible on le rendoit en même tems plus susceptible de passions violentes. Voilà les argumens rebattus de nos anciens et modernes visionnaires' (Several moralists, who believe that harshness is equivalent to virtue and that boredom is commendable, have reasoned so poorly in the cold solitude of their cloister or their study that they have claimed that making the heart sensitive also makes it more susceptible to violent passions. These are the hackneyed arguments of our old and modern visionaries); see ibid., 13. See, by contrast, the ecstatic image which Mercier sketched of the *homme de lettres* meditating in his study, in *Le bonheur des gens de lettres* (1766).

Diderot ended the introduction to his *Entretiens sur le fils naturel* with a similar contrast between the cold solitude of the *cabinet* and the passion of real-life interaction: 'Voici nos entretiens. Mais quelle différence entre ce que Dorval me disait, et ce que j'écris! . . . Ce sont peut-être les mêmes idées; mais le génie de l'homme n'y est plus . . . C'est en vain que je cherche en moi l'impression que le spectacle de la nature et la présence de Dorval y faisaient. Je ne la retrouve point; je ne vois plus Dorval; je ne l'entends plus. Je suis seul, parmi la poussière des livres et dans l'ombre d'un cabinet . . . et j'écris des lignes faibles, tristes et froides' (Those were our conversations. But what a difference between what Dorval said to me, and what I am writing! . . . They may be the same ideas, but the genius of the man is no longer there . . . I search in vain to recreate the impression that the spectacle of nature and the presence of Dorval made upon me. I can't find it; I can no longer see Dorval; I can no longer hear him. I am alone, amidst the dust of books and in the shadow of a library . . . and I am writing weak, sad, cold lines); Diderot, *Oeuvres esthétiques* (Paris, 1966), 78–9.

54 On 20 October 1765, Diderot, for example, reported to his mistress Sophie Volland: 'Il y aura dimanche huit jours que je ne suis sorti du cabinet: l'ouvrage avance; il est sérieux, il est gai; il y a des connoissances, des

plaisanteries, des méchancetés, de la vérité; il m'amuse moi-même; j'en ai pris un goût si vif pour l'étude, l'application et la vie avec moi-même, que je ne suis pas loin du projet de m'y tenir. Tout se compense sans doute en société avec ses amis; une gaieté plus vive, quelque chose de plus intéressant, de plus varié; on se communique aux autres; ils vous tirent hors de vous; voilà le beau côté. Mais combien de fois l'amour-propre blessé, la délicatesse révoltée, et une infinité d'autres petits dégoûts! Rien de cela dans la retraite et la solitude. Les voilà tout autour de moi, ceux dont je ne me suis jamais plaint' (By Sunday, I will have gone eight days without leaving the study: the work is progressing, it is serious, it is merry; it contains knowledge, jokes, nasty jibes, truth; it amuses me myself. Because of it, I have developed such a keen taste for study, application, and solitary living that I am not far from resolving to stick to them. Everything is undoubtedly compensated for in society with one's friends; there is a livelier merriment, something more interesting, more varied, and one communicates with others; they pull you out of yourself, that's the nice side. But how many times one's pride is wounded, one's delicateness offended, and an infinity of other small distastes are triggered! There is none of that in retreat and in solitude. There they are all round me, those of whom I have never had anything to complain); Diderot, *Correspondance* (Paris, 1997), 5:541–2. The editor of the *Correspondance* speculates that the work on which Diderot was writing at the time of this letter was *Le neveu de Rameau.*

55 In contrast to what he maintained in his *Encyclopédie* article 'Gens de lettres,' Voltaire championed solitary intellectual pursuit in the article by the same name which he wrote for his *Dictionnaire philosophique* (1764), 'Les gens de lettres qui ont rendu le plus de service au petit nombre d'êtres pensants répandus dans le monde, sont les lettrés isolés, les vrais savants renfermés dans leur cabinet, qui n'ont ni argumenté sur les bancs des universités, ni dit les choses à moitié dans les académies; et ceux-là ont presque tous été persécutés. Notre misérable espèce est tellement faite que ceux qui marchent dans le chemin battu jettent toujours des pierres à ceux qui enseignent un chemin nouveau' (The men of letters who have rendered the greatest service to the small number of thinking beings spread around the world are the isolated authors, the true scholars enclosed in their study, who have neither argued on university benches nor made half-expressed pronouncements in the academies; and those of this sort have almost all been persecuted. Our miserable species is so made that those who walk the beaten path always throw stones at those who are uncovering a new way); quotation from Voltaire, 'David-Vertu,' in *Dictionnaire philosophique*, in *Oeuvres complètes de Voltaire*, 36:285.

56 Ribard, *Raconter, vivre, penser,* 130.

57 'Quand Leibniz s'enferme à l'âge de vingt ans, et passe trente ans sous sa robe de chambre, enfoncé dans les profondeurs de la géométrie ou perdu dans les ténèbres de la métaphysique, il ne pense non plus à obtenir un poste, à coucher avec une femme, à remplir d'or un vieux bahut, que s'il touchait à son dernier moment. C'est une machine à réflexion, comme le métier à bas est une machine à ourdissage, c'est un être qui se plaît à méditer; c'est un sage ou un fou, comme il vous plaira, qui fait un cas infini de la louange de ses semblables, qui aime le son de l'éloge comme l'avare le son d'un écu'; *Réfutation suivie de l'ouvrage d'Helvétius intitulé 'de l'Homme,'* in Diderot, *Oeuvres philosophiques* (Paris, 1964), 568.

58 Ibid., 570.

59 See *Le rêve de d'Alembert,* in Diderot, *Oeuvres philosophiques,* 362–3; *Salon de 1767,* ed. J. Seznec and J. Adhemar (Oxford, 1963), 148–50. As Diderot put it in the *Éléments de physiologie,* 'Point de penseurs profonds, point d'imaginations ardentes qui ne soient sujets à des catalepsies momentanées. Une idée singuliere se presente, un rapport bizarre distrait, et voila la tête perdue, on revient de là comme d'un reve: on demande à ses auditeurs, où en etais-je? Que disais-je?' (There are no deep thinkers, no ardent imaginations that are not subject to momentary catalepsies. A singular idea presents itself, a bizarre connection distracts, and one's head is lost, and one comes out of it as from a dream: one asks one's listeners, 'Where was I? What was I saying?') Diderot, *Éléments de physiologie* (Paris, 1964), 51.

According to Jean Starobinski, Diderot's predilection for comparing abstract thinkers to automatons stems from a more general tendency (particularly evident in his later works) to describe human beings as objectified entities; see Jean Starobinski, 'Diderot et la parole des autres,' in Denis Diderot, *Oeuvres complètes,* 25 vols. to date (Paris, 1972–), 23:iii–xxi, esp. xvi. I would add that it also involves a spatial conception of selfhood, particularly evident in *Le rêve de d'Alembert*: the self of the absorbed thinker occupies a reduced space.

chapter four

The Eccentric Centre: Selfhood and Sociability at the Heart of England's Culture of Enlightenment Print[1]

DAVID S. SHIELDS

Of the fantasies that fired the imaginations of classical republicans at the close of the eighteenth century, none flamed more brightly than the dream of printing presses stamping virtue onto the characters of the citizenry. The reading citizen, like the philosopher's tabula rasa, was a passive receptacle, absorbing instruction in morality, politeness, and rationality. Print performed this instruction, inscribing into the mind, memory, conscience, and will models for emulation, laws for internalization, wisdom for illumination, and lexicons for judgment and communication in order to shape an integral character. My purpose here is not to amplify the chorus of scholars announcing the contradictory and fanciful nature of the republican faith in print's beneficial influence upon human character and the body politic. Instead, I will examine a special historical setting – a time, place, and community in which print may have reached the greatest possible saturation in social life – to show that it was precisely there that character as an organizing concept of personhood in the English-speaking world fell apart. Yet the collapse of character did not give rise to a Grub Street dystopia of immorality, crudity, and madness; rather, it occasioned the emergence of a new organization of selfhood, 'personality,' that cherished eccentricity rather than normalcy, genius rather than common sense, and a comity of appetite and shared interest. The time was the last half of the eighteenth century, the place was the Chapter Coffeehouse, Paternoster Row, London, and the community was the Witenagamot, a club of booksellers, printers, authors, and readers that met daily in two sessions until its dissolution some time in 1808.

'Witenagemot'[2] – Anglo-Saxon for the 'gathering of wise heads' – was the name given to England's earliest putative legislature – the proto-parliament that met in the various kingdoms from the seventh century until the Norman invasion. Since the early seventeenth century, the Witenagemot had been an object of political fantasy. (The facts were few enough to permit rather daring projection.) In the imaginings of the first sect of English historians, the Elizabethan Antiquaries, it was where the yeomanry voiced its will and advised the king – the commons before there was a commons. Its existence, documented in the Anglo-Saxon library assembled by antiquarian Sir Robert Bruce Cotton, contradicted King Charles I's claims that Parliament lacked antiquity and that the Crown by precedent had authority to govern and secure revenue without its advice and consent. In political fantasy, the Witenagemot was where the *vox populi* sounded, untrammelled by aristocracy and Crown, a haven where opinion sounded with primordial force. The Witenagemot could determine regal succession and depose unworthy rulers. What is of interest about the latter-day Witenagemot is that far from accepting the station of 'unacknowledged legislators' of the land, the men of letters who met at the Chapter – publishers-writers-readers – declared themselves *in camera* and *ex cathedra* to be 'the legislators.' This assumed status became particularly interesting in the 1790s, when the ministry – as John Barrell tells us – shut down clubs and associations of political tendency.[3] The Witenagamot sat uninterrupted throughout the decade, despite the fact that its members included an affiliate of the Jacobin Club of Paris and the three most radical publishers in English.

Yet the Chapter Coffeehouse's mock parliament was no cabal of radical republicans. Just as its membership included persons with every sort of relationship to print – writer, reader, printer, bookseller, editor, collector – so it contained individuals of every political stripe. Indeed, its promiscuity of political outlook and tolerance of disparate opinion about religion, state, and society show it to have been an incarnation of that entity so frequently invoked in periodicals early in the eighteenth century, but rarely, if ever, instituted in the social world: a friendly society, a company that promoted catholicity of expression. The conceit of *The Tatler*, *The Spectator*, and so many other magazines couched as club ruminations was made flesh in this long-lived assembly.[4] But with a difference. By meeting as a phantom national legislature, the members of the Witenagamot projected for themselves the roles of actors, testifiers, representatives, rather than assuming the sideline stance of an ocular witness or an oral reporter. So – what did the daily moots of the Witenagamot mean for our sense of the way print culture was organized in the metropolis, and how it mediated selfhood? And what should we make of its disparate composition?

First, we should recognize that this society was active, not nominal, with regular fellowship, conversation, and exchange taking place for a half-century. This last aspect deserves emphasis because there is a temptation among cultural historians to inject into the latter half of the eighteenth century the picture of the impersonal workings of the later print market, in which rivalry and predation among competing booksellers dominated publishing – a picture of the world of producers and sellers as an aggregate of autonomous actors rather than a society of colleagues. The picture of capitalist competition that Rosalind Remer paints of the print world of Philadelphia in the early 1800s does not map easily onto the doings of the Witenagamot.[5] Nor does the club's activity accord well with the impersonal regime of print power that Michael Warner draws in *The Letters of the Republic*, in which the imprint obtrudes between author, publisher, and reader, assuming a kind of sovereign power of instruction.[6] At the Chapter Coffeehouse the readers, authors, publishers, and printers sat at the same table and argued about the contents of new papers, magazines, and books while the ink was still wet. In these conversations, texts became pretexts for inquiry, not autonomous declarations.

This is not to say that certain of the booksellers in the Witenagamot did not make use of the image of sociable fellowship to sell magazines. The old promise of a provincial reader being incorporated through print into a cosmopolitan friendly society, enunciated by *The Tatler* and *The Spectator* early in the century, was re-proclaimed in the issues of the *Monthly Magazine* and other periodicals written at the Chapter Coffeehouse.[7] Nominal clubs – like those invoked in magazines – gave a personal face to the relation of subscriber to editor, often rendered even more sociable by the invitation to correspond and contribute contents to the club's 'proceedings.' But it would be an anachronism to think that the virtual sociability of the world of periodicals masked an effort to expand an impersonal regime of print power by printers and booksellers whose primary concern was personal profit and cultural-political influence. First of all, this view projects too adamantly an image of publisher as independent economic actor. The commercial custom in the metropolitan world of print through much of the eighteenth century made publishers seek partners and form relationships of mutual dependence with other persons in the trade. Richard B. Sher's documentation of booksellers' frequent recourse to congers (that is, concerted projects by groups of booksellers) in eighteenth-century London, Edinburgh, and Dublin shows that sharing risk and profit often outweighed a desire for personal pre-eminence in the market.[8] The Witenagamot emerged from what might be the conger of congers, a company of booksellers, comprising the initial Conger Club and members of the rival New Conger, who, in 1734, designated themselves the Chapter, after the Chapter Coffeehouse, where they met.[9]

The Chapter group created and maintained the register book of printed titles. This record, kept on the Coffeehouse premises, announced every member's publications; inclusion of a title in the register established, by an informal contract of all signatories of the record, a perpetual copyright for that volume.[10] The Courts in 1774 may have confirmed the 'Statute of Anne,' ruling that copyright had only a fourteen-year duration, with one renewal by a living holder, but the brotherhood of booksellers used its title book to keep control of a literary property in perpetuity.[11] Those who violated the pact had all their issued titles banned from sale in the signatories' bookstores. Protecting its market against the incursions of Scottish publishers and Dublin print pirates, the Chapter was a trade association, constraining rivalry among its membership by regulation and the partitioning of rights and profits. They would also partner in underwriting large-scale projects such as Dr Samuel Johnson's *Lives of the English Poets*. Some time before 1762, the booksellers supplemented the notice of a book's existence in the register book with the presence of the book on the shelves that lined the walls of the first floor of the Coffeehouse. Indeed, during the 1750s, it became a communal practice of the habitués of the house to bring in every item issued from the London press, no matter how fugitive, forming the first library in England that collected imprints promiscuously rather than selectively. (The Worshipful Company of Stationers did not keep copies of the totality of imprints registered in their records. The Bodleian and Cambridge University Libraries did not collect fugitive and clandestine issues of the press, which grew increasingly numerous after the lapse of the Licensing Act in 1695.) Beginning in the late 1750s, this library attracted another population besides booksellers and printers into the Chapter Coffeehouse, a host of news junkies, readers, writers, and would-be writers. Testimonies survive from several of these men seeking print. Perhaps the most revealing is a 1775 memorandum by Dr Thomas Campbell, a Scot touring England:

> Strolled into the Chapter Coffeehouse, Ave Mary Lane, which I heard was remarkable for a large collection of books, and a reading society. I subscribed a shilling for the right of a year's reading, and found all the new publications I sought, and I believe, that all the new books are laid in, some

> of which, to be sure, may be lost or mislaid. Here I saw a specimen of English freedom, viz. a whitesmith in his apron, and some of his saws under his arm, and called for his glass of punch, and his paper, both which he used with as much ease as a Lord.[12]

Campbell noted the existence of a 'reading club' – this was the Witenagamot, the most vibrant of several sodalities that coalesced out of the Coffeehouse clientele. When certain of the booksellers, readers, printers, and authors began calling themselves the Witenagamot, cannot precisely be determined – certainly after the English world of letters embraced the fashion for literary primitivism and indulged in the Ossianic craze of the later 1760s. Before we enter into the doings of this club and consider its peculiar significance in English cultural history, we must first answer the question, Why did the people and books gather in this particular place?

Because of its convenience. In the bookscape of late eighteenth-century London mapped so carefully by James Raven, Paternoster Row was the most ink-saturated of the six streets closest to St Paul's Cathedral and Stationer's Hall in London where printers and publishers congregated. It paralleled the north side of the cathedral, the first lane north from the street called 'St Paul's Churchyard.' In the four-storey-high brick townhouses, a multitude of printers, binders, and booksellers lived and worked, often in crammed quarters in subleased spaces. There was a definite hierarchy at play in spatial arrangements: booksellers owned buildings on the Row, with printers and binders off back alleys or leasing space in their attics or ground floors.[13] The more prosperous booksellers clustered about Amen Corner.[14] The lane had its virtual counterpart in the literary renderings of London's bookscape. After the ruin of the actual Grub Street (originally Grape Street, an avenue of taverns and dramshops in Moorfields celebrated by Ned Ward and Tom Brown in the 1690s) in 1735, the hacks gravitated to Paternoster Row, to join the booksellers, the printers, and the literary projectors. All that was commercial about the world of print radiated from the row houses there, and its eminent characters and style of business were captured in humorous surveys such as bookseller Henry Dell's 1766 poem 'The Booksellers.'[15] Paternoster Row took on the literary habiliments of old Grub Street: the hacks, the critics, the drinking, the antic yet melancholy atmosphere, the fantasy that commerce seduced genius to whoredom for the public's penny.[16]

The Chapter stood at 50 Paternoster Row, the street's very centre. It was a sturdy, brick building with a shallow attic renowned for its dim windows. Mrs Gaskell, who saw the building during the last months of its existence in 1856, described it as being a sort of provincial townhouse: 'It had the appearance of a dwelling-house two hundred years old or so, such as one sometimes sees in ancient country towns; the ceilings of the small rooms were low, and had heavy beams running across them; the walls were wainscoted, breast high; the stairs were shallow, broad and dark, taking up much space in the centre of the house.'[17] During its heyday the large first-floor coffee room sported banks of shelves, holding a library containing every English paper from 1762 onwards, a near comprehensive collection of new imprints, and the Chapter's register books.[18] The first floor also housed several stalls, or boxes. These were capacious cubicles with wood partitions, benches, a table, and an open front. Each cubicle became the haunt of a circle of persons. The north-east box housed the Witenagamot, which held it from nine in the morning to nine at night. Other boxes at various times held other sodalities. In 1774, the Humane Society formed at the Chapter in the south-west box.[19] In the 1780s, the Chapter Coffeehouse Chemical Society organized itself, the first company devoted to the experimental conduct of chemistry.[20] The upper floors contained a few bedrooms and several meeting rooms (Mrs Gaskell's 'small rooms'). Here the editors of magazines and papers met to assemble issues. Few in the eighteenth century used the Chapter for lodgings. The clientele was almost exclusively male in its latter decades. For weeks on end, the only female presence was the hostess, Miss Brun. The house rules announced that anyone with three pence could gain admittance for a day and read the papers; few women understood themselves to be included in 'anyone.' As Campbell indicated, the premises served alcohol as well as coffee.

The daily rhythm of the print trade governed the sittings of the company. Members of the Witenagamot first appeared at 9:00 a.m., when the printers brought the wet sheets of the papers to the Coffeehouse for reading. A fixture at this first sitting was the Reverend William Murray, a Scots Episcopal minister with an eidetic imagination, who could recall the contents of every paper in London published in the previous thirty years, a man who incarnated the ephemeral print culture of his day and stood in judgment on the accuracy of the wet papers as they were read daily, in the morning session of the club. His remarks delighted the politicos in the wet-paper contingent, for his ideas reproduced exactly the chaotic miscellaneousness of all the views captured in periodical print. He parroted the multitude of voices echoing in his head, and so became the spirit of self-contradiction. During the midday hours, when booksellers and printers were occupied with business, the Coffeehouse was given over to solitary caffeine addicts and readers. Then at 5:00 p.m. in the afternoon company began to assemble for the colloquy of the club. This rite occurred daily, from the late 1750s well into the first decade of the nineteenth century, with a relatively stable membership, characterized by its diversity of interests and abilities.

Dr Campbell's surprise at seeing a whitesmith (a metalworker specializing in the manufacture and finishing of shiny-surfaced items in iron and steel) in his work clothes amid the print tradesmen and literati suggests something of the permission found in this meeting house of the devotees of print. Moreover, the differences found within the Chapter's precincts were more than simply the disparate class origins of the readers, for disparities in station, taste, and genius were not only tolerated but were celebrated in the Chapter's stalls. It is not hyperbolic to claim that in this literary company occurred a transformation in the cultural judgment of personal difference, even eccentricity. We should recall that in Grub Street portraits of the sociable world during the first half of the eighteenth century (Ned Ward's *Secret History of Clubs*, for instance), behaviours such as indulging personal peculiarity and asserting self-interest, ruling passion, or desire appeared as moral deformities.[21] These wilful perversions were emblematized by Ward in the program of the 'Ugly Club.' Ward's Billingsgate burlesques of the associational world recognized the city clubs as the social spaces in which a new style of individual presentation emerged, insulated by rules of secrecy from the cultural demand to perform as a virtuous, public-spirited citizen or a pious follower of Jesus. This new mode of performing individuality did not get named in English until mid-century, when Samuel Richardson termed it, in *Clarissa Harlowe*, 'personality.'[22] He used it in a negative way to speak of innate or habituated traits of an individual that disrupt an education in virtue.[23]

Grub Street accounts of clubdom and the sort of insular personality it bred envisioned the membership in clubs being composed of like-minded persons – sharers in ugliness or brothers in inebriety. In a Tory funhouse mirror, Ward refracted the Earl of Shaftesbury's vision of sociability as a fellow feeling, a *sensus communis* discovered when a sally of wit provokes spontaneous laughter in a room of strangers, revealing those who do and do not share one's sense of humour.[24] The likeness of club membership, a unanimity rendered emphatic by its deviance from normative piety or civic virtue, made it seem something integral while being something dissident – what later theorists have termed a 'counter-public.'[25] I call attention to this because this picture of shared difference stands in marked distinction to the nature of the company that met in the Chapter Coffeehouse. A common interest in print did not breed a common personality; rather, the club was an assortment of different types, an assembly of distinctive fellows, whose likeness lay only in their common gender, taste for beverages, and hunger for news. In taste, in genius, even in politics, they differed. It was a company that thrived for half a century on diversity.

Numbers of glimpses of the club and its members appeared during the latter years of its existence, when its longevity and peculiarity became a matter of general interest. The most ample and influential of the club portraits was a memoir by editor Alexander Stephens sketching its character at the end of the eighteenth century, published in the *Monthly Magazine* and republished repeatedly during the nineteenth century, including an American printing in *The Port-Folio* by Joseph Dennie, a visitor to the Witenagamot and admirer of its practices.[26]

Four physicians were among the regulars. Three were noted practitioners in London: Doctors Buchan, Fordyce, and Gower. 'On subjects of medicine they seldom agreed, and when such were started, they generally laughed at one another's opinions.'[27] The elegant, white-haired Buchan presided over the assembly when he was present. The fourth physician, Francis Lowndes, was a more speculative fellow, penning *Observations on Medical Electricity* in 1787. Two men of finance belonged: the banker Blake and the stock speculator Mr Patterson. Several members were in manufacturing – Baker from Spitalfields, the coal merchant Hennell, and Hammond from Coventry, who sat religiously in the evening sessions of the club for forty-five years. The tea merchant James sat regularly in the 1790s. Among those involved in publishing were George Robinson (1737–1801), the 'king of the booksellers,' and his brother and partner, John. Also publisher Joseph Johnson (1738–1809), who printed scientific works and controversial writings by Blake, Priestley, Godwin, Fuseli, and Paine.[28] There were James Parry, publisher of *The Courier*, and Alexander Philips, editor of *The Monthly Magazine*. Alexander Chalmers, editor of many book projects of the 1790s, also attended regularly. Then there was an assortment of writers, each with his peculiar niche in the cosmopolitan world – Captain William Skinner (1759–99), ex-officer of the Marines, ex-member of the Jacobin Club in Paris, translator of French writings, and commentator on post-Revolutionary politics; John Walker (1732–1807), sometime actor, sometime teacher, who became a force in the history of English rhetoric with *The Elements of Elocution*

(1781); Dr Thomas Busby (1755–1838), organist, composer, music historian, and, when music didn't pay, parliamentary speech transcriber for the London journals; Robert MacFarlane, a political reporter turned historian, who surprised the nation with his account of the extent of the monarch's mental illness in *The History of the First Ten Years of the Reign of George III.*[29] There were contingents of talkers-raconteurs who specialized in tales of the bon ton, and controversialists who delighted in confuting their fellows. The most delightful talkers were 'Long-bow' Wilson, who magnetized the crowd with his tales of the secret lives of the aristocracy, and Dr Samuel Berdimore (1732–1807), master of Charterhouse School and master also of the anecdote and of enlivened conversation. Least loved was 'growling' Dobson, an asthmatic who 'vented his spleen on both sides.'[30] Finally there were the readers – in two instalments. An Irish schoolmaster, Arthur Kelly, sat in evening sessions scanning papers and political pamphlets. But the most famous reader, indeed the 'chronicler' of the Witenagamot was the Reverend William Murray, the Scots Episcopal minister who, for the last quarter of the eighteenth century, worked as a pick-up preacher for any suddenly open pulpit in London. He 'generally sat in one place from nine in the morning till nine at night,' and because of his phenomenal memory, 'he was appealed to whenever any point of fact within the memory of man happened to be disputed. It was often remarked, however, that such incessant daily reading did not tend to clear his views.'[31]

Though the name Witenagamot suggests that the club espoused the sort of proto-republican sympathies that had thrived in London's club world since the heyday of William Camden's Society of Antiquaries in the 1590s, the political sympathies of the membership were as various as their talents and tastes. Dr Buchan, the club's moderator, was a Tory. So were Dr Berdimore, Dr Towers, MacFarlane, Blake, and Long-bow Wilson. Among the Whigs numbered Hammond, Baker, Lowndes, Patterson, and Alexander Chalmers. Then there were the Jacobin radicals – Captain Skinner, Joseph Johnston, Parry, and Robinson. Several members were temporizers, switching sides in debates, much to the dismay of the company: Dobson, Kelly, Alderman Jacob, and the Reverend Murray. The point was the debate. As Walter Besant observed, 'They all sat together; people came to hear them talk.'[32]

The Witenagamot, though it operated through conversation, installed itself into memory and into writing because of the novelty of its comity. It did not aspire to a utopian harmony, or even to consensus. It thrived on the clash of interest and the amusement of entertaining the marked differences of personality. It was a society of odd fellows in which complementarity meant more than commonness. It incarnated a possibility first glimpsed in print, in magazines. In the second decade of the eighteenth century, the Spectator Club fantasized a disparity of points of view tolerated in a table community. As Roy Porter has reminded us, however, the variety around the club table was invoked in order to suggest a discipline of behaviour healing social divisions. 'Whigs and Tories, High Church and Low Church, town and country, gentry and commerce, men and women,' by fitting into the conversation of the Spectator Club, would become 'agreeable, conformist social actors.'[33] The Witenagamot marked an evolution beyond this formation. It found division tolerable, and nonconformity a beneficial feature of social coexistence.

Even the most obvious putative commonality shared by the members – an interest in print – did not instil coherence in the assembly, for the members had strikingly different relationships to the processes of publication: they were press technicians, authors, editors, sellers, consumers. And their involvement in the world of print did not lead, necessarily, to personal edification, clarification, or wisdom. Stephens's most remarkable observation, already alluded to, concerning the Reverend Murray, the man who incarnated English newsprint, was that 'such incessant daily reading did not tend to clear his views.' Against the cherished hope of republican ideology, that public immersion in print would lead to an enlightened populace capable of performing citizenship, the Witenagamot entertained the possibility that the welter of voices and views coming into print might not resolve into any understanding or *sensus communis.*

What most interests about the glimpses of the Witenagamot that came into print in the late eighteenth and early nineteenth centuries is the emphasis on personal oddity. When we turn to the prose portraits of the physicians of the club, for instance, this tendency to caricature becomes pronounced. We probably should ignore the caricatures of the club moderator, the Edinburgh-educated Dr William Buchan, for his famous book, *Domestic Medicine* (1770, with twenty subsequent editions before 1805), communicating the secrets of his profession to the public, provoked extraordinary professional jealousy. So let us consider his colleagues Fordyce and Gower. Here is the brief portrait of Dr George Fordyce supplied in *Physic and Physicians,* a compendium of eighteenth-century English medical luminaries:

> Dr. George Fordyce was one of the most eminent and successful lecturers of the day . . . He was much censured for his intemperate habits. He frequently

> has been known to have been up all night, and to have lectured to his class for three hours next morning, without having undressed himself. He had a most retentive memory. He read but little, but what he did read he remembered. His appearance was by no means prepossessing. His countenance was dull and heavy, and not at all indicative of his mind. This celebrated lecturer dined every day for more than twenty years at Dolly's Chop House. His researches in comparative anatomy had led him to conclude, that man, through custom, eats oftener than nature requires, one meal a day being sufficient for that noble animal, the Lion.[34]

Here is the 1822 obituary reflection upon Fordyce's fellow physician and table companion Dr Charles Gower. Richard Reese comments on the first of Gower's two periods as practitioner in London:

> Having added to his stock of classic lore, as much practical knowledge of modern medicine as he could collect in one year at this hospital, he became a Fellow of the College of Physicians, and boldly commenced the fee trade. The Doctor soon found, that to make a Practice adequate to the support of the establishment of an Oxford physician, something more than a practical knowledge of the practice of medicine was necessary. The interior of his head may be well furnished at Oxford and a London hospital, but the medical phiz, the bow, and the art of pleasing, so necessary to ensure success in this enlightened age, were only to be obtained at Edinburgh. Sooner than submit to be drilled by a dancing-master . . . he gave up the practice of medicine, and embarked with a few friends in a medical concern . . . Being now a proud merchant of London, he pretended to hold in great contempt the practice of medicine . . . He would now often contend that the art of medicine had not advanced since the time of Hippocrates, and lament that his system was not universally adopted.[35]

Both appear as eccentrics – not creatures of vice, but of whimsical genius. They inhabit a space no longer controlled by characterology, yet haunted by its old normative language. They are *personalities* whose strangeness is amplified by the ghost of Locke's educated and cultivated whole man.

There is no way of disentangling the Witenagamot as an institution from print. Print invoked the fellowship into existence. Shelves and shelves of print surrounded it during its existence, cocooning the members in a cloud of stories, opinions, and imaginings. Print absorbed the club, transmuted it to written legend, and has preserved its memory since its last sitting in 1808. The club's history suggests that once an assembly of persons becomes an entity (or body) and locates itself within the space of print's multifarious meanings, it can embody extremities of difference. The club's name gestured at a national representativeness. As a parliament of British eccentrics, it prefigured the nineteenth-century myth about the Anglo print world, the one in which the collision of eccentric personalities in Britain somehow maintains a structure of community.[36] We should not forget that the most popular author of the nineteenth century first won his audience recounting the projects of the Pickwick Club, a community of eccentrics adventuring through the English countryside. Or that John Stuart Mill opened *On Liberty* with a plaint about the loss of eccentricity:

> In this age, the mere example of nonconformity, the mere refusal to bend the knee to custom, is itself a service. Precisely because the tyranny of opinion is such as to make eccentricity a reproach, it is desirable, in order to break through that tyranny, that people should be eccentric. Eccentricity has always abounded when and where strength of character has abounded; and the amount of eccentricity in a society has generally been proportional to the amount of genius, mental vigour, and moral courage it contained. That so few now dare to be eccentric marks the chief danger of the time.[37]

Nor should we forget that the historian of the nineteenth century who most industriously kept the image of the Witenagamot before the public, John Timbs, publishing notices of its membership and doings in three books – *The Romance of London*, *Club Life of London*, and *A Century of Anecdote* – began his career as a writer working for a periodical, *The Monthly Magazine*, born in the Chapter Coffeehouse, and culminated it with his 1866 masterwork of antiquarian recovery, *English Eccentrics and Eccentricity*.

What are we to make of the eccentricity at the centre? When Paul Gilroy's *Post-Colonial Melancholia* came out, I remember resisting his account of romantic British nationalism being constructed from a sense of loss of the first British Empire after the American Revolution. Imperial consciousness seemed merely to morph from the first English Empire to the second, with nationalism manifesting itself in name only. But now I wonder. Early in the eighteenth century, there was an expansive imperial consciousness evinced in Defoe's 'True Born Englishman' that embraced the contributions of Dutch and Huguenots to the work of England, positing a cosmopolitan diversity of identity. But here in the Witenagamot, diversity is refigured as the comity of eccentrics whose Englishness is underscored by Anglo-Saxon archaism. The foreigners have left the island. Perhaps Gilroy was right and an ethnic national identity reigned.

In conclusion, let me return to the western side of the Atlantic. I mentioned that Stephens's memoir of the Witenagamot was printed and commended in the pages of *The Port-Folio* in 1822. This is a resonant fact. The magazine had been founded in the wake of Jefferson's Democratic-Republican takeover of the federal government in 1800. As William Dowling has noted, *The Port-Folio* became a fantasy space in which Dennie and his group of contributors promulgated a new politics of personality and a homosocial fantasy of the nation as the Harvard common room writ large.[38] Dennie promoted anglophilia, celebrated genius, and experimented with self-consciously outré and queer personae. Though popular, the magazine viewed itself as marginal to the commercial, republican, practical spirit of the United States. Its eccentricities constituted a counter-cultural critique of Democratic republicanism, heterosexuality, domesticity, and evangelical Protestantism.[39] The self-confessed marginality of Dennie's coterie of odd fellows puts into relief the absolute centrality of the Witenagamot's presentation of communal eccentricity to the cultural space of Great Britain. There at the centre of the print culture of the metropolis, the odd fellows were doing just fine. No emulation please, we're British. No women need apply.[40]

NOTES

1 This article is dedicated to the memory of my friend Jay Fliegelman. It takes up the subject of our last conversation in Oakland, California, in October 2006 – the role of print in the emergence of modern formations of personality.

2 The spelling 'Witenagemot' refers to the old Anglo-Saxon institution, but the spelling 'Witenag*a*mot' is used to denote the Chapter Coffeehouse conger.

3 John Barrell, *Imagining the Death of the King: Figurative Treason, Fantasies of Regicide, 1793–1796* (Oxford and New York, 2000).

4 George Justice, *The Manufacturers of Literature: Writing and the Literary Marketplace in Eighteenth-Century England* (Newark, DE, 2002), 34–40.

5 See Rosalind Remer, *Printers and Men of Capital: Philadelphia Book Publishers in the New Republic* (Philadelphia, 1996), 65, 78–9.

6 Michael Warner, *The Letters of the Republic* (Cambridge, MA, 1990). I do not, however, take issue with Warner's argument concerning the increasingly rhetorical manipulation of the author, to the point that the author's personhood became entirely instrumental in its relation to an audience.

7 Justice, *Manufacturers*, 34–40.

8 Richard B. Sher, 'Corporatism and Consensus in the Late Eighteenth-Century Book Trade: The Edinburgh Booksellers' Society in Comparative Perspective,' *Book History* 1, 1 (1998), 32–90. The Conger was organized in 1719 in an effort to supplant the Stationers' Company control of publishing. Five partners agreed to mutually recognize the rights to certain titles. Mirror entities quickly emerged, sometimes with the additional purpose of undertaking a large-scale publishing enterprise too risky for any single publisher to put through the press. The origin of the name is obscure, although some reference to the conger eel and its rapaciousness is thought to exist or is suspected behind the term. See chapter 8 of Lyman Ray Patterson, *Copyright in Historical Perspective* (Nashville, TN, 1968), 151–5.

9 Maurice Couturier, *Textual Communication* (London and New York, 1990), 22.

10 Graham Pollard, 'The English Market for Printed Books: The Sandars Lectures, 1959,' *Publishing History* 4 (1978), 33.

11 Richard B. Sher, *The Enlightenment and the Book: Scottish Authors and Their Publishers in Eighteenth-Century Britain, Ireland, and America* (Chicago and London, 2006), 353–4.

12 James A. Clifford, ed., *Dr. Campbell's Diary of a Visit to England in 1775* (Cambridge, 1947).

13 James Raven, 'Constructing Bookscape: Experiments in Mapping the Sites and Activities of the London Booktrades of the Eighteenth Century,' in Jacqueline Murray, ed., *Mappa Mundi: Mapping Culture / Mapping the World* (Windsor, ON, 2001).

14 Adrian Johns, *The Nature of the Book: Print and Knowledge in the Making* (Chicago, 1998), 66.

15 The poem is treated in Terry Belanger, 'A Directory of the London Book Trade, 1766,' *Publishing History* 1 (1977), 7–48.

16 Pat Rogers, *Grub Street: Studies in a Subculture* (London, 1972).

17 Herbert E. Wroot, *The Persons and Places of the Bronte Novels*, Transactions and Other Publications of the Bronte Society 3 (Bradford, UK, 1906), 159.

18 Sher, 'Corporatism and Consensus,' 43.

19 Newton Bosworth, *The Accidents of Human Life; With Hints for Their Prevention* (London, 1834), 100.

20 Trevor Harvey Levere and Gerald L'Estrange Turner, eds, *Discussing Chemistry and Steam: The Minutes of a Coffee House Philosophical Society* (Oxford, 2002).

21 Edward [Ned] Ward's *Secret History* was one of his more elaborate satires of city manners and institutions, going through several print incarnations, among them *The Secret history of clubs: particularly the Kit-cat, Beef-stake, Vertuosos, Quacks, Knights of the Golden-fleece, Florists, Beaus, &c: with their original, and the characters of the most noted members thereof* (London, 1709); *Satyrical reflections on clubs: in twenty nine chapters . . . by the author of The London-spy* (London, 1719); and *A compleat and humorous account of all the remarkable clubs and societies in the cities of London and Westminster* (London, 1756).

22 See letter 27, 'Miss Clarissa Harlowe to Miss Howe,' in Samuel Richardson, *Clarissa, or, the History of a Young Lady* (London, 1748). Jay Fliegelman, during our final conversation, argued the pivotal role of the novel in the evolution of personality as a concept in Britain.

23 See Richard Sennett, *The Fall of Public Man* (New York, 1992), 149–54, for a summary analysis of the distinctions between character and personality as they emerged at the end of the eighteenth century.

24 Anthony Ashley Cooper, 3rd Earl of Shaftesbury, 'Sensus Communis, an essay on freedom of wit and humour in a letter to a friend,' in Lawrence Klein, ed., *Characteristics of Men, Manners, Opinions, Times* (1711; Cambridge, 1999), 29–69. For its relation to the world of private society, see my *Civil Tongues and Polite Letters in British America* (Chapel Hill, NC, 1997), 36–8.

25 Michael Warner, 'Publics and Counter Publics,' *Public Culture* 14, 1 (2002), 1–49.

26 John Timbs, 'Recollections of Sir Richard Phillips,' in *Walks and Talks about London* (London, 1865), 100, claims that Phillips, editor of *The Monthly Magazine*, who was one of the few boarders at the Chapter Coffeehouse in the 1790s, provided the bulk of the recollections of the Witenagamot and Chapter Coffeehouse that he published in 1821 among the instalments of Alexander Stephen's memoranda, entitled 'Stephensiana,' in volume 52 of *The Monthly Magazine*. For the American reprint, see 'Literary Life in London: From the Mss of the Late Alexander Stephens,' *The Port-Folio* 23 (January–July 1822), 298–302.

27 Stephens, 'Stephensiana,' 300.

28 Gerald P. Tyson, *Joseph Johnson: A Liberal Publisher* (Iowa City, 1979).

29 On Skinner, see his obituary in *The Monthly Magazine* 2 (September 1799), 658. On Busby, see K.G.F. Spence, 'The Learned Dr. Busby,' *Music and Letters* 37, 2 (April 1956), 141–53.

30 Stephens, 'Stephensiana,' 301.

31 Ibid.

32 Walter Besant, 'Paternoster Row,' *The Book Lover: A Magazine of Book Lore* (Summer 1900), 220.

33 Roy Porter, *Flesh in the Age of Reason* (New York, 2004), 117.

34 [F.B. Winslow], *Physic and Physicians; a Medical Sketch Book . . .*, 2 vols. (London, 1839), 2:56–8.

35 Richard Reese, *The Monthly Gazette of Health* 7 (1822), 281.

36 Paul Langford, *Englishness Identified: Manners and Character, 1650–1850* (Oxford, 2001), 267–300, supplies a survey of the perceived eccentricity of the English.

37 John Stuart Mill, 'Of Individuality,' in *On Liberty* (London, 1859), 120.

38 William C. Dowling, *Literary Federalism in the Age of Jefferson: Joseph Dennie and the Port Folio 1801–1811* (Columbia, SC, 1999).

39 See the chapter on Joseph Dennie and his circle in Catherine O'Donnell Kaplan, Men of Letters in the Early Republic: Cultivating Forums of Citizenship, 1790–1812 (Chapel Hill, NC, 2008), 140–83.

40 I have not commented directly on the role of gender in the creation of this print-bolstered domain of masculine eccentricity in large measure because the space required to engage the arguments of Mary Poovey and Nancy Armstrong concerning the centrality of the figure of the woman in the emergence of personality would require an additional fifteen pages of discussion. Suffice it to say that logo-phallo-centrism had no more ink-soaked a domain than the Witenagamot.

chapter five

Theatrical Identities and Political Allegories: Fashioning Subjects through Drama in the Household of Cardinal Richelieu (1635–1643)

DÉBORAH BLOCKER

It is remarkable that, in Anglo-Saxon countries, questions of selfhood, subjectivity, and identity should be so largely the domain of what is generally called 'cultural studies.' In Europe, for instance, questions of identity are associated mainly with problems of social status or nationality and thus left primarily to social historians, sociologists, and political scientists. But, in searching the system-wide University of California libraries' catalogue, one finds some two hundred and fifty books under the heading 'subjectivity in literature,' which indicates that, in the Anglo-Saxon world, problems of selfhood and subjectivity have mainly been taken up – in the last twenty to thirty years – by those scholars who, within literary disciplines, devote themselves to cultural studies. It is true that, in historical studies, the history of the self seems to be a budding field, in which interesting work has recently been produced.[1] This rather new historical field is still marginal, however, when compared to the productions in cultural studies on the same topic: in the same University of California libraries' catalogue, a subject heading such as 'Self – Social aspects – History' pulls up only forty-nine books, many of which do not actually deal directly with the question of selfhood.

In the literature produced within cultural studies, novels, dramas, and autobiographical writings become privileged sources from which to document the historical transformations of our conceptions of the self, while archival materials (legal documents such as wills and contracts, or any form of testimony written in front of a legal authority) are rarely viewed in this light.[2] To a substantial extent, the development of such a subfield within literary studies is due to the specific disciplinary geographies which characterize humanistic inquiry in Anglo-Saxon countries.

Indeed, as feminist theorist Elaine Marks has pointed out, literary and cultural studies as practised in the English-speaking world seem particularly disposed to ask 'the big metaphysical questions that [have] dropped out of Anglo-Saxon philosophy' – such as the nature of reality, language, gender, sexuality, the body, and, last but not least, the self – as if these studies were compensating for the disinterest analytical philosophy has generally shown for such problems.[3]

Another striking characteristic of the literature produced by literary scholars within cultural studies is that much of it is centred on the question of the origins of the modern self – whatever that configuration might be. This is especially visible in works dealing with the early modern period which, no matter what their individual focus, rarely seem to escape the Burckhardtian impetus to search, in one form or another, for the seeds of modern subjectivity in the social, cultural, and political practices of early modernity. Although no one today would assert, as Burckhardt did, that individualism was born in the Italian cities of the Renaissance, scholars from Stephen Greenblatt to Anthony Low through Catherine Belsey and Mitchell Greenberg continue to claim that fundamental changes occurred during the early modern period in the way subjectivity was construed and acted out.[4] And this assumption may well be true, at least when formulated from the perspective from which the question of subjectivity is almost always asked; that is, from the standpoint of modernity. Here, however, an attempt has been made to set that perspective aside.

My move originates from a desire to make room for a better historical understanding of past practices and realities. Because the existing research in cultural studies is generally framed though a specifically modern understanding of the word 'subject' – one that explicitly links the word to questions of selfhood and inwardness – too little attention is generally paid to the understanding early modern societies had of the word. In seventeenth-century France, for instance, the words *moi* or *soi* (the modern French equivalents for what in modern English is referred to as the 'self'), though sometimes used in specific contexts by philosophers such as Descartes or Pascal, do not generally appear in dictionaries, which define a *subject* exclusively as someone who submits to a higher form of power, whether familial, societal, or political – or even the power of the elements. Antoine Furetière, in his *Dictionnaire universel* (1690), for instance, defines a subject as follows: 'He who is born naturally subjected to a sovereign Prince, or to a Republic. Kings have *subjects* and have no parents . . . He who is forced by his nature or his condition, or by his duty to do and bear a variety of things. Men, by birth, are *subject* to the injuries of the weather, they are *subject* to a thousand ills and discomforts.'[5] This definition highlights docility, subservience, and/or submissiveness as the principal characteristics of the subject, reminding us that, in the early modern period, subjectivity was not defined as reflexivity and self-awareness but rather as a form of acceptance of a higher order or even, more generally, as a self-imposed passivity in front of anything more powerful than oneself.

To be sure, the works of Stephen Greenblatt and Mitchell Greenberg constitute notable exceptions to the trend which has seemingly made the early modern subject – that is, the individual as subjected to power and hierarchies – disappear behind the self-reflexive consciousness of modernity. Indeed, in his study *Renaissance Self-Fashioning*, Stephen Greenblatt is particularly attentive to the 'relations of power' in which the subjects he observes were bound; and he reminds us in the conclusion of his book that the 'choice' to fashion one's self as a subject 'was always [tied up] among possibilities whose range w[as] strictly delineated by the social and ideological systems in force.'[6] In his book *Subjectivity and Subjugation in Seventeenth-Century Drama and Prose*, Mitchell Greenberg, relying heavily on psychoanalytic theory, pushes the analysis of the constraints, real or imagined, weighing on subjects considerably further, suggesting – as formulated in the printed summary on his book cover – that, on the French classical scene, 'a new subjectivity is formed in and through the representation of the family as the mediating locus of a patriarchal ideology of sexual and political containment.' This reading, which explicitly portrays the spectacle of subjection exhibited in French public theatres as one of the birthplaces of the modern subject, is seductive. But the book is also somewhat frustrating in that it fails to adequately document in historical terms how the representations of subjugation that it discusses actually produce, in society, the new types of subjective freedom that the author values and calls for.

Another disquieting element in Greenberg's work is its teleological quality. Because teleology – or the tendency to see the past solely as a prefiguration of the present – is more pronounced in Greenberg's book than in much of the existing work on early modern subjectivity, his study constitutes a telling example of the types of problems that arise when modern conceptions of the subject are conflated with earlier ones. This is because Greenberg's analysis leans heavily, albeit indirectly, on Hegel's tale of the emergence of self-consciousness, as told in the *Phenomenology of the Spirit* (1807). Greenberg's argument draws specifically on a version of the Master/Slave dialectic that was popularized in a variety of twentieth-century psychoanalytic discourses inspired by Hegel's analysis. This would be the case in particular with the work of Jacques Lacan, whose debt towards Hegel has often been pointed out.[7] In some theories more or less loosely inspired by Lacan's work, modern subjectivity seems to have taken the place of Hegel's Spirit or Absolute Knowledge. But, like all Hegelian tales, the tale of the advent of consciousness by way of its successive denials is oriented towards a goal: the evolution the German philosopher was tracing made sense only from the perspective of the ultimate manifestation of the Spirit. Or, more exactly, this very evolution was sketched out with this hypothetical reading and its accomplishment in mind. In the same way, because of its Hegelian overtones, Greenberg's argument never really allows for an understanding of past practices as anything else but an anticipation of present ones.

Yet power and hierarchies in early modernity deserve our interest, if only for what they tell us about how relationships of authority were conceived, represented, and exerted in a different historical configuration. In this perspective, one needs to take the time and trouble to explore forms of subjection at this specific time, in a variety of different places. As Furetière's definition suggests, there are few better places to observe these interactions than in the king's immediate surroundings, as the vicinity of the monarch was, in early modern Europe, the primary symbolic space where political power was exercised and represented. Technically, of course, courts can rarely be construed as actual spaces, as they were often itinerant, moving continuously from place to place at the monarch's will. However, during early modernity, the various places they visited became more and more restricted, and the surroundings of the prince appeared with an ever greater frequency as a specific place, separate, at least in *ethos*, from the rest of the nation, because obeying, socially and politically, its own rules.[8] This perception was just beginning to emerge in France during the reign of Louis XIII, but it is probably fair to say that its rapid spreading was at least to some extent due to the courtly practices examined here, that is to say, the theatre performances produced by Cardinal Richelieu in his household (by which is meant here the sum of his domestic surroundings, as well as the cohort of his clients and protégés, whether he was sojourning in his Parisian palace – the Palais Cardinal – in his castle of Richelieu, or at his country mansion in Rueil) and, more generally, for the court, between 1635 and 1643.[9]

Scholars working on the English Renaissance have often interpreted theatre as a social practice central to the definition of modern or even pre-modern forms of subjectivity, stressing that, in England, the public display of theatrical characters, backed up by such dramaturgical conventions as the monologue, both displayed and encouraged new understandings of the self.[10] Such claims are of course difficult to document because we have virtually no testimonies as to how these plays were received, but, provided one is prepared to consider early modernity mainly as a building ground for our own modernity, they are certainly not implausible. However, as Mitchell Greenberg suggests in *Subjectivity and Subjugation*, things seemed to have functioned somewhat differently on the French stage, where representations of the family often aimed either directly or indirectly at disciplining social and political conducts. Greenberg offers readings of a number of classical plays which display this tendency in various guises, but he does not actually clarify the particular historical circumstances which might have prompted the French stage to develop in the seventeenth century as a form of what the book calls 'containment.'

This is why it is necessary, before discussing court theatre and its claims of fashioning subjects through drama, to say a few words about the various political interventions which led, in the first half of the century, to the institution of the French stage. For the development of court theatre in his household was in fact only one of the means through which Richelieu strove to shape theatrical practice, as well as social and political conduct, not only at court but also in the capital.[11] In France, theatre was formalized as a practice at a much later date than in England or in Spain, with public playhouses coming into existence in Paris only around 1630.[12] To explain the rapid establishment of specific norms for theatrical practice – codified genres are a case in point – historians of French literature have traditionally emphasized the role played by an emerging 'classical doctrine.'[13] Their account generally tells how, by implementing a conception of drama handed down to them by the Italian commentators of Aristotle's *Poetics*, French theorists and dramatists essentially worked together (though sometimes not without disagreement) towards the establishment of what these literary historians – regrettably reusing here the vocabulary and concepts of their sources without questioning them – described as a stage freed of moral and political improprieties, rationalized in its forms, and altogether more orderly in its spectacles. The problem with this way of describing the evolution of theatrical practices is not just that it takes at face value the beliefs of those who, more or less openly, attempted to bring it about. This narrative also leaves out of the story the political interventions through which, by supporting and encouraging these very theorists and dramatists, Richelieu and his entourage played a crucial role in the development of French theatre.

This political attempt to tame or even discipline the emerging Parisian stages, while more generally transforming theatre into a means of political action, seems to have first taken shape in the wake of the quarrel over Corneille's *Le Cid.* In early 1637, Corneille's first tragi-comedy, based on a work of the Spanish playwright Guillén de Castro, was a roaring success, but it quickly generated critics among his peers, as well as theoretical oppositions, on the grounds that the play was morally inappropriate, politically unfit for the French stage, and messy in its management of the dramaturgical unities of action, time, and space.[14] Richelieu put an end to the quarrel, while reframing it to his advantage, when he commissioned the newly founded French Academy to publish an opinion on the play. In the aftermath of the quarrel, the cardinal began both to intervene quite directly in the affairs of the stage and to experiment actively with theatre in his household and, more widely, in larger court settings. This is essentially because the success of Corneille's daring play created great anxiety in the entourage of the minister about the circulation of 'bad examples' in public theatres. Such fears were voiced in particular by one of the cardinal's protégés, Jean Chapelain, who was commissioned to express the point of view of the Academy (and of those in power) in what became the *Sentimens de l'Académie française sur la tragi-comédie du* Cid. In the ultimate version of this text (1637), Chapelain writes:

> Bad examples are contagious, even on the stage; make-believe representations provoke more than enough true crimes and there is great danger in entertaining the crowd with pleasures which can one day produce public unsettlements. We must be very careful to refrain from accustoming the eyes and ears of the mob to actions it had better remain ignorant of, if we do not simultaneously teach it the punishment such feats must receive and if, returning from these spectacles, the people do not bring home at least a small amount of fear among a lot of contentment.[15]

The fear that is expressed in this text is a fear that the representations of what we now understand as fiction might directly contaminate, through the evil force of their example, the political reality of the kingdom, in the same way that a small amount of poison might infect and corrupt the entire human body. The spectacle of adequate chastisement – that is, of discipline and proper subjection – is presented as the universal cure to this ill, as Chapelain argues quite directly, because it allows for a form of theatre where the existing political order is constantly buttressed by the actions represented on stage.

While this set of clauses in Chapelain's text is one of the clearest formulations of the kind of understanding of the political uses of theatre that Richelieu was attempting to circulate, it is by no means the only expression of such a vision. Rather, such ideas were voiced over and over, albeit sometimes indirectly, in the years after the argument over Corneille's play died down (1638–40). For Richelieu soon convinced a handful of authors (Georges de Scudéry, Jean-François Sarasin, Hippolyte-Jules de La Mesnardière, and François Hédelin d'Aubignac), many of whom also wrote plays for the court theatre the minister was simultaneously attempting to set up, to write and publish a variety of different texts on theatre.[16] On these texts was later based the theory which presumed the coordinated elaboration of a 'classical doctrine.' However, as texts commissioned by the minister, the nature and power of such books were considerably more complex. Ranging from an apology of theatre to considerations on a play by Scudéry, originally conceived as a refutation of *Le Cid*, this set of doctrinal writings also included two longer attempts at formalizing, for the first time, a set of poetic codes for crafting plays. But all of them carried a call for a theatre respectful of established ways (the word used by contemporaries is *bienséances*, which could be translated as 'propriety') and buttressing the existing political order.

In the treatises by La Mesnardière (1639) and d'Aubignac (1657, but started in 1640), the effort to discipline theatrical practices was in fact completely indistinguishable from the larger goal of regulating social and political conduct. This was true ultimately because, as the fear of bad examples shows clearly – albeit in the negative – representations (theatrical or otherwise) were then generally conceived on a rhetorical model, as devices designed to act upon the world in which they appeared, via the circulation of the images they produced of their surroundings. In this perspective, an orderly performance was considered capable of bringing about orderly conduct in the world (whether due to the play's rationalized treatment of plot, or to its display of obedient behaviour and disciplined discourse, or to the modesty exhibited in the actors' performances), simply because it projected outside of itself images and values which were seen as upholding existing hierarchies. This understanding also explains why Richelieu's efforts to discipline theatrical genres through the circulation of rules and codes were accompanied with attempts to regulate the conduct of actors on the stage. To this end, in 1641, the minister had a royal declaration published which stated that if actors kept their performances within the realm of good morality, they were not to be considered infamous.[17] In this text, the power of immoral gestures or actions is once again designated as endangering the public good, and the infamy of comedians – by which was meant their exclusion from the religious community, as well as from the civil realm – is considered as the direct consequence of such reprehensible behaviour.[18] Ultimately, what this understanding of the rhetorical force of fictional transgressions suggests is the absence of a clear distinction between reality and representation: images of things or conducts are considered an active and powerful part of the world they represent.

But the simultaneous production of doctrines defining theatrical representation and of laws framing the behaviour of actors was not the only way Richelieu attempted to codify the theatre while trying to set it to direct political use. At the very same time, the minister was actively developing theatrical models inside his own household and more widely at court, something he had started to do as early as March 1635 with the staging of a play entitled *La comédie des Tuileries.* A number of the plays he produced, written first by a group of playwrights called the 'Cinq Auteurs,' and then by Desmarets de Saint-Sorlin, were an attempt to develop a new kind of theatre both in courtly settings and in the city. For the cardinal simultaneously endeavoured, most notably through the publication of doctrinal considerations of the type just mentioned, to have some of the models with which he was experimenting in his household adopted on the public stages of Paris. This effort was upheld by the systematic circulation in print of the plays staged in Richelieu's household (with the exception of *La grande pastorale,* which was apparently judged too mediocre), with the assumption that they would then reach a much larger audience than the courtly one.[19] This is why, if Richelieu's theatre can be seen as an experiment in the art of fashioning subjects through drama – as I hope to demonstrate below – the implications of such practice should not be too hastily restricted to the life of the court. The cardinal's endeavours to shape subjection within the court – by the performance of allegories of disciplined courtly conduct – were also designed, once print circulated them more widely, to serve as examples of the disciplined, as well as disciplining, forms of theatre that the minister and his entourage hoped to see taken up in Paris.

From 1635 to 1643, Richelieu produced a variety of different plays for courtiers to see, generally speaking, in two different contexts.[20] In the first of these contexts, which was the largest and the more formal of the two, the plays were offered to the court at large. Until 1641, such performances took place in the small theatre Richelieu had established in his Palais Cardinal in Paris. After 1641, these court plays were shown in the first Italianate playhouse in France, the Grande Salle of the Palais Cardinal, which was designed and constructed at Richelieu's own expense. This second playhouse, which could accommodate machinery as well as decors exhibiting perspective, gathered several thousand people, a number of which were probably not regular courtiers. Indeed, the upper classes of Parisian society seemed to have been at least occasionally convened as well, such as in the case of *Mirame*, the first play represented in the Grande Salle.[21]

In both the Palais Cardinal theatres, Richelieu staged what Jean Chapelain referred to in a letter as 'comedies of pageantry' (*comédies d'apparat*).[22] By this he meant spectacles attended by the whole court, as well as by foreign envoys, and generally performed in the presence of the king himself. In this context, the cardinal proposed a specific kind of play, in which all plots – comic or tragic-comic – revolved around the question of the submission of the main characters to higher forms of authority, whether father, king, or God Himself. Indirectly, this type of performance allowed Richelieu to extol the authority of the king – whom he himself was constantly courting – while setting before the eyes of the courtiers in attendance illustrations of the need to abide by the will of those with authority over them. Such plays thus suggested to the men and women surrounding the king models of subjection that they were implicitly encouraged to adopt in their own behaviours, at court and beyond.

La comédie des Tuileries (1635), *L'aveugle de Smyrne* (1636), *Aspasie* (1636), and *Mirame* (1641) all fall into this category. But *Aspasie*, the first play by Desmarets de Saint-Sorlin – who soon after became Richelieu's main court dramatist – probably offers the best example of how the cardinal attempted to use representations of submission in the court. The play was staged in the Palais Cardinal in March 1636. In it, Aspasie and Lysis, two children of prosperous families, are in love; but Lysis's father, Argiléon, also loves Aspasie and manages to ask for her hand before his son dares do so. Aspasie is very disappointed, but wilfully submits to her parents' desires, marrying Argiléon, who immediately takes her to his home. There Lysis learns from the mouth of his beloved that she is now married to his father. However, Aspasie asks nothing of Lysis but that he show a submission equal to the one she herself demonstrates – and she obtains this sacrifice from her lover. Meanwhile Argiléon learns that his son is in love with the woman he has just married. He returns home only to find the two lovers together, whereupon he banishes his son from his sight and locks his wife up in the garden. Lysis revolts only briefly, declaring almost immediately that he will abide by his father's orders. Yet the young man then goes and finds Aspasie in the garden, where both lovers vow to part, but ultimately fall into a swoon at the very thought of a possible separation. Their parents find them unconscious, embracing chastely. At the sight of such an example of persevering obedience, Argiléon finally renounces his wife and authorizes the marriage of the young lovers.[23]

Such an outcome implicitly depicts personal happiness as the consequence of an unquestioning obedience to authority: it is by submitting – at least formally – that Aspasie and Lysis bring upon themselves the goodwill and generosity of those who have power over them. The importance of getting such a point across to courtiers in the year 1636 had to do with the specific political situation the French crown happened to be in: having led France into the Thirty Years' War, Richelieu was now particularly worried that the high nobility would revolt against the king's power. As Arlette Jouanna and Jean-Marie Constant have shown, the cardinal and his entourage were especially afraid that those nobles voicing dissatisfaction or disagreement with the king's policies might seek the support of France's enemies – most notably Spain – to threaten the *régime*.[24] In such a context, promoting models of relationships to authority that showed the need to both accept established hierarchies (depicted as natural and legitimate) and search for solutions capable of satisfying all parties, was a political necessity.

Written by a group of playwrights specially commissioned by the minister, *La comédie des Tuileries* and *L'aveugle de Smyrne* functioned on the same level, using domestic plots to circulate rules for political conduct. *Mirame*, the first play to be represented in the Grande Salle of the Palais Cardinal, was a tragi-comedy, reflecting the search for a nobler tone more appropriate to this grand new venue. But, in essence, the play was similar in its rhetoric to the others Richelieu had staged up to that time – its plot once again showing a couple opposing the will of a father who also happens to be a king. Eventually all tensions are appeased through a providential outcome, and the spectacle manages to praise indirectly the virtues both of submission and of patience.

When the king was not present and the audience for the performances was Richelieu's own retinue, rather than the entire court assembled around the monarch and his minister, different sorts of spectacles were staged. We have far less information regarding the plays presented in this context than we do for the pageantry plays because the latter were, at the time, highly publicized in the first official French periodical, the *Gazette*, whereas the former were not given the same kind of publicity. It is probable that these plays were often though not exclusively performed in the smaller theatre of the Palais Cardinal, which had been in existence since 1635 at least. A good indication of the specific status of such performances is that some were also produced in a much more confined or, more exactly, domestic, setting, sometimes restricted to the small group of followers Richelieu customarily invited to his country house in Rueil. For we know that this *château*, at the time it was in his possession, contained at least one large well-equipped room that was able to function as a playhouse.[25] In these relatively more secluded spaces, the minister encouraged the performance of a different type of play from the ones performed in the king's presence.

Though a variety of different plays were staged in these settings, two core dramatic structures stand out when it comes to fashioning subjects. In plots of the first type, which were staged mainly in the years immediately following the quarrel over Corneille's *Le Cid*, the central question seems to have been how to master one's passions in a political environment. For instance, in *Scipion* by Desmarets, staged in the spring of 1638, the eponymous hero is depicted as an incarnation of virtue, whose moral strength is tested both by love and by the complex political situation he finds himself in. But Richelieu's dramatic rhetoric also utilized counter-examples, as can be seen in Scudéry's *L'amour tyrannique*, performed the same year in his household, before being staged in an urban setting. This play portrays a king momentarily overcome by his passions. Such dramatized portraits of good and bad rulers mobilized the rhetoric of the books which, in early modernity, were commonly referred to as mirrors of the prince.[26] But the staging of such commonplaces within a courtly playhouse conferred a different meaning upon them, for, in such a setting, they no longer constituted discourses addressed to the king by a courtier. Rather, these representations were now tied into the discourse the monarchy circulated about itself in order to preserve and enhance its own power. In the case of the drama produced in Richelieu's household, while indirectly praising the commissioner of these performances – just as printed mirrors of the prince normally praised their patron – the plays also functioned as exemplifiers: they invited Richelieu's spectators to reform their behaviour according to the models (or counter-models) developed in front of them. For, like most of the theatre of the time, these plots were allegorical: in showing admirable leaders, they were attempting to circulate models (and counter-models) of political virtue which could be imitated or shunned, if at a lesser level, by most courtiers.

The same can be said of the plays produced during the years 1640–2, though these later performances also included some new elements, in particular an emphasis on a form of political sacrifice. To courtiers, this move must have been clearly recognizable, because Richelieu, especially in the second part of his ministry, liked to be portrayed as devoting himself entirely to France and its king.[27] *La pucelle d'Orléans*, a historical tragedy, and *Cyminde*, a tragi-comedy, both prose plays written by d'Aubignac in 1641 (and published in prose and verse versions in 1642), constitute good examples of these attempts to indirectly stage their commissioner's sacrifices. Written and published simultaneously, they were clearly meant to function together, as variations on the theme of political sacrifice.

The first depicts Joan of Arc as a prisoner solely of the English (and not of the Burgundians), showing her confrontations with them during a trial that drags on over two acts. In the end, Joan triumphs rhetorically over her enemies but is nonetheless sent to the pyre. And because her death cannot be attributed to the complicity of Frenchmen, it is possible to transform her into a convenient figure of political self-abnegation who sacrifices herself for France and its future kings. Joan's devotion is thus portrayed as one of the historical events that allowed for the establishment of the kingdom inherited by Louis XIII. By virtue of the setting, Richelieu was thus indirectly presented as a heroic figure in the manner of Joan of Arc: he was implicitly depicted as a saint willing to give up his life to preserve both his faith and his country.

The companion play to *La pucelle d'Orléans*, *Cyminde*, because it was entirely fictional, allowed for a much more direct rhetoric of sacrifice. In the city of Astur, Neptune claims a yearly sacrifice. Mysteriously, an oracle prophesies that this will continue until the day when a crime shall put the angry god in a position of having to refuse the sacrifice of two 'victims of love.' Ostane, Neptune's principal priest, loves Cyminde, the wife of Arincidas, the king's prime minister. The priest manages to get Arincidas designated as Neptune's victim. Arincidas wilfully submits, but the king is afraid of losing his most precious support. Cyminde then offers herself as victim, in order to save her husband and the kingdom. But when the lovers give themselves to Neptune, the maritime god rejects their sacrifices and returns them to the shore: the oracle is accomplished and the kingdom is saved thanks to the generosity of the two victims. *Cyminde* points, often quite directly, to the various sacrifices Richelieu was claiming to have made for the prosperity of the realm. In particular, the king of Astur repeatedly states that the people of his kingdom do not feel enough gratitude for the self-sacrifice of their prime minister, Arincidas. As Arincidas is offering himself as a victim, the king, for instance, complains that none of his subjects offers to take the place of his faithful minister:

> Here is indeed a noteworthy effect of the destiny of ministers who work incessantly for the people they govern. Such Princes suffer under the pressure of public affairs, they are worn out by wars, they expose their life a hundred times fighting for the welfare of the State and afterwards, if they need it, the populace does not recognize their name, their virtues or their exploits. The people think that the Princes owe them everything, and that it owes them nothing but a useless homage. What good does it do you to have defended my State so many times, against so many enemies? To have solicited my favours for so many people? To have embraced every occasion to benefit my subjects? These ungrateful wretches will not even sacrifice themselves for you? What, not even one slave in an entire Empire which has so many times owed its safety to you?[28]

The model at work here suggests a chain of sacrifices where the self-sacrifice of the most powerful is necessarily to be met with the submissive compliance of the governed. In this way, the play encouraged in its viewers a self-effacing form of subjection very much reminiscent of Joan of Arc's behaviour when she walks to the pyre. *La pucelle* and *Cyminde* thus constituted a diptych in which Richelieu's dramatist was allegorically suggesting to his courtiers two things, which were later made explicit by Guillaume Colletet in the dedicatory epistle of the play.[29] First, it was underscored that Richelieu's devotion to the welfare of France was precisely what preserved the country from the chaos it had suffered and of which *La pucelle* offered an indirect image. But something else was also mirrored in *Cyminde.* Indeed, in this play, the minister was implicitly setting himself up as an example to be imitated in his sacrificial ways: his generosity – which included producing these performances in his household – and his self-denial were proposed to all the king's subjects as standards of the proper political conduct.

It is thus difficult to see where in Richelieu's theatre there would have been a place for what we call the self, or any prototype thereof. This theatre was about creating obedience and devotion to the kingdom in the courtiers' practices. To that end, this court drama fashioned personae – fictional or historical, but generally allegorical – which were destined to serve as models for the spectators.[30] Though these characters often spoke through monologues and openly questioned their own actions or their passions, they were not created to depict, or ponder on, any kind of inwardness or reflexivity. Rather they were crafted as examples designed to encourage the audience to act in a particular way. Nor was Richelieu actually saying anything specific about himself in *La pucelle* or *Cyminde*. He was conveying something to his courtiers, by producing fictional representations of the kinds of power dynamics he wanted them to enter into.

Clearly, the types of plays just described were specific to this particular court and moment. Nonetheless, these usages of theatre invite us more generally to be cautious about assuming that, in early modern plays, theatrical elements such as monologues or even characters were designed as fictional devices to reflect on what we now call the self, or that they were even perceived as addressing questions of identity by early modern spectators. For when Richelieu attempted to moralize via the stage in his house or at court, he was actually only taking advantage of a capacity commonly ascribed to theatre: the ability to represent moral, social, and political behaviours and, in some cases, to reform them through the sheer force of the images put into circulation by the performance. Furthermore, insofar as these plots and characters were destined to function as examples, one must also remember that examples are rarely reflexive or focused on singularity: they point outside of themselves to illustrate general ideas, to serve as models, or both.[31] Finally, because Richelieu was not only mobilizing an established characteristic of theatre, but also more specifically attempting to reform the practice of drama in public playhouses according to the particular understanding he had of its political utility, it is not impossible that what his experimentations tell us about the functioning of theatre as a social and political practice in his household and, more widely, at court could be extended, at least to a certain extent, to some of the plays produced at that time for an urban audience.

There is good reason to believe, however, that while the cardinal was eager to see the forms of theatre he experimented with at court implemented on the Parisian stages as well, exporting them to another context or space proved generally difficult. For one thing, though urban dramatists were often pensioned by the minister – this was the case for instance with Corneille and Mairet – the pressure put on them to produce drama attuned to the specific kind of moral and political *bienséances* Richelieu was striving for could never be as great as on someone such as Desmarets de Saint-Sorlin, whose entire career and livelihood revolved around the cardinal. Furthermore, whereas in Richelieu's various playhouses the minister or the king was at the centre of attention, with all interpretations of the drama necessarily pointing back toward one of them, in urban playhouses the monarchy was still only perceived as a very distant patron of the stage – something that was to change with the institution of privileged theatres around 1680.[32] Finally, because in court the power of the minister's theatre to discipline was inseparable from his power to favour and protect those who knew how to comply – and chastise those who did not – theatre created after such models in an urban setting would always lack the same authority, possibly making city audiences more difficult to seduce or convince. We do not have very many testimonies of courtiers voicing their opposition or suspicion after viewing Richelieu's courtly plays.[33] But the implementation on Parisian stages of the poetics and theatrical models that Richelieu put into circulation generated numerous examples of ambivalence towards the minister's policies regarding theatre (starting with Corneille himself), as well, perhaps, as towards the political conceptions he was trying to advance through them.

NOTES

1 See, for instance, Jan Goldstein, *The Post-Revolutionary Self: Politics and Psyche in France, 1750–1850* (Cambridge, MA, and London, 2005) and Jerrold Seigel, *The Idea of the Self: Thought and Experience in Western Europe since the Seventeenth Century* (Cambridge, 2005).

2 This assumption is spelled out clearly in the preface of Catherine Belsey's book *The Subject of Tragedy: Identity and Difference in Renaissance Drama* (London and New York, 1985): 'Fictional texts also address themselves to readers and audiences, offering them subject positions from which the texts most readily make sense. In that it defines subjectivity and addresses the subject, fiction is a primary location of the production of meaning of and for the subject' (x).

3 Elaine Marks, 'Some Final Words: An Interview with Elaine Marks,' in Donald E. Hall, ed., *Professions and Conversations on the Future of Literary and Cultural Studies* (Urbana, 2001), 277. See also Joe Moran, *Interdisciplinarity* (London, 2002), 83, which stresses that, because the analytical bias of current Anglo-Saxon philosophy makes its concepts of little use when attempting to phrase

such wide questions, literary and cultural historians or theorists working in Anglo-Saxon countries end up relying mainly on Continental thinkers, such as Foucault or Lacan, when elaborating theoretical and historical models for their research. Both authors are quoted in Donald E. Hall, *Subjectivity* (London, 2004), 4.

4 See Jacob Burckhardt, 'The Development of the Individual,' pt. 2 of *The Civilization of the Renaissance in Italy* ([Basel, 1860; first English trans. 1878], Oxford, 1945), 81–103. Stephen Greenblatt, *Renaissance Self-Fashioning from More to Shakespeare* (Chicago, 1980), 2, claims that change resides in 'an increased self-consciousness about the fashioning of human identity as a manageable, artful process'; Anthony Low, *Aspects of Subjectivity: Society and Individuality from the Middle Ages to Shakespeare and Milton* (Pittsburgh, 2003), xi, states that, in early modernity, there was 'a change in attitude regarding the significance and desirability of th[e] inner world'; Belsey, *The Subject of Tragedy*, 4, defines her project as an attempt to 'chart in the drama of the sixteenth and seventeenth centuries the eventual construction of an order of subjectivity which is recognizably modern'; Mitchell Greenberg, *Subjectivity and Subjugation in Seventeenth-Century Drama and Prose: The Family Romance of French Classicism* (Cambridge, 1992), xi, claims that, in the 'family romance of French Classicism' as it was represented on stage, the modern 'subject,' characterized as a 'psychological' being with a sense of the self, was given its first delineation. Greenberg hypothesizes that this subjectivization of the individual is a consequence of the repeated spectacle of his subjugation on the public stage.

5 Antoine Furetière, 'Sujet,' in *Dictionnaire universel concernant généralement tous les mots françois, tant vieux que modernes, & les Termes de toutes les sciences et des arts* . . ., 3 vols. (The Hague and Rotterdam, 1690): 'Qui est né soumis naturellement à un Prince souverain, ou à une République. Les Rois ont des *sujets* & n'ont point de parents . . . Qui est obligé par sa nature ou sa condition, ou par son devoir, à faire & à souffrir plusieurs choses. Les hommes en naissant sont *sujets* à souffrir les injures de l'air, sont *sujets* à mille maux et incommoditez.' The English translation is mine, as in all that follows.

6 Greenblatt, *Renaissance Self-Fashioning*, 256.

7 See, for instance, Slavoj Žižek, 'Lacan: At What Point Is He Hegelian?' trans. Rex Butler and Scott Stephens, at http://www.lacan.com/zizlacan1.htm, as well as Žižek, *How to Read Lacan* (New York, 2007).

8 A good example of this perception of the court as a specific *locus* would be La Bruyère's description of Versailles, which he portrays as a strange and foreign 'country.' See Jean de La Bruyère, 'De la cour,' in *Les Caractères*, ed. Robert Garapon (Paris, 1990), §§ 74, 244–5.

9 My description of the uses of court theatre in Richelieu's household and, more generally, at court is taken from the third chapter of my study of the institution of the 'art' of theatre in early modern France, '"L'art" et l'action: Les théâtres de Richelieu,' in *Instituer un 'art': Politiques du théâtre dans la France du premier XVIIe siècle* (Paris, 2009), 185–278.

10 See, in particular, Belsey, *The Subject of Tragedy*; Katharine Eisaman Maus, *Inwardness and Theater in the English Renaissance* (Chicago, 1995); and Richard Hillman, *Self-Speaking in Medieval and Early Modern Drama: Subjectivity, Discourse and the Stage* (London, 1997).

11 To liken Richelieu's household theatre to court theatre is clearly problematic given that, as 'principal minister,' he was neither in right nor in fact the institutional or ceremonial centre of court life. Furthermore, all the plays he staged were performed in one of his own properties or palaces (two successive theatres were developed in Richelieu's Parisian Palais Cardinal, and one was installed in his country mansion in Rueil). In this respect, it might seem more accurate to describe these plays as the domestic productions of a high-ranking aristocrat. However, both because Richelieu was commonly perceived as the most powerful individual at court after the king and because his household plays were often played not only in the king's presence but also in front of the entire court, describing them as court theatre is the only way to understand the impact they had on court life and beyond. It is also the best way of capturing how a performance of one of these plays in Richelieu's household might have differed, in meaning, from the staging of the same play in a public playhouse (some of these plays were indeed taken up subsequently in a public context). This designation also allows us to pinpoint how specific political readings could consistently be embedded or perceived in a play, in a particular setting, in connection with the actions and values of the principal patron of the performance. For a much more extensive and detailed treatment of this question, please see my above-mentioned chapter '"L'art" et l'action,' in Blocker, *Instituer un 'art,'* 206–12.

12 See, for instance, Melveena McKendrick, *Theatre in Spain, 1490–1700* (Cambridge, 1989) and Janette Dillon, *The Cambridge Introduction to Early English Theatre* (Cambridge, 2006). Sara Beam, *Laughing Matters: Farce and the Making of Absolutism in France* (Ithaca, 2007) gives a renewed account of the emergence of the French public stage in the years preceding 1630.

13 Two books were instrumental in developing this myth: René Bray, *La formation de la doctrine classique en France* (Paris, 1927) and Jacques Scherer, *La dramaturgie classique en France* (Paris, 1962).

14 The principal sources related to this quarrel can be found in Jean-Marc Civardi, ed., *La querelle du Cid* (Paris, 2004).

15 'Les mauvais exemples sont contagieux, mesmes sur les theatres; les feintes representations ne causent que trop de veritables crimes, il y a grand peril à divertir le Peuple par des plaisirs qui peuvent produire un jour des douleurs publiques. Il nous faut bien garder d'accoustumer ny ses yeux ny ses oreilles à des actions qu'il doit ignorer, si nous ne luy apprenons en mesme temps la punition, et si, au retour de ces spectacles il ne remporte du moins un peu de crainte parmy beaucoup de contentement'; from [Jean Chapelain], *Les sentiments de l'Académie française sur la tragi-comédie du* Cid, ed. Colbert Searles, Studies in Language and Literature (University of Minnesota) 3 (March 1916): 20–1 [E].

16 Georges de Scudéry, *L'Apologie du théâtre* (Paris, 1639); [J.-Fr. Sarasin], *Discours de la tragédie ou Remarques sur* L'Amour tirannique *de Monsieur de Scudéry par M. de Sillac d'Arbois,* in Georges de Scudéry, *L'Amour tyrannique, tragicomédie* (Paris, 1639) (for a modern edition, see Jean-François Sarasin, *Oeuvres,* ed. Paul Festugière, 2 vols. [Paris, 1926], 2:1–36); Hippolyte-Jules Pilet de La Mesnardière, *La poëtique* ([Paris, 1639]; Geneva, 1972); and François Hédelin, abbé d'Aubignac, *La Pratique du théâtre, oeuvre tres-necessaire à tous ceux qui veulent s'appliquer à la Composition des Poëmes Dramatiques, qui font profession de les Reciter en public, ou qui prennent plaisir d'en voir les Representations* (Paris, 1657), which was recently re-edited by Hélène Baby (Paris, 2001).

17 Anathase-Jean-Léger Jourdan, M. Decrusy, François-André Isambert, and Alphonse-Honoré Taillandier, eds, *Recueil général des anciennes lois françaises depuis l'an 420, jusqu'à la révolution de 1789,* 29 vols. (Paris, 1821–33), here vol. 16, covering the years 1610–43, text no. 346, 'DÉCLARATION sur la profession des comédiens, qui leur défend les paroles lascives et déshonnêtes,' 536–7. See in particular the following passages: '[1] A ces causes nous avons fait et faisons très expresses inhibitions et défenses, par ces présentes signées de notre main, à tous comédiens de représenter aucunes actions malhonnêtes, ni d'user d'aucunes paroles lascives ou à double entente qui puissent blesser l'honnêteté publique, et ce sur peine d'être déclarés infâmes et autres peines qu'il écherra . . . [4] Et en cas que lesdits comédiens règlent tellement les actions du théâtre qu'elles soient, du tout, exemptes d'impuretés, nous voulons que leur exercice qui peut innocemment divertir nos peuples de diverses occupations mauvaises, ne leur puisse être imputé à blâme, ni préjudice de leur réputation dans le commerce public . . .' ([1] For this reason we have forbidden and continue to forbid, by this text signed by our hand, all actors to represent dishonest actions or to use on stage lascivious or equivocal wording that might offend public honesty, lest they should be declared infamous, with all the penalties that accompany this status . . . [4] And if the above-mentioned actors so regulate

the actions of the theatre that they are absolutely free of impurities, we want that their activities, which can innocently divert our peoples from a variety of bad occupations, not be held against them in public interactions . . .).

18 'Infamy' was an extremely complex juridical notion in early modern France, in part because it was active in both canon and civil law. Richelieu, in having the 1641 declaration published, was in some way attempting to play on this ambiguity: in conditionally suppressing the civil infamy of actors, he was also trying, albeit very indirectly, to delegitimize their infamy in canon law. However, it seems this declaration had mostly the opposite effect. On this complicated subject, I also venture to refer the reader to Blocker, *Instituer un 'art,'* 279–363.

19 Richelieu's Palais Cardinal housed two theatres. The first one was set up around 1635 and could accommodate about six hundred spectators. The second venue, the Grande Salle, opened in 1641 and was much larger and grander. It could house an audience of three to four thousand spectators. Richelieu's theatre in Rueil was probably quite modest in size. The theatre existing in the Louvre before Richelieu's accession to power was smaller and much more impractical than the one in the Grande Salle. The dance hall available in the Arsenal had therefore often been thought of as more adequate to produce a ballet or a masque (which the court usually valued over theatre).

20 Quite a bit of research has been done on these plays, with the first of the contexts discussed here – namely, the theatre produced in the Grande Salle for a larger audience – having generally been privileged over the more intimate context of Richelieu's retinue, which he sometimes gathered around a play in his country house in Rueil or even in the smaller venue of the Palais Cardinal, after the larger theatre was created there. See Léopold Lacour, *Richelieu dramaturge et ses collaborateurs: Les imbroglios romanesques, les pièces politiques* (Paris, 1926), 13–15; Timothy Murray, 'Richelieu's Theater: The Mirror of a Prince,' *Renaissance Drama* (1977): 275–98; Georges Couton, 'Richelieu et le théâtre,' in *Richelieu et la culture: Actes du Colloque international en Sorbonne les mardi et mercredi 19 et 20 novembre 1985*, ed. Roland Mousnier (Paris, 1987) and *Richelieu et le théâtre* (Lyon, 1986); Hugh Gaston Hall, *Richelieu's Desmarets and the Century of Louis XIV* (Oxford, 1990); C.E.J. Caldicott, 'Richelieu and the Arts,' in Joseph Bergin and Lawrence Brockliss, eds, *Richelieu and His Age* (Oxford, 1992), 203–35; Marie-Claude Canova Green, *La politique-spectacle au Grand Siècle: Les rapports franco-anglais*, pref. Alain Viala (Paris/Seattle/Tübingen, 1993). Christian Jouhaud's 'Desmarets, Richelieu, Roxane et Alexandre: Sur le service de plume,' *XVIIe Siècle* 193, 4 (1996), 859–74, republished in *Les pouvoirs de la littérature: Histoire d'un*

paradoxe (Paris, 2000), 269–92, is a rare contribution on one of the plays produced in Richelieu's entourage which was probably not intended for a staging in the king's presence.

21 See Murray, 'Richelieu's Theater,' 285, who, basing himself on the memoirs of Michel de Marolle, describes how all spectators that night were assigned places according to their rank, from the highest aristocrats and princes of the church to the more modest men of law (*gens de justice*), who could scarcely have been regular courtiers.

22 See Jean Chapelain to François Le Métel de Boisrobert, 24 January 1635, letter 59 in *Lettres de Jean Chapelain de l'Académie française*, ed. Philippe de Tamizey de Larroque, Collection des documents inédits sur l'histoire de France, n.s., vol. 1 (Paris, 1880), on the subject of the *Comédie des Tuileries*: 'Monsieur, je ne vous diray point avec quel respect et quelle joye je receus le commandement que Monseigneur me faisait de travailler au dessein d'une comédie d'apparat dont il se veut divertir, puisque ce fust vous qui me le portaste' (Sir, I will not tell you with what respect and joy I received the order His Eminence has given me to write the canvas of a comedy he wants to entertain himself with, as you are the one who communicated his will to me).

23 Though such a decision would seem to violate church law directly, the character of Argiléon seems completely unbothered by the problem. The lines which Jean Desmarets de Saint-Sorlin places in his mouth are very clear : 'Les Dieux à mon hymen n'avoient point consenty / Moy-mesme ie le romps; et vous unis ensemble' (The gods had not agreed to my marriage / I myself dissolve it and join the two of you in marriage); see Jean Desmarets de Saint-Sorlin, *Aspasie* (Paris, 1636), 93.

24 See Jean-Marie Constant, *Les conjurateurs: Le premier libéralisme politique sous Richelieu* (Paris, 1987); and Arlette Jouanna, *Le devoir de révolte: La noblesse française et la gestation de l'État moderne, 1559–1661* (Paris, 1989).

25 See Honor Levi and Dominique Helot-Lécroart, 'Le Château de Rueil du temps de Jean de Moisset et du Cardinal de Richelieu, 1606–1642,' *Fédération des sociétés historiques et archéologiques de Paris et d'Ile de France* 36 (1985): 19–95.

26 On these books, see Michel Senellart, *Les arts de gouverner: Du regimen médiéval au concept de gouvernement* (Paris, 1995).

27 See Christian Jouhaud, *La main de Richelieu ou le pouvoir cardinal* (Paris, 1991), 49–84.

28 [D'Aubignac], *Cyminde ou les deux victimes* (Paris, 1642): 'Voilà certes un effet bien notable du destin des Grands qui travaillent incessamment pour les peuples soumis à leur ministere. Ils souffrent dans la presse des affaires publiques, ils se consomment dans les fatigues de la guerre, ils exposent

cent fois leur vie dans les combats pour le bien d'un Estat: & puis si apres ils ont besoin du peuple, on ne connoist plus leur nom, leurs vertus, ni leurs exploicts. Il [le Peuple] s'imagine que les Princes lui doivent tout, & qu'il ne leur doit rien qu'un hommage inutile. Que vous sert maintenant d'avoir défendu mon Estat tant de fois contre tant d'ennemis? d'avoir sollicité mes graces pour tant de personnes? d'avoir embrassé toutes les occasions de faire du bien à tous mes sujets? . . . Ces ingrats ne racheteront pas vostre vie? . . . Quoy? pas un esclave pour un Empire entier qui vous doit tant de fois son salut?' (32–4).

29 Guillaume Colletet, *Cyminde ou les deux victimes, tragi-comédie* (Paris, 1642), dedicatory epistle to Richelieu, no pagination.

30 Inherited from the practice of biblical interpretation, allegory remained the dominant mode of expression and decipherment in the literature of seventeenth-century France. This allegorical manner was however protean in its practices and should not be reduced to keyed writings or readings (*lectures à clef*), which constitute but an element of it. On allegory and keyed literature in seventeenth-century France, see B. Beugnot, 'Oedipe et le Sphinx: Essai de mise au point sur le problème des clefs au XVIIe siècle,' in M. Fumaroli, ed., *Le statut de la littérature: Mélanges offerts à Paul Bénichou* (Geneva, 1982), 71–85, repub. in B. Beugnot, *La mémoire du texte: Essais de poétique classique* (Paris, 1994), 227–42; G. Couton, *Écritures codées: Essais sur l'allégorie au XVIIe siècle* (Paris, 1990); and M. Bombart and M. Escola, 'Clés et usages de clés: Pour servir à l'histoire et à la théorie d'une pratique de lecture,' *Littératures classiques* 54 (2005), 5–21.

31 The bibliography on exemplarity is extensive. See in particular Claude Brémond, Jacques Le Goff, and Jean-Claude Schmitt, *L'exemplum: Typologie des sources du Moyen Age Occidental*, fasc. 40 (Turnhout, 1982); John D. Lyons, *Exemplum: The Rhetoric of Example in Early Modern France and Italy* (Princeton, 1989); Timothy Hampton, *Writing from History: The Rhetoric of Exemplarity in Renaissance Literature* (Ithaca, 1990); and Laurence Giavarini, ed., *Construire l'exemplarité: Pratiques littéraires et discours historiens* (Dijon, 2008).

32 These theatres were awarded a royal monopoly on certain types of spectacle. Their troupes were increasingly administered by the First Gentlemen of the king's household, who sometimes also decided what they staged. In exchange for their service to the Crown, these playhouses also received generous subventions from the monarch, which often ensured their viability well into the eighteenth century. A prime example of these privileged venues is the Théâtre-Français, better known today as the Comédie-Française.

33 We do have, however, a set of reactions to *Mirame* by courtiers who were generally in opposition to Richelieu. They tended to read the play as a

performance staged to embarrass Anne of Austria: the plot is deciphered as allegorically depicting the queen's presumed romance with the Duke of Buckingham. See Charles de Montchal, *Mémoires de M. de Montchal, archevêque de Toulouse contenant des particularitez de la vie et du ministère du cardinal de Richelieu* (Rotterdam, 1718), 1:107; Antoine Arnauld, *Mémoires*, in *Collection des Mémoires relatifs à l'histoire de France avec des notices sur chaque auteur par M. Petitot*, 2 vols. (Paris, 1824), 2:199–200; as well as the reading offered by the satirist Tallemant des Réaux, *Historiettes*, ed. Antoine Adam, 2 vols. (Paris, 1960–1), 1:236–7. These readings, which see Richelieu's efforts to impose his authority as directed solely at the queen, are not entirely convincing: the play was probably intended more as a self-serving discourse, in the manner of the rest of Richelieu's theatrical experiments. However, the documented existence of these other readings of the text, which distance themselves from the discourses Richelieu was in the habit of having staged both about the king's power and about his own, is an important fact, because it points to the difficulty of controlling the production and circulation of allegorical interpretations in such settings.

chapter six

Noble Selfhood and the Nature Poetry of Saint-Amant

MICHAEL TAORMINA

Alcidon, for whom I proudly
Make only beautiful things,
Accept this fantastical tableau
Painted with vivid images.
I seek out the wilderness
Where dreaming, alone, I enjoy
The eloquent discourse
Between my Genius and the Muse:
But my most loving occupation
Is remembering your conversation.

Saint-Amant, 'La solitude,' 1629[1]

The contradictions inherent in noble identity were particularly glaring in early modern France.[2] By the mid-sixteenth century, nobles were no longer primarily identified by military service, and were increasingly sidelined from affairs of state. Nor were they distinguishable on account of immemorial familial ties to the land. Ennobling offices, titles, and property had long been for sale. New families were continually filling noble ranks, and urban nobles were developing manners and ways of talking considerably different from those of their country peers. After the Wars of Religion, new questions were raised about the relevance of a caste held responsible for the devastation of France. At issue was whether the privileged-by-birth deserved their social station. Thus, nobles went looking for new ways to define themselves. How could they show that they were noble by right?

The emergence of a new social identity for the nobility in the early seventeenth century in France has been well documented.[3] Increasing emphasis was placed on cultural refinement, or *honnêteté*, as a marker of caste membership. Provenance began to take a back seat to performance. Historians of early modern French culture, most notably Norbert Elias, recognize the crucial role played by the spaces of sociability in the formation of noble selfhood.[4] At the king's court, in the salons of their urban residences, or on their country estates, nobles performed their social and personal identities for one another. Conversation, fashion, belles-lettres – pastimes typical of the aristocracy in its idleness – held out the promise of social distinction and, potentially, advancement. To be noble was to be recognized as such by one's peers. Of course, this situation only further opened the door to ambitious commoners with expertise or talent in these cultural areas – many of whom usurped titles – but there was no going back.

Such was the case with Saint-Amant's self-fashioning in and through his nature poetry.[5] Of Norman, Protestant, and common origins, Antoine Girard de Saint-Amant enjoyed a successful career as a poet until he was laughed out of the court of Louis XIV in 1661. While his poetry as a whole presents a variety of locations, his nature poetry uses the description of natural places to give an idealized portrait of noble selfhood. The natural settings are meant to be sites that the poet himself inhabits, often in solitude, sometimes in fellowship, but always thanks to the generosity of his aristocratic patrons. Saint-Amant's nature poetry thus *appears* to describe natural places imbued with values prized by the nobility – a space of freedom, pleasure, independence, leisure – a noble way of life. In reality, however, Saint-Amant fashions a noble self by projecting poetic topoi on to natural places. His noble self appears to be grounded in nature when it is in fact *rhetorically* fashioned by his discourse.

Poetry and the Spaces of Noble Sociability

The spaces of noble sociability were private in the sense of 'personal,' but since this social life was, in this instance, so crucial to social standing and self-image, these 'private' settings were in fact the other face of the 'public.' Nobles spent a good part of their waking hours together: conversing, drinking, dining – generally amusing themselves. These places of *otium* were separate from the more serious face of their public life, the arena of *negotium* spent in the service of church and state. At the same time, this leisurely social life *was* in many ways their business. It was through social contact that opportunities for advancement presented themselves: the acquisition of a royal office or honorary title, an advantageous marriage proposal, or a favourable position among a noble clientele. Whence derives the importance of social distinction, of performing one's nobility, of pleasing one's peers through conversation and pastimes: this is how one secured increasingly scarce opportunities for social advancement. The spaces of noble sociability were thus quite public, and the *otium* enjoyed there was inseparable from noble reputation and standing.

These were the contexts in which Saint-Amant and other poets of his day lived and worked. Although many of them were outsiders of non-noble origins, their writing talents secured them positions in aristocratic patronage networks. The personal ties between patron and poet mimicked the broader social relations that existed between the grandees and their clients from lower noble ranks. The patron offered political and financial protection to the poet, and in return the poet contributed to the patron's reputation and social standing. The lavishness of having a poet in one's clientele and the expenditure it implied were considered in themselves to demonstrate a patron's generosity and his commitment to all things fine, two qualities prized as markers of noble distinction. In addition, and most important, the poet wrote poems explicitly celebrating the patron's merits. Even poems devoted to themes seemingly unrelated to patronage – love, drinking, gardens, friendship, and so on – implied that the noble way of life depicted in them was made possible and sustained by the patron's generosity. Poets and poetry thus fulfilled a social need. They celebrated rival patrons and rival social networks and, ultimately, rival conceptions of what it was to be noble.

Poetry was an integral part of the settings of *otium*, but it could also migrate to the political arena of *negotium*. Poetry anthologies and individual books brought aristocratic claims and ideals to the other sectors of the ruling elite. Of course, members of the clergy and the Parlement were no strangers to the royal court, to households of great lords, or to salons. Many of them were noble, too, or at least recently ennobled. However, it is one thing to hear a poem read aloud in the household of a powerful lord and another thing to see it published at large. In the latter form, a poem could make its way into less sympathetic, more contested territory. The aesthetic pleasure, the ideals expressed and claims made in and through poetry, could then be challenged as part of public discourse. This is surely what happened to Théophile de Viau, who became an unwilling spokesman for aristocrats with libertine proclivities. Publicly condemned by the Jesuit Père Garasse, de Viau was tried in absentia by the Paris Parlement, and subsequently arrested and imprisoned.[6] His is an extreme case. Nonetheless, if aristocratic values or beliefs espoused in poetry were taken seriously enough by sectors of the ruling elite to warrant his condemnation, it shows that poetry had a very public audience and could generate political effects. Aristocratic values and beliefs expressed in public needed to be taken seriously, for different expressions of what was considered fine, honourable, or noble (*to kalon* in Aristotelian rhetoric) could imply different political actions and policies and alternative distributions of power.[7] By extending the reach of noble sociability, poetry anthologies and individual books potentially transformed poets into spokespersons. Therefore, when a poet wrote, he necessarily aimed at a very public audience, even when addressing an ode to an individual patron.

The rhetorical education of the day thus served poets well. Poets either came into direct contact with ancient rhetorical manuals or assimilated the basic tenets second-hand through contemporary manuals.[8] From rhetoric manuals, poets learned how to win the goodwill of an audience, how to increase credibility in their eyes, and how to uncover topics, themes, and arguments likely to be effective with them. They did this by adapting their character to fit the character of the audience or, perhaps, to correspond with some cherished ideal representation the audience had of itself. This persuasive technique, called 'ethos' and usually translated as 'character' or 'kind of person,' is perhaps the most important aspect of the triadic principle of accommodation known as decorum.[9] It works for self-presentation as well as for the presentation of another person. The persuasive power of ethos derives from its close association of place, kind of person, and soul.[10] That is, while ethos is related to the places one haunts and to one's innermost nature, it is also manifested by the kind of things one says and the way one says them.[11]

Saint-Amant's nature poetry presents a nobiliary ethos, an aesthetic and ethical ideal of what it was to be noble in early seventeenth-century France. This ideal character type is what I take to be a social self, for the individual aristocrat's sense of self was derived from his membership in the group. However, because noble identity was changing, and because social distinction was so crucial, a contrary impulse was pushing the representation of character towards singularity. Nobles wanted to distinguish themselves from commoners, but they also wanted to distinguish themselves from one another. This drive to assert one's difference, one's individual nature, may also be subsumed by ethos, connoting in this sense the singular soul, something like a metaphysical self. It is what I take Montaigne to mean when he says: 'It is myself that I portray.'[12]

The link between character and soul, I will argue, is voluntary decision, especially the sort we find in stylistic choices. Thus, analysing the ethos portrayed in Saint-Amant's nature poetry will be tantamount to analysing one version of noble selfhood in early seventeenth-century France.

Nature and Noble Nostalgia

Nature, as an expression of nostalgia for a Golden Age, occupied a special place in the imagination of the early modern French nobility. Here, the nostalgia did not represent any acute historical crisis, but rather a way of looking at the world typical of nobility. For, as historian Jonathan Dewald suggests, the nobility had never enjoyed unchallenged dominance.[13] What was acute was the migration of aristocratic families to urban centres. As ties to the provincial manor were severed, there was a yearning for their preservation. In imagination, the lands of the provincial manor represented the difference of nature that supposedly separated the noble from the commoner and the old families from the new. The fief had allegedly been awarded to an illustrious ancestor whose virtue was passed to his heirs with the land and family name. Thus, the urban residence had to absorb and reflect the provincial manor. 'While the estate residence is still present,' says Elias, 'of all its functions it [the urban residence] has retained only its approach and its prestigious appearance. The stables, storerooms, and servants' quarters are still there, but they have merged with the manor house, and of the surrounding nature only the gardens are left.'[14] The urban garden expressed a nostalgia for the natural setting of the provincial manor. Pastoral literature also reflected this in its own way. The aristocratic shepherds and shepherdesses of d'Urfé's *L'Astrée* (1607–24), for instance, pine away in a pristine valley whose wholesome air and fertile soil are one with 'their native gentleness.'[15] The atmosphere and land give them their noble character. Such nostalgic representations of nature – gardens and pastoral poetry – did not accurately portray the early seventeenth-century nobility or how they lived, but the yearning they expressed gave the nobility a sense of identity. 'This was an identity free from change,' says Dewald, 'because it rested on possessions immune from challenges or control by others.'[16] Nature represented the nostalgia for noble difference and autonomy formerly embodied in the land attached to the family name.

'Solitude' (La solitude), the poem that made Saint-Amant famous, plays on this noble nostalgia associated with nature.[17] Its conceit is that the poet is taking a solitary stroll through natural surroundings as he describes and meditates on their beauty, variety, and mystery: the woods, mountains, a swamp, the sea. These natural settings and the way Saint-Amant shows himself in them portray the speaker as noble and are calculated to appeal to an aristocratic patron and community at large. There is no doubt that the poem enjoyed a favourable reception from the public and exerted a powerful effect on its readers. In his preface to Saint-Amant's 1629 *Oeuvres,* Nicolas Faret observes:

> Indeed who can read his beautiful 'Solitude,' so unanimously acclaimed in France, without being tempted to go daydream in the wilderness, and if all those who admire it had given free rein to their initial impulses on reading it, would not Solitude herself have been destroyed by her very praise, and would she not now be more populated than the City?[18]

In the same preface Faret also notes how Saint-Amant was acclaimed by contemporaries as a poet with a genius for vivid descriptions of nature:

> The fire which the Ancients call Genius is vouchsafed to few minds, and may be remarked principally in the Descriptions, which are like rich Paintings where Nature is represented, whence it is that Poetry has been dubbed a speaking Picture.[19]

Indeed, so vivid are the descriptions in 'Solitude' that modern editors and critics have been unable to resist the temptation to look to nature as the source of Saint-Amant's inspiration.[20] The actual places they believe are portrayed in the poem include 'Belle-Isle,' an island off the coast of La Rochelle where Saint-Amant accompanied the Duc de Retz in 1629, and the countryside of Normandy where the poet grew up. But Edwin M. Duval has persuasively shown that the vivid descriptions of nature in this instance are lifted from passages in Latin, Italian, and French poetry. For example, Duval shows how the themes, vocabulary, and imagery of the poem's opening stanzas come from Ovid's story of the Four Ages in book 1 of the *Metamorphoses,* by way of the French influence of d'Urfé's *L'Astrée.*[21] Saint-Amant plays on the expectation that poetry is a picture with the capacity to give a visual representation of the world. And yet in 'Solitude' he depicts a natural world that mirrors the pages of Ovid and d'Urfé, two authors whose nostalgia for the Golden Age must have struck a chord. Saint-Amant is probably writing in the solitude of his study, but his poem shows him gadding about in a natural setting imbued with noble nostalgia. In a sly reversal, he has projected poetic topoi onto natural places to invest nature with noble values and transform it into a utopian space of nobility. What 'Solitude' truly affords the nobility is a way of looking at nature, a way of living the natural world symbolically, as the expression of noble nostalgia. If we take Faret at his word, the noble community was eager to indulge the conceit.

Saint-Amant's Ethos of Diversity

Saint-Amant's nature poetry pretends to report a way of life, when, in fact, the poet depicts the natural setting in such a way as to fashion a speaker meant to be a model of nobility. While this strategy appears to ground the characteristics of the speaker in nature, these traits are in fact rhetorically determined by the poet's stylistic choices. This is especially clear in 'The Contemplator' (Le contemplateur), the companion poem to 'Solitude.' Specific topics mark the speaker as noble, and the desultory way the topics are arranged is meant to be an expression of the noble way of life which the poet claims to live.

'The Contemplator' is an epistle addressed to 'Sir Philippes Cospean [Cospeau], Bishop of Nantes.' The bishop receives hyperbolic praise in the opening stanzas: 'You . . . Salvation of my soul, / Divine Prelate, holy Orator . . . True minister of Heaven's gate, / Noble heart, Man without rancor.'[22] The poem implies that the bishop is the poet's spiritual director. He is also someone who takes an interest in poetry: 'You, who deign to cherish / The noble work of the Muse, / Have been so good to inquire / How I amuse myself these days.'[23] The bishop *deigns* not only because of the difference in social station between him and the poet, but also because a bishop is occupied with the more serious business of salvation. Saint-Amant will therefore use this occasion to show the bishop what essential purpose 'the noble work of the Muse' may serve. Given the public nature of poetry's audience, he indeed proposes to show the whole noble community. In the process, moreover, he will portray himself as a devout Catholic, a loyal client of the Duc de Retz, and a man whose worldly pastimes qualify him as noble.

The poem attempts to achieve these ambitious objectives by depicting how the poet spends his days wandering through a utopian nature. Duval did not track down the sources of the pertinent allusions in 'The Contemplator,' but we may be fairly sure they remain Ovid and d'Urfé: 'All that I formerly sang / About the Sea in my Solitude / Is represented to me in this place / Where I often make my study.'[24] The middle stanzas are like a gallery of pictures showing the poet's activities, divided between the devout and the worldly. For instance, we see the poet engaged in hunting (vv. 191–200), fishing (201–10), reading (211–14), music making (291–300), and writing love poetry (281–90), and in dinner conversation with his patron, de Retz (252–60). Elsewhere, in his contemplation of the Belle-Isle 's natural wonders, the poet finds symbolic evidence of God's presence in the world: the tide (vv. 91–100) and the glow-worm (221–30). The sunrise witnessed by him towards the end of the poem (301ff.) provokes a vision of the Resurrection and Last Judgment. The nature imagery of this final sequence – 'The Stars fall from the Sky,' 'The Sea burns like eau de vie,' 'Molten metals / Make precious rivers,' – is not nostalgic but eschatological.[25] The utopian nature of the Golden Age of Ovid and of d'Urfé gives way to that of the Last Days of the Book of Revelation: 'Nature is exterminated.'[26] Eden meets apocalypse. This comes as a surprise, certainly, but it is a choice consistent with the devout turn of the nobility typified by François de Sales's *Introduction à la vie dévote*, an immensely popular work that sought to reconcile religious devotion with the worldly life led by nobles. In addition to being a manual of *politesse*, the *Introduction* followed in the footsteps of Ignatius's *Spiritual Exercises* by offering vivid verbal pictures that the faithful were to contemplate in prayer.[27] In the final sequence of 'The Contemplator,' then, Saint-Amant embraces Salesian spirituality. These final stanzas are ingenious tableaux of sacred truths. They are meant to entertain and to inspire. In this way the poet displays his love of God – 'I burn with no other flame / Than the flame of your love'[28] – and declares his loyalty to the apostolic church through his devotion to the bishop: 'You, whose eloquence, / Accompanied by good examples, / Bears such fruit that true Altars / Triumph over all false Temples.'[29]

The wandering organization of topics, descriptions, and vivid imagery in 'The Contemplator' gives one the impression of a walk in a natural setting. This seemingly random succession of elements is also accompanied by vertical changes in stylistic register, mixing high, middle, and low – as in the vision of the Resurrection, where bodies awake from the grave in a rather bawdy and comic sequence. Critics, beginning with Boileau, never quite approved. 'The Contemplator' is at once devotional and worldly, sublime and burlesque, descriptive and allusive, flitting from topic to topic, from high to low, from serious to comic, without warning or transition. This is typical of Saint-Amant's best work. It is the hallmark of his style.

The desultory arrangement is especially integral to Saint-Amant's ethos, that is, both the kind of person he wants to portray himself as and the social function and value of this person. At one point in 'The Contemplator,' the speaker addresses the question of the poem's arrangement and assigns it this purpose:

So it is according to its object
That my mind changes its project,
Flitting from thought to thought:
Diversity most pleases the eye,
And the gaze ends up fatigued
That focuses too much on Heaven.[30]

This remark about heaven will become clear in a moment. The above passage echoes a similar passage in 'Solitude':

Now joyful, now mournful,
According to the fury of my inspiration
And the object that falls under my gaze,
My soul gives birth to words
In perfect liberty, without constraint . . .[31]

And just a few lines later in the same poem:

Oh how I love Solitude!
It is the Element of excellent Minds;
Where else could I have learned
The Art of Apollo without study . . .[32]

'Diversity' is the name Saint-Amant gives the apparently random organization of topics, as well as the mixing of registers, and it is no accident that this term recalls an ideal quality of Ciceronian eloquence articulated in *Orator*. Cicero, defining the truly Attic orator, assigns an end to each level of style and leaves it up to the orator's judgment to decide what is needed at any moment within the same speech.[33] We need only suppose that Saint-Amant has transposed this Ciceronian ideal to poetry, which, it may be argued, partakes of epideictic eloquence, whose end is *to kalon* (what is fine, noble, or honourable), a concept that ties moral goodness to aesthetic pleasure.[34] To judge from the above passages, Saint-Amant's diversity is associated with an aesthetics of pleasure (it 'most pleases the eye') as well as with an ethics of 'liberty' practised by 'excellent Minds,' and naturalness ('without study'). Diversity here is a version of *sprezzatura*, an aristocratic quality implying freedom, independence, leisure, spontaneity, and naturalness. It sums up the noble way of life represented in Saint-Amant's poetry.

Above all, diversity is intended to give pleasure and to entertain. To Cospeau, the bishop, it offers recreation. The pleasure of poetry offers relief from a too steady religious devotion that might otherwise drive the bishop to melancholy. It offers a similar recreation to de Retz, the duke. Unrelieved political responsibilities, such as being on the lookout for an English invasion at Belle-Isle, might weigh down the duke with worry and care. But it does not allow him – or the larger aristocratic community – to forget the devotion they owe 'the Author of Nature.'[35] The diversity of Saint-Amant's poetry thus serves a noble purpose. It contributes, however indirectly, to the more serious civic activities of the bishop and the duke. The poet shoulders his share of the burden by entertaining them. The ethos thus portrayed is noble, not only because it is a type, a kind of person with certain characteristics, but also because its function and value are determined by its relation to elites of church and state. In this respect, Saint-Amant could be said to create an early version of the *honnête homme* – the honourable gentleman. Nicolas Faret, Saint-Amant's friend, published *L'honnête homme, ou l'art de plaire à la cour* in 1630, one year after Saint-Amant's initial collected works. For Faret, the honnête homme pursuing a career at court serves the Prince and the 'Patrie' 'by making himself pleasing to everyone,' being obliged 'to profit not just himself, but also the public, especially his friends, who are the virtuous men.'[36] Saint-Amant's 'diversity' aims to please a wide audience, particularly two virtuous men who are his 'friends,' and in the process offers the poet himself as a model honnête homme to the larger noble community.

Ethos and the Self-Portrait

The natural setting from which Saint-Amant chooses to address the audience can also serve to portray something like a metaphysical self, that is, the soul. To grasp how such a self-portrait could work, we need only recall that Aristotelian ethos, or character, is largely determined by voluntary decision. One character is distinguished from another, and one kind of person from another kind, in virtue of the end being aimed at – in what way, for what reason, etc.[37] Voluntary decision, moreover, is a distinguishing characteristic of the rational part of the soul.[38] Hence voluntary decision is the link between character and the soul. Individual character and soul are what they are in virtue of the same principle. One soul differs from another not in virtue of its capacity to make voluntary decisions, but rather in virtue of the actual decisions being made; in other words, its specific choices and the way it makes those choices.

It follows that Saint-Amant's choice of topics, arrangement, and figurative language could be considered a symbolic image of his soul, provided that these choices represent operations characteristic of what it is to be Saint-Amant and no one else. However tendentious this line of reasoning might be, and however problematic its assumptions, Saint-Amant apparently espouses this view of poetic language. His poem 'À Théophile' designates poets and the representational powers of poetry in these terms:

Painters whose talking brushes
In excellent traits
Draw invisible things,
Noises, thoughts, harmonies,
Angry or peaceful winds,
And the soul through its body.[39]

If poetry is a speaking picture, the soul is one of the invisible things it has the power to paint in and through its speaking. A poem is like a picture of the soul.

An excellent example of how an external natural place corresponds to the inner state of the poet's soul can be found in the sonnet 'Alpine Winter' (L'hiver des Alpes).

These atoms of fire that sparkle on the Snow,
These sparks of gold, silver, and crystal,
Decorating the white hair of Winter, strewn about
By the Winds, with oriental brilliance in the sun:

This beautiful Cloth of Heaven, in which mountains dress,
This transparent road, made of the second metal,
And this crisp and healthy air, conducive to vital spirits,
Are so sweet a sight, my eyes sparkle with pleasure.

This Season is my pleasure, I love its frost:
Its Robes of innocence and pure splendour
Almost cover over the crimes of the Earth:

Thus the Olympian views us with a humane brow,
His anger spares us, and never will the thunder
Fly from his hands to desolate our days.[40]

Although it has a picture postcard quality to it, we may be fairly certain that the description of the snowy Alps in this sonnet resorts to allusion. The opening image of the sunlight on the snow, 'These atoms of fire,' and the reference to thunder in the final tercet should probably be traced to Lucretius's *De rerum natura*, book 6, where the causes of lighting and snow, indeed all meteorological phenomena, are attributed to seeds of fire torn from the clouds by the wind. The allusion signals that the speaker is an epicurean. The character of a hedonist, for whom the good is pleasure, does not conflict with a noble identity increasingly defined by its pursuit of pleasure. Nor is it fundamentally at odds with the ideal of the honnête homme. On the other hand, *this* epicurean also appears to be a materialist. The correspondence between the inner and the outer world is signalled by the 'fire,' the 'sparks,' and the 'sparkling eyes.' A materialist philosophy would explain the fact that the speaker's soul appears to be made of the same stuff as the natural world. In this respect, Saint-Amant pushes the boundaries of the type and begins to cross into the singular – at the very least into an elite. Gassendi had rehabilitated epicurean philosophy for the intellectual elite, and these elites sometimes included members of the upper nobility who considered themselves above orthodox beliefs and morality.

What is singular is the way the speaker's soul is portrayed. Saint-Amant uses the imagery of sun and snow to create the impression of movement – a defining characteristic of the soul – and he achieves it by presenting the imagery in a list. The soul's movement is thus portrayed not just by the sparkling, but especially by the succession of images. The appositions astonish by their diversity, but it is done with a certain elegance and naturalness. While the speaker's eyes sparkle with pleasure at the sight of the sun and snow, his soul flashes with brilliance in and through the figurative language of his poetry. The speaker's soul thus mirrors his surroundings: he is all fire and elevation and vitality. A spark passes between the Alps and the speaker, and this spark is then relayed to the reader via the sonnet. The reader is invited to admire and to approve these material qualities as moral, that is, as qualities of the *noble* soul. The ideal of this ethos is the nonchalance of *sprezzatura*, here given an epicurean turn: it is freedom from pain, from effort, and freedom for spontaneity and naturalness. It is a cool tranquillity imbued with a sparkling vitality.

Is there an implicit political statement in this self-portrait? Not unlike 'The Contemplator,' the sonnet articulates an ethical purpose for pleasure. The last two stanzas suggest that pleasure serves to assuage the avenging anger provoked by 'the crimes of the Earth.' What crimes? It is not stated. But the Alps as a topos connote struggle and war. They recall Mount Olympus – indeed 'the Olympian' overlooks them here – the site of a primal struggle, a War in Heaven, between the Titans and the Gods, Chronos and Zeus, heralding the end of the Golden Age. They also recall illustrious military campaigns: Caesar, Hannibal, or Charlemagne. Or, in more recent memory, François I crossing the Alps to press his claims in Italy, Louis XIII bringing the French army to the 'Pas de Suse.' Whether Saint-Amant was actually there or not, the sonnet portrays a soul discovering pleasure and tranquillity against a background of struggle and war. The sonnet not only holds up for admiration noble ideals and values – elevation, repose, spontaneity, vitality, naturalness – but it also becomes an expression of them, offering itself as a performance of them. Just as the pleasure of the snow assuages the avenging anger of 'the Olympian,' so the pleasure afforded by Saint-Amant's poetry smoothes over resentment. Whose? The monarch's? The nobility's? Saint-Amant leaves it open. What is clear, however, is that the pleasure of poetry is meant to relieve the passion for vengeance born of struggle and war.

One could say that Saint-Amant's nature poetry as a whole performs nobility even as it appeals to provenance, a natural world imbued with poetry, a utopian space where nobility discovers itself and engages in suitably noble acts. But Saint-Amant's idea of nobility, his ethos, inclined too much towards singularity. Faret had already cautioned the would-be honnête homme to avoid writing poetry, since poetry admitted nothing 'mediocre.'[41] In fact, however, the honnête homme was mediocre in the sense of 'moderate' and 'modest.' By adapting himself and his discourse to reflect the concerns of his individual interlocutors, the honnête homme would evolve not towards singularity but towards a universal quality. A poet, it turned out, was too exceptional, too singular, to qualify as *honnête.* Pascal grasped this later development and articulated it in two fragments in his *Pensées.* 'A poet and not an honnête homme,' he observes. The honnête homme is 'not a mathematician, not a preacher, not eloquent, but honnête. His universal quality alone is pleasing. When a man enters a room and they remember his book, that's a bad sign.'[42] Not only did Saint-Amant define and perform nobility in and through poetry, but its stylistic diversity and astonishing imagery made this noble ethos seem too extravagant. As Boileau was to say of him years later in 'Chant III' of the *Art poétique*: 'Don't imitate that madman.'[43]

NOTES

1 Saint-Amant, 'La solitude,' in *Oeuvres,* 5 vols. (Paris, 1971), 1:46–7, vv. 171–80: 'Alcidon, pour qui je me vante / De ne rien faire que de beau, / Reçoy ce fantasque tableau / Fait d'une peinture vivante. / Je ne cherche que les deserts, / Où révant tout seul, je m'amuse / A des discours assez disserts / De mon Genie avec la Muse: / Mais mon plus aymable entretien / C'est le ressouvenir du tien.' Translations are my own, except where otherwise indicated.

2 Jonathan Dewald, *The European Nobility* (Cambridge, 1996), 33; see also Ellery Schalk, *From Valor to Pedigree: Ideas of Nobility in France in the Sixteenth and Seventeenth Centuries* (Princeton, 1986).

3 See Emanuel Bury, *Littérature et politesse: L'invention de l'honnête homme* (Paris, 1996).

4 See Faith E. Beasley, *Salons, History, and the Creation of 17th-Century France* (Burlington, VT, 2006); Benedetta Craveri, *The Age of Conversation* (New York, 2005); Norbert Elias, *The Court Society* (New York, 1983).

5 For recent criticism on Saint-Amant's poetry, see Guillaume Peureux, *Le rendez-vous des enfans sans soucy: La poétique de Saint-Amant* (Paris, 2002). Other excellent studies of Saint-Amant include John D. Lyons, *The Listening Voice: An Essay on the Rhetoric of Saint-Amant* (Kentucky, 1982); Edwin M. Duval, *Poesis and Poetic Tradition in the Early Works of Saint-Amant: Four Essays in Contextual Reading* (York, SC, 1981); and Robert T. Corum, Jr, *Other World and Other Seas: Art and Vision in Saint-Amant's Nature Poetry* (Kentucky, 1979).

6 See Christian Jouhaud, *Les pouvoirs de la littérature* (Paris, 2000), 47–52.

7 Aristotle, *On Rhetoric* 1.9.35–6; here trans. George A. Kennedy (Oxford, 1991), 5.

8 See Marc Fumaroli, *L'âge de l'éloquence* (Paris, 1980).

9 Aristotle, *On Rhetoric* 1.2.4, 2.1.5, 2.13.16 (trans. Kennedy, 38, 120–1, 168). Kathy Eden, *Hermeneutics and the Rhetorical Tradition* (New Haven, 1997), 26. Decorum is the accommodation of (1) time, (2) place, and (3) persons.

10 See Eugene Garver, *Aristotle's 'Rhetoric': An Art of Character* (Chicago, 1994); and Charles Chamberlain, 'From "Haunts" to "Character": The Meaning of *Ethos* and Its Relation to Ethics,' *Helios* 11, 2 (1984), 97–108.

11 Aristotle, *On Rhetoric* 1.2.3–4 (trans. Kennedy, 37–8).

12 Montaigne, *The Complete Essays*, trans. Donald M. Frame (Stanford, 2002), 2.
13 Dewald, *European Nobility*, xv, 9.
14 Elias, *The Court Society*, 44–5.
15 Honoré d'Urfé, *L'Astrée* (Paris, 1984), 35: 'leur douceur naturelle.'
16 Dewald, *European Nobility*, 12.
17 For a dated but useful review of 'la solitude' tradition in early seventeenth-century French poetry, see Richard A. Maza, 'Théophile de Viau, Saint-Amant, and the Spanish Soledad,' *Kentucky Romance Quarterly* 14 (1967), 393–404.
18 Nicolas Faret, 'Preface sur les Oeuvres de Mr. de Saint-Amant par son fidelle amy Faret,' in Saint-Amant, *Oeuvres*, 1:16–17: 'Et certes, qui peut voir ceste belle Solitude, à qui toute la France a donné sa voix, sans estre tenté d'aller resver dans les deserts, & si tous ceux qui l'ont admirée s'estoient laissé aller aux premiers mouvemens qu'ils ont eus en la lisant, la Solitude mesme n'auroit-elle pas esté destruitte par sa propre loüange, & ne seroit-elle pas aujourd'hui plus frequentée que les Villes?'
19 Ibid., 1:15: 'Ceste chaleur que les Anciens ont appelée Genie, ne se communique qu'à fort peu d'esprits, & ne se fait principalement remarquer qu'aux Descriptions, qui sont comme de riches Tableaux où la Nature est representée, d'où vient que l'on a nommé la Poësie une Peinture parlante.'
20 See Corum, *Other Worlds and Other Seas.*
21 Duval, *Poesis and Poetic Tradition*, 17.
22 Saint-Amant, 'Le contemplateur,' in *Oeuvres*, 1:49, vv. 1–5: 'Vous . . ./ Cause du salut de mon Ame, / Divin Prélat, sainct Orateur'; and 50, vv. 15–16: 'Vray Ministre d'Estat du Ciel, / Coeur debonnaire, Homme sans fiel.'
23 Ibid., 50, vv. 21–4: 'Vous, dis-je, qui daignant cherir / Les nobles travaux de la Muse, / Avez voulu vous enquerir / A quoy maintainant je m'amuse.'
24 Ibid., 56, vv. 151–4: 'Tout ce qu'autrefois j'ay chanté / De la Mer en ma Solitude, / En ce lieu m'est representé, / Où souvent je fay mon estude.'
25 Ibid., 67–8, v. 411: 'Les Estoilles tombent des Cieux'; v. 417: 'La Mer brusle comme eau-de-vie'; and vv. 421–2: 'Les Metaux ensemble fondus / Font des rivieres precieuses.'
26 Ibid., 68, v. 432: 'La Nature est exterminée.'
27 For the *Introduction*'s connection to *politesse*, see Benedetta Craveri, *The Age of Conversation* (New York, 2005), 16–20. For its connection to Jesuit rhetorical manuals in the tradition of Ignatius's *Spiritual Exercises*, see Fumaroli, *L'âge de l'éloquence*, 265.
28 Saint-Amant, 'Le contemplateur,' 69, vv. 449–50: 'Je ne brusle point d'autre flame / Que de celle de ton amour.'

29 Ibid., 69, vv. 451–4: 'Et vous, dont les discours sont tels, / Accompagnez des bons exemples, / Que par leur fruit les vrais Autels / Triomphent de tous les faux Temples.'

30 Ibid., 55, vv. 135–40: 'Voilà comme selon l'objét / Mon esprit changeant de projét / Saute de pensée en pensée: / La diversité plaist aux yeux, / Et la veuë en fin est lassée / De ne regarder que les Cieux.'

31 Saint-Amant, 'La solitude,' in *Oeuvres*, 1:47, vv. 185–9: 'Tantost chagrin, tantost joyeux, / Selon que la fureur m'enflamme, / Et que l'objet s'offre à mes yeux, / Les propos me naissent en l'ame, / Sans contraindre la liberté . . .'

32 Ibid., 47, vv. 191–4: 'O que j'ayme la Solitude! / C'est l'Element des bons Esprits, / C'est par elle que j'ay compris / L'Art d'Apollon sans nulle estude.'

33 Cicero, *Orator* 21.70 (Cambridge, 1997).

34 Aristotle, *On Rhetoric* 1.3.5 and 1.9.3 (trans. Kennedy, 49, 79). On the connection between eloquence and poetry, see Fumaroli, *L'âge de l'éloquence*, 66.

35 Saint-Amant, 'Le contemplateur,' 63, v. 309: 'l'Autheur de la Nature.'

36 Nicolas Faret, *L'honnête homme, ou l'art de plaire à la cour* (Geneva, 1970).

37 See Aristotle, *Nicomachean Ethics* 3.3.1111b5 and 3.5.1114b25; here trans. Terence Irwin (Indianapolis, 1985), 59, 70.

38 Ibid., 1.13.1102a30–1103a5 (trans. Irwin, 30–2).

39 Saint-Amant, 'À Théophile,' in *Oeuvres*, 1:4, vv. 19–24: 'Peintres dont les pinceaux parlans / Avecques des traicts excellens / Tirent les choses invisibles, / Les bruits, les pensers, les accords, / Les vents courroucez ou paisibles, / Et l'ame au travers de son corps.'

40 Saint-Amant, 'L'hiver des Alpes,' in *Oeuvres*, 2:124–5 (here with alternate final tercet): 'Ces atômes de feu, qui sur la Neige brillent, / Ces estincelles d'or, d'azur, et de cristal, / Dont l'Hiver, au Soleil, d'un lustre oriental / Pare ses Cheveux blancs, que les Vents esparpillent: /
'Ce beau Cotton du ciel, de quoy les monts s'habillent, / Ce pavé transparant, fait du second metal, / Et cet air net, et sain, propre à l'esprit vital, / Sont si doux à mes yeux, que d'aise ils en pétillent. /
'Cette Saison me plaist, j'en ayme la froideur, / Sa Robbe d'innocence, et de pure splendeur, / Couvre en quelque façon les crimes de la Terre: /
'Aussi l'Olympien la void d'un front humain; / Sa collere l'espargne, et jamais le tonnerre / Pour desoler ses jours ne partit de sa main.'

41 Faret, *L'honnête homme*, 31.

42 Blaise Pascal, *Pensées* (Paris, 1963), 585, no. 611: 'Poète et non honnête homme'; and 588, no. 647: '*Honnête homme.* Il faut qu'on n'en puisse (dire)

ni il est mathématicien, ni prédicateur, ni éloquent mais il est honnête homme. Cette qualité universelle me plaît seule. Quand en voyant un homme on se souvient de son livre c'est mauvais signe.'

43 Nicolas Boileau, *Satires, epîtres, art poétique* (Paris, 1985), 246, v. 261: 'N'imitez pas ce fou.'

PART II

PLOTTING THE BODY: TRAJECTORIES AND PROJECTIONS

chapter seven

Divine Grace, the Humoral Body, and the 'Inner Self' in Seventeenth-Century France and England

ROBERT DIMIT

Catherine Belsey presented herself in 1985 as arguing against what she saw as the dominant 'liberal-humanist' belief that 'in its essence the subject does not change,' claiming instead that the European self of 1600 was radically different from the self we know today.[1] Little more than a decade later, however, Roy Porter edited a collection of essays whose initial premise was roughly the opposite of Belsey's: belief in a self that changes over time is common, so much so that there exists a standard account of the self's history – the 'Authorized Version,' in Porter's words – that is ripe for revision, if not outright refutation.[2] Porter's position is consistent with the many historical accounts of the self that have appeared in recent years, and it is safe to say that few scholars in the humanities today continue to assume that the nature of personal identity has been always and everywhere the same.[3]

As Porter notes, histories of the self have often located the 'great divide' separating the pre-modern from the modern self within the seventeenth century.[4] Specifically, our modern sense of personal inwardness as an attribute of the self is often supposed to have arisen during this century. Thus, Belsey, building on an account offered by Francis Barker, has argued that the sense of personal interiority suggested by Hamlet's claim to have 'that within which passes show' is an anachronism, a hallmark of later bourgeois subjectivity projected onto Shakespeare's character by liberal-humanist critics. According to Belsey and Barker, the interiority attributed to Hamlet was impossible before the end of the seventeenth century.[5] Against Belsey and Barker's position, Katherine Eisaman Maus has cited numerous references to personal interiority in British works published in the early seventeenth century. Her examples, as she insists, make it 'difficult to claim that Hamlet's boast of "that within" is anachronistic.'[6] Nicholas Paige has offered abundant evidence from French religious autobiographical writings that there is before the middle of the seventeenth century a clear sense in France, too, of something like our present-day conception of mental interiority.[7]

While the examples offered by Maus and Paige leave little room for the outright denial that a sense of personal interiority was possible in Europe before 1700, I believe nevertheless that their positions must be qualified in important ways. Focusing particularly on early seventeenth-century Britain and France, I will show that there was then no 'inner self' in the full sense in which that term is now commonly understood. What was inner about the early modern self was not what differentiated it from other selves, while features that we today closely identify with the inner self were then attributed to external factors. Today, mental interiority is associated with psychological depth, which in turn is associated with both obscurity of motivation, on the one hand, and individuality and authenticity, on the other. Seventeenth-century conceptions of personal inwardness do not generally encompass these attributes, nor even psychological depth in our late modern sense. Instead, both the differentiation among selves (judged neither authentic nor inauthentic) and the obscure sources of motivation were most often attributed to the effects of divine grace and the functions of the physical body, both of which were forces or processes external to the period's understanding of the inner self.

In any comparison of early and late modernity, our own ideas about the nature of a person are often more difficult to characterize than those of the earlier period. Recent developments in cognitive psychology and neuroscience are at odds with our folk psychologies, and those folk psychologies can vary substantially among the inhabitants of, for example, Paris, Kansas City, or Havana. Bracketing these differences, and drawing on my own experiences as a US American, I take as a working premise that most late modern non-specialist accounts of mental interiority follow psychoanalysis and other depth psychologies in understanding the inward self as the site of that which is concealed, repressed, or otherwise difficult to know. According to these models, actions of the outer, visible self originate more or less obscurely in the volitions of an authentic, more or less unknowable inner self. Our late modern structural models or metaphors of personal interiority are informative in this regard. Freud frequently wrote of psychoanalysis as an analogue to archaeology. He likened the work of analysis to the excavation and reconstruction of the ruins of an ancient city. This archaeological metaphor accounts for the stratification of the psyche and the ways that this stratification is built up over time, with the oldest memories in the deepest layers. As Donald Spence has argued, Freud's depth metaphor has become reified in our contemporary belief that the human mind is structured in layers, each of which is successively more difficult of access.[8]

Freud's model of layered depth has also been assimilated to a discourse of authenticity which contrasts an authentic inner self to the inauthentic outward selves required to fulfil social roles. There are many different models of authenticity in our time, of course, and Alessandro Ferrara has made the point that not all such models are tied to individual difference. Ethnic group membership, as he notes, is considered a source of authenticity in certain forms of identity politics, and authenticity is sometimes attributed to blues and country music performers based on their regional or rural origins.[9] But our dominant concepts of personal authenticity do tend to focus on individual differences. Ferrara writes:

> All *normative* conceptions of authenticity share the assumption that a life in which the deepest and most significant motifs that resonate within us find expression is . . . a kind of 'ought' that binds all of us. Furthermore, all conceptions of authenticity share an aversion to the reason-centered view of subjectivity typical of the Western tradition and especially to the hierarchical structuring of human subjectivity into a higher rational component and a lower one, constituted by the realm of affects, emotions, feelings and the passions.[10]

I quote this passage at length because it so clearly articulates the ethical value placed on personal authenticity today, the linkage of authenticity and affect, and the late modern assumption that the expression of the 'deepest' and (not coincidentally) 'most significant' motifs 'within us' is what is at stake in the project of authenticity. While Ferrara is concerned with contemporary philosophical accounts of authenticity, the themes he identifies as being common to all of them are easily recognized in self-help and other pop-cultural discourses as well.[11] In late modern North America, this authentic inner self is closely linked to feelings or emotions, or even taken to be constituted by feelings.

By contrast, early moderns who wrote of personal interiority may have conceived of it in terms of vastness or openness, but they seldom attributed to it successive depths or layers of hiddenness.[12] Neither did the early moderns think that the inner self was the site of personal authenticity or individuality.[13] On the contrary, to the extent that such an inner self was thought praiseworthy, its value was seen in its more or less direct connection to God rather than in its authenticity.[14] And differences among people were credited mainly to differences in their bodies or to influences from the external, material world rather than to the immaterial inner self.

Of the sixteenth and early seventeenth centuries, Timothy Reiss has written, 'Everyone shared the idea that all souls had one identical nature and the consequent problem it posed with regard to differences in mental ability.'[15] If all souls are alike, how does one explain the evident differences among people in performing those functions that belong to the soul? A key text treating this question was Juan Huarte's *Examen de ingenios* (1575; translated into French, Italian, and English before 1600). Huarte acknowledged that in special cases certain 'Wits [and] Abilities' are miraculously given by God, such as 'the wisdom of the Prophets, and of all those to whom God granted some grace infused.' In less exceptional cases, he reasoned that 'all souls being of equal perfection (as well that of the wiser, as that of the foolish),' observable differences in mental ability cannot be attributed to differences in men's rational souls.[16] Instead, he attributed those differences in ability to differences in the body, differences which he explained in terms of Galenic humoral theory. In *The Optick Glasse of Humours* (1607), Thomas Walkington also credited the 'diversity of wits' primarily to 'the diverse temperature of the body.'[17] More generally, Walkington wrote that the soul 'sympathizes' with the body and follows the body's 'crasis,' or humoral mixture: 'The heavenly soul of man . . . doth feel . . . by a certain deficiency the ill affected crasis of the body, so that if this be annoyed or infected with any feculent humors, it fairs not well with the soul, the soul herself as maladious feels some want of her excellency, and yet impatible in regard of her substance.'[18]

This idea that souls are immune to imperfection is repeated by Thomas Browne in 1657 when he argues that if bodies have a soul, 'they must have it perfectly, because the soul doth not receive more or less of quantity, but is the very perfection and absolution of a thing.'[19] Edward Reynolds (1640) attributes the 'inequality and difference of men's understandings' to the soul's dependence on the body, but he also acknowledges that it has been questioned 'in the Schools' whether men's souls might not have 'in their Nature degrees of perfection and weakness.' One explanation for this, he suggests, could be that the soul as well as the body suffered the 'corruption' that ensued after the Fall. Reynolds seems to reject this possibility, but his account is ambiguous. He first suggests that differences in the operations of the soul come 'principally . . . from the sundry constitutions of men's bodies.' Then, after citing Aristotle's claim that the soul is 'impassible from any corporeal agent,' Reynolds writes, 'So then it is manifest, that this weakness of apprehension in the Souls of men, doth not come from any immediate and proper darkness belonging unto them; but only from the coexistence which they have with a Body ill disposed for assistance and information.'[20] Although Reynolds ends by affirming that all souls are equal, and that their differences arise from the bodies with which they are conjoined, his reasoning suggests that it could not be taken for granted in the mid-seventeenth century that everyone agreed.

Unlike the texts of Huarte, Walkington, and Browne, which are grounded in medical lore and aim at practical ends, Reynolds's treatise is grounded in theology and philosophical speculation, and aims at ethical ends. That he explicitly explains the limitations the body places on the soul's functions as resulting from the body's corruption in a fallen world is significant here, as it explains one potential role of grace in determining the differences in understanding among people.

My point in citing these sixteenth- and seventeenth-century authors is to show that the sort of individuation we today associate with an authentic (inner) self was not an attribute of early modern inwardness. For them it was attributable to the fallen, material body with which the soul was conjoined and on which it depended, a body which is certainly outside the inner self. Setting aside Reynolds's seeming ambiguity, it appears that Reiss is largely correct to suggest that 'everyone' then thought that all souls were the same. What distinguished one self from another was external to the soul.

Still, all the texts considered so far are concerned with differences in ability, primarily the ability to reason or understand. Our conceptions of an inner self are not limited to reasoning alone, but include affect as well. And, as Ferrara tells us, our accounts of individual authenticity quite specifically involve emotion. How, then, did these early moderns understand the relationship between the inner self and, to use the period's language, the passions?

The most useful guide to the passional aspects of seventeenth-century interiority is Descartes's *Les passions de l'âme* (1649), not because of its originality or influence, but because of its clear and detailed analysis of the soul's and the body's interaction within the soul-body compound. A consideration of his treatment of the passions confirms the disjuncture between late and early modern conceptions of the inner self: where affect is concerned, individuation was then considered external to the soul.

This is not the place to consider the relationship of Descartes's treatise on the passions to his earlier work, but one passage in the *Discours de la méthode* should be mentioned in this context. There, Descartes repeated the claim that reason is the same in all people, but wrote that 'the diversity of our opinions . . . [arises] solely because we direct our thoughts along different paths and do not attend to the same things' (la diversité de nos opinions . . . vient . . . seulement de ce que nous conduisons nos pensées par diverses voies, et ne considérons pas les mêmes choses).[21] While this passage conforms to the then widely shared belief that the soul is the same in all people, it fails to mention the body as the primary source of observable differences in mental abilities. Given the emphasis in *Les passions de l'âme* on the body's role as a limiter of the soul's faculties, the failure to acknowledge this factor in the *Discours* is surprising. Still, the two treatises were written many years apart (they were the first and last of Descartes's works published during his lifetime), and the confidence concerning reason's perfectibility in the *Discours* should perhaps be read as a rhetorical gesture in support of the Cartesian method rather than as the product of careful reasoning.

Before considering those sections of *Les passions de l'âme* that are most relevant to the present discussion, it will be useful to remind ourselves of a few details from Descartes's account of the mechanisms through which the body and soul interact. The most important elements in this account are the *esprits animaux*, or animal spirits, and the pineal gland. According to Descartes, perception of any object sets the animal spirits within the brain in motion according to a certain pattern. The movements of the animal spirits cause the gland to move in a certain way, and this movement, communicated through the gland to the soul, elicits an associated thought. Also, the movements within the brain that represent specific objects to the soul are naturally accompanied by movements that excite particular passions. Conversely, volitions can also move the gland, which in turn moves the spirits so as to produce bodily motion. There is much more to Descartes's account of soul–body interaction – motion of the animal spirits can cause the body to move without the soul's participation, the soul can represent passional objects to itself and thereby cause motions in the gland and spirits corresponding to passions, and so on – but we can safely ignore those aspects that are not directly relevant to our concerns.[22]

In explaining how passions are excited in the soul, Descartes mentions in passing that different people may experience different passions in response to the same object, 'according to the differing temperament of the body or the strength of the soul' (selon le divers tempérament du corps, ou la force de l'âme) and according to past experiences in similar situations.[23] The reference to temperament aligns Descartes's account with Galenic theories of character, but, as will become apparent, his explanation of the body's role in passional differences is based on mechanics rather than humoral balance. Before considering the body, however, it will be useful to address some difficulties raised by Descartes's passing reference to the soul's strength.

In another passage, Descartes describes those with the strongest souls as 'those in whom the will can naturally conquer the passions most easily and stop the accompanying movements of the body' (ceux en qui naturellement la volonté peut le plus aisément vaincre les passions & arrêter les mouvements du corps qui les accompagnent). For Descartes, strength of soul is demonstrated by a person who follows judgments rather than present passions (though he adds that strength of soul is ethically insufficient if it is not accompanied by a knowledge of the truth).[24] Elsewhere, Descartes writes, 'although . . . it is easy to believe that all the souls God puts in our bodies are not equally noble and strong . . . it is certain nevertheless that good education is very useful for correcting deficiencies of birth' (encore . . . qu'il soit aisé à croire, que toutes les âmes que Dieu met en nos corps, ne sont pas également nobles & fortes . . . il est certain néanmoins que la bonne institution sert beaucoup, pour corriger les défauts de la naissance).[25] While the idea that God has placed souls of varying strengths in different people's bodies contradicts the widely shared belief that all souls are identical in their perfection, it is also another instance of the role of divine grace as a source of difference among selves. Still, Descartes does not claim that God has done this, only that this idea is easy to believe. On the other hand, there is no further explanation in *Les passions de l'âme* as to how these unequally strong souls might come about. The suggestion that souls might be made weaker or stronger by education or other experience would similarly contradict the doctrine that the immaterial soul cannot be changed by the world of matter (the soul is 'impatible in regard of her substance,' 'impassible from any corporeal agent,' as Walkington and Reynolds wrote).[26]

Descartes never explicitly resolves these apparent contradictions, but their resolution may lie in the fact that a person's strength of soul is judged on the outcome of a process involving the soul-body compound. He describes a situation where the pineal gland is being pushed in one direction by the animal spirits and in the opposite direction by the soul, that is, in which the movements of the spirits are such as to evoke a passion in the soul and the soul's volition resists that passion. In such a situation, a person's strength of soul can never be measured absolutely, but only in relation to the strength of his or her animal spirits. As Descartes makes abundantly clear in other passages, differences among bodies are of much greater significance to our understanding and management of the passions. His comment in this context that a good education is useful in 'correcting deficiencies of birth' – a proposition which he says is certain and not merely 'easy to believe' – also points towards the body, or the soul-body compound, rather than the (impassible) soul.

In fact, aside from these and a few other passing mentions of the strength of souls, Descartes attributes the differences in people's passional responses primarily to differences in their bodies. Article 39 of *Les passions de l'âme*, in which Descartes explains how the same object can provoke different passions in different people, says that these differences arise because human brains are not all configured the same way ('tous les cerveaux ne sont pas disposez en même façon'), and the flow of animal spirits in different brains is consequently varied. Although he mentions the movement of the pineal gland – which is necessarily communicated to the soul – and the passion that may result, he does not mention the soul as such.[27]

Ultimately, Descartes aims in *Les passions de l'âme* to give advice with regard to the control of the passions. Despite the abundance of technical material in the treatise, his purpose is ethical. When he turns his attention to this goal, he predicates his advice for managing the passions on the centrality of the body's functions in the production of the passions. Descartes claims that 'there is no soul so weak that it cannot, when well guided, acquire an absolute power over its passions' (il n'y a point d'âme si faible qu'elle ne puisse, étant bien conduite, acquérir un pouvoir absolu sur ses passions). This is so, he writes, because 'although each movement of the gland seems to have been joined by nature to each of our thoughts from the beginning of our life, one can nevertheless join them to others by habituation' (encore que chaque mouvement de la glande semble avoir été joint par la nature à chacune de nos pensées, dès le commencement de nôtre vie, on les peut toutefois joindre à d'autres par habitude). He offers our use of language as one example, where the movement of the gland that is naturally associated only with the sound of the word, for example, 'cat,' comes to be associated with the idea of the small house pet known by that name. Furthermore, though movements within the brain that excite certain passions in the soul naturally accompany the movements that represent certain objects to the soul, by habituation the passional movements can be separated from the image-representing movements and others substituted in their place. Descartes notes that this change of association can be accomplished very quickly, by a single event: 'Thus when someone unexpectedly comes upon something very foul in food he is eating with relish, the surprise of this encounter can so change the disposition of the brain that he will no longer be able to see any such food afterwards without abhorrence' (Ainsi, lorsqu'on rencontre inopinément quelque chose de fort sale en une viande qu'on mange avec appétit, la surprise de cette rencontre peut tellement changer la disposition du cerveau qu'on ne pourra plus voir par après de telle viande qu'avec horreur). Thus, the links between particular movements of the gland and spirits and particular thoughts in the soul, and the links between the movements that represent particular objects to the soul and the accompanying movements that evoke passions, can be altered.[28] The first sort of possible alteration, though important for Descartes's analysis, is relatively unimportant for a discussion of the early modern self. The possible alteration of the relationships between passions and their objects, on the contrary, is important for the difference it reveals between this aspect of the inner self then and now.

Descartes has already established that (setting aside the ambiguously described strength of the soul) the differences among individual persons where the passions are concerned lie in the body rather than the soul. Thus, just as this period's opinion held that the faculty of reason is the same in all souls and varies only because of the soul's reliance on the corrupt body, so, too, the passional function was seen as the same in all souls, varying only according to differences among the bodies to which they were joined. Additionally, Descartes suggests here the means by which interpersonal differences in the passions might develop. In a seeming anticipation of psychoanalytic theory, Descartes believes that past experiences contribute to the constitution of present desires. But where Freudian and post-Freudian late moderns see the past's influence in our psyches, Descartes saw it in our bodies. His example of the once delectable, now disgusting, dish may seem trivial in this respect, but a more apt example may be found in his letter to Hector Pierre Chanut of 6 June 1647.

Chanut had apparently asked Descartes to explain how it is that we can love one person instead of another even before we know their true worth. Descartes writes that there are two reasons, one pertaining to the mind and one to the body. That pertaining to the mind he declines to explain in a letter, seemingly out of fear that the orthodoxy of his answer regarding the soul might be challenged. Of the reason pertaining to the body, he writes: 'It consists in the arrangement of the parts of our brain . . . The objects which strike our senses move parts of our brain . . ., and there make as it were folds, which undo themselves when the object ceases to operate; but afterwards the place where they were made has a tendency to be folded again in the same manner by another object resembling even incompletely the original object.'[29] By way of example, Descartes tells the story of his having as a boy loved a cross-eyed girl, after which the visual 'impression' of her eyes in his brain became connected to the impressions of the accompanying passion of love. Long after, he found that he had an 'inclination' to love persons with a similar condition, and only gradually realized the reason for this preference. The similarities between the process Descartes describes here and those posited by psychoanalysis are obvious enough, and indeed Henri Ellenberger cites this letter as a sort of precursor to Freud's insights.[30] But a crucial difference lies in the fact that Descartes explains this phenomenon entirely in terms of the body. In his account there is nothing like the process by which repression constitutes the unconscious. Rather, physical changes in the brain account for these instances of apparently unexplained desire: no inner self is involved.

These, then, are a few ways that early seventeenth-century discourse about personal interiority diverges from late modern assumptions about the inner self. Today, authenticity, individuality, and the obscurity of the unconscious are all associated with the interior self. For the earlier period, authenticity was not a concern, while both individuation and the inscrutable sources of motivation were primarily attributed to the body. Of course, not everyone today shares the understanding of interiority I have here attributed to late modernity, and not all seventeenth-century texts are consistent with those I have cited. But, while I have no wish to join those utopians who would rigidly 'maintain the absolute otherness of the premodern past,' I hope that I have shown why we should hesitate to assimilate all our preconceptions about the inner self to early modern discourses on interiority based on partial similarities.[31]

NOTES

1 Catherine Belsey, *The Subject of Tragedy: Identity and Difference in Renaissance Drama* (London, 1985), ix–x, 13–18.

2 Roy Porter, 'Introduction,' in Roy Porter, ed., *Rewriting the Self: Histories from the Renaissance to the Present* (London and New York, 1997), 1.

3 See, in addition to Porter's volume, Charles Taylor, *Sources of the Self: The Making of the Modern Identity* (Cambridge, MA, 1989); M. James C. Crabbe, ed., *From Soul to Self* (London and New York, 1999); Timothy J. Reiss, *Mirages of the Selfe: Patterns of Personhood in Ancient and Early Modern Europe* (Stanford, 2003); Dror Wahrman, *The Making of the Modern Self: Identity and Culture in Eighteenth-Century England* (New Haven and London, 2004); Raymond Martin and John Barresi, *The Rise and Fall of Soul and Self: An Intellectual History of Personal Identity* (New York, 2006).

4 Porter, 'Introduction,' 3.

5 Belsey, *Subject*, 40–2; Francis Barker, *The Tremulous Private Body* (London, 1984), 36, 57, passim; both citing *Hamlet* 1.1.76–86.

6 Katharine Eisaman Maus, *Inwardness and Theater in the English Renaissance* (Chicago, 1995), 3–12.

7 Nicholas D. Paige, *Being Interior: Autobiography and the Contradictions of Modernity in Seventeenth-Century France* (Philadelphia, 2001), 1–4, passim.

8 Donald P. Spence, *The Freudian Metaphor: Toward Paradigm Change in Psychoanalysis* (New York and London, 1987), 11–16, passim. See also Donald Kuspit, 'A Mighty Metaphor: The Analogy of Archaeology and Psychoanalysis,' in Lynn Gamwell and Richard Wells, eds, *Sigmund Freud and Art: His Personal Collection of Antiquities* (New York, 1989), 133–51.

9 Alessandro Ferrara, *Reflective Authenticity: Rethinking the Project of Modernity* (London and New York, 1998), 57.

10 Ibid., 53.

11 Ferrara's description of the various 'models of authentic subjectivity' (ibid., 53–60) is preliminary to an argument in support of his own alternative model.

12 Paige, *Being Interior*, 3, passim.

13 It is worth noting that not all early modern instances of the language of interiority are necessarily metaphorical, or at least not in the way that our own recourse to such language most often is. In some instances, particularly in physiological or medical discussions, writers are concerned with changes in the body's interior that accompany, for example, passional events in the soul. In such cases the language of interiority may be literal or may refer metonymically to the accompanying processes in the soul.

14 Taylor, *Sources,* 127–42; Paige, *Being Interior,* 12–13, passim.
15 Reiss, *Mirages,* 366.
16 Juan Huarte, *Examen de Ingenios: The Examination of Mens Wits* (1594) (Gainesville, FL, 1959), 19–20. Here and throughout, I have silently modernized spelling in quotations from early modern editions, with the exception of capitalization.
17 Thomas Walkington, *The Optick Glasse of Humours* (London, 1607), A4v, 41v–49r.
18 Ibid., 9v.
19 Thomas Browne, *Nature's Cabinet Unlock'd* (London, 1657), 12.
20 Edward Reynolds, *A Treatise of the Passions and Faculties of the Soule of Man* (London, 1640), 5–7.
21 René Descartes, *Discourse on the Method,* in *The Philosophical Writings of Descartes,* trans. John Cottingham, Robert Stoothoff, and Dugald Murdoch, vol. 1 (Cambridge, 1985), 111; *Discours de la méthode,* in *Oeuvres de Descartes,* ed. Charles Adam and Paul Tannery, 11 vols. (Paris, 1996), 6:1–2; this Adam and Tannery edition will be cited hereafter as *Oeuvres de Descartes.*
22 René Descartes, *The Passions of the Soul,* trans. Stephen Voss (Indianapolis and Cambridge, 1989), 37–9, cited hereafter as *PS*; *Les passions de l'âme,* in *Oeuvres de Descartes,* 11:354–7, cited hereafter as *PA.*
23 *PS,* 39; *PA,* 356.
24 *PS,* 46–7; *PA,* 366–8.
25 *PS,* 109; *PA,* 453.
26 Walkington, *Optick Glasse,* 9v; Reynolds, *Treatise,* 7.
27 *PS,* 40; *PA,* 356–7.
28 *PS,* 46–9; *PA,* 366–70.
29 'Elle consiste dans la disposition des parties de notre cerveau . . . Car les objets qui touchent nos sens meuvent . . . quelques parties de notre cerveau, & y font comme certains plis, qui se défont lorsque l'objet cesse d'agir; mais la partie où ils ont été faits demeure par après disposée à être pliée derechef en la même façon par un autre objet qui ressemble en quelque chose au précédent, encore qu'il ne lui ressemble pas en tout': René Descartes, Letter to Chanut, 6 June 1647, in *The Correspondence,* trans. John Cottingham, Robert Stoothoff, Dugald Murdoch, and Anthony Kenny, *The Philosophical Writings of Descartes,* vol. 3 (Cambridge, 1991), 322; Descartes à Chanut, La Haye, 6 juin 1647, in *Oeuvres de Descartes,* 5:56–7.
30 Henri F. Ellenberger, *The Discovery of the Unconscious: The History and Evolution of Dynamic Psychiatry* (New York, 1970), 523.
31 Paige, *Being Interior,* 18.

chapter eight

Nicole and Hobbes: Materiality, Motion, and the Passions

EREC R. KOCH

In an essay titled 'De la charité et de l'amour-propre,' Pierre Nicole turns to vortices (*tourbillons*), which organize and direct celestial motion in Descartes's mechanistic account of the cosmos, in order to represent the mobilizing passions of individuals emplaced in society.[1] Few devices are more common to seventeenth-century French moralist rhetoric than physical figures of interiority and subjectivity, but I will argue that the literal supersedes the figurative value of Nicole's celestial image.[2] Nicole's importation of a mechanical model of physics to morals reveals one trend in French seventeenth-century 'moralist' writing: this rapprochement draws physics together with physiology and the work of the human body together with the production of passions. Significantly, mechanics, medicine, and *morale* are the three correlative branches of science that stem from Descartes's tree of knowledge.[3] The celestial mechanical model that Nicole deploys below is drawn from Descartes's *Principia philosophiae*, and it represents civil and political life in terms of particulate motion and impact, contact, or 'touch.' I will argue that such touch provokes, at least residually, the primal political passions, especially fear. Nicole asserts:

> Nothing more properly represents this spiritual world created by concupiscence than the material world created by nature; that is, that mass of bodies that constitute the universe. For we observe similarly in the latter case that every part of matter tends naturally to move, to extend itself, and to leave its original place, but, being pressed by other bodies, every part is reduced to a sort of prison, from which it escapes as soon as it manages to acquire more force than the matter that surrounds it. This is the image of the constraint to which the self-love of each individual is reduced by the others' self-love,

> which does not allow it to move about as freely as it would like. And we will witness all of the other movements represented in the rest of this comparison. For, just as those small and imprisoned bodies, chancing to unite their forces and their movements, create large clusters of matter that are called vortices, which are like states and kingdoms; and just as those vortices being themselves pressed and imprisoned by other vortices, as if by neighbouring kingdoms, within each large vortex there are created small vortices that, following the general movement of the large body that draws them along, continue nevertheless to have their own particular movement and to force still other small bodies to rotate around them; so too the nobles of a state follow the general motion in such a way that they maintain their own individual interests and are, as it were, the centre for a number of people who attach themselves to their fortune. Finally, just as those small bodies drawn along by the vortices continue to turn, as much as they can, around their centre, so too they of lower rank who follow the nobles' fortune and the State's still look after themselves and always have in sight their own interests in performing duties and services for the others.[4]

This developmental stage of civil and political life follows closely in the wake of a detailed excursus into the Hobbesian state of nature: unrestrained self-love (*amour-propre*) fuels the war of all against all, but fear of death prompts individuals to band together so that they may, by peaceful means, meet their necessarily more restrained needs and desires.[5] Civil society and the emerging political order consequently accommodate as much as necessary the self-love of all.[6] Clearly, Nicole attempts to naturalize the socio-political order. That sustained metaphor depicts the restrictions of impulses of self-interest and self-love in terms of physical force, motion, and interactive collision or contact. The image of the Cartesian vortices also displays the restriction of motion to an orderly and predictable pattern that is inscribed within the laws of causality. This image is held against the natural chaos and unsystematic action that precedes the courtly organization of vortices: random motion and violent collisions occur that are dictated by the whims and passions of individual 'particles.' What is at stake in Nicole's model is the opposition of the ordered movement and graded causal interaction of parts constructing a totalizing whole, on the one hand, and chaos and violence, on the other. In an age in which natural law was given considerable priority over positive law in political theory, the reference to the laws of nature in describing the curbing of self-love and other passions that fosters social order is illuminating.[7] Moreover, the selection of 'motions' to represent the passions that drive individuals is hardly a coincidence.

The system of ordered and centred turnings within a hierarchical system of centres in centres and vortices in vortices represents the accommodation of individual self-love to that of others. The concealment of self-love, which still operates effectively as the primary motive of action, is, of course, the cornerstone of the ethos of *honnêteté*.[8] That representation associates a moral and political imperative with the natural necessity of physical law. The accommodation of self-love to that of others and especially to the centre of each hierarchical system produces the individual's necessary comportment and action at all levels of social and political organization. Nicole's reference to vortices presupposes the convergence of public and private interests.[9] Individual movements converge with the swirling motions of the vortices in which they are installed. Like Hobbes, Nicole turns unrestrained self-love, here represented as chaotic movement, as it was, incidentally, in the Hobbesian war of all against all, into repressed, concealed, and redirected self-love in civil and political life – the very definition of *honnêteté*. Nicole himself makes this point later in the essay when he observes that 'this suppression of self-love is properly what makes human *honnêteté*,' a suppression – he will note – that by its very concealment allows self-love to act more efficaciously than if it operated without dissimulation.[10] This remark is followed by a confirming reference to Pascal and his comparison of self-love and charity, in which the latter necessitates the destruction of the moral-appetitive centrality of the self and the former its repression by concealment. This is the main thrust of the image of the vortices, which inscribes the civil life of the private individual (*le particulier*) within the system of the political order, and, moreover, resolves the apparent conflict between the two.

This Cartesian system of vortices coheres and functions via causal contact. External causality of the action of particles on particles, which, subsumed within vortices that in turn act one on the other, is productive of fear (*crainte*).[11] Nicole suggests that fear, this primal passion of the state of nature, is what frequently provokes the sentiments of admiration, trust, confidence (*confiance*), and even love.[12] Fear continues to be a principal passion in society after the founding of the socio-political order and the institution of enlightened self-love (*amour-propre éclairé*); the three principal 'movements' of self-love attendant on the causal contact of the particles are fear, interest, and esteem or the desire to be loved.[13] Fear of punishment motivates obedience and ensures the smooth functioning of the vortices.[14] Fear is one of the principal passions caused by contact of the particles that circulate in the vortices. As is the case for Hobbes, fear lies at the origins of the socio-political order and motivates its creation, but it also continues in society, driven by enlightened self-love.[15]

What is even more essential in this analogy with celestial bodies is that Nicole, echoing contemporary thinkers, including Pascal, situates political and social life in the order of the human body. The human body navigates public socio-political space, while shielding the private world of conscience and thought. In Nicole's analogical model, comportment, action, and display of the body, motivated by an inner passion, act in turn on other bodies and produce passions that shape the psychic states of those that are touched.[16] The outward signs of authority or social standing are intended to provoke an affective response and the appropriate corresponding comportment. One of the principal passions stirred in this way is that necessary effect of self-love, fear, which is in turn shaped by self-love into productive action. This is one of the important ways in which self-love allows socio-political comportment to be based in the individual and her/his passions, rather than in pure mechanical coercion and application of authority from above.[17] The key passion for Nicole is clearly self-love, and its primary movement fear.

In the system of interacting vortices and their constituent particles, just as the motion at every level of the system is driven by exterior causality, in other terms by elements striking, pushing, and impelling other elements, so too, in the civil and political body, the motivating passions and consequent actions of each individual are provoked and sustained by causal contact, by touch. The forces acting in the vortices and the laws of cause and effect are physical and moral, as the bivalent rhetoric of force in other parts of the essay 'De la charité et de l'amour-propre' implies. Other essays as well suggest, in the socio-political order of the body, the corporal birth and sustenance of the passions: they are provoked by actions on the body, which in turn drive the moral comportment and action of the individual. For example, in 'De l'éducation d'un prince,' Nicole asserts that it is necessary not only to direct their young minds to virtue, but also 'to bend [the princes'] bodies to it,' otherwise those bodies will serve as obstacles to virtue that, by their very 'weight,' risk drawing the princes to actions demonstrating their 'immorality and . . . disorder': he states that 'a bad fold that is given to the body in youth is often a very great obstacle to piety later in life. There are those who become accustomed to being so unruly, so impatient, so quick to react that they are incapable of all regular and tranquil occupations. Others are so sensitive that they cannot endure anything that is the least bit difficult.'[18]

Nicole denies that movements of passions and the actions that they set in motion are the products of the mind; instead, 'they have a permanent cause residing in the body.'[19] His analysis of the example of ennui clarifies the corporal mechanism: if we are accustomed to excessive stimulation, we will suffer ennui when 'the objects that present themselves to us do not stir us vigorously enough.'[20] In section 39 of the essay, Nicole elaborates further the corporal mechanism that is at work here in the ability of the object to strike and stir the sensibility of the body. In echoing Descartes's analysis in the *Passions de l'âme,* Nicole asserts that 'impressions' in the body will generate passions. Such impressions are excited in the body 'when these objects [of fear, anger, and impatience] present themselves, and [the impression] is communicated to the mind to some extent.'[21] Like Descartes, Nicole recommends, in the formation of the prince, not a regimen of spiritual or psychic ascesis to control the passions, but the habituation of the body so that it will not adopt the vicious *pli* (fold) of passionate excess.[22]

In the essay 'De la grandeur,' Nicole develops the familiar argument that, after the institution of socio-political order and consequent inequality of subjects, it becomes necessary to reaffirm socio-political hierarchy in the order of the body. Pomp, riches, and other external displays of the body and ceremonial behaviour, especially ceremonies of respect, are necessary for concupiscent man to maintain peaceful civil society and political order.[23] Displays of wealth and power prove efficacious by creating an impression upon the senses and in provoking consequent passions realized in the psyche. They stir awe and admiration, but they also provoke fear. It is, to extend the analogy of the vortices, in striking, stimulating, stirring other bodies by causal contact that such displays can affirm the socio-political order. In this way, by acting on the body and provoking the consequent passions, the founding of the socio-political order is constantly re-enacted:

> Besides the pomp and splendour, external respects that inferiors pay to the mighty are still another of the legitimate consequences of their condition.
>
> . . .
>
> Now men are so opposed to humbling themselves beneath others and to recognizing them as loftier than they are that, in order to habituate their souls, they must in some fashion habituate their bodies, so that the soul will assume without notice the fold and the position, and pass from ceremony to truth.[24]

It is through machine-like repetition and action on the body that the appropriate passions are developed before people of noble birth, and that awe in their presence, admiration, and fear can be experienced so that the corporal bent (*pli*) will become an affective habit.

In 'Des moyens de conserver la paix avec les hommes,' Nicole asserts, again following Hobbes, that peace is the prime value of life in society and among nations and individuals. The avoidance of the state of nature – a Hobbesian formulation that Nicole does not use – and of the war of all against all require a restriction of the excessive movements of transgressive passions, which trouble the peace of the self and of society: 'We procure peace for ourselves by regulating our thoughts and our passions. And by that interiorized peace, we contribute greatly to the peace of the society in which we live, for there is nothing other than passions that troubles that peace.'[25] He goes on to note that if we demand love and recognition from others – as we did in the state in which all men were equal – we will tend instead to alienate them. Nicole opposes to the primal state a vision of socio-political life that links and binds subjects together. Significantly, this binding is associated with needs fuelled by passions which must be restrained in order to allow men to sustain the spatial proximity of society, as opposed to the violent motion of unbridled passions:

> We must consider to that end that men are bound to one another by an infinite number of needs, which require them of necessity to live in society, and each individual cannot dispense with the others. And that society conforms to the order of God, since He allows those needs for that end. Everything that is necessary to maintain that end conforms to that order, and God rules in a way by that natural law that obliges each part to contribute to the conservation of the totality.[26]

This image is congruent with that of the vortices, in which the restrained motion of passion-driven individuals allows for productive interaction and causal action, whereas the release of unrestrained passions would otherwise lead to chaos and the 'separation' of its constituent elements.

Nicole's own example drawn from the *Essais de morale* would seem to be consistent not only with Cartesian mechanical models of the universe, but also with contemporary physiology of the production of passions. The causal contact of particles in the vortices, and even of vortices among each other, is effective in that it produces and sustains such passions as self-love, and notably the species of fear, which motivate and subtend future 'predictable' action. I would suggest that the extensive references to Hobbes that astute commentators like Laurent Thirouin and E.D. James have discerned are less to the thematics of the state of nature and the founding and perpetuation of civil society and more to a corporal-physiological account of the production of passions – passions whose sustenance and control are essential to the regulation of peaceful life in civil society. In other words, Nicole refers also to the doctrine of physiology and motion common to many advocates of mechanical physics, including Descartes. There is as much Hobbesian as Cartesian mechanics at work in Nicole's thought when we unpack the analogy of celestial mechanics.[27]

For Hobbes too, motion and contact account for the production of passion and the socio-political life of the individual. From his early writings, Hobbes attributes the stimulation of organs of sense by external objects to motion. The exemplary mode of such influence is touch. In the *Little Treatise* (1630), Hobbes observes that 'that which is in no way touch'd by another, hath nothing added to it or taken away.' To produce sensation, the organ must have something 'added or taken away,' and this occurs by motion and impact, that is, 'by touching, which constitutes the only way' for an object to provoke sensation.[28] In the *Elementorum philosophiae sectio prima, De corpore* (1655), on which Hobbes had worked for at least ten years before its publication, that materialist philosopher uses 'tangere' (to touch) to designate the stimulation of organs by matter in motion, and the same generic verb describes the process of sensation.[29] In Hobbes's political writings, motion, impact, and passion are primary valences for the emergence of civil society from the state of nature.

As we have seen, Nicole draws into relation motion and contact, social interaction, and the passions, and thus provides an intriguing point of intersection between Descartes's physics and Hobbes's social and political analysis. It is illuminating to see how those three factors play a role and are developed in Hobbes's political writings.[30] For Hobbes, civil society, ruled by the laws of nature (that is, of reason), is set against the state of nature, characterized as one of passion.[31] Hobbes draws an important distinction between the determination of the good by reason, in civil society, and its determination by the whims of passion, in the state of nature:

> For when we voluntarily contract society, in all manner of Society we look after the object of the Will, i.e. that, which every one of those who gather together, propounds to himselfe as good; now whatsoever seemes good, is pleasant, and relates either to the senses of the mind, but all the mindes

> pleasure is either Glory, (or to have a good opinion of ones selfe) or referres to Glory in the end; the rest are Sensuall, or conducing to Sensuality, which may be all comprehended under the word Conveniences.[32]

Against the good determined by reason for gain and glory of all stands a good that is sensuous, variable, and determined by individual passions. In the state of nature, 'the natural proclivity of men, to hurt each other . . . [derives] from their Passions.'[33] Since the state of nature is one of absolute equality – inequality stems from the establishment of civil society and property rights – the violence of all against all is its necessary consequence.[34] Violence ensues, represented as the chaos of forceful collisions and conflicts among individuals. The circulation of individuals in the state of nature is a chaotic motion that results in collisions and conflict. In the state of nature, there are no limits to action and passions because of the de facto equality of all and because might makes right.[35] In this configuration, one cannot overemphasize the place of passion that precedes the emergence of the state. Chaos, violence, and unpredictable motion in the state of nature are linked to the domination of the passions in each man. In a concise description of the opposition of the state of nature and civil society, Hobbes asserts that 'out of it [civil society], there is a Dominion of Passions, war[,] fear, poverty, slovinlinesse, solitude, barbarisme, ignorance, cruelty. In it, the Dominion of reason, peace, security, riches, decency, society, elegancy, sciences, and benevolence.'[36]

Hobbes finds it necessary to introduce the origins of civil society by an analysis of motion, impact-touch, sensation, and passion. Since the state of nature is first a state of passion, Hobbes must give a detailed account of the production and maintenance of that state, which begins with physiological psychology. Motion produces motion: action on the body, sensation, and consequent passion. In these violent collisions, touch is the privileged sense by which the exterior world acts on the body to produce sensation and passion. If the state of nature consists of a violent and chaotic war of all against all, it is because it is fuelled by external motion that in turn produces internal effects. Such motion makes passion the primary driver of action in people, that is, of the unrestrained motion of each individual. In a world in which all are equal and have equal claim to objects of satisfaction, there can be no restriction of the individual's wilful motion, provoked by the motion of the external world. Motion, impact, contact-touch, and sensation-passion are the fundamental forces of nature. For this reason, early in *Leviathan* Hobbes asserts that the most general subject of science is body (entities) and its two principal accidents, magnitude and motion.[37] Moreover, all science, all knowledge, is founded on the study of motion, visible and invisible, the domain of physics or natural philosophy. The humanistic study of man and his faculties in the sciences of ethics, logic, rhetoric, and the consummation of those disciplines in politics and civil philosophy, must begin with the study of motion and forces acting on the body.[38]

It is for this reason also that, in emerging from the state of nature and of passion, subjection takes the form of the restraint of motion. When subjects submit to the law of nature dictated by reason, when they enter into the body of what will later become Leviathan, the images multiplied are those of restraint of motion and integration. In *De cive*, drawing on the well-worn architectural metaphor of the immovable foundation of knowledge, Hobbes compares the establishment of civil society to the placement of stones into a static structure. Such a process also involves the casting aside of those that do not fit,

> not unlike that which is found in stones, brought together in the Building, by reason of the diversity of their matter, and figure. For as a stone, which in regard to its sharp and angular form takes up more room from other stones than it fills up it selfe, neither because of the hardnesse of its matter cannot well be prest together, or easily cut, and would hinder the building from being fitly compacted, is cast away, *as not fit for use*: so a man who for harshness of his disposition in retaining superfluities for himself, and detaining of necessaries from others, and being incorrigible, by reason of the stubbornnesse of his affections, is commonly said to be uselesse, and troublesome to others.[39]

Although Hobbes qualifies liberty in *Leviathan* as the (relative) absence of impediments to motion, the image above instead emphasizes restraint within an ordered structure as the principal feature of civil life. The stasis of that structure is opposed to the passion-driven state of nature.[40] Spragens notes that, for Hobbes, such liberty is opposed to the state of nature, in which passions left unrestricted make life a matter of 'colliding power drives' that are another manifestation of the 'boundlessness and disorderliness of nature as a whole.' Politics is primarily a task of containment of natural forces and passions, a move motivated by the pre-eminent fear of death. Most significantly, a residual desire for self-preservation and the fear of death continue in society and politics: they bind individuals to the founding covenant over time.[41]

Hobbes maintains that a fundamental law of nature is that every man accommodate himself to others and – in a manner that anticipates Nicole's image of the vortices – that his motions and emotions fit with those of others. To be subject to the laws of nature dictated by reason, much like the laws that govern the visible movements of objects of nature, requires integration and restraint by the individual and his adjustment to others: motion and contact-touch must converge in a non-violent, non-conflictual way. For this reason Hobbes emphasizes in *De cive*, for example in the fourth precept of nature, that every man should 'render himself useful unto others,' although the diversity of men's dispositions is brought about by the 'diversity of their affections.'[42] Motion, both literal and metaphorical, must submit to the natural law of reason. This is the way in which subjects accommodate their passions and dispositions to those of others. This restricted integration of the individual within a system is summarized both by the corporal model of the Leviathan and the metaphor of the structure referred to above. Such an ordered system anticipates Nicole's image of the vortices, in which society is integrated within the totality of the state.

Restraint of motion within an ordered system governed by law serves as a model for the restraint of passion and stands against the transgressive excess of the state of nature. This point is further underscored by a negative example. In chapter 12 of *De cive*, entitled 'Of the internall causes tending to the dissolution of any government,' Hobbes compares the role of passions in sedition to the unrestricted motion of bodies:

> Now as in the motion of naturall bodies, three things are to be considered, namely, *internall disposition*, that they be susceptible of the motion to be produced; the *externall Agent*, whereby a certain and determined motion may in act be produced; and the *action it selfe*: so also in a Common-weale where the subjects begin to raise tumults, three things present themselves to our regard; First the *Doctrines* of the *Passions* contrary to Peace, wherewith the mindes of men are fitted and disposed; next their quality and condition who sollicite, assemble, and direct them already thus disposed, to take up armes, and quit their allegiance; Lastly, the manner how this is done, or the *faction* it selfe.[43]

Hobbes goes on to assert that seditious subjects have not renounced their right to determine good and evil, dictated by individual and variable passions. Those passions disrupt the motion of the system as a whole and lead to the excessive agitation of individuals driven by them, which in turn provokes the whole to disintegrate into chaos, by initiating collisions, strikings, and violence that characterize the state of nature.

For Hobbes, who inspired, in part, Nicole's cosmological analogy, motion that defines all interactions in civil society produces sensation and passion by impact and touch: external motion provokes internal affective and sensory motion that subtends and motivates human action. One of the goals of life in civil society is to restrict or constrain those affective motions so that they can be productive for the social whole. These same passions drive the actions of the individual as part of civil society. Although integrated within the totalizing state, its subjects forfeit the excessive affective motions and consequent actions that characterize the state of nature, and the motion of passion continues in civil society, if only in restrained and disguised form. In his own autobiographical account, Hobbes reserves a special role for fear as the central passion produced by motion and interaction in society. Fear, repeatedly excited by the contact-touch of life in civil society, helps to found but also to sustain the state. It directs the actions of the individual within the constraints imposed by civil society. There is a residue of fear, by Hobbes's own admission, involved in every action on the individual body. It is this very model of contact-touch that articulates the individual and the socio-political order in which he participates. Touch of the body produces fear and the system of constraints in society. Ultimately, civil society restricts individual affective motion and approaches the stasis of the building, a seminal image of affective civilized constraint. This phenomenon is the source of socio-political coercive power: passions provoked by 'contact' with the social and material world necessitate the creation of the state and the restriction of individuals' motions. Fear continues to be the affective by-product of social contact and touch.

This observation brings into focus the convergence of the Hobbesian source with Nicole's cosmological analogy, in which socio-political reality can be represented by an image of causal action in the physical universe, or, in Nicole's formulation, the material world can represent spiritual, affective experience. Although Nicole's use of Cartesian vortices as a figure for political and civil life may lead us to conclude in favour of a coercive mechanism for driving the political order, a further investigation of the web of associations of that image leads us necessarily to the sensibility of the body. That body situated in society is affected by the force of contact-touch, which provokes passion and, most notably, fear. Touch is the principal modality of sensation in a world that subjects bodies to strikings, impacts, and so on. The rule of 'reason' and law consists in restricting and channelling affective motion in such a way that it motivates appropriate comportment and action. Fear is always already present as an affective product. That affect is present, Hobbes reminds us, as the source of the socio-political order, and it continues to be the principal affect, if only in a residual manner, of life in society. The mechanical model underscores not only the natural necessity of the socio-political order, but also the means by which it produces sensibility and passion. This observation should remind us of the importance of affectivity in seventeenth-century political theory and representations of life in society.

NOTES

1 Pierre Nicole, 'De la charité et de l'amour-propre,' in *Essais de morale*, ed. Laurent Thirouin (Paris, 1999), 381–415; all subsequent references to Nicole's *Essais de morale* are to this edition. All translations of Nicole's works are my own. A Jansenist theologian, polemicist, and moralist, Pierre Nicole (1625–95) studied and taught at the school for the young located in the Jansenist abbey of Port-Royal. In 1654 he became the informal secretary to Antoine Arnauld, the most vocal defender of the neo-Augustinian Jansenist movement. He collaborated on the preparation of Blaise Pascal's *Lettres provinciales* (1657), and co-authored with Arnauld the celebrated *La logique, ou l'art de penser* (1662). Nicole is credited with writing the chapters of the *Logique* that address moral questions. That interest is more extensively represented in his most celebrated work, the *Essais de morale.* Composed over several years, the *Essais* were largely complete by 1675, when the first edition was published. They were reissued in various editions over the course of the next century, read by Mme de Sévigné, Saint-Pierre, and Voltaire (who admired Nicole), and translated by Locke for the Countess of Shaftesbury.

2 An extended version of this essay appears in my study *The Aesthetic Body: Passion, Sensibility, and Corporeality in Seventeenth-Century France* (Newark, 2008) and is partially reproduced here with the permission of the publisher.

3 René Descartes, *Principes de la philosophie,* vol. 9, pt. 2, in *Oeuvres,* ed. Charles Adam and Paul Tannery (Paris, 1904), 14: 'Ainsi toute la philosophie est comme un arbre, dont les racines sont la métaphysique, le tronc est la physique, et les branches qui sortent de ce tronc sont toutes les sciences, qui se réduisent à trois principales, à savoir la médecine, la mécanique et la morale; j'entends la plus haute et la plus parfaite morale, qui présupposant une entière connaissance des autres sciences, est le dernier degré de la sagesse.'

4 Nicole, 'De la charité et de l'amour-propre,' 385–6: 'Rien n'est plus propre pour représenter ce monde spirituel formé par la concupiscence, que le monde matériel formé par la nature, c'est-à-dire cet assemblage de corps qui composent l'univers. Car l'on y voit de même que chaque partie de la matière tend naturellement à se mouvoir, à s'étendre et à sortir de sa place; mais qu'étant pressée par les autres corps, elle est réduite à une espèce de prison, dont elle s'échappe sitôt qu'elle se trouve avoir plus de force que la matière qui l'environne. C'est l'image de la contrainte où l'amour-propre de chaque particulier est réduit par celui des autres, qui ne lui permet pas de se mettre au large autant qu'il voudrait. Et l'on va voir tous les autres mouvements représentés dans la suite de cette comparaison. Car, comme ces petits corps emprisonnés venant à unir leurs forces et leurs mouvements forment de grands amas de matière que l'on appelle des tourbillons, qui sont comme les Etats et les royaumes; et que ces tourbillons étant eux-mêmes pressés et emprisonnés par d'autres tourbillons, comme par des royaumes voisins, il se forme de petits tourbillons dans chaque grand tourbillon, qui suivant le mouvement général du grand corps qui les entraîne, ne laissent pas d'avoir un mouvement particulier et de forcer encore d'autres petits corps de tourbilloner autour d'eux: de même les Grands d'un Etat suivent tellement le mouvement, qu'ils ont leurs intérêts particuliers, et sont comme le centre de quantité de gens qui s'attachent à leur fortune. Enfin, comme tous ces petits corps entraînés par les tourbillons tournent encore autant qu'ils peuvent autour de leur centre, de même les petits qui suivent la fortune des Grands et celle de l'Etat ne laissent pas, dans tous les devoirs et les services qu'ils rendent aux autres, de se regarder eux-mêmes, et d'avoir toujours en vue leur propre intérêt.'

5 Thirouin details many indisputable allusions in Nicole's essay to Hobbes and Hobbesian themes, such as the representation of the state of nature, the role of fear in the founding of the state, the fulfilment of individual interests in the state, and the repressive function of the state: see Nicole, 'De la charité et de l'amour-propre,' 382–3n1, 388n1). Hobbes's *De cive* (1642) was published in Paris and quickly translated into French by Samuel Sorbière. E.D. James, *Pierre Nicole, Jansenist and Humanist: A Study of His Thought* (The Hague, 1972), also documents the clear influence of Hobbes on Nicole's analysis of the dawn of civil and political order. James reminds us that Hobbes's *De cive* (1642) and *Leviathan* (1651) were written in Paris, and the former, at least, was known at Port-Royal. Hobbes, like Nicole's colleague and mentor Antoine Arnauld, was a member of Marin Mersenne's informal academic circle. James also cites references to Hugo Grotius's *De jure belli et pacis* (1625), also written in Paris and known at Port-Royal. James details the clear influence of

such secular political thought on the author of the *Essais de morale*: 'Nicole, who, in a rationalistic age, set out to show the rationality, the reasonableness of the good life, not only availed himself of traditional conceptions of natural law but did not fail to be influenced by contemporary lay rationalism' (*Pierre Nicole*, 137). Nicole's essay 'De la charité et de l'amour-propre' echoes the Hobbesian discourse of the sublimation of force deployed in the war of all against all when the social and political order is founded. Fear of death, for Nicole as for Hobbes, is at the origin of that initiative: 'la crainte de la mort est donc le premier lien de la société civile, et le premier frein à l'amour-propre' (fear of death is thus the first bond of civil society, and the first restraint on self-love): Nicole, 'De la charité et de l'amour-propre,' 384. Artifice is substituted for force and violence: accommodation of the individual's self-love to the self-love of others allows public interaction (*le commerce du monde*) to take place. Nicole notes that the desire to dominate is still present in those newly created subjects of the state, but that desire functions under a system of constraints that is illustrated by the *tourbillon* analogy (ibid., 385).

Similar thematic resonances of Hobbes can be found in Nicole's essay 'De la grandeur,' in *Essais de morale*, 197–243. For example, Nicole asserts there that if the state of nature had been preserved, men would have remained equal. Concupiscence and the Fall make inequality and the elevation of the Grandees necessary when men enter into civil society (ibid., 201–2). Nicole also cites Hobbesian natural reason as the faculty that motivates and justifies the creation of the state and the socio-political order (ibid., 202).

6 The concept of enlightened self-love (*amour-propre éclairé*) – that is, of self-love that conceals itself and serves the desires and needs of the individual by accommodating itself to the desires and needs of others – is developed and extended throughout Nicole's *Essais de morale*. For example, in 'De la grandeur,' Nicole elaborates the ways in which ceremonies and actions demonstrating respect for the high nobility are not simply coercive requirements of civil and political life but serve the self-love of the individual for the 'advantages that one derives therefrom' (212). Similarly, in 'Des moyens de conserver la paix avec les hommes,' Nicole, describing the individual's accommodation of others' passions so that she/he may live in peace, states, 'Il faut donc s'appliquer à ce que l'on doit aux inclinations des autres, parce qu'autrement il est impossible d'éviter les plaintes, les murmures, les querelles, qui sont contraires à la tanquilité de l'esprit et à la charité, et par conséquent à l'état d'une vie vraiment chrétienne' (we must be attentive to the inclinations of others, because otherwise it is impossible to avoid complaints, murmurings, quarrels, which are opposed to tranquillity of mind and to charity, and consequently

to the state of a truly Christian life): Nicole, 'Des moyens de conserver la paix avec les hommes,' in *Essais de morale*, 141.

7 See Nannerl Keohane's compelling argument on this question in *Philosophy and the State in France: The Renaissance to the Enlightenment* (Princeton, 1980), 282–302.

8 In seventeenth-century France, *honnêteté* was the principal aristocratic ideal of social performance, and politeness was its exemplary component. Politeness connotes both the promotion of self-interest and the accommodation to others' interest.

9 Keohane refers to the image as a representation of the broad efforts of political philosophers of the seventeenth century 'to reinterpret the public interests in such a way that the interests of individuals within the state are encompassed by them, realized through them, rather than being quite separate entities, opposed to the interests of the whole' (*Philosophy and the State in France*, 182).

10 Nicole, 'De la charité et de l'amour-propre,' 389: 'Cette suppression de l'amour-propre est proprement ce qui fait l'honnêteté humaine, et en quoi elle consiste.'

11 Ibid., 387.

12 Ibid., 387.

13 Ibid., 388.

14 Ibid.

15 In 'De la grandeur,' Nicole traces a similar dawn of the socio-political order. He notes again the essential role of fear in the establishment of that order, but he also asserts that fear of punishment, of the 'gibbet and the wheels of torture' [gibet et roues] (383), is essential to the maintenance of order. See also Keohane, who notes that 'once it has been formed, the political union is cemented by the fear of punishment, and especially by the fear of death' (*Philosophy and the State in France*, 298).

16 E.D. James has noted this recourse to sensibility in the socio-political thought of both Pascal and Nicole as a post-lapsarian loss of reason. See especially James, *Pierre Nicole, Jansenist and Humanist*, 142: 'Both Nicole and Pascal see the relations between superior and inferior as very much an affair of externals. Men have ceased to be guided by their highest faculty, reason, and are turned towards the things of sense. That is their normal condition, so that even the loftiest side of their nature must in general be reached by way of the senses.'

17 See also James, *Pierre Nicole*, 148: 'For Nicole society does not subsist merely by a system of subordination and coercion from above. Into the whole social fabric is woven a pattern of human desires and needs.'

18 Nicole, 'Traité de l'éducation d'un prince,' in *Essais de morale,* 278: 'D'y plier leur corps'; 'dérèglement et . . . désordre'; 'Le mauvais pli que l'on donne au corps dans la jeunesse est souvent dans la suite de la vie un très grand obstacle pour la piété. Il y en a qui s'habituent à être si remuants, si impatients, et si prompts, qu'ils deviennent incapables de toutes les occupations uniformes et tranquilles; d'autres qui sont si délicats, qu'ils ne sauraient souffrir tout ce qui est tant soit peu pénible.'

19 Ibid., 278: 'Ils ont une cause permanente dans le corps.'

20 Ibid., 279: 'Les objets qui se présentent à nous ne nous remuent pas assez vivement.'

21 Ibid., 280: 'Lorsque ces objets [de la crainte, de la colère, et de l'impatience] se présentent, et [que l'impression] se communique à l'esprit jusqu'à quelque degré.'

22 It is noteworthy that Nicole adopts the Cartesian term *pli,* which Descartes associated with a default psychic state triggered by the habitual coursing of the *esprits animaux* (animal spirits). It is also worth remarking that one of the areas that Nicole recommends to the young prince and that is not part of the traditional cursus is anatomy; see Nicole, 'Traité de l'éducation d'un prince,' 280. That study of the body will help in his mastery of the passions. Nicole makes a similar point in the 'Traité de la comédie,' where he deploys the rhetoric of 'impression' and 'striking' [*frapper*] to describe the way in which the spectacle and 'external objects' viewed on the stage act on the senses and stir dangerous and illicit passions in the spectator of theatre; see Nicole, 'Traité de la comédie,' in *Essais de morale,* 1733–71 (repr. Geneva, 1971), 1:267).

23 Nicole, 'De la grandeur,' 207.

24 Ibid., 208: 'Outre la pompe et l'éclat, les respects extérieurs que les inférieurs rendent aux Grands sont encore une des suites légitimes de leur condition . . . Or les hommes ont une telle opposition à s'humilier sous les autres et à les reconnaître pour plus grands qu'eux, que pour y accoutumer leur âme, il faut en quelque sorte y accoutumer leur corps, afin que l'âme en prenne insensiblement le pli et la posture, et passe de la cérémonie à la vérité.'

25 Nicole, 'Des moyens de conserver la paix avec les hommes,' 111: 'On se procure la paix à soi-même en réglant ses pensées et ses passions. Et par cette paix intérieure, on contribue beaucoup à la paix de la société dans laquelle on vit, parce qu'il n'y a guère que les passions qui la troublent.'

26 Ibid., 148: 'Il faut considérer pour cela que les hommes sont liés entre eux par une infinité de besoins, qui les obligent par necessité de vivre en société, chacun en particulier ne se pouvant passer des autres: et cette société

est conforme à l'ordre de Dieu, puisqu'il permet ces besoins pour cette fin. Tout ce qui est donc nécessaire pour la maintenir est dans cet ordre, et Dieu commande en quelque sorte par cette loi naturelle qui oblige chaque partie à la conservation du tout.'

27 Contemporaries discerned more similarities than differences between Hobbes's and Descartes's mechanics. For example, Seth Ward, in *Vindiciae academiarum* (1654), assesses Hobbes's doctrines of motion and sensation as follows: 'The theory explaining sence upon the grounds of motion, was almost generally received here before his Book [*Leviathan*] came forth. Being sufficiently taught by des Cartes, Gassendus, Sir K[enelm] Digby': quoted in John Bowle, *Hobbes and His Critics: A Study in Seventeenth Century Constitutionalism* (London, 1951), 73.

28 Quoted in Frithiof Brandt, *Thomas Hobbes's Mechanical Conception of Nature* (Copenhagen, 1928), 193.

29 Thomas Hobbes, *Elementorum philosophiae sectio prima, De corpore*, in *Thomae Hobbes Malmesburiensis opera philosophica quae latine scripsit omnia*, vol. 1 (London, 1839), 318, 320. Chapter 29 of the book, 'De sonore, odore, sapere, et tactile' (On Sound, Smell, Taste, and Touch), bears the title 'Tactus, organum primum' (Touch, the First Sense). Here, Hobbes grants priority to touch because it affects the whole body and it exemplifies the other modalities of sensation that are produced and sustained via the movement of matter: see esp. 412.

30 For an argument that articulates Hobbes's natural philosophy and political theory, and an account of critical debate on that point, see T.A. Spragens, Jr, *The Politics of Motion: The World of Thomas Hobbes* (Lexington, KY, 1973), esp. 163–97. My point is not to enter into the debate about whether or not Hobbes's mechanico-materialist account of the body and passions makes civil and political order necessary. I wish simply to acknowledge and investigate the fact that physiological mechanics is part of the account of the functioning of man in the state of nature and in civil society, and that this is linked to touch and to passions, which motivate his actions. Although it would be misguided to argue that civil society is the product of necessary mechanical laws, it would also be an error to discount their presence and role in motivating man in the state of nature and civil society.

31 Hobbes frequently uses 'laws of nature' and 'laws of reason' interchangeably. Matthew W. Kramer clarifies that for Hobbes the laws of nature are natural in that all adults can grasp those imperatives by way of reason; see Kramer, *Hobbes and the Paradoxes of Political Origins* (New York, 1997), 80.

32 Thomas Hobbes, *De cive*, ed. Howard Warrender (Oxford, 1983), 43.

33 Ibid., 49.

34 Ibid., 45.

35 Ibid., 48.

36 Ibid., 130. Hobbes makes a similar point in *De homine.* After describing appetite and aversion (expected pleasure and pain), as they are associated respectively with good and evil, he notes that 'emotions or perturbations of the mind are species of appetite and aversion, their differences having been taken from the diversity and circumstances of the objects that we desire or shun. They are called perturbations because they frequently obstruct right reasoning in this, that they militate against the real good and in favor of the apparent and most immediate good, which turns out frequently to be evil when everything associated with it hath been considered': see *Man and Citizen: De Homine and De Cive,* ed. Bernard Gert (Indianapolis and Cambridge, 1991), 55.

37 Thomas Hobbes, *Leviathan,* ed. Edwin Curley (Indianapolis and Cambridge, 1994), 49.

38 Ibid., 50. Motion, force, and action of the body also ground ethics, for, as Hobbes will claim in chapter 9 of *Leviathan,* 'The Difference of Manners' – and contrary to the tradition of classical philosophy, especially in its stoic branch – felicity resides in the perpetuation of motion rather than in stasis.

39 Hobbes, *De cive,* 66.

40 Hobbes, *Leviathan,* 136.

41 Spragens, *Politics of Motion,* 192–7.

42 Hobbes, *De cive,* 66.

43 Ibid., 145–6.

chapter nine

Loci Theologici: Authority, the Fall, and the Theology of the Puritan Self

FRÉDÉRIC GABRIEL

De locis theologicis (Of Theological Places) is the title of the great work of the Spanish Dominican Melchior Cano, renovator of scholastic theology.[1] His purpose was to firmly determine a hierarchical scale of arguments, but this title also shows us the importance of rhetorical and controversial 'space' in the early modern period. Cano's work was one of the emblems of the Counter-Reformation and the standard manual of argumentation and of topic choices. The early modern Puritans were among the most radical sceptics of this theory of hierarchy and theological spaces linked to a Roman theory of church authority. Known for their rejection of all pontifical residues and of every type of hierarchy issuing from them, they wished to reform the Reformation. As Michael Walzer has shown, the Puritans were directly opposed to the notion of hierarchy.[2] This is one of the reasons for the differences between Puritan and Catholic theological constructions and rhetorical arguments regarding the status of the self. In Cano's work, as in Catholic sermons, the primary source is Scripture, but the other sources he lists give pride of place to institutions and to their authority. By contrast, in the Puritan texts that will be examined here, we may observe a 'face-to-face' debate between Scripture and the self. Puritans in seventeenth-century England concentrated on the relationship between these two 'spaces,' especially as they developed autobiographical writing.[3] Historians, among them Dean Ebner, have argued that such writing of the self grew directly out of the Puritan movement.[4] The pertinence of the theme of 'self' for the Puritans has become well recognized, and in one of the latest studies to go over the terrain, Charles Taylor's *Sources of the Self,* the Puritans play a central role.[5] Despite this long and impressive historiographical tradition, I want to re-examine the notion of the self in seventeenth-century Puritan texts, in particular in a corpus that is absent from these earlier studies, and ask just what value and position the self has in these texts.

In this literature, we find the self so radically questioned that we have to come to a new understanding of its role in the Puritan Reformation. I will examine a coherent grouping of theological texts (treatises and sermons) whose emphasis on 'self-denial' is already apparent in their titles: Henry Burton (1578–1648), *A most Godly Sermon . . . shewing the necessity of Selfe-denyall* (1641); Thomas Brightman (1562–1607), *The Art of Self-Deniall* (1646); Theophilus Polwheile (d. 1689), *Treatise of self-denial* (1658); and Thomas Watson (d. 1686), *The Duty of Self-denial* (1675). The authors of these texts – like Daniel Cawdrey (1587–1664) and Edmund Calamy (1600–66), who will be cited below – have in common that they studied at Cambridge, a well-known centre of Puritanism, which developed on the margins of its colleges, especially under the influence of the famous William Perkins (1558–1602). Their texts reveal with precision the place occupied by the self within sacred space and the self's relationship to this space. How is the self localized as a topic and constituted as a rhetorical and theological space?

Theology of the Self: Self-Examination and Christian Duty

The examination of conscience, rejected by the early great Protestant reformers, is a peculiarity of English Protestantism.[6] The particular attention that Puritans paid to introspective discipline and self-control is well known.[7] Cawdrey, in *Selfe-examination required in every one*, begins with the verse of St Paul 'But let a man examine himself' (1 Cor. 11:28).[8] Cawdrey sees in it a 'way of preparation' that distinguishes the 'matter' (himself) and the 'manner' (examine).[9] The context of these words is the institution of the Lord's Supper and the imperative necessity of man's preparation: 'For as often as ye shall eat this bread, and drinke this cup, ye shewe the Lords death till he come. Wherefore, whosoever shal eat this bread, and drinke the cup of the Lord unworthely, shalbe giltie of the bodie, and blood of the Lord. Let a man therefore examine him self, and let him eat of this bread, and drinke of this cup. For he that eateth and drinketh unworthily, eateth and drinketh his owne damnation (because) he discerneth not the Lords bodie.'[10] This *examination*, argues Cawdrey, is necessary because if one ignores this injunction, one comes directly under God's judgment.[11] Obedience to it is of absolute necessity: it is a 'precept, or command.'[12]

The result of this imperative self-examination should be a meditation on the self that reveals the true nature of one's 'qualifications' – this is how Cawdrey understands the self with this passage from Paul. He who examines himself will necessarily be confronted with a corrupted object and its qualifications: 'What blindnesse and darknesse there is upon his minde, what weakness in his memorie, what pervernesse in his judgment, what stubbornnesse in his will, what distemper in his affections, what a sinck of sin is in his heart . . . he that examines himself, shall find all this.'[13] Self-examination (the self is here detailed by the language of faculties: mind, memory, judgment, will, affections, heart) is an awakening of the conscience and a first response to the corruption of human nature through original sin. Obviously, for most Puritans, one of the essential sources for the doctrine of self-examination and of the Fall is the Augustinian model.[14] Brian Stock sees in St Augustine's *Confessions* an innovation and a reinvention of the soliloquy genre (*soliloquium*): 'This was envisaged as a type of discourse in which a person and his rational spirit entered into debate in the interior of the soul on the preconditions and limitations of self-knowledge.'[15]

Self-examination is only the first step on a long road to perfection. The objective is not for the Christian to examine himself in order to write about himself, but rather the reverse, to praise his denial. Self-examination is immediately followed by 'self-denial,' which is also expressed imperatively and considered an inevitable consequence of a Christian's contemplation of his corrupted self. This is one of the meanings of the Reformation for these writers: Burton declares, 'We are in the expectation of a true *Reformation,* and in the very *Reformation, selfe-denyall* is to be used.'[16] Polwheile, in an original fashion, links self-denial to three types of arguments representing as many institutional places where authority is affirmed: 'Scholis,' location of the *argumentativa negatio* ('arraignment and conviction of Self'), 'Foro,' location of the *judicialis negatio* ('sentencing and condemnation of Self'), and 'Castris,' location of the *hostilis negatio* ('actual execution of self').[17] In this text, each place is equally emblematic of a *duty* to be accomplished. Similarly, Brightman writes that the 'denyall of our selves' is the first 'own duty of the Christian.' When he gives a portrait of the Christian, he focuses on two dimensions: 'There are two parts of our Christian profession to which we are called: the first concerns things to be beleeved, the other duties to be performed Faith and Obedience.'[18] The Christian finds himself under the authority of the Bible, and all the more so of those passages conveying the words of Christ. These are the words heard by people listening to a sermon by a 'Puritan divine' in the same modality as they were first pronounced: an injunction to be followed, the *first lesson* of God and of Christ.[19] Burton, in the opening words of his sermon, is insistent: 'The first Lesson is the *A. B. C.* that CHRIST teacheth us in his School, is this, *For a man to deny himself.*'[20]

Starting with the preface to his *Duty of Self-denial*, Watson also accentuates the importance of this precept and affirms: 'Self-denial is the first principle of Christianity; it is the life-blood, which must run through the whole body of Religion. Self-denial is learned not out of the *Topicks* of Philosophy, but out of the *Oracles* of Scripture.'[21] He thus directly links this principle to the primary theological 'space,' Scripture, as a religious and corporeal expression that touches the self more nearly than a simple philosophical topic; self-denial is not only a 'topic' but part of the 'oracle.'[22] Like Burton and Brightman, Watson uses an excerpt from the Gospel of Luke (9:23) as an incipit, as a text to be commentated, and as a divine law: 'And he said to them all, If any man will come after me, let him deny himself.'[23] This textual starting point is one of the factors that gives unity to the Puritan corpus on the self. It is also what allows these authors to create a discourse that takes the form of a simple development of Christ's own words. Quoting another passage from Luke, Watson comments: 'These words are dropped from the lips of Christ, the *ORACLE* of *TRUTH.*'[24] These words are recorded and repeated not only for their literal meaning but also for their effectiveness, for self-denial is a '*Practice*,' as Watson emphasizes.[25] Here again, Christ is the supreme model of the performative word: 'The Lord Jesus not only spake as never man spake, but acted as never man acted; he was not a *Pencil* in his tongue, and a *Sponge* in his conversation, but a *walking Commentary* upon his own Doctrin, especially this of Self-denial.'[26] The Word *is* an act, its 'commentary' is a spatial action, and, following its example, the Christian must submit to a practical imperative: 'Christ doth not only *command* us Self-denial in his Doctrine, but *commend* it to us in his practice, he propounds himself as a Pattern of it, *follow me.*'[27]

This perspective indicates clearly that the Puritan and his listeners position themselves between the two key 'dramatic' moments of the Bible, on the one side the Fall of Adam and, on the other, the life of Christ. They place themselves directly in the intensity of biblical Revelation, of the possibility of Salvation, and of the battle between Good and Evil. In Puritan writings of this period, England is often described as a land full of sin and compared to the territories of the Apostles' missions in an attempt to render the text and biblical actions into the present and to superimpose the two narratives.[28] Every word of the Testaments or referring to the Testaments is thus perceived in this double context in which, by definition, 'a good Christian must be a Self-denier.'[29]

Self(-Denial) in Context

Self-denial is not so simple and easy to carry out when one considers its precise modalities and consequences. The dangers of the self are illustrated by Calamy in a treatise with an eloquent title: *The Monster of sinful self-seeking anatomized.* He begins with 'Paul's complaint': 'Phil. 2.21 *For all seek their owne, not the things which are Jesus Christs.*'[30] Although Paul elsewhere has painted an ideal portrait of the very young Church ('Christians . . . were sodered together in Love and Unity'), here his words designate a reality that is even more deplorable in the present, affirms Calamy. With Paul, he draws 'the blackest bill of indictment.'[31] The most accusatory word that Paul uses is the adjective 'own': self-seekers think of themselves (and of all that is related to themselves) in terms of property, whereas we are merely overseers: 'We our selves are not our owne. I. *Cor.* 6:19 *You are not your owne.*'[32] Among all those who call themselves Christians, many are in fact 'self-seekers' and very few 'Christ-seekers.'[33] Several elements can explain this remark: first of all, to speak in the tone of Calamy, most men are guilty of self-idolatry, for as Brightman emphasizes: 'What is deerer and neerer of a man than himself?'[34] However, the self is in truth a screen between man and his Salvation rather than the usual mark of individuation. According to Polwheile, 'It is the nature of Self, to work for it self, and not for another.'[35] It is difficult to disengage oneself from one's *self* (which is by definition reflexive), a self that some men worship as their individual God.[36]

Among the things that work to prevent this disengagement are self-love, ignorance, fancy, and illusion.[37] The general solipsistic reversal is illustrated by the figure of Narcissus: 'Every man by nature, is (*Narcissus* like) in love with himself, blinde in his own cause, and apt to think that he seeks the things of Christ, when he doth not.'[38] This mirrored self only reflects back to man his 'self-deceit' and 'self-delusion.'[39] This vicious circle can be combined with hypocrisy 'when a Christian seeks his *owne things* in seeking the *things of Christ,* when he *pretends* to seek the things of Christ, and yet intends no such thing, but seeks *himselfe* even under *colour* of seeking the things of Christ.'[40] However, as Polwheile repeats: 'There are not two greater enemies in the world than Self and Christ, and their counsels are mutually destructive one of the other.'[41]

Calamy warns his listeners against 'that *hypocrisie, insincerity, and rottennesse of heart,* which is in all men by nature, hence it is that men pretend Jesus Christ, but intend their own private interest, because of the hypocrisie and falsenesse of their hearts.'[42] Asserting the 'grievousnesse and mischievousnesse of the sinfull selfe-seeking,' he concludes that a bad self is a '*sin* of the *first magnitudo*' or is even 'self-destroying.'[43]

All these wanderings, blindnesses, and labyrinths of error result from the Fall, hence the importance of meditating on sins, the fruit of original sin: this implies not only meditating on one's own corruption but also understanding all that was at stake at the moment of the Fall within Adam, who is qualified by Cawdrey as a 'publick person' – and thus as representative, by anticipation, of every man.[44] Before original sin, Adam 'was the Oracle of Wisdom . . . a kind of earthly Angel,' but the Fall sealed his exile, characterized in the first place by his exclusion from the holy space of the Garden of Eden.[45] When the Christian meditates upon Adam, he contemplates both Adam's exile and the exile within his own self that excludes him from holy ground and projects him into a land of suffering. He contemplates human nature, corrupted and stigmatized by this exile, in the figure of Adam and within himself. The topography of the Fall in the Bible is the land of the Christian.

The importance conferred by Puritans on the theology of the Fall follows the radical and inflexible path laid out by Augustine in *De peccato originali* and developed by Calvin and the Rhineland theologians (Bulliger, Bucer, Oecolampadius), who were opposed to the supple path of Origen and Tatian or the moderate path advocated by Thomas Aquinas and the Council of Trent.[46] The Calvinism of the Puritans no longer needs to be demonstrated: in addition to the famous Marian Exiles, proof is evidenced in the facts that there are more translations of the Genevan theologian into English than into any other language and that the Geneva Bible (1560) was dethroned only after many years by the King James version.[47]

The exile, renewed in every man, is not only spatial but also gnoseological and psychological. The self is defined by enumerating all its aspects that must be 'put off,' such as 'all humane affections and naturall desires.'[48] According to Brightman, 'This denyall is to be practised according to all the parts and powers of the Soule, as Mind, Will, Desire, Affection, Appetite, &c.'[49] Watson provides the most detailed list: it is necessary to 'denie the reason' that cannot understand the mysteries of theology (Trinity, Incarnation, Resurrection); furthermore, 'the Doctrines of Faith do not oppose Reason but transcend it'; 'we have to denie our will, which in innocency was the echo to Gods Will,' but is now no more than 'impotency, obstinacy'; 'we have also to denie' 'self-confidence,' 'self-conceit,' 'appetite,' 'ease,' 'inordinate passions,' 'sinfull fashions,' 'self-applause,' 'superstition,' 'heterodoxy,' and of course, 'carnal policy' and 'carnal part,' which he also calls 'Carnal Self.'[50] The self does not only involve the soul; rather, following a logical Pauline heritage, the body, too, attracts every kind of Puritanical attack: 'The Body of Man is the worst halfe of Man, *vilissima pars hominis,* The shell, the box, the carcasse of Man.'[51]

Yet this is not all that denial covers. It also involves social space in its entirety, for 'a Christian must deny his *Relations,*' which are a part or extension of the self, and a context for it.[52] Just like the men chosen by God in the Old Testament and the Apostles in the New, the Christian must be able to leave everything and follow Christ. Theological theses are systematically supported by biblical exegesis examining each character in Scripture who submits to the imperatives of self-denial, such as Noah, Abraham, and Moses.

Of absolute salvific necessity, self-denial (involving the self in a broad sense and in a social context) is a dispossession that echoes in reverse the original dispossession caused by the Fall: man finds a new nature.[53] This is why, in this denial of loss, 'there is nothing lost by self-denial.'[54] Self-denial is an 'extirpation of the old Adam.'[55] We must rid ourselves of our corrupted nature, 'renouncing of all this is in us.'[56] Watson hammers on: 'He who cannot deny his life for Christ, will deny Christ.'[57] For Brightman just as for Watson, 'Self-denial is a kind of Self-annihilation.'[58]

The post-lapsarian anthropology that guides the Puritans also leads them to discern and specify the conditions and guarantees of true self-denial: to guard against hypocrisy and affectation, all these operations of self-denial are held to purity of *intention* and *scrupulous* implementation.[59] Intention is of central importance in breaking the vicious cycle of the self, for the Christian must 'consent,' must decide consciously and intentionally to submit himself to self-denial and to the law of the Gospels. The intention behind the act is just as determining as the *factual* aspect of its accomplishment. 'Suffering for Christ must be free and spontaneous.'[60] The intention must be primary, sincere, and zealous.[61] It is the intensity of the Christian's commitment and the conscientiousness of his undertaking that guide him towards the right path: Thomas Brightman exhorts us to be 'Martyres of our selves.'[62] Sincerity of intention is a burning question, all the more so in matters of *imitatio Christi.*

How then should self-denial lead us to consider the Christian self? What does self-denial teach us about the Puritan theology of the self?

The Self: From Annihilation and Exile to Divine Body

In general, classical philosophy conceives of the self as a stable structure and as a primary reference for comprehending reflexivity and the humanity that results from it. However, discourses of self-denial work from the contrary assumption. The subject is not the starting point for an individual in search of intellection and liberty; it is rather through giving up one's self that one finds the path to salvation. In denying loss, one dispossesses oneself of what constitutes the centre of possessive consciousness in order to follow Christ, who says: 'Follow me.' Brightman concludes: 'So that to deny our selves, is to renounce to proper motion.' Indeed, only 'the will of Christ and God [is] the square of right.'[63] To follow Christ is to give oneself over to Him entirely, and as a conversion the *imitatio Christi* touches first on the self. The very term 'conversion' indicates the movement that this implies: to convert is to follow Christ as the Apostles followed Him.[64] This must be the only motion of the Christian.

Conversion brings about a reversal in perspective, illustrated by Edmund Calamy: 'I may truly say, he that is the greatest selfe-denier, is the greatest selfe-seeker.'[65] This is obviously not a confusion in terms or a paradox. Calamy instead recognizes the *inherent* contradiction of the self, for it is in denying it that one finds it. This notion suggests the possibility of seeking oneself by remaining on the path of righteousness through identifying with Christ or with God, 'divine and sublimated self-seeking.'[66] 'The more a man serves God out of pure love, without reflection to selfe, the more he seeks himselfe.'[67] Conversion concerns not only faith but also the very notion of the self, which from this moment acquires an entirely different nature. Calamy affirms: '*Intus est, quod homo est,* The Soule of Man is the Man of Man. *Animus uniuscujusque is est quisque.* And therefore he that seeks to get his Soule *beautified* with *grace,* to be made *Christs picture,* and a reall member of his body, this Man, and this Man onely, seeks himselfe.'[68] In a few decisive words, Calamy gives the true meaning of conversion: the saint is the image of Christ – which is why, in seeking himself, he also seeks Christ – and is a part of Christ's mystical body. This presence of Christ in us is itself the sign that we belong to His body.[69] These two models, that of Christ dwelling within us and that of the Christian as a member of the divine body, echo and complete one another. The self is thus situated in (theological and mystical) spaces that are completely different from those previously evoked. There can be no more narcissism, for it is the Christly image of ourselves that we find instead of – in place of – ourselves; nor can the body be sinful, for we are only parts of a saintly body.

The *sacred* space that the Puritans desire here takes on its full meaning. In technical Latin literature, in Festus's *De verborum significatione* for example, the word 'sacred' applies to a place or an edifice. The 'sacred' judicially limits an object or a space, a place that is consecrated and hence constantly localized by the act of consecration.[70] In the Augustinian tradition, however, sacred topography is closely related to the self as an edifice or as part of the edifice. It is in fact in a sermon for the dedication of a church that St Augustine mentions that we are ourselves the house of God, that we are in God and that God lives within us.[71] This exchange of qualities makes Christians the 'living stones' of the Church (1 Peter 2:5), as long as they are previously qualified as images of Christ. Conversion brings the Christian into the space in which the edifice is built and consecrated, but sacred space is above all an interior space and, as Augustine says on several occasions, 'His Temple [is] built of soules and not of stones.'[72] The structure previously designated as the self, called in this context the soul (whereas Augustine's Latin speaks of men: 'hominibus'), is thus the meeting point between the sacred text of man's creation (in the image of God) and the mission of the Word of God, the building of an interior Church and the advent of the Law.[73] This inner construction ends in the Pauline theme of the body of Christ, which reaches its culmination in the inner law. This is 'a law written in the heart of Man, and is consonant to Reason.'[74] The new evangelical law is integrated within the body. Puritans were motivated by a reformation of religion, man, and society, all at once: the inner law strongly links the individual to both the ecclesial and the civil space. Calamy's frequent association of 'Church and State' reveals the strength of the consequences of the Christian's self-disciplinary reformation on the life of the commonwealth.[75]

Following Christ as a living presence in contemporary England is the psychological and discursive equivalent of self-denial. These Puritan texts place otherness within a present territory of identity and insist on the theological commonplaces that link the personal and ethical commitment of an individual to a theological and political activity.[76] The self is a metaphor but also, in a way, an actual territory to be converted. In all the displacements brought about by his conversion, man becomes himself, through self-denial, a theological *locus* of sermons, a place uniting reformation, a return to biblical space, an *imitatio Christi*, and the construction of the mystical and social body.

The self refers first of all to properties, to qualifications that determine a physical space (here the body) and a mental topic (psychology). The spaces of the self delimit and emphasize the geography of these borders as well as their connections with other spaces close to Puritan literary themes favouring pilgrimage, conflict, or exile: biblical spaces (Paradise, the exile of original sin), moral ones (self-condemnation), *terra incognita*, and so on.[77] All these dimensions may refer to invasion, colonization, expropriation, change of territory, and exile, either biblical, psychological, or social. The 'self' is contained in three dimensions: foundational and theological, personal and identifying, contextual and civil. Thus, denying the self and all the 'properties' and possessions of the self allows one to take a step back, the better to view one's entire territory.

'Spaces of the self' expresses the extent to which the self is defined, first of all, by its borders (its human limits, for example, which determine its post-lapsarian status) and, second, by the new relationship that is implied by the necessary abolition of the former properties (the 'old man,' limited, imprisoned in sin), so that the self may enter into a new kind of space. From this moment its borders delimit a 'sacred' space, in so far as the man is now truly in the image of God.[78] Sacred space is no longer characterized by an immutable border separating the two realms. Self-denial transforms it from a closing space into an opening space and from a post-lapsarian space into one with a soteriological dimension.

The uniqueness of the Puritan theology of the self is that it situates displacement – 'splitting' would be a better word – within the self itself, within the reflexive structure that usually serves as a fixed observation point. Its constitution is therefore antithetical. The distance that determines reflexivity (and thus the identity-forging operation of the self) is, for these theologians, the occasion of a double operation that both maximizes and minimizes the distance by lodging divine transcendence (the infinite) in the centre of the self (the intimate).[79] Within himself the Christian finds the image of God, *is* the image of God; in other words, a human reflection of the divine perfection that gives him being. The self becomes 'He.' For the Puritans, the self is not a real place that procures autonomy, as it is in most philosophical traditions, but is rather the result of a process. Conversion is the complete upheaval of mental topography as one discovers oneself as a sacred internal space, a member of a divine body, and thus a depository of an internal law. A sacred space and its logic of relationships have replaced the self. This is the price of grace.

NOTES

Thanks to Sarah Novak for the translation.

1 Melchior Cano, *De locis theologicis libri duodecim* (Salamanticae, 1563). It should be noted, as Thils has done, that Cano's *De locis theologicis* 'is not a summary of Christian faith, like many Catholic and Protestant *Loci communes* of this period, but rather a sort of "theological topic" constructed according to the "dialectical spaces" proposed by the humanists.' On this, see Gustave Thils, *L'infaillibilité du peuple chrétien 'in credendo': Notes de théologie posttridentine* (Paris-Louvain, 1963), 9. Cano's book became famous for the quality of his Latin, which broke away from scholastic Latin, judged mediocre. He was able to combine the Counter-Reformation with Latin humanism.

2 Michael Walzer, *The Revolution of the Saints: A Study in the Origins of Radical Politics* (New York, 1976), chap. 5; see also G.B. Tatham, *The Puritans in Power: A Study in the History of the English Church from 1640 to 1660* (Cambridge, 1913), 3. Each commonplace (*locus*) in Cano corresponds to a source of knowledge and authority that determines a textual space of discussion and invention.

3 Dean Ebner, *Autobiography in Seventeenth-Century England: Theology and the Self* (The Hague–Paris, 1971), 'It was during the Seventeenth Century that autobiography first began to flourish in England, and it did so under the aegis of the theological modes of thought which then prevailed' (11). Ebner concentrates on several well known figures: John Bunyan, Herbert of Cherbury, George Fox, Richard Baxter. See also Roger Sharrock, 'Modes of Self-Representation: Herbert of Cherbury, Kenelm Digby, Pepys,' *The Seventeenth Century* 3, 1 (1988), 14. Cf. Michael Mascuch, *Origins of the Individualist Self: Autobiography and Self-Identity in England, 1591–1791* (Stanford, 1996), which does not deal much with Puritans. For general notions, without consequence for the subject at hand, see Roy Porter, ed., *Rewriting the Self: Histories from the Renaissance to the Present* (London, 1997), pt. 1; Joan Webber, *The Eloquent 'I': Style and Self in Seventeenth-Century Prose* (Madison, WI, 1968).

4 Ebner, *Autobiography*, 17, and 18: 'By the close of the century, Puritans of all types had swollen the number of English autobiographies to slightly over one hundred.'

5 Charles Taylor, *Sources of the Self: The Making of Modern Identity* (Cambridge, MA, 1989), 45, 184, 194, 227–31. However, the author only cites Puritan sources from the classic work of Michael Walzer, which seems to be his only 'source' on the subject.

6 'Examen de conscience,' in *Dictionnaire de spiritualité ascétique et mystique*, vol. 4, pt. 2, col. 1826 (Paris, 1937–95, here 1961).

7 As Yan Thomas remarks: 'Le réfléchi, en latin juridique, souligne l'indépendance comme maîtrise de soi sur soi' (The reflexive, in legal Latin, emphasizes independence as a mastery of the self over the self). For this quotation, see Yan Thomas, 'Du sien au soi: Questions romaines dans la langue du droit,' *L'écrit du temps* 14–15 (1987), 167.

8 D[aniel] C[awdrey], *Selfe-examination required in every one . . . first, delivered in a Sermon . . .* (London, 1646), 1. Richard Baxter uses another passage from St Paul, 'Examine yourselves, Whether ye be in the faith, prove your owne selves. Know ye not your own selves, how that Jesus Christ is in you, except ye he reprobates?' (2 Cor. 13:5). Richard Baxter, *The mischiefs of Self-Ignorance, and the benefits of Self-Acquaintance . . .* (London, 1662), 2.

9 Cawdrey, *Selfe-examination,* 3–4.

10 *The Newe Testament of our Lord Iesus Christ,* trans. William Whittingham (Geneva, 1560), fol. 309.

11 Cawdrey, *Selfe-examination,* 12.

12 Ibid., 4, 14.

13 Ibid., 22. Daniel Dyke, who will be the subject of a forthcoming article, is the author of a treatise with a significant title, *The mystery of Self-Deceiving or a discourse and discovery of the deceitfullnesse of Mans Heart* (London, 1614), in which he lists in precise detail all the passions that alienate man. His book was translated into French by Jean Verneuil and published in Geneva in 1630, transposed under another interesting title: *La sonde de la conscience* (The Probe of Conscience).

14 Robert J. O'Connell, *St. Augustine: Early Theory of Man,* A.D. *386–391* (Cambridge, MA, 1968), pt. 2; Peter Dennis Bathory, *Politic Theory as Public Confession: The Social and Political Thought of St. Augustine of Hippo* (New Brunswick, NJ, and London, 1981), chaps. 1–2. Taylor, *Sources,* 178, underlines, along with others, the capital importance of St Augustine for this model. On its reception, see Åke Bergvall, *Augustinian Perspectives in the Renaissance* (Uppsala, 2001), who devotes his first chapter to 'The Divided Self'; however, he concentrates exclusively on Petrarch.

15 Brian Stock, *After Augustine: The Meditative Reader and the Text* (Philadelphia, 2001), 11.

16 Henry Burton, *A most Godly Sermon: Preached at St. Albons in Woodstreet on Sunday last, being the 10 of Octobre 1641: Shewing the necessity of Self-denyall and Humiliation, by Prayer and Fasting before de Lord . . .* (London, 1641), fol. 3v. All italics and capitals in quotations are original.

17 Theophilus Polwheile, *Authentes, or a Treatise of Self-deniall wherein the Necessity and Excellency of it is Demonstrated . . .* (London, 1658), 22–3.

18 Tho[mas] Brightman, *The Art of Self-Deniall: or a Christians first lesson* (London, 1646), 1–3, 22.
19 Ibid., 50.
20 Burton, *A most Godly Sermon*, fol. 1v. The title of Thomas Brightman's volume could not be clearer.
21 Thomas Watson, *The Duty of Self-denial briefly Opened and Urged* (London, 1675), fol. 2r. Cf. Polwheile, *Authēntes*, 18: 'Self-denial is a duty that must of necessity bee throughly practiced by every one that will come after the Lord Jesus, in the way of holyness, unto eternal happiness.' Earlier (p. 10), Polwheile confirms that self-denial is a divine doctrine (*è coelo descendit*).
22 The first words of Thomas Watson's chapter 1 repeat 2 Tim. 3:16: 'All Scripture is given by inspiration of God.'
23 Watson, *The Duty*, 1. Watson's quotation from *The Newe Testament* (Whittingham), fol. 32v. Thomas Brightman chooses the version 'He that will be my Disciple, let him deny himselfe,' and like Thomas Hooker in *Heautonaparnumenos: Or a Treatise of Self-Denyall* (London, 1646), 3, Theophilus Polwheile in *Authēntes*, 1, chooses the parallel passage, Matt. 16:24: 'If any man will come after me, let him deny himself, and take up his cross, and follow me.'
24 Watson, *The Duty*, 2.
25 Ibid., fol. 2r. See also Polwheile, *Authēntes*, 18.
26 Polwheile, *Authēntes*, 16–17.
27 Ibid., 17. On Christ as a 'pattern' and an 'exemplum,' see Edmund Calamy, *The Monster of sinful self-seeking* . . . (London, 1655), 18–19.
28 Cawdrey, *Selfe-examination*, 2; Calamy, *The Monster*, 2, 5. For a historical study of Calamy, see Richard L. Greaves, *Saints and Rebels: Seven Nonconformists in Stuart England* (Macon, GA, 1985), chap. 1.
29 Watson, *The Duty*, 4.
30 Calamy, *The Monster*, 1. See also, ibid., 22: 'There are three sorts of men whom I indict as guilty of this sinfull and cursed selfe-seeking. 1. Such as seek their owne things, and not at all the things of Christ. 2. Such as seek their own things before, and more than the things of Christ. 3. Such as pretend to seek the things of Christ, but seek their owne things, under the colour of seeking the things of Christ.'
31 Ibid., 2.
32 Ibid., 2 § 1: 'Not the *honor* of Christ, but their *owne* honor, their *owne private gaine and advantage*, not the profit of Religion, but their *owne* profit; their *owne delights, pleasures, and recreation*; their *owne* ease, safety and security, not the safety of the *Gospel*, but their *owne* safety, their *owne* wills, lusts, and carnall contentments. Not to please Christ and doe his will, but to doe their

owne wills, and to please themselves. And to speak according to the language of our times, *Their owne private, carnall, and Creature interest*'; and see, ibid., 3. On the equivalency between *proprius* and *suus ipsius*, see, in another context, Giambattista Vico, *The New Science*, trans. Thomas Goddard Bergin and Max Harold Fish (Baltimore, 1976), bk. 2, chap.2, 121 § 386.

33 Calamy, *The Monster*, 5, 15.

34 Ibid., 19; Brightman, *The Art*, 41.

35 Polwheile, *Authēntes*, 25; also, Calamy, *The Monster*, 13: The self-seeker 'makes himselfe the *principle*, *rule*, and *end* of all his undertakings, acting from *self* as a principle, by *selfe* as a rule, for *self* as an end.'

36 Brightman, *The Art*, 30: 'our selves being our owne God.'

37 Calamy, *The Monster*, 16: 'As the love of Christ is the *root* of Christ-seeking, so the love of our selves is the *root* of sinfull self-seeking.' Brightman, *The Art*, 21 on *philautia*, and 31: 'this self-love being contrary to the love of GOD, the fountain of all Holy duties.' Calamy, *The Monster*, 17: 'The sinfull self-seeking ariseth from that *spirituall ignorance and blindnesse* which is in all men by nature.' Ibid., 18: 'So there are multitudes of Christians, who fancy to themselves.' On illusion: ibid., esp. 16–18.

38 Calamy, *The Monster*, 18.

39 Ibid., 18.

40 Ibid., 14.

41 Polwheile, *Authēntes*, 24.

42 Calamy, *The Monster*, 16.

43 Ibid., 18, 17, in that order.

44 The concept 'publick person' is from Cawdrey, *Selfe-examination*, 21.

45 Quotation from Watson, *The Duty*, 18.

46 Frank Livingston Huntley, *Jeremy Taylor and the Great Rebellion: A Study of His Mind and Temper in Controversy* (Ann Arbor, 1970), 69–70.

47 On the Puritan's Calvinism, see for example Frits G.M. Broeyer, 'A Pure City: Calvin's Geneva,' in Walter E.A. van Beek, ed., *The Quest for Purity: Dynamics of Puritan Movements* (Berlin, Amsterdam, 1988). On the dissemination of Calvin's work in English, see Francis Higman, 'Calvin's Work in Translation,' in Andrew Pettegree, Alastair Duke, and Gillian Lewis, eds, *Calvinism in Europe, 1540–1620* (Cambridge, 1994), 87.

48 Brightman, *The Art*, 5.

49 Ibid., 6. Burton (*A most Godly Sermon*, fol. 1v) summarizes all these dimensions with the Augustinian triad: 'understanding, will, and affection.'

50 On the necessity to deny the reason that cannot understand the mysteries of theology, see Watson, *The Duty*, 6–8; also Brightman, *The Art*, 24. For the remaining quotations here, see Watson, *The Duty*, 9, 10–38, 48.

51 Calamy, *The Monster*, 8. On body versus soul, see ibid., 15, and 17: 'If he seeks the good of his body with the neglect of his soule, he seeks himself.' Also, see Watson, *The Duty*, 5, 27. In all these writings, St Paul is constantly cited; Burton goes so far as to say: 'We should deny our selves with *Paul*' (fol. 3r). For a general study, see John S. Coolidge, *The Pauline Renaissance in England: Puritanism and the Bible* (Oxford, 1970). On the philosophical heritage of dualism in Calvin, see Charles Partee, 'Soul and Body in Anthropology,' in *Calvin and Classical Philosophy* (Leiden, 1977), chap. 5. This kind of trenchant opposition (found, for example, between 'elect' and 'reprobate') may be attributed to the influence of Ramus (Pierre de la Ramée, 1515–72), who promoted a dialectical method of analysis by distinctions that were easy to picture mentally and to memorize. Roland MacIlmaine's and Dudley Fenner's translations played an important role in Ramus's reception among the Puritans. See in particular Perry Miller, *The New England Mind: The Seventeenth Century* (Cambridge, MA, 1963), appendix A; Leon Howard, *Essays on Puritans and Puritanism* (Albuquerque, NM, 1986), pt. 3.

52 Watson, *The Duty*, 40. This passage continues: 'Luke 14.26, *If any man come to me, and hate not father, and mother, and wife, and children, he cannot be my Disciple.* The meaning is, when carnal relations come in competition with, or stand in opposition to Christ, we must hate them.' Also, Burton, *A most Godly Sermon*, fols. 2v–3r; fol. 3r: 'A Christian must deny himself in all civill Relation.'

53 On salvific necessity, see Watson, *The Duty*, 47: 'Without self-denial, we can never come up to Christs terms. If the World be not denied, Christ cannot be loved. If self-righteousness be not denied, Christ cannot be trusted; if the will be not denied, Christ cannot be obeyed: Therefore self-denial is of as absolute necessity as Heaven.'

54 Watson, *The Duty*, 55.

55 Calamy, *The Monster*, 9.

56 Brightman, *The Art*, 5.

57 Watson, *The Duty*, 46, 43, in that order.

58 Ibid., 3, 48. The vocabulary of annihilation is also found in Brightman, *The Art*, 18: 'We must abase and annihilate our selves.'

59 In this, Puritan usage recovers the original meaning of *religio*: scruple. See Maurice Sachot, '*Religio/Superstitio*, Historique d'une subversion et d'un retournement,' *Revue de l'Histoire des Religions* 208, 4 (1991), 366.

60 Watson, *The Duty*, 43.

61 Calamy, *The Monster*, 4. On the negligence of the sinner, see ibid., 23.

62 Brightman, *The Art*, 50. On the subject of commitment, one should note the capital importance of a contract (*foedus*) for Puritans.

63 For the two quotations, see Brightman, *The Art*, 5–6 and 13.

64 As Brian Stock remarks, this is also Augustine's perspective: 'Augustine left his own readers the transcript of this experience in the narrative books of the *Confessions*, doubtless in order to encourage them to try his method of conversion for themselves.' See Stock, *After Augustine*, 3; cf. 9, 14, and generally chap. 1. Coolidge, *The Pauline Renaissance*, affirms: 'The dynamically Christocentric apprehension of the Bible is the originally distinctive element of Puritanism' (145).

65 Calamy, *The Monster*, 10.

66 Ibid., 8.

67 Ibid., 11; same page: 'That man who seeks the glory and honour of God, above his owne glory and honour, is a Divine self-seeker.'

68 Ibid., 8.

69 Ibid.: 'a Christ-seeker, and a true self-seeker are termes convertibles.'

70 Cf. Robert Schilling, *Rites, cultes, dieux de Rome* (Paris, 1979), 54–70; Huguette Fugier, *Recherches sur l'expression du sacré dans la langue latine* (Paris, 1963); Dominique Iogna-Prat, *La maison Dieu: Une histoire monumentale de l'église au moyen âge* (Paris, 2006), 53–8.

71 Augustine, *Sermo* 336, 'In dedicacione ecclesiae,' § 1. On this sermon, see Iogna-Prat, *La maison Dieu*, 37.

72 St Augustine, *Of the Citie of God* (London, 1620), bk. 17, chap. 12, 602.

73 Augustine's Latin text is: 'Templum Dei de hominibus factum, non de lapidibus': the body itself is considered, at this stage of conversion, as a mystical body.

74 Watson, *The Duty*, 5.

75 For Calamy's associations of church and state, see Calamy, *The Monster*, 11: 'He that loves the publique good more than his owne private good, that seeks the prosperity of Sion and Jerusalem, of Church and State more than his owne, is a Divine selfe-seeker.' Cf. ibid., 13, 19, 21, 29. In all communities, Calamy notes, the wicked self-seeker only serves himself: ibid., 13. See also Coolidge, *The Pauline Renaissance*, 148: 'Christian liberty as Paul conceives it, and the Puritans after him, knits individual conscience to communal consciousness indissolubly.'

76 Brightman, *The Art*, 33–4.

77 As Baudouin de Gaiffier remarks: 'Primitivement *peregrinus* (*peregrinatio*, *peregrinor*) signifie l'étranger, celui qui a quitté son pays d'origine et se trouve loin de sa patrie' (Originally, *peregrinus* [*peregrinatio*, *peregrinor*] signified foreigner, one who has left the place of his origins and is far from

his homeland). For this quote, see Baudouin de Gaiffier, *Études critiques d'hagiographie et d'iconologie* (Bruxelles, 1976), 31.

78 For Puritans, the self is now no more than a primary territory, no longer one's property, and is transformed into an *operation* or process that allows one to free oneself from the exile that affects all mankind.

79 In this sense, self-consciousness is truly theological.

chapter ten

Exile in the Reformation

LEE PALMER WANDEL

> Locating human actions in space remains the greatest intellectual achievement of the map as a form of knowledge.
>
> J.B. Harley[1]

In the study of the sixteenth century, cartography and Reformation have been treated as two utterly separate phenomena. There is evidence, however, that the two were, in fact, deeply intertwined:

- In 1544, in Louvain, Gerardus Mercator was arrested and imprisoned on suspicion of being a 'Lutheran.'[2] It took his friends and supporters seven months to convince the regent to free him. Most of those who were captured with him were executed: decapitated, hanged, burned at the stake. One other, Christiaen Broyaerts, also survived, but was banished 'in perpetuity, on pain of death.'[3]
- In 1579, Abraham Ortelius included the 'Peregrinations of Saint Paul' in the *Theatrum orbis terrarum*, a map based, he said, upon Mercator's 1554 and 1572 maps of Europe, both of which included an engraved text of the travels of St Paul.[4]
- In 1584, Ortelius published an account of his travels in Belgium, which he called *Itinerarium per nonnullas Galliae Belgicae partes*, and dedicated to Gerard Mercator, 'cosmographer.'
- In 1585, Mercator published the first detailed maps of France and of what he called 'Upper Belgium.'
- Some time between 1585 and 1590, Mercator wrote a commentary on Paul's Epistle to the Romans, in which he explicitly rejected Calvin's particular formulation of predestination.[5]

In the magnificent third volume of Harley and Woodward's *History of Cartography*, which encompasses more than two thousand pages and sixty contributors, only one, twenty-page piece addresses 'the European religious worldview,' gathering together the ideas of such diverse individuals as Roger Bacon, Hartmut Schedel, Martin Luther, and John Calvin under that notion, and maps that 'all, in one way or another, present or allude to the unfolding of the divine plan for human redemption in a postlapsarian time and space.'[6] No chapter directly addresses the Reformation as bearing somehow on the transformation of cartography in the sixteenth century.[7] If one follows one of the threads of research into sixteenth-century cartography, that exclusion makes sense: most of the influential cartographers seem not to have entered into the religious polemics of the time, in print, or in spoken or written word such as we can find today. Even those who imprisoned Mercator ultimately could bring no evidence to demonstrate what he believed – nor could his friends prove his orthodoxy. David Woodward called most cartographers 'humanists,' separating them from the religious polemics of the period.[8] Cartography, following his conceptualization, moves from 'Renaissance' directly to 'Enlightenment' – in keeping with his sense that cartography affiliates with the history of science, through its rootedness in mathematics and particularly geometry, and that, following Richard Westfall, it is therefore conceptually and personally removed from religion.

If, however, we take up Brian Harley's definition of a map with which this essay opens, then another way of thinking about self and space in the Reformation may be possible. Setting aside the traces of evidence we have for individual cartographers' scriptural engagements, such as Mercator's commentary on Romans, or Ortelius's maps of Paul's peregrinations, there is the larger context within which those cartographers pursued maps of such precision that one could locate oneself within them. Mercator's capture and imprisonment is a reminder that his own landscape was a place of violent religious division, where Europeans of many different understandings of Christianity were being brought forcibly into religious conformity. Mercator was born near, and Ortelius in, Antwerp, which in their lifetimes witnessed unprecedented iconoclasm, the slaughter of thousands of its citizens, siege, and the expulsion of all Protestants.[9] Mercator's cellmate's banishment is another reminder of thousands of Europeans who were forced from their homes – expelled, banished, driven out – in extraordinary numbers: Jews in 1492, Muslims by 1501, and, then, throughout the sixteenth century, Christians who were not Christian in the ways their sovereigns demanded.

In the past few years, scholars have taken up a number of ways religion and space were mutually implicated in the sixteenth century.[10] Catholics reconsecrated the churches and the altars they recaptured from Protestants.[11] Reformed Protestants removed images and altars from within the space of their churches and placed the table for the Supper beneath the pulpit.[12] Cities sought to restrict the movement of relics and monstrances through their streets, seeking to delineate a boundary between the inner sanctified space of a church and the outer civic space of the urban landscape. Jesuits travelled alone and in pairs to 'the remote corners' of the earth, sometimes providing other cartographers with the information they accrued, other times drawing their own maps.[13]

Perhaps the most pervasive, albeit the least studied, connection between religion and space was exile. The fragmentation of Christianity engendered movement. Movement was in and of itself not new.[14] The Crusades had mobilized thousands, predominantly men, but they had chosen to go, and all of them could return, if they survived and so chose. Pilgrimage, too, had set Europeans in motion, but this was geographically teleological – whether Compostella, Rome, or Jerusalem, one had an end-point. It was also, luck prevailing, a closed loop: most pilgrims returned 'home' – to a place familiar physically, climactically, and socially. Nor were expulsion and exile new: Jews, Muslims, Waldensians, Hussites, Lollards had all already been forced to leave their homes. Furthermore, not all Europeans had been sedentary: the poor and the more dangerous vagrants and mercenaries had long been itinerant. The movement of Europeans in the sixteenth century differed.[15] Unlike Crusaders or pilgrims, most refugees had no telos, no end point, nor was their itinerary a circuit or loop. So, too, the groups forced onto the roads differed from the poor, those seeking work, or the marginal or vagrant: entire families of artisans, shop-keepers, even nobles found themselves without residence, adrift in waters of unpredictable currents.

One such noble refugee was James, Lord of Falais and of Breda in Brabant, the natural grandson of Philip the Good, Duke of Burgundy. Falais had converted to that understanding of Christianity Calvin was promulgating in Geneva. When Spain imposed conformity to Catholicism on the Burgundian Netherlands, Calvin wrote him in 1543, charting the path of exile:

> Monsieur, Although I rely with confidence in our gracious God, that He has guided you hitherto, bestowing grace to overcome many difficulties, which

> might have turned you aside out of the straight road, He will also in time coming vouchsafe you strength to resist all the assaults which Satan can muster up against you, nevertheless, when I consider the danger wherein you now are, already harassed by so many temptations, as I see them arrayed and set in order, I could not refrain from reminding you, that the benefits which God hath bestowed upon us, indeed require that we should prefer His honour to all the world besides, and that the hope of salvation which we have by His Evangel is so precious, that we ought readily to forego all meaner considerations, in so far as they hinder us from reaching forward to that hope, and that we ought to have such contentment in conforming ourselves to His will, that whensoever the question arises of our displeasing the whole world, that we may obey His pleasure, it is good for us.[16]

Embedded in Calvin's exhortation is a notion of a 'straight road' which is not only a moral path. It is also spatial. Within a generation, from the Iberian Peninsula to Poland, from Stockholm to Rome, Europeans could no longer speak of 'Christendom' as geographically homogeneous, continuous, or unified. Persecutions, expulsions, and forced conversions put hundreds on the road, as they left one place within the former 'Christendom' that no longer permitted their particular understanding of Christianity, in search of another which did. Conversos settled briefly in Portugal, then more permanently in Amsterdam. Reformed Christians emigrated to London, Leiden, ultimately across the Atlantic. Catholics fled Imperial Free Cities and England. Anabaptists were more difficult to discern, travelling as they did from conventicle to conventicle, but travel they did, as court records attest. Falais left his natal lands and dwelt successively in Cologne, Strasbourg, and Basel. Neither persecution nor coexistence was constant over geographic expanse, but sporadic, as Anabaptists' testimonies document.[17] Across Europe, European Christians encountered places where their presence might be tolerated, interspersed with places of persecution.[18]

But to speak of 'across Europe' is to invoke a perception of space that was not available to sixteenth-century refugees. The places of safety as well as the places of danger were known only verbally – by word of mouth. There were no two-dimensional cartographic representations a refugee might carry. Each had to rely upon names, written or spoken, place and personal names, which identified havens. No one, from Falais to the poorest of journeymen, could see where he or she was to go. Refugees heard – by word of mouth – from their preachers, from their friends, from co-religionists. But they did not see.

Like Mercator, Calvin was a refugee. Unlike Mercator, he chose words to articulate what he understood exile to mean. He wrote letters, hundreds of letters, forming an extraordinary epistolary network among Christians driven from their homes.[19] Calvin's letters testify to far more than the numbers of refugees. His words, I hope, will help us to read what Harley calls the text of maps, to link the experience of exile to the spatial representations of Mercator's cartography. This cartography sought accuracy in distance and direction; privileged no space over another, whether land over water, or Jerusalem over Africa; and organized the entire surface of the globe according to the regularities of the geometry of longitude and latitude.

Calvin documented many of the consequences of exile. Groups lived as strangers in lands of unknown political and social landscapes, among speakers of a language they frequently did not understand, and in contact with unfamiliar devotional practices. A number of Calvin's letters address the problems that displacement engendered. In 1552, for example, he wrote to the refugee church in London:[20]

> If those who have stirred up these conflicts have taken occasion to do so from the diversity of ceremonies, as M.A. Lasco has informed me, they have but ill understood in what the true unity of Christians consists, and how every member is bound to conform himself to the body of the Church in which he lives. It is true, that if a different form has been seen and preferred, it is quite allowable in communicating first of all with the pastor, to tell him what is thought of it, provided one accommodates one's-self to the usages of the place where one lives, without clamouring for novelty, but peaceably conforming to any order that is not repugnant to the Word of God.[21]

Communities that received exiles were transformed. In 1551, Calvin wrote to his colleague in Geneva, William Farel, of 'foreigners, who daily pass through this place in great numbers, or who have come hither to take up their abode' – two different kinds of refugees, those who were still in transit and those who were settling. Refugees swelled the number of inhabitants within city walls, often to the point of tension. It was, Calvin said, 'a pleasing spectacle to me, if they do not overwhelm me with their visits.'[22] Refugees had different needs from existing residents: housing, the many acts of translation.[23] As they moved in, cities were no longer coherent places of shared customs and familiar traditions. As the letter to the Church in London revealed, viewed by strangers, local devotional customs were strange. Misunderstandings in the small and the large marked the sites where strangers settled among older residents.

Refugees who found themselves among the faithful, as Calvin wrote, were the fortunate ones. They had each other, and in that collectivity they had the affirmation of what constituted proper worship and faithfulness for each individual and for the group. Adversity gave the group its boundary, a line at once separating it from hostile environments and affirming its identity, its integrity over against that hostility. Even in martyrdom, as Calvin wrote to five prisoners in Lyon, they were not alone: they were embraced in the geographically dispersed 'all children of God' and 'the mutual compassion which ought to exist between members of the same body'; other Reformed Christians, he noted, 'know well that you labour for them, in maintaining the cause of their salvation.' The five in Lyon could see in one another that to which God had 'called' them: 'Doubt not, therefore, that according as He employs you, He will give you strength to fulfill His work, for He has promised this, and we know by experience that He has never failed those who allow themselves to be governed by Him.'[24] Even in martyrdom, the prisoners could look at one another and witness the working of divine providence.

In the early years, exile was far likelier to be solitary or, at best, with those members of one's family who could travel. Solitary exile placed one in a singular relationship to landscape. In a letter to Martin Bucer, dated 4 September 1532, Calvin described an unnamed refugee:

> He so conducted himself as to be beloved among the men of our profession, if any one was. Esteemed as such among men who were endowed with some degree of authority, and so as to be neither a shame nor a disgrace to them. At length, when he could no longer bow the neck to that voluntary bondage which even yet we bear, he departed to take up his residence with you, having no prospect of return. But, as the matter stands, it fell out, contrary to his expectation, like the shifting scene of a play, and he could find no settled abode, whither he might betake himself.[25]

Exile placed Europeans on roads across unknown terrain. In letters to the ministers in Basel, dated 13 November 1537, to Peter Viret, written towards the end of May 1538, and to William Farel, dated September 1538 and 4 May 1545, Calvin detailed the treacherous landscape of a Europe religiously fractured – the spontaneous and savage outbreaks of violence, the rescinding of letters of safe passage, shifting regional and national alliances, allies unwilling to commit, the arbitrary withdrawal of support, even the means to travel.[26] He wrote to the ministers of Neuchâtel, on 5 September 1551, of 'Hugues, with five other brethren, and a lady of rank, [who] had been seized in the neighbourhood of Maçon.'[27] He informed Heinrich Bullinger, one of his regular correspondents, on Whitsunday 1552, of the disappearance of two mutual friends.[28]

It was not simply that these were people driven from their native homes, or that exile propelled individuals from familiar landscapes into dangerous terrain. The fragmentation of religion transformed the landscape of Europe from a place traversed by pilgrimage and trade routes, with large patches of the darknesses of forests, into an uncharted and shifting archipelago of safe havens surrounded by seas of potential arrest, imprisonment, and execution. Space had become broken, discontinuous. It was not merely that one might be set upon by bandits, but that one could no longer rest easily in human settlements – one might disappear entirely.

Individually, exile transformed the landscape of Europe into space of uncertain extension. One never knew, after leaving home, whether another was friend or foe; and, as Calvin captured in many of his letters, one never knew who might attach to one's person a reputation both inconceivable at home among those who had known one, and deeply at odds with one's own sense of who one was. And, as Calvin represented it, that reputation enveloped a person, creating distance between oneself and those with whom one thought one had fundamental beliefs in common. In a letter to Farel, written in Strasbourg in 1538, Calvin intimated something of the psychology of exile, an experience of being a solitary point, singular, bounded, without affiliation in or to any place:

> My departure from Basle was so hurried and disorderly, that I brought away with me, stuffed aside in the innumerable traveling-pouches of the brain, the letter which I promised would be left for you; nor indeed was there at the time, anything that required my writing sooner. Three days after my arrival a messenger presented himself, and there was already somewhat worth communicating. But as I was afraid to run the risk of sending my letter by that channel, I chose rather to put it off until now.[29]

Exile was, for Calvin, far more than a social fact. As he wrote to the ministers of the Church of Montbeliard, 'Your lot, however hard, will be more blessed than if you maintained a name and a place where the Son of God was exiled.'[30] That sense, that Christ was 'exiled,' at once echoed the experience of those who had been driven out and intimated something more in Calvin's understanding of exile. There were places from which the Son of God could not, in that mechanical sense of physical force, be forced, by anyone or anything, no matter how powerful – one was 'exiled,' not because others had the authority or the physical means to drive one out, but because one did not belong in that place, and that not-belonging had the force of expulsion. In so many of his letters – to Viret, to Falais, to Madame Budé, to the ministers of Montbeliard – Calvin wrote that it was better to move, to feel the inner force that propelled one away, than to remain where Christ's presence could not or no longer be found.

In a letter to Bullinger, dated January 1552, Calvin spoke of 'our Pharaoh,' invoking at once a people of God oppressed by political power and a people forced to leave everything behind, to wander for forty years in waste and uncertainty.[31] The havens for the faithful were not quite the Promised Land – 'You shall enter here no earthly paradise, where you may rejoice in God without molestation: you will find the people unmannerly enough' – but the faithful were certainly being forced to wander, at times seemingly aimlessly, across a landscape frequently denying them food or shelter.[32] Like the children of Israel, they were called to abandon everything in obedience to God, to leave behind all that they could not carry. Like the children of Israel, the faithful were confronted with the seductions of idols and gold. And they had no maps, nothing to show them that line – a series of points – connecting Egypt to the River Jordan, nothing to show them, simultaneously, where they had left, the course they were to follow, and where they were going.

> However, your departure must be like that out of Egypt, bringing all of your effects along with you. For all this, I believe you will need stedfast and very determined courage. But you are able to do all in Him who strengthens you. When He has brought you hither, you shall see how He will guide you farther. For my part, I would gladly help thereunto cheerfully and steadily, as bound as I am to do. I am confident, that after leading you by the hand in greater things, He will not fail you on this occasion. But he is sometimes pleased to exercise and try our faith, so that while quitting hold of that which is within our grasp, we know not what we shall receive in place of it. We have an example of this in our father Abraham. After having commanded him to forsake his country, his kindred, and everything else, He shewed him no present reward, but put that off to another time. 'Get thee out,' said He, 'into the land which I shall shew thee.' Should it please Him at this time to do the like with us, that we must quit the land of our birth, and betake ourselves into an unknown country, without knowing how it may fare with us there, let us surrender ourselves to Him, that He may direct our way, and let us honour Him, by trusting that He will steer us to a safe harbour.[33]

Mercator's first map, published in 1537, was of the Holy Land.[34] Evidence of his biblical scholarship, it also manifested his own emerging sense of the visual capacity of maps: it possessed more detail, both topographical and historical, than earlier maps; it was oriented north-west, in order to reduce the space on the plane of the paper that was otherwise useless (*inutilia*). The organization of the plane of the map was governed by the twin values of utility and symmetry. The map's title, 'Amplissima Terrae Sanctae descriptio ad vtrivsqve testamenti intelligentiam,' gave its purpose: for 'the understanding of both testaments.'[35] In the central cartouche at the top of the map, Mercator inscribed texts from Micah: 'O my people, what I have done unto thee? and wherein have I wearied thee? testify against me.' And from Deuteronomy: 'For the Lord thy God bringeth thee into a good land, a land of brooks of water, of fountains and depths that spring out of valleys and hills; a land of wheat, and barley, and vines, and fig trees, and pomegranates . . . a land whose stones are iron, and out of whose hills thou mayest dig brass.' On the map, Mercator charted the Exodus route. He was unable to locate all forty-two camps of the people of Israel named in the Book of Numbers, but he gathered information, predominantly from Jacob Ziegler's *Quae intus continentur* published five years earlier, and, possibly, from Holbein's map published in the Coverdale Bible, as well as Cranach's, published with the Liesvelt Antwerp edition of Luther's German New Testament. Using the capacity of maps to represent discrete historical events simultaneously on the same plane, Mercator engraved both the path of the flight from Egypt and the person of Christ on Mount Tabor.

When Calvin fled France in 1533 and Geneva in 1538, he moved from one landmark to the next, along routes known through verbal description – word of mouth or letters – that connected not simply clusters of human settlement, which any merchant might know, but safe havens, particular points in a landscape of danger. Among the earliest to flee the physical threat of persecution, he stayed with sympathetic friends, moved from one town to the next – Basel, Strasbourg, Geneva – places known to offer, legally or privately, safe haven for someone of his convictions. But he had no map. It is not that he owned no map; there were no maps of the kind he would need. There were no atlases – no portable maps – until the 1560s, long after Calvin and many others had settled in Geneva or London.[36] Nor would the kind of cartographic detail and precision of measurement that travellers could use be produced until much later in the century, arguably not until Mercator's maps of the 1580s.

Calvin did not situate himself as a point on a plane marked by symbols to stand for rivers, forests, human settlements, although at times, as we have seen, he did indeed consider himself very much a point, a solitary one not situated on a surface or within a larger representation of contiguous space. The image that pervades so much of Calvin's writing is that of a 'path,' a line neither so frequently travelled nor so well marked as pilgrimage or trade routes, a line, in fact, that might not ever be marked on a map at all. As Calvin wrote in his address 'To the Reader,' which prefaced the 1559 edition of the *Institutes*, 'For I trust that God out of his infinite goodness will permit me to persevere with unwavering patience in the path [*cursu*] of his holy calling.'[37] Calvin's path was personal, individual, and, in keeping with his understanding of providence, unmarked to his human eyes.[38] God calls the faithful individual to a journey which he or she walks, without cartographic knowledge. God had laid the line, like that of Moses and Abraham, without indicating its future course. The map could only be drawn in retrospect.

The three biblical figures who caught the attention of sixteenth-century cartographers – Abraham, Moses, and Paul – were not the only biblical figures in movement.[39] Like Calvin and those to whom he wrote, these three left everything behind to follow a line as yet undrawn across strange landscapes unknown to them before they arrived. They were known for their stories of exile and exodus. All three placed themselves in trust of God; trust was their location, marking and distinguishing their lives. Abraham and Moses reiterate that trust, underline it as they put themselves in motion, towards a goal God has spoken, but they have not seen.

In 1544, Mercator was arrested for 'Lutherey,' a term broadly used to designate those who seemed not orthodox in their speaking.[40] Scholars have found it difficult to situate Mercator in the modern mapping of confessions, with their patches of uniform colour and their clear boundaries. Vermij affiliated Mercator with Erasmus.[41] Carlo de Clerq argued that in his commentary on Paul's Letter to the Romans, Mercator rejected Calvin's particular formulation of predestination, making Mercator, therefore, Catholic.[42] Certainly, Mercator disagreed with Calvin on a specific point of doctrine, but he did not ally himself with the decrees of Trent or any other public declaration of Catholic orthodoxy.[43] For him, the problem with predestination was the constraint it placed upon God's will to choose freedom for humankind.

Europe was, perhaps, a baffling place for someone who could envision it all at once, with trees and rivers, small towns and major commercial centres, trade routes and oceans. In keeping with the configuration of the history of cartography, Mercator's religious beliefs have been kept apart from his map-making, the former the focus of a handful of studies – after all, he left almost no conventional texts explicating his beliefs – the latter the focus of volumes, all of which take up his mathematics but not his religious thinking. Mercator, as Vermij rightly notes, got lost in the construction of national narratives of the Reformation. But I think Vermij is wrong: neither Mercator nor Erasmus was backward looking. Rather, let me suggest, Erasmus and Mercator each held a vision unintelligible in the polemics of the sixteenth century. Throughout his writings, Erasmus posits a plurality of humankind that does not ever divide simply into two categories, right and wrong, but that shares sin and frailty and expresses faith diversely. Mercator sought accuracy, which, like the line he drew on a surface, took into account divergent readings of a text and sought not affiliation of belief, but that position which best accommodated conflicting information. He wrote not polemically, but along a line drawn between positions. His commentary on Paul and his maps share a theological commitment to a Creator who disposes according to his will and an orientation with regard to Creation. For Mercator, human information enables greater precision in charting Creation, in sharpening a sense of what is inaccurate and enhancing a sense of Creation's sheer magnificence.[44] He called his great life's work *Atlas, or Cosmographical Meditations upon the Creation of the Universe.*

Such an approach did not have a 'church' in the sixteenth century. It was not 'heretical' in the traditional sense, as a conscious divergence or setting out on a path away from orthodoxy. It was heretical in the emerging sense of the sixteenth century: not obedient to ecclesiastical authority, not acquiescent to the readings of others. Mercator may well have been surprised by his arrest, as some scholars have it: he was not charting a divergent path, but gathering information to etch the most accurate line.[45] By 1544, such a position shared no terrain with any of the settlements – Lutheran, Reformed, Catholic, or even Anabaptist, all of which had their confessions and their boundaries. Cartographically, Mercator's position might best be conceptualized as a point, but it had no place. Like Calvin, Mercator eschewed citizenship in the place where he resided: unlike Calvin, who accepted citizenship at the end of his life, Mercator remained for forty years, legally, a stranger within the place he lived until his death.

In the second century CE, Ptolemy developed the means to situate a human being anywhere on the globe. The geometry of projection

Figure 10.1 Ptolemy, *Cosmographia*, Ulm, 1482. Photo courtesy of The Newberry Library, Chicago [Ayer 6 F9 1482a].

permits precisely the ability to locate any point – a person, a fortress, a town, a village – on land conceived as a two-dimensional plane. Like so much else of the Greek tradition, Ptolemy's geometry – the systematic measurement of the earth – was lost to the West for centuries and, alongside Plato, Galen, and other authors, rediscovered in the fifteenth century with electrifying results (see figure 10.1). Navigators, such as Columbus, found in Ptolemy a way of conceptualizing distance across unknown bodies of water, and in the sixteenth century, cartographers, such as Mercator, found a way of conceptualizing the globe, but the great majority of Europeans did not 'situate' themselves in any abstract matrix, upon any graphic representation, within any system of signs to designate roads, rivers, mountains, and bodies of water. They walked the land, and when they walked beyond familiar landscape, they relied upon the words of others to describe for them their way.

In cartography, the relationship between a human being and space is 'representational,' drawing upon changing conventions of symbols to invoke three dimensional experiences – of trees, rivers, specific settlements (figure 10.2).[46] That relationship was utterly different from the face-to-face experience of the world of late medieval Europe. One imagined oneself in this or that place, but it was an act of imagination, in part because at any one time, one could only be in one place, in part because the cartographic system of representation had not achieved the kind of specificity of walking a town. A map lifts the viewer above the terrain. One could see, as Ortelius showed in his *Itinerarium per nonnullas Galliae Belgicae partes*, on the surface of a map, where one had been, at any one moment, even as one could see, simultaneously, the terminus of the itinerary – where one would end – with all the points in-between.[47]

Perhaps no one invoked Paul more fully in the sixteenth century than did Calvin. He wrote commentaries on all the Pauline epistles. He drew the four offices of the Church and his definition of the ministry from Paul.[48] Like Paul, Calvin found himself on the road as a young man. Born in Picardy, he was forced to flee France at the age of twenty-four. His first haven was Basel. Within two years, however, when he tried to return there after a trip to Strasbourg, he found his route blocked – his convictions had made of him a persecuted minority in the borderlands between France and the Swiss cantons. In 1536, therefore, by a circuitous route, he found a temporary safe haven in Geneva, where, like Paul, he preached to communities 'under the cross,' that is, suffering persecution. In 1538, he fled to Strasbourg. In 1541, he returned to Geneva,

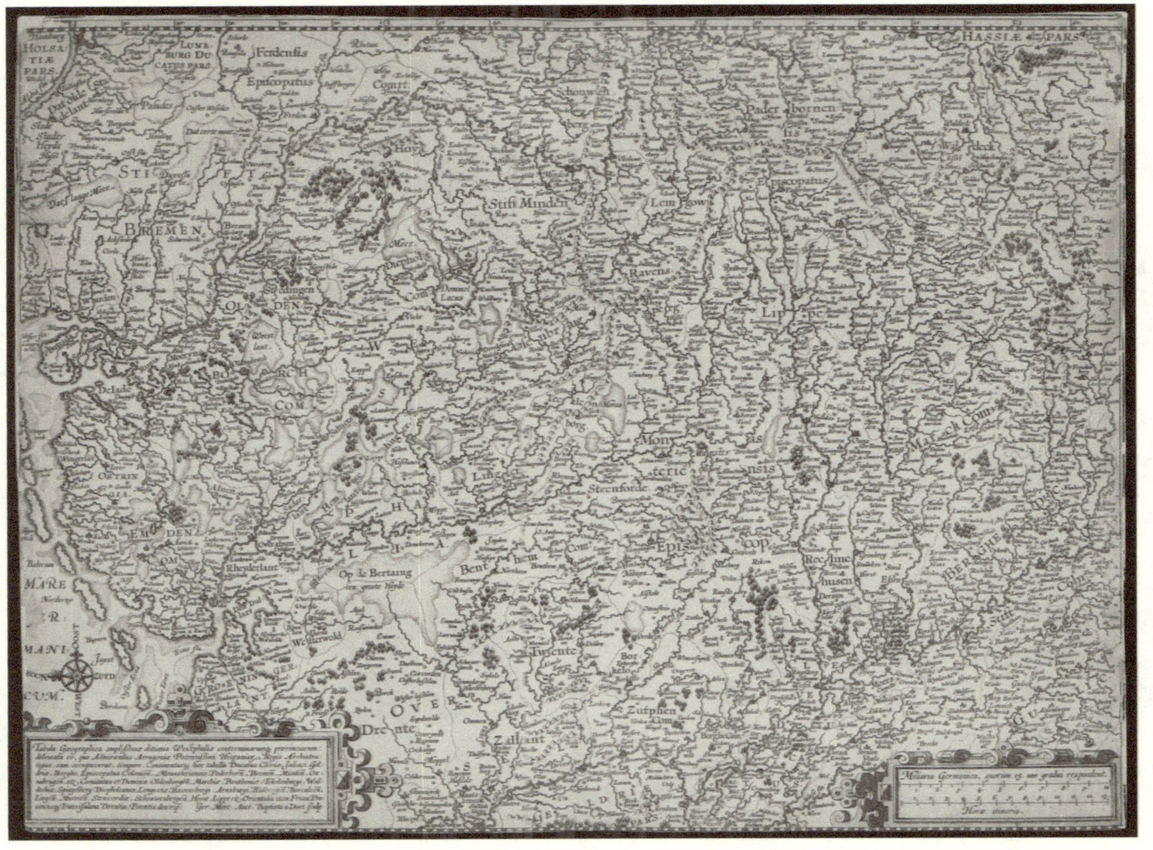

Figure 10.2 Gerardus Mercator, *Tabula Gaeographica amplissima editionis Westphaliae conterminarumque provinciarum*, 1589. Photograph reproduced by permission from Special Collections, University of Amsterdam.

Figure 10.3 Rumoldus Mercator, after Gerardus Mercator, *Orbis terrae compendiosa descriptio,* 1587. Photograph reproduced by permission from Special Collections, University of Amsterdam.

where he died in 1564, some 650 kilometres from his birthplace. Thus, also like Paul, Calvin was called to preach far away from his birthplace.

Calvin gave voice to a sense of self as solitary point abstracted from immediate physical surroundings and in motion, following in obedience a path God was inscribing on a much larger landscape – the landscape of all of Europe and the Americas. He found the biblical analogy for that experience in the same letters of Saint Paul that Ortelius used to chart Paul's 'peregrinations,' using the geometry of cartography. Mercator, for his part, developed a cartography that rendered a plane surface without any orientation marked on that surface, without pre-marked itineraries, in which all points are equal and all space is uniform (figure 10.3). He found the geometry that in its very abstraction allowed each solitary soul to find him or herself on the plane surface of all Creation. Sixteenth-century Europeans were in motion, isolated, on a surface, which, thanks to Mercator's geometry, they could then imaginatively view from outside themselves. They could see themselves in motion, negotiating, but not a part of, the landscape they were traversing. They could place their lives, as points, on the map of Creation, and, at the same time, view those lives from above, see them as paths.

NOTES

1 J.B. Harley, 'Texts and Contexts in the Interpretation of Early Maps,' in Paul Laxton, ed., *The New Nature of Maps: Essays in the History of Cartography* (Baltimore and London, 2001), 35.

2 See, for example, Mary of Hungary's letter to the guardian of the Friars Minor at Malines, dated 21 May 1544, in M. Van Durme, ed., *Correspondance Mercatorienne* (Antwerp, 1959), 24–5.

3 C.-A. Campan, *Mémoires de Francisco de Enzinas: Texte latin inédit avec la traduction française du XVIe siècle en regard 1543–1545*, vol. 1 (Brussels, 1862), 302n3, quoted in Nicholas Crane, *Mercator: The Man Who Mapped the Planet* (New York, 2003), 160.

4 Ortelius made his claim about his sources in his 'Parergon.' See Robert W. Karrow, Jr, *Mapmakers of the Sixteenth Century and Their Maps: Bio-Bibliographies of the Cartographers of Abraham Ortelius, 1570* (Chicago, 1993), 406.

5 Carlo de Clercq, 'Le commentaire de Gérard Mercator sur l'Épître aux Romains de saint Paul,' in *Festschrift zum 450. Geburtstag Gerhard Mercators*, Duisburger Forschungen 6 (Duisburg-Ruhrort, 1962), 233–43.

6 Pauline Moffitt Watt, 'The European Religious Worldview and Its Influence on Mapping,' in David Woodward, ed., *Cartography in the European Renaissance*, vol. 3 of *The History of Cartography*, ed. J.B. Harley and David Woodward (Chicago, 1987–2007), 400.

7 'There has been no comprehensive study of the relationship of cartography to the Catholic and Protestant reform movements of early modern Europe.' Watt, 'The European Religious Worldview,' 387.

8 David Woodward, 'Introduction,' in *Cartography in the European Renaissance.*

9 For details of individual cartographers' lives, see Karrow, *Mapmakers.*

10 See, for example, Will Coster and Andrew Spicer, eds, *Sacred Space in Early Modern Europe* (Cambridge, 2005); Andrew Spicer and Sarah Hamilton, eds, *Defining the Holy: Sacred Space in Medieval and Early Modern Europe* (Aldershot, 2005).

11 Lee Palmer Wandel, 'Religion, Raum, und Ort,' in Johannes Burkhardt, Thomas Max Safley, and Sabine Ullmann, eds, *Geschichte in Räumen: Festschrift für Rolf Kießling zum 65. Geburtstag* (Constance, 2006), 279–92.

12 On the removal of images, see foremost Olivier Christin, *Une révolution symbolique: L'iconoclasme huguenot et la reconstruction catholique* (Paris, 1991); Solange Deyon and Alain Lottin, *Les casseurs de l'été 1566* (Westhoek and Lille, 1986); Eamon Duffy, *The Stripping of the Altars* (New Haven, 1992); and Lee Palmer Wandel, *Voracious Idols and Violent Hands: Iconoclasm in Reformation Zurich, Strasbourg, and Basel* (New York, 1995). On the placement of the table, see Lee Palmer Wandel, *The Eucharist in the Reformation: Incarnation and Liturgy* (New York, 2006), 183, 203.

13 See, for example, 'Rome Reborn: The Vatican Library and Renaissance Culture,' Exhibition at the Library of Congress, http://www.loc.gov/exhibits/vatican/; in particular, the Jesuit Michael Boym's *Magni Catay* (1652) and the edition of Ortelius's *Asia orbis partium maximae nova descriptio* (1567), which Jesuits carried with them to China.

14 See Dirk Hoerder, *Cultures in Contact: World Migrations in the Second Millennium* (Durham and London, 2002), esp. chap. 3.

15 Hoerder's project is a study of migration on a global scale over two millennia. As such, he gives the Reformation of the sixteenth century roughly 3 pages of 582. That said, however, Hoerder charts the demographic transformation of Europe, from the emigration of the Bohemian Brethren to Silesia, Poland, Hungary, Berlin, and ultimately, the United States, to the departures of Irish Catholics and Huguenots, the last, 'the largest group of refugees within Christendom.' Ibid., 106.

16 *Letters of John Calvin . . .* , ed. Jules Bonnet, trans. David Constable, 2 vols. (Edinburgh, 1855), 1:377; cited hereafter as *Letters.*

17 See Michele Zelinsky, 'Religion as a Civic Virtue: Religious Identity and Communal Relations in Augsburg, 1517–1555,' PhD diss., University of Pennsylvania, 2000.

18 Benjamin Kaplan has found evidence of religious freedom and coexistence. See his *Divided by Faith: Religious Conflict and the Practice of Toleration in Early Modern Europe* (Cambridge, MA, 2007).

19 Robert Kingdon, *Geneva and the Coming of the Wars of Religion in France, 1555–1563* (Geneva, 1956; repr. with a new foreword and afterword, 2007).

20 On the refugee church in London, see Andrew Pettegree, *Foreign Protestant Communities in Sixteenth-Century London* (Oxford, 1986).

21 Calvin to the Church in London, 1552, in *Letters*, 2:346.

22 Calvin to William Farel, 1551, in *Letters*, 2:298.

23 See, for example, Calvin to Viret, 20 November 1553 (no. 331) and Calvin to Farel, 30 December 1553 (no. 335), in *Letters*, 2:421–2 and 430–1, respectively.

24 Calvin to Lyons prisoners, in *Letters*, 2:335–6.

25 Calvin to Martin Bucer, 4 September 1532, in *Letters*, 1:9–10.

26 To the ministers of Basel, in *Letters*, 1:34–6, 45–6, 56–8, 434–5.

27 Calvin to the ministers of Neuchatel, 5 September 1551, in *Letters*, 2:303.

28 Calvin to Heinrich Bullinger, Whitsunday 1552, in *Letters*, 2:334.

29 Calvin to Farel, 1538, in *Letters*, 1:56.

30 Calvin to the ministers at Monbeliard, 1549, in *Letters*, 2:195.

31 Calvin to Bullinger, January 1552, in *Letters*, 2:317.

32 Calvin to a French seigneur, in *Letters*, 2:167.

33 Calvin to a French seigneur, 18 October 1548, in *Letters*, 2:167.

34 Ortelius recorded the existence of the map, but no copy was believed to have survived, until the 1920s, when one was discovered in Italy (Karrow, *Mapmakers*, 377). For a description, I have relied upon Antoine de Smet, 'Mercator à Louvain (1530–1552),' in *Festschrift zum 450. Geburtstag Gerhard Mercators*, 39–43; Crane, *Mercator*, 97–105. On Mercator's maps more generally, see *Le cartographe Gerard Mercator 1512–1594* (Brussels, 1994).

35 Karrow, *Mapmakers*, 377.

36 Ibid., 4.

37 'quia Deum pro immensa sua bonitate daturum mihi confido, ut in cursu sanctae suae vocationis aequabili tolerantia perseverem.' *Ioannis Calvini opera quae supersunt omnia*, vol. 2, *Institutio Christianae religionis*, ed. Wilhelm Baum, Edward Cunitz, and Edward Reuss (Braunschweig, 1864), 2; in English: *Institutes of the Christian Religion*, ed. John T. McNeill, trans. Ford Lewis Battles, 2 vols. (Philadelphia, 1960), vol. 1, bk. 1, chap. 4.

38 On the indefinite duration of suffering, see Jean-Daniel Benoit, *Calvin in His Letters: A Study of Calvin's Pastoral Counselling, Mainly from His Letters*, trans. Richard Haig (Oxford, 1991), 125–6.

39 In addition to the *Peregrinationis divi Pavli*, Ortelius also published *Abrahami Patriarchae peregrinatio, et vita* with the *Theatrum* of 1586. For a discussion of that map, see Marcel P.R. van der Broecke and Deborah Günzburger, 'The Wanderings of Patriarch Abraham,' in Marcel van den Broecke, Peter van der Krogt, and Peter Meuter, eds, *Abraham Ortelius and the First Atlas: Essays Commemorating the Quadricentennial of His Death 1598–1998* (Utrecht, 1998), 319–29.

40 For a discussion of Mercator's arrest, see Rienk Vermij, 'Mercator and the Reformation,' in Manfred Büttner and René Dirven, eds, *Mercator und Wandlungen der Wissenschaften im 16. und 17. Jahrhundert*, Duisburger Mercator-Studien 1 (Bochum, 1993), esp. 81. See also De Smet, 'Mercator à Louvain,' 75–9.

41 Ironically and, I think, unintentionally affiliating Mercator with that humanism which remains apart from the Reformation. Vermij, 'Mercator and the Reformation,' 79ff.

42 De Clercq, 'Le commentaire de Gérard Mercator,' 233–43.

43 Karl Schmitz-Moormann argues a similar independence in 'Mercator und die Entwicklung der Exegese im sechzehnten Jahrhundert,' in Hans H. Blotevogel and Rienk Vermij, eds, *Gerhard Mercator und die geistigen Strömungen des 16. und 17. Jahrhunderts*, Duisburger Mercator-Studien 3 (Bochum, 1995), esp. 211–18.

44 Cf. Karl Schmitz-Moormann, 'Mercator vor dem Horizont der mittelalterlichen Wissenschaften, insbesondere der Theologie,' in *Mercator und Wandlungen der Wissenschaften im 16. und 17. Jahrhundert*, Duisburger Mercator-Studien 1 (Bochum, 1993), 93–101; Giorgio Mangani, 'La signification providentielle du *Theatrum orbis terrarum*,' in *Abraham Ortelius (1527–1598): Cartographe et humaniste* (Brussels, 1998), 93–103.

45 See, most recently, Crane, *Mercator*, chap. 15.

46 See, broadly, Harley, *The New Nature of Maps*, esp. chaps. 1–3.

47 On the *Itinerarium*, see Klaus Schmidt-Ott, 'The *Itinerarium per nonnullas Galliae Belgicae partes* by Abraham Ortelius and Johannes Vivianus,' in van den Broecke et al., eds, *Abraham Ortelius and the First Atlas*, 363–77.

48 Calvin, *Institutes of the Christian Religion*, vol. 2, bk. 4, chap. 3.

chapter eleven

Spaces of Dreaming: Self-Constitution in Early Modern Dream Narratives

ANDREAS BÄHR

Battista Moduco and Paolo Gasparutto were charged with heresy and brought to trial by the Holy Inquisition in March 1575, in Cividale, Friuli. They were accused of being *benandanti*, that is, 'good vagabonds,' who claimed to be leaving their bodies at night in order to fight their adversaries, the *stregoni* or *malandanti*. 'I am benandante,' Moduco had the inquisitor put on record, 'because I go with the others to fight four times a year, that is during the Ember Days, at night; I go invisibly in spirit and the body remains behind; we go forth in the service of Christ, and the witches of the devil; we fight each other, we with bundles of fennel and they with sorghum stalks. And if we are the victors, that year there is abundance, but if we lose there is famine.'[1] Both Moduco and Gasparutto asserted that this fight took place in their dreams. When travelling at night Moduco did as he was told by a 'certain invisible thing' in his dream. Gasparutto was convinced that he had been led by an 'angel'; to Moduco, however, after he had come to think that Gasparutto's idea was heretical, the 'thing' seemed to have the 'form of a man.' Moduco is reported as having added: 'I thought I was asleep but I was not, and it seemed to me that he was from Trivignano . . . I thought I heard him say "You must come with me" . . . and so I told him that if I had to go, I would, but that I did not want to depart from God; and since he said this was God's work, I went at age twenty-two, or twenty-three.'[2]

Moduco and Gasparutto claimed that they were dreaming when they moved against the *malandanti*, yet at the same time, they stressed that their excursions were real. These fights were in their dreams but they were not just dream battles. Moduco was sleeping, and, at the same time, he was not: his body was sleeping, and his spirit was awake. While their bodies were left behind, the *benandanti*'s souls met the others in order to carry on an imaginary fight that was more than fantasy. It was this idea of the spirit actually departing the body that the theologians of the Inquisition attacked most of all. In the course of the trial, they induced the accused to confess that this notion was heretical. Moduco again: 'Ever since I heard from that friend of mine who is in prison that an angel appeared to him, I have come to think that this is a diabolical thing, because our Lord God does not send angels to lead spirits out of bodies, but only to provide them with good inspiration.'[3] With that, the Inquisition succeeded in removing the opposition of ben*andanti* and mal*andanti*, of good and evil, which was fundamental for the *benandanti*'s voyages. In the end, Moduco and Gasparutto were convinced that it was the devil himself who had tempted them to go out – the very devil against whom they had believed they were fighting at night. The Inquisition *patres* had attained their goal: they had fit the heretofore unfamiliar phenomenon of the *benandanti* into the demonology of the Witches' Sabbath.[4]

Further details can be found in Carlo Ginzburg's book *Night Battles.* In this chapter, I will focus on the spatial structure of the dreams depicted here. In the *benandanti*'s dreams, the soul was leaving the body, it was transgressing its limit; it was leaving the house in which the body was sleeping, in order to enter an imaginary place – the field where it met the others. The spatiality of this dream, however, is closely related to its temporal structure. Gasparutto's and Moduco's dreams were divinatory ones: at their dream destinations, their souls saw the future of their village communities, and, at the same time, they saw that they themselves determined its fate. This set of beliefs must not be interpreted as a mere 'relic' of pagan magic; the *benandanti* actually professed a Christian faith. What is more, aspects of their beliefs were shared by the theologians who accused them of heresy. The inquisitors were bothered by the idea of a human spirit going *out,* but they believed in a divine spirit going *in.* That is, they did not deny that there were spirits able to move through space and cross the limits of the body. Against this background many Christians believed that God might reveal the future by means of divinatory dreams. Such dreams were discussed in theological and 'scientific' treatises, which tried to differentiate them from natural and demonic ones.[5] Furthermore, with the help of published dream books people could decipher their nocturnal dream images after waking up in the morning, and, what is most interesting, authors of numerous life narratives and autobiographies could remember their lives as the fulfilment of a divinatory dream imagination.

In what follows, I will attempt to show that divinatory dreaming presupposes specific historical concepts, not only of time, but also of space and place. Divinatory dreams seem to have been constitutive of many autobiographies and self-narratives in the early modern era. Here I shall analyse the historical ideas of space that underlie the ideas of self expressed in these texts. I will explore not only the space of the self (and borders, boundaries, and limits), but also the concept 'space' itself, as it was then understood. In so doing, I show that the specific spatiality of early modern processes of self-constitution becomes particularly manifest in instances when people believed they were dreaming about their own future.

This question of the space–self relationship has two different aspects: the relationship between space and person on the one hand, and that between space and dream on the other. In modern times, psychoanalysts usually hold dreams to be the fulfilment of unconscious desires that cannot be articulated consciously and fulfilled in reality.[6] The psychoanalytical interpretation of dreams is epistemologically associated with a conceptualization of the 'person' as an individual self, psycho-physically closed. The modern self is usually formed and constituted as an inner space which is strongly and qualitatively separated from its outer world. In early modern times, however, a separation of this kind cannot be found.[7] The things, bodies, and souls of this world appeared to be connected by spiritual beings. Against this background the dream imagination could be considered a mediator between microcosm and macrocosm able to reveal the future to the dreamer. The imaginary transgression of limits, however, was based on the idea of a divine and cosmic space which itself seemed to have material effects in the world. Kant and Einstein had not yet been born.

It was on condition of this effectiveness that people were able not only to dream their own future but also to bring about this future by dreaming it, and that meant being able to enter this future as a place in space. This capacity attributed to space became particularly relevant when the dreamers' imaginations were affected by fear; in other words, when dreamers were experiencing that affect held to be the necessary precondition for the salvation of souls. All this has to be explained in detail.

Many early modern definitions of space and place are based on the Aristotelian metaphor of the container.[8] This metaphor was used to describe the world as a whole filled with objects. One of them was a person's body, which itself was conceived as the container or the house of the soul. This imagery separated the soul from the body that housed it and allowed it to enter and leave its home. This 'body' was bounded or limited quite differently from its late eighteenth-century successor. As Claudia Benthien has pointed out, the human skin was presumed to be a permeable membrane with various elements flowing in and out: fluids and humours, emanations of a living nature, good and evil spirits, and divine messages.[9] The skin was held to be an interface between microcosm and macrocosm, which were closely and materially connected. Only when the skin became an 'organ' during the eighteenth century can we find a strong epistemological dichotomy between an internal and an external self, a conceptualization of the person as an individual psycho-physical system, a 'notion of self being *inside* a fleshy container.'[10]

It was on condition of the permeability of the skin that the early modern imagination attained its specific power. By linking body and soul, the imagination itself seemed to be able to bring about what it was imagining. This idea can be found not only in natural and demonic magic, but also, and in particular, in the debate about the origins of the plague: many people thought that timorously imagining the plague might cause the malady.[11] Divinatory dreaming seemed to be one sort of such imagination. In 1714, the Lutheran preacher Johann Christoph Männling wrote in his dream book: 'Terror and impression suck into the mind more deeply than oil into cloth. As the famous physician Olaus Borrichius tells us, there was a woman who fell ill whenever she had seen him in her dreams.'[12] We can also read about the English knight Rutger of Oxstey:

> Once upon a time, after going to bed in the best of health, [Rutger] dreamt that he was knocked down by, and fought with, a naked and enraged plague sufferer. Finally, this man, sitting on Rutger's body, spat his plague into the dreamer's face. Woken up and filled with great horror, the knight was convinced that he would soon die from the plague. This idea was engraved in his mind so deeply that he was unable to drive it out of his memory. Three days later, he indeed contracted the plague, suffering from great anxiety and high temperature, and no medicine could help him. After four days he died.[13]

This dream imagination proved to be not only an image but also a cause of the event it indicated. How can this be explained? In early modern cosmology and semiology, the things and occurrences of the world were connected by relations of analogy and similarity. These relations were indicated by signs which were more than only signs: they seemed to be things themselves, and as such they brought about the things they signified.[14] Thus, the images of the divinatory dream, which appeared to be similar to the things and events they stood for, indicated a sympathetic and causal relation between themselves and the future they represented.

As these relations were indicated by *similarities* (not identities), they could not be recognized with absolute certainty. Since the divinatory dream, though revealing the future, symbolically encoded the events it prophesied, only very few of its signs could be read without any doubt. This is why it was quite difficult to find out both what a dream was foretelling and whether it was divinatory at all. The two cases quoted above obviously were clear: Rutger of Oxstey dreamt that he was contracting the plague by dreaming its causes, and Borrichius's patient foresaw her illness by seeing the man who had previously healed her when she was ill. In other instances, however, there were errors and misunderstandings, occasionally with fatal consequences. In order to be certain of the meaning of their dreams, people had to wait to see how things would turn out. Männling tells us that in Florence

> there was a man dreaming that he was being deadly injured by a stone lion which was standing in the entrance of a church with his jaws wide open. When going to church in the morning, the good fellow saw the statue of the animal, laughed at his dream, told his friends about it, and put his hand into the mouth of the lion, saying to it: 'Bite me, you evil enemy, and strangle me, if you can.' Hardly had he said this when he was stung by a scorpion which was hiding in the jaws of the lion, and thus he had to die.[15]

The Florentine had been mistaken about the type of similarity: it became evident that the stone lion had not indicated a living animal but a deadly attack close to it.[16]

Regardless of these constitutive uncertainties and limits of interpretation, people could dream the future only on condition that their dream images appeared to be clear. This feature is important with regard to the spatiality of dream and dreaming. The 'internal' events represented in divinatory dreams took place within the same spatial structures as the 'external' realities of the day, even if they were partly symbolically encoded. As we can read in Männling's book, one Georg von Schleinitz dreamt that he was a bear dying in a forest fire, although virgins rushed to extinguish it. Nobody was able to explain this dream until the dreamer really died: not long before von Schleinitz's wedding day, a nobleman, dressed up like a bear, caused a fire at a Shrovetide dance; von Schleinitz's bride threw herself at him in order to protect her groom, but she did not succeed.[17] In contrast to many modern dream narratives, the space–time relation remained undisturbed here; it corresponded to the logic of daytime perception.[18] The event which was dreamt might bring about what it represented because both unfolded within a unified space, that is, because in terms of spatiality the inner space of the person and its outer world did not differ from each other.

From dream images like these, we can detect both the concepts of space at the base of the dream imagination and the related category of time. The events revealed in divinatory dreams were future events. Divinely inspired people were able to see them because these events appeared to be part of all-embracing Providence: they had already taken place. The time of Providence was not yet considered to be open towards the future, as it would be in the eighteenth century, but to be closed in divine eternity. Correspondingly, the divine cosmos, which contained events happening in time, was presumed to be closed in a spatial sense. Within this framework, the future event had its place in a cosmic space: it was already present.[19] This place was not simply a metaphor, since it was based on concepts of space very different from ours. And this space was not the mere category of perception of modernity, but rather a container which itself had material effects, irrespective of the fact that it might be conceptualized as either finite or infinite, filled or empty, independent of material things or part of them.[20] People who were dreaming the future were entering its place in a timeless space, and, in so doing, they caused – that is, they realized – the things they saw and experienced in their imagination.

How can this conceptual framework be demonstrated on the basis of autobiographical texts? It was not until the Renaissance and the Reformation that Christian dreams began to be narrated first and foremost as stories of the dreaming person's life on earth.[21] Despite references to ancient texts and traditions, innovations did take place. First of all, the dream book itself changed. Dream books in the tradition of Artemidorus Daldianus, a late antiquity author, were reference books, composed of nothing but general meanings and interpretations of separate dream images. In 1562, however, the Italian humanist and physician Jerome Cardan published such a book which additionally contained a chapter on his own dreams.[22] Even though these 'personal' images were common historical-cultural dream symbols, they could not be interpreted without the dreamer's experiences of his own individual biography. Only in remembering his own life was Cardan able to recognize whether his dreams in the past had predicted the events of his future. And that means that this chapter of Cardan's dream book offered not just an interpretation of its readers' nocturnal images, but a new model to assist them in making their own interpretations.

In order to search for meaning, people had to record not only their lives but also their dreams; already in late antiquity, Synesius of Cyrene had recommended keeping a 'night book.'[23] Many authors of autobiographical texts took this advice, looking back and remembering their lives as the fulfilment of past divinatory dreams. Writing their lives now required understanding the meaning of their past dreams. In this way, dream narratives came to have an important place in autobiographical writing. Life and dream explained and interpreted one another. In order to illustrate this I will give two particularly instructive examples of early modern life writing: Jerome Cardan's sixteenth-century *De vita propria* (Book of My Life), and Augustin Güntzer's mid-seventeenth-century *Kleines Biechlin von meinem gantzen Leben* (Little Book about My Whole Life).[24] These texts offer a key to numerous other dream records that can be found in early modern self-narratives.[25]

One night Cardan dreamed that his professional honour as a physician was in serious danger.[26] In retrospect, however, he realized that the dream had protected him from losing this honour. In his nocturnal imagination, Cardan found himself threatened by a huge snake, which was about to swallow him. Awakened with great fear and horror, Cardan knew that his dream was predicting a mortal danger. What the danger was, however, it did not reveal; this had to be proved by the future, and the future was coming soon. Next day, Cardan declared himself willing to attend to Count Camillo Borromeo's son, who had fallen ill from an unknown fever. As he tells us, he should have known that it would have been better to refuse the count's request, for, as he realized afterwards, in their coat of arms, which was hung up everywhere, the Borromei bore the face of a snake. This had been the first sign, but Cardan had failed to notice it. Thus, he started attending an illness the symptoms of which he was unable to interpret; only later did he learn from Galen's *De praesagitione ex pulsibus* that the young Borromeo's illness could not be cured.[27] Since Cardan was unsure about the right therapy, he prescribed a stronger medicine in order to be on the safe side. However, having sent out a servant to the chemist's shop, Cardan remembered his nocturnal dream, and intuitively realized that he had made a dangerous decision. Thus, he abandoned those plans and chose a milder cure instead. In so doing he elected an intervention that could not save the young patient from dying but that did avert his own social death: had he actually administered the much stronger medicine, his colleagues in Milan, as unsure as he was about the diagnosis in this case, might have held him responsible for the boy's death. The warning dream had served its purpose. When the boy died, the colleagues thought this was not *because of* but *in spite of* Cardan's medication, which was the one they too would have chosen and had actually prescribed after Cardan left the scene. Cardan noted that the warning of the snake occurring in his dream not only had prevented permanent loss of his honour as a physician, but also had served as a basis and starting point for his scientific oeuvre and his later medical successes, motivating him to remember and write down this lucky development. It was not until Cardan looked back on the events of his life that he was able to understand their meaning and to recognize the relevance of his dreaming for his personal fate. As witnessed by this narrative, when authors constructed their own lives, dreams obtained their meanings from the memory of the life they predicted, and, conversely, that life achieved its biographical coherence from the power of divinatory dreaming.[28]

When Cardan was writing about dreaming his own life, the pre-modern providential concept of time and related notion of space were at work. He wrote about himself:

> It seemed to me that my naked soul was in the Heaven of the Moon, liberated from my body and solitary, when, as I seemed to be lamenting on account of my state, I heard the voice of my father speaking to me: 'I have been appointed guardian to you by God; all these spaces are filled with spirits, but you see them not, even as I am invisible to you, nor is it lawful for you to address them. You will remain in this Heaven seven thousand years, and the same number in star after star until you reach the eighth; after the eighth you will come into the Kingdom of God.' Of this dream I have made the following interpretation: the soul of my father is my tutelary spirit; what more loving or more gracious interpretation could there be? The Moon signified grammar; Mercury, geometry and arithmetic; Venus, music, the art of divination, and poesy; the Sun, the moral life, and Jupiter, the natural. Mars represented medicine, and Saturn, agriculture, knowledge of plants and of the remaining simple arts. The eighth orb stood for the final harvest of all understanding, for natural science and various studies. And after these things I shall rest serenely with my Prince, the Lord. This dream was, as it were, set forth – even though I did not notice it at the time – in the seven divisions of the *Problemata*, for which the time of completion for publication was at hand.[29]

As Cardan tells us, he dreamt this around 1534, more than four decades before he died. Though in the end this dream promised the wise man's reward in the next world (alluding to Cicero's *Somnium Scipionis* and Dante's *Divina commedia*), it was not a dream about his afterlife. Rather it was a dream about what would happen to him in his further life as a scholar. The whereabouts of his soul was not heaven or hell but a celestial sphere, a macrocosmic 'space.' Cardan dreamed his future on earth, and he did it in Neoplatonic terms: he dreamed its celestial place, and his soul actually entered this place by dreaming it. Cardan imagined himself as becoming wholly soul, by imagining the (cosmic) steps and stages of his life. This reflects the contemporary idea that every field of knowledge and each phase of the scholar's life and work is influenced by the stars. Step by step, life ascended the cosmic ladder until it reached divine perfection and redemption.

This dream proves to be particular, since Cardan was dreaming not only the future of his life but also the personal divine spirit who was the protector of this future. Whenever he had to make decisions, whenever he had to act to defy the arbitrariness of fate, this tutelary spirit was at his side, warning him and directing his vision towards things, events, and developments he was otherwise unable to see, and it did so first and foremost by means of divinatory dreams.[30] That spirit who protected Cardan by revealing the future to the dreamer also revealed itself in a dream as being protective. Thus, in a sense, in this case, Cardan was dreaming about his own divinatory dreaming. Compared to so many other instances, the pictures of this dream are relatively abstract: they do not tell a real daytime story taking place in time and space; rather, they describe the preconditions for divinatory dreams, which are represented as stories from daily life.

By describing his own life as the fulfilment of divinatory dreams, Cardan located himself in a closed cosmic space constructed of concentric spheres. The spheres and indeed all the elements of this space were connected by sympathetic relations of cause and effect, but such relations could only be assumed because this closed space itself was held to be able to have effects on matter. It was on condition of this effectiveness that the soul in its dreams was able to see the truth. When one was dreaming future events, his or her soul was physically touching the divine sphere, crossing the limits of the body, either by leaving it or by astral influence and the inspiration of a divine spirit (and that means that both directions of movement proved to be just two sides of the same coin).[31] The materiality of space, therefore, was the precondition both of divinatory dreaming and of the power of such dreams to realize what they were imagining.

From this we can conclude that religious-theological, magical, and 'scientific' interpretations of dreaming were not to be separated from each other, at least in the terms of then commonly accepted epistemology. On the one hand, Cardan advocated Neoplatonic ideas, saying that the wandering soul not only saw what happened at remote places but also brought about there what it was seeing – simply by seeing it.[32] On the other hand, Cardan always tried to interpret divinely inspired dreaming as a 'natural' process, basing his interpretation on an Aristotelian concept of space and referring to a human capability of having premonitions which had more to do with medical diagnosis and prognosis than with divine inspiration.[33] Both approaches have more in common than seems to be the case at first sight. Those who dreamed an Aristotelian dream did not look immediately into the future but read the signs of nature: they 'felt' 'natural' causes of future effects to be present; this nature, however, was God's creation.[34] God made people dream the future by enabling the (virtuous) soul to perceive and feel the signs He was sending.[35] When combining Plato with Aristotle, Cardan did not contradict himself; it becomes clear, rather, that both interpretations had the same epistemological roots.

The epistemology underlying acceptance of divinatory dreaming was common not only among different philosophical traditions but also among different Christian denominations. This can be demonstrated by comparing the text of a professed Catholic, Cardan, with autobiographical texts written by Protestant authors. Protestant critics of traditional practices in dream interpretation did not deny that it was possible to have divinatory dreams; first and foremost they stressed the practical difficulties in recognizing whether a dream had to be considered as divine truth or diabolical deception.[36] In addition, they interpreted dreams from God as reminders to reflect on their own sinful lives and as warnings to do penance. These positions are manifest not only in theological discussion (Luther, Melanchthon, Conrad Dieterich, and Männling may be cited here) but also, in particular, in autobiographies like Calvinist tradesman Güntzer's *Kleines Biechlin von meinem gantzen Leben*.[37]

Güntzer, like Cardan, dreamt his own life. In 1606, when he was approximately ten years old, the devil appeared in one of his dreams: the family was sitting at the lunch table when a 'dreadful black man' rang the door bell and demanded that Güntzer come out and fight. He refused, but the unwelcome guest did not take no for an answer; hence, the young boy took up a stick and courageously beat his adversary. Angels were at his side, and therefore he was victorious. Looking back on his life as he wrote his autobiography, Güntzer saw that this dream had come true: his whole life had turned out to be a constant fight with evil powers, the Christian soldier's struggle against his enemies in the world and within himself.[38] This battle, however, he was unable to win, for even though he defeated his enemies in the world, he could not vanquish his own sin. But this plight was no cause for despair: if he was aware of his impotence before sin, and if he accepted that God would be merciful to those who knew they needed His grace, then he had always and already won.[39] God proved his grace by sending fearful dreams of the devil. By means of the imaginary fight, He promised future victory to the good. Güntzer's dream had threatened him with a lifelong and terrifying struggle against Satan and had also promised him eventual triumph.

Though it presented the dreamer with an image of the devil, this dream, related as a remembered future in Güntzer's autobiography, was not a diabolical one, but a divine reminder and providential warning, constitutive of his life. This is what Güntzer and Cardan had in common. Moreover, regardless of many differences, Güntzer's story had much in common with the *benandanti* narrative related at the beginning of this essay: the imaginary fight between good and evil, the specific spatiality of dream images, and its connection with time. Though Güntzer was not dreaming the fate of the village community but rather his own development, he, too, left his home: he saw himself going outside for the fight with the waiting devil. Just like the *benandanti*, Güntzer stepped outside from within; he proceeded to that dangerous place where the battle was going to be held, where it was to be decided which future was going to come. In leaving his shelter to fight with the 'dreadful black man,' Güntzer was not only stepping out of his home but also envisioning and beginning a new life.[40]

Güntzer's 'night battle' can be considered as a narrative of its author's struggle to protect himself and secure his spiritual welfare. Against this background, in the relationship between self-constitution, divinatory dream, and historical concepts of space, the *terrifying* imagination appears to be crucial. We can see this both in Güntzer and in Cardan. In order to draw a conclusion I am going to explain this aspect in detail.

The power of imagination, which I have been discussing above, became particularly relevant when it was affected by fear. Like imagining and dreaming, fearing also entailed looking into the future, touching the future, and bringing it about by touching it. However, since from a religious perspective fear was an affect indicating the person's estrangement from God, the presence of fear in a dream proved that the terrifying future being imagined was the one that divine reprisal and revenge would actually bring to pass. It was God, then, who was acting here, through and by means of space. Paracelsus's writings provide one of the best examples of this sort of interpretative framework. According to him, people afraid of the plague obviously had no fear of God; they did not trust in his power. This is why their fear was able to cause the plague they feared. God punished the fearful by inflicting on them the very thing they most feared – as a punishment for fearing.[41] Therefore fear itself often appeared to be the most terrifying of experiences. 'What I am mostly afraid of,' Michel de Montaigne wrote in his *Essais*, 'is fear. Its violence exceeds any other harm.'[42]

Against this background, it becomes clear why fear also seemed to be the most relevant affect for processes of self-constitution in the early modern era. Fear was viewed as a sort of violence that could have serious consequences: the disintegration and the loss of self, which, in some instances, could even lead to insanity. Precisely because of its violent character, however, fear, at the same time, was considered as the precondition of salvation. Fear and fearlessness could not be separated but were constituent of each other. Thus, talking about fearlessness meant talking about fear, and vice versa. If one wanted to describe oneself as fearlessly fearing God, then one had to turn away from the fear that came from sin, the others' and one's own, and admit that one feared God while fearlessly trusting in his mercy. In the face of that, people usually described their own fear as being currently absent: those who talked about their anxieties in the past introduced themselves as being 'converted' in the present, into fearless and God-fearing believers. Anyone able to talk about the sin of fear and the fear of sin already seemed to have defeated and overcome both. Against this background, in terms of both theology and textuality, in early modern self-descriptions the presence of fear is the precondition for its being overcome. This is no tautology: God sent fear to men in order to free them from fear; and authors of life-narratives depicted their fear in order to announce what the Lord had done in them. In that respect, in writing about their fearlessness, the authors of these texts in the first place created the fear from which, as they tell us, they were released.[43]

The constituent opposition of fear and fearlessness was conceptualized also in spatial categories. God-fearing people knew that fear was born from earthly crampedness or confinement and the depth of sin and, at the same time, that divine grace led to the vastness and height of heaven; they knew that the gates of sin and fear were opened to those who were aware that this anxious and sinful life was a 'dungeon' (*Kerker*). To the influential baroque poet Andreas Gryphius, for example, the world seemed to be a 'house of anxiety' (*Angsthaus*) and a 'hall of torture' (*Folter-Sal*); consequently, 'anxiety' mostly meant to him the 'anxiety of the world' (*Angst der Welt*): confinement to a frail earthly existence.[44] Students of this period will find a host of concepts in which anxiety and space are closely associated. These concepts demonstrate that anxiety itself seemed to be not an emotional but rather a spatial phenomenon. People who were suffering from fear felt physically oppressed and strained; by means of the Latin *angor* and *anxius* this affect found its etymological way into the German *Angst* (meaning 'narrowness') and the English words *anxiety* and *anxious.*

Given all these facts, we can see that when describing their own fearsome dreams, early modern authors located themselves neither in a closed inwardness of individual subjectivity nor in an interiority of feelings, but in a cosmic space of divine Providence, which made fear achieve what was terrifying, and fearlessness drive it out. Both Cardan and Güntzer dreamed their fearful life to come, and in doing so, they dreamed the defeat of their fear as well. Examples like this, closely connecting fear and dream imagination, can demonstrate in a special way that the early modern authors writing about themselves and their anxieties must not be conceptualized and characterized according to the modern subject and 'inner self' as it is usually done in academic literature.[45]

NOTES

This essay is a modified and extended version of Andreas Bähr, 'Träumen von sich: Imaginative Selbstverortung und der Raum der "Person" in Traumerzählungen der europäischen Frühen Neuzeit,' in Andreas Bähr, Peter Burschel, Gabriele Jancke, eds, *Räume des Selbst: Selbstzeugnisforschung transkulturell,* Selbstzeugnisse der Neuzeit 19 (Cologne, Weimar, Vienna, 2007), 273–87. Many thanks to Peter Carrier (Braunschweig, Berlin), Marie-Luise Baehr (Washington, DC), the editors, and Ellen Wilson (Los Angeles), for comments and corrections.

1 Quoted from the transcript of the trial against Paolo Gasparutto and Battista Moduco, printed as the appendix in Carlo Ginzburg, *The Night Battles: Witchcraft and Agrarian Cults in the Sixteenth and Seventeenth Centuries,* trans. John and Anne Tedeschi (Baltimore, 1992), 153.

2 Ginzburg, *Night Battles*, 160; see also 157.

3 Ibid., 160. On early modern concepts of spirit and soul, see Michaela Boenke, *Körper, Spiritus, Geist: Psychologie vor Descartes*, Humanistische Bibliothek: Texte und Abhandlungen, 1st ser. 57 (Munich, 2005).

4 In doing so, however, the *patres* initially helped the *benandanti*'s ideas spread all through Friuli; see Ginzburg, *Night Battles*, 94–7. Only during the seventeenth century did the Inquisition succeed in suppressing to a large extent the *benandanti*'s knowledge and memory; ibid., 99–145.

5 See, for example, Stuart Clark, *Vanities of the Eye: Vision in Early Modern European Culture* (Oxford, 2007), 300–28.

6 See Sigmund Freud, *The Interpretation of Dreams* [1900], Standard Edition of the Complete Psychological Works of Sigmund Freud 4/5 (London, 2001).

7 Cf. Michel Foucault, *The Order of Things: An Archaeology of the Human Sciences* ([Paris, 1966] London and New York, 2002). Cf. also Clifford Geertz, '"From the Native's Point of View": On the Nature of Anthropological Understanding,' in Janet L. Dolgin, David S. Kemnitzer, David Murray Schneider, eds, *Symbolic Anthropology: A Reader in the Study of Symbols and Meanings* (New York, 1977), 483; Ralf Konersmann, *Kulturelle Tatsachen* (Frankfurt am Main, 2006), 188.

8 See Aristotle, *The Physics*, trans. Philip H. Wicksteed and Francis M. Cornford, Aristotle in Twenty-three Volumes 4/5 (Cambridge, MA, and London, 1980), §§ 209b–12a.

9 Claudia Benthien, *Haut. Literaturgeschichte – Körperbilder – Grenzdiskurse* (Reinbek b. Hamburg, 1999).

10 Mike Crang and Nigel Thrift, 'Introduction,' in *Thinking Space*, Critical Geographies 9 (London and New York, 2000), 7; my italics.

11 Cf. esp. Johann Werfring, *Der Ursprung der Pestilenz: Zur Ätiologie der Pest im loimographischen Diskurs der frühen Neuzeit*, 2nd ed., Medizin, Kultur und Gesellschaft 2 (Vienna, 1999), 174–222. For a semantic analysis see Andreas Bähr, 'Vom Nutzen der Paradoxie für die Kulturhistorie: Furchtlose Furcht in frühneuzeitlichen Selbstbeschreibungen,' in Franz X. Eder, ed., *Historische Diskursanalysen: Genealogie, Theorie, Anwendungen* (Wiesbaden, 2006), 305–21. Since in the early modern era, illness could always be regarded as a means of divine power and a scourge of God, this is also relevant for historical research on violence; see Andreas Bähr, 'Die Semantik der Ungarischen Krankheit: Imaginationen von Gewalt als Krankheitsursache zwischen Reformation und Aufklärung,' in Claudia Ulbrich, Claudia Jarzebowski, and Michaela Hohkamp, eds, *Gewalt in der Frühen Neuzeit: Beiträge zur 5. Tagung der Arbeitsgemeinschaft Frühe Neuzeit im VHD*, Historische Forschungen 81 (Berlin, 2005), 359–73.

12 Johann Christoph Männling, *Außerlesenster Curiositaeten Merck=wuerdiger Traum=Tempel* . . . (Frankfurt and Leipzig, 1714), 204; my translation. German: 'In kein Tuch zieht das Oehl so tieff ein, als das Schrecken und Impression in das Gemüthe. Der berühmte Medicus, Olaus Borrichius, erzehlt von einer Frau, so offt ihr von ihm geträumt, ware sie allemahl kranck worden.'

13 Ibid., 345–6. Männling cites from Ysbrand van Diemerbroeck, 'Tractatus de peste, In quatuor libros distinctus; truculentissimi morbi historiam ratione et experientia confirmatam exhibens,' in *Opera omnia, anatomica et medica* (Utrecht, 1685), 2:233. The quotation is my translation of Diemerbroeck's text.

14 Cf. Foucault, *The Order of Things*, 19–38.

15 Männling, *Traum=Tempel*, 53.

16 For the four types of similarity (*convenientia, aemulatio,* analogy, and sympathy) cf. Foucault, *The Order of Things*, 28.

17 Männling, *Traum=Tempel*, 295–7.

18 Cf. esp. the literary dream narratives in the work of Franz Kafka; cf. Peter André Alt, *Der Schlaf der Vernunft: Literatur und Traum in der Kulturgeschichte der Neuzeit* (Munich, 2002), 350–64.

19 See Lucian Hölscher, *Die Entdeckung der Zukunft* (Frankfurt am Main, 1999), 35–9.

20 For the physical effectiveness of space and place see Ernst Cassirer, *The Individual and the Cosmos in Renaissance Philosophy* [1927], trans. and intro. Mario Domandi (New York and Evanston, IL, 1963), 117; Wolfgang Breidert, 'Raum II: Mittelalter bis zum Beginn des 18. Jh.,' in *Historisches Wörterbuch der Philosophie* vol. 8, col. 85. For the debates on vacuum and the infinity of space see Max Jammer, *Das Problem des Raumes: Die Entwicklung der Raumtheorien* (Darmstadt, 1960); Alexandre Koyré, *From the Closed World to the Infinite Universe,* Publications of the Institute of the History of Medicine, Johns Hopkins University, 3rd ser., Hideyo Noguchi Lectures 7 (Baltimore, 1957); Stephan Günzel, 'Introduction to Part I,' in Stephan Günzel and Jörg Dünne, eds, *Raumtheorie: Grundlagentexte aus Philosophie und Kulturwissenschaften* (Frankfurt am Main, 2006), 19–43, esp. 19–33.

21 In the Middle Ages, theologians considered dreams to be divinatory only when they appeared as part of conversion processes or when they beheld the space of the hereafter. For medieval dream narratives see esp. Steven F. Kruger, *Dreaming in the Middle Ages,* Cambridge Studies in Medieval Literature 14 (Cambridge, 1992); Annette Gerok-Reiter and Christine Walde, eds, *Vision in der Vormoderne: Traditionen, Diskussionen, Perspektiven* (Berlin, 2012). Jacques Le Goff argues in terms of psychoanalysis:

Le Goff, *Time, Work and Culture in the Middle Ages* (Chicago and London, 1995), chap. 7, and *The Medieval Imagination* (Chicago and London, 1988), chap. 5.

22 [Artemidor von Daldis,] *Des Griechischen Philosophen Artemidori Grosses und vollkommenes Traum=Buch, In dem der Ursprung, Unterschied und die Bedeutung allerhand Träume, die einem im Schlafe vorkommen können, aus natürlichen Ursachen hergeleitet wird, Nebst einer Erinnerung Philipp Melanchthons vom Unterschied der Träume und angehängtem Berichte, was von Träumen zu halten sey* [1540, trans. into German by Walter Hermann Ryff]. Neue verbesserte und mit einem vollständigem Register und einer Astronomischen Traum= Tafel vermehrte Auflage (Leipzig, 1753; repr. Darmstadt, 1969), hereafter cited as Artemidor, *Traum=Buch*; Jerome Cardan, 'Synesiorum Somniorum, omnis generis insomnia explicantes, Libri IV' [1562], in *Opera omnia: The 1663 Lvgdvni-Edition*, intro. August Buck (New York and London, 1967), 5:715–27; cited hereafter as Cardan, 'Synesiorum somniorum.'

23 Wolfram Lang, *Das Traumbuch des Synesius von Kyrene: Uebersetzung und Analyse der philosophischen Grundlagen*, Heidelberger Abhandlungen zur Philosophie und ihrer Geschichte 10 (Tübingen, 1926), § 153A. The recommendation was taken by Cardan, 'Synesiorum somniorum,' 601–3.

24 Jerome Cardan, *The Book of My Life (De Vita Propria Liber)*, trans. Jean Stoner (New York, 1962), 135–7. The best accessible edition of the Latin original is Cardan, 'De propria vita, liber,' in *Opera omnia*, vol. 1. Augustin Güntzer, *Kleines Biechlin von meinem gantzen Leben: Die Autobiographie eines Elsässer Kannengießers aus dem 17. Jahrhundert*, ed. Fabian Brändle and Dominik Sieber, Selbstzeugnisse der Neuzeit 8 (Cologne, Weimar, and Vienna, 2002).

25 Esp. 'Paul Winkler's Selbstbiographie,' ed. August Kahlert, *Zeitschrift für Geschichte und Alterthum Schlesiens* 3 (1860), 92–3; 'Aufzeichnungen des Pfarrers Plebanus von Miehlen aus den Jahren 1636/37,' ed. Ferdinand Heymach, *Nassauische Annalen* 38 (1908), 269, 271, 282–5; Johann Valentin Andreae, *Selbstbiographie*, in *Selbstbiographien berühmter Männer*, ed. David Christoph Seybold (Winterthur, 1799), 2:21–2; August Hermann Francke, 'Lebensnachrichten über A. H. Francke, von ihm selbst zusammengestellt,' in Gustav Kramer, ed., *Beiträge zur Geschichte August Hermann Francke's, enthaltend den Briefwechsel Francke's und Spener's* (Halle/Saale, 1861), 77–9. Furthermore, see the Pietistic dream narratives in Hans Ludwig Nehrlich, *Erlebnisse eines frommen Handwerkers im späten 17. Jahrhundert*, ed. Rainer Lächele, Hallesche Quellenpublikationen und Repertorien 1 (Tübingen, 1997), 28, 32–3, 60–1; Johann Henrich Reitz, ed., *Historie Der Wiedergebohrnen: Vollständige Ausgabe der Erstdrucke aller sieben Teile der pietistischen Sammelbiographie (1698–1745) mit einem werkgeschichtlichen Anhang der Varianten*

und Ergänzungen aus den späteren Auflagen, ed. Hans-Jürgen Schrader, 4 vols. (Tübingen 1984), esp. vol. 1, pt. 1, p. 144; vol. 1, pt. 2, p. 229; vol. 1, pt. 3, pp. 53–9, 171ff.; Johanna Eleonora Petersen, *Leben, von ihr selbst mit eigener Hand aufgesetzet: Autobiographie* [1718], ed. Prisca Guglielmetti, Kleine Texte des Pietismus 8 (Leipzig, 2003), §§ 15, 24, 33–6, and 38. For English self-narratives cf. Kaspar von Greyerz, *Vorsehungsglaube und Kosmologie: Studien zu englischen Selbstzeugnissen des 17. Jahrhunderts*, Publications of the German Historical Institute London 25 (Göttingen and Zurich, 1990), 131–6.

26 Cardan, *My Life*, 135–7. This dream narrative can be found also in Cardan's 'Synesiorum somniorum,' 723–5. For Cardan's autobiographical writing cf. also Anthony Grafton, *Cardano's Cosmos: The Worlds and Works of a Renaissance Astrologer* (Cambridge, MA, and London, 1999), 178–98.

27 Claudius Galenus, 'De praesagitione ex pulsibus,' in *Opera omnia*, ed. C.G. Kühn (Leipzig, 1825; repr. Hildesheim, 1965), 9:205–430; Galenus, 'Synopsis librorum de pulsibus,' ibid., 9:543–6.

28 For further details see Andreas Bähr, 'Furcht, divinatorischer Traum und autobiographisches Schreiben in der Frühen Neuzeit,' *Zeitschrift für Historische Forschung* 34, 1 (2007), 1–32.

29 Cardan, *My Life*, 158–9.

30 Cf. the chapter on the tutelary spirit and guardian angel, ibid., 240–7.

31 Cf. Cardan, 'Synesiorum somniorum,' 598–9, and *My Life*, 241–3.

32 Cf. Theophrastus von Hohenheim, called Paracelsus, 'Practica in scientiam divinationis,' in *Sämtliche Werke*, ed. Karl Sudhoff, sect. 1: *Medizinische, naturwissenschaftliche und philosophische Schriften*, 14 vols. (Munich, 1922–33), 12:490–1, and 'De virtute imaginativa fragmentum,' ibid., 14:315. For critical discussions cf. the article 'Einbildungs = Kraft,' in Johann Georg Walch, *Philosophisches Lexicon*, 2nd ed. (Leipzig, 1740), 688, and the article 'Einbildungs = Krafft,' in Johann Heinrich Zedler, ed., *Großes vollständiges Universal Lexicon Aller Wissenschafften und Künste* (Halle, Leipzig, 1732–54; repr. Graz, 1993–9), vol. 8, col. 535, referring e.g. to Thomas Fienus, *De viribus imaginationis*, 2nd ed. (Leiden, 1635).

33 And thus he denied the existence of a vacuum: Jerome Cardan, 'De subtilitate,' in *Opera omnia*, vol. 3, bk. 1, cols. 359b, 367b–8a; cf. Jammer, *Problem*, 90, and Markus Fierz, *Girolamo Cardano, 1501–1576: Physician, Natural Philosopher, Mathematician, Astrologer, and Interpreter of Dreams* (Boston, Basel, Stuttgart, 1983), 93–4.

34 Cardan, 'De propria vita,' 39: 'vnum satis est harum rerum conscientiam & sensum, vniuersi orbis (sanctè iuro) regno etiam diuturno, cariorem mihi esse.' Stoner's translation (Cardan, *My Life*, 213) is too imprecise here. Cf. Aristotle, *On the Soul. Parva Naturalia. On Breath*, trans. W.S. Hett,

Aristotle in Twenty-three Volumes 8 (Cambridge, MA, and London, 1964), §§ 458b–64b.

35 Cf. Cardan, 'Synesiorum somniorum,' 594, 601–2, and *My Life*, 199–203 (concerning Artistotle, see 200) and 240–7; cf. also Carol Schreier Rupprecht, 'Divinity, Insanity, Creativity: A Renaissance Contribution to the History and Theory of Dream/Text(s),' in *The Dream and the Text: Essays on Literature and Language* (Albany, NY, 1993), 118. It was on condition of the Aristotelian concept of place and space that the things in the world might be connected by sympathy (see Hans Günter Zekl, 'Raum I: Griechische Antike,' in *Historisches Wörterbuch der Philosophie*, vol. 8, col. 76), and that the early modern imagination attained its power. But note that this idea cannot be found among the ancients; see Esther Fischer-Homberger, 'On the Medical History of the Doctrine of Imagination,' *Psychological Medicine* 9 (1979), 619–28.

36 This is one more proof for the fact that Protestant religion of the sixteenth and seventeenth centuries does not indicate a Weberian rationalization and 'disenchantment of the world.' Cf. esp. Robert W. Scribner, 'The Reformation, Popular Magic, and the "Disenchantment" of the World,' *Journal of Interdisciplinary History* 23 (1993), 475–94; Kaspar von Greyerz, 'Grenzen zwischen Religion, Magie und Konfession aus der Sicht der frühneuzeitlichen Mentalitätsgeschichte,' in Guy P. Marchal, ed., *Grenzen und Raumvorstellungen (11.–20. Jh.) – Frontières et conceptions de l'espace (11e–20e siècles)* (Zurich, 1996), 329–43; also Ulinka Rublack, *Reformation Europe*, New Approaches to European History 28 (Cambridge, 2005), who detects a 'Protestant "super-enchantment" of the early modern world until c. 1650' (10–11).

37 Martin Luther, 'Predigten des Jahres 1524,' in *D. Martin Luthers Werke: Kritische Gesamtausgabe (Weimarer Ausgabe)*, Abt. I, *Schriften* (Weimar, 1883–), 15:620–22; idem, 'Vorlesungen über 1. Mose Kap. 17,' in *Luthers Werke*, 42:668; idem, 'Vorlesungen über 1. Mose Kap. 28,' in *Luthers Werke*, 43:593; idem, 'Vorlesungen über 1. Mose Kap. 37,' in *Luthers Werke*, 44:249; Philipp Melanchthon, 'Erinnerung . . . Von mancherley Geschlechtern der Träume, samt ihrer Bedeutung,' in Artemidor, *Traum=Buch*, 17–29; Conrad Dieterich, *Philosophischer vnd Theologischer Traum Discurß / Von den Nächtlichen Träumen . . .* (Ulm, 1625).

38 Güntzer, *Kleines Biechlin*, fol. 14r–15v, 102r–v, 217v–19r; my translation. For further details see Bähr, 'Furcht, divinatorischer Traum und autobiographisches Schreiben.'

39 Thus, Güntzer was certain of being chosen by God; see Güntzer, *Kleines Biechlin*, fol. 175r.

40 Against this background, what the dreaming person *saw in his dreams* and what he *did when he was dreaming* were closely associated, not only in Cardan but also in Güntzer – regardless of the fact that Güntzer as a Protestant does not tell us that his soul is leaving its home: the body. The house appearing in Güntzer's dream is significant, because the sleeping body could be regarded as the house of the dreaming soul (see Männling, *Traum=Tempel*, 44) and the person's body as the home of the spirit of God (see Güntzer, *Kleines Biechlin*, fol. 213r). The early modern house constituted a space of the good life, protecting it from harmful powers and spirits which were threatening outside. That boundary, which was drawn by walls and thresholds, had an ontological character. It separated one geographical unit from another, good from evil, the profane life from the holy, the mundane world from the supernatural, and it also distinguished between different parts of life. See Robert W. Scribner, 'Symbolizing Boundaries: Defining Social Space in the Daily Life of Early Modern Germany,' in Lyndal Roper, ed., *Religion and Culture in Germany (1400–1800)*, Studies in Medieval and Reformation Thought 81 (1992; repr., Leiden, 2001), 302–22. For the threshold as 'a sort of sacred boundary between two spaces, where the antagonistic principles confront one another and the world is reversed,' see also Pierre Bourdieu, *Outline of a Theory of Practice*, trans. Richard Nice, Cambridge Studies in Social Anthropology 16 (Cambridge, London, New York, and Melbourne, 1977), 130.

41 Theophrastus Paracelsus, 'De pestilitate,' in *Pansophische, magische und gabalische Schriften*, vol. 5 of Theophrastus Paracelsus, *Werke*, ed. Will-Erich Peuckert, 2nd ed. (Basel and Stuttgart, 1982), 240–1.

42 'C'est ce dequoy j'ay le plus de peur que la peur. Aussi surmonte elle en aigreur tous autres accidents.' Michel de Montaigne, *Les Essais*, ed. Jean Balsamo, Bibliothèque de la Pléiade 14 (Paris, 2007), bk. 1, chap. 17, p. 78; my translation.

43 For further details and bibliographical references see Bähr, 'Vom Nutzen der Paradoxie' and '"Unaussprechliche Furcht" und Theodizee: Geschichtsbewusstsein im Dreißigjährigen Krieg,' *WerkstattGeschichte* 49 (2008): 9–31.

44 Andreas Gryphius, *Catharina von Georgien: Trauerspiel*, ed. Alois Maria Haas, 2nd ed. (Stuttgart, 1995), 4:59 and 501, and ibid., 5:180; Gryphius, 'Grabschrifft Marianae Gryphiae seines Brudern Pauli Töchterlein,' in *Gesamtausgabe der deutschsprachigen Werke*, vol. 2 of *Oden und Epigramme*, ed. Marian Szyrocki, Neudrucke Deutscher Literaturwerke N.F. 10 (Tübingen, 1964), 209; my translation. For the concept of 'Welt=Angst' see also the article 'Angst,' in Zedler, ed., *Universal Lexicon*, vol. 2, col. 301.

45 A modernist view can even be found in John Jeffries Martin, *Myths of Renaissance Individualism* (Houndmills/Basingstoke, 2004). For further bibliographical references see Bähr, 'Furcht, divinatorischer Traum und autobiographisches Schreiben'; Andreas Bähr, Peter Burschel, and Gabriele Jancke, 'Räume des Selbst: Eine Einleitung,' in *Räume des Selbst*, 6–9.

chapter twelve

Cartography and the Melancholic Self

CHRISTOPHER WILD

Melancholic Subjects and Objects

In the section 'Doctrine of Justification, *Apatheia*, Melancholy' of his Habilitationsschrift, *Origin of the German Tragic Drama* (*Ursprung des deutschen Trauerspiels*), Walter Benjamin develops a phenomenology of emotions, namely, those of mourning and melancholy, through a reading of obscure German baroque dramas. His methodological observations and conclusions, however, need not be confined to the baroque and provide a useful framework in which to unfold a different narrative of melancholic iconography. According to Benjamin, 'every feeling is bound to an *a priori* object, and the representation of this object is its phenomenology.'[1] Thus, melancholy is made visible through the world and its objects as they appear under the melancholic gaze. The relationship of emotion and corresponding object, or object and corresponding emotion, is described by Benjamin as necessary and mechanical. 'For feelings, however vague they may seem when perceived by the self, respond like a motoric reaction to a concretely structured world.'[2] Consequently, these feelings are not bound to a specific author or audience, but are 'released from any empirical subject and are intimately bound to the fullness of an object.'[3] Thus, this correspondence of objects and emotions is grounded in the latter's essentially intentional structure. Feelings, including those of mourning and melancholy, are not merely accidental to intentional acts of cognition, but are oriented towards an object and therefore intimately associated with it. In fact, for Benjamin the two emotions of love and mourning are ostentatiously and obsessively intentional. Because emotions objectify themselves in and as the world, the description of this world as it appears to and is represented by the melancholic subject is the only adequate description of the subject's affective state. Since the emotional constitution of the subject has shaped the world in which it finds its inner state reflected, the world can be considered an objectification of this inner state. Insofar as the melancholic world and the artefacts of melancholy are produced by the melancholic gaze, Benjamin can consider the objects corresponding to a specific affective state as a priori objects. In other words, he explores the 'concretely structured world' corresponding to baroque melancholy and mourning.

Benjamin's 'phenomenology of emotions' provides a theoretical framework in which to situate the long practised iconographical approach to melancholic imagery inaugurated by Klibansky, Panofsky, and Saxl with their monumental study *Saturn and Melancholy* in 1964, the revised and enlarged English version of Panofsky and Saxl's 1923 monograph on Dürer's *Melencolia I* – which Benjamin knew well.[4] Benjamin's reflections, I would like to suggest, delineate the specific relation between melancholic subjects and objects and thus account for the semiotic status of melancholic requisites and props. Thereby, the detailed historical and philological work of Klibansky, Panofsky, and Saxl on melancholic artefacts can be given an epistemological and hermeneutical grounding. By drawing on both these traditional iconographic studies of melancholy and on Benjamin's analysis of the baroque, I will explore the relation between the affect of melancholy and a particular set of melancholic requisites or props, namely, geometrical bodies and instruments of measure employed in astronomy, the science of perspective, and, in particular, cartography. This set of melancholic markers points – at least on the iconographic level – to an implicit correlation between melancholy and geometric space and the practices producing it. In order to take seriously this iconographic conjunction between melancholy and geometrically constructed space and to explore further its deeper structural and epistemological implications, I will first turn to a pictorial document which proposes that cartography is born from the humour of melancholy: an engraving by Maarten van Heemskerck (see figure 12.1).

Maarten van Heemskerck's Children of Saturn

Over the course of six years, Maarten van Heemskerck (1498–1574) produced designs for three series of prints with closely related themes: *The Four Seasons, The Four Temperaments*, and *The Seven Planets.*[5] The plates for the *Four Temperaments* were engraved by Herman Jansz. Muller and published in 1566, without mention of the publisher.[6] As in the case of the *Four Seasons*, it appears that Hadrianus Junius, the philologist and town physician of Haarlem, Heemskerck's home, was the author of two lines of Latin verse at the bottom of each print. The order of the prints follows the traditional classical system of humoral pathology, which also embraces the seasons, the elements, and the planets: there is the sanguine disposition, associated with Jupiter and Venus, spring, air, warmth, and humidity; the choleric, linked to Mars, summer, fire, heat, and dryness; the melancholic, affiliated with Saturn, autumn, earth, cold, and dryness; and finally the phlegmatic, related to Luna (the moon), winter, water, cold, and humidity. Since the composition is remarkably similar to Heemskerck's series of *Seven Planets*, one would almost think that the subjects of these engravings were children of the planets if the prints had not been provided with titles and inscriptions. The personified planets are seen up in the clouds surrounded by the associated signs of the zodiac, and down on earth figures are depicted which are engaged in the activities specific to their temperaments.

My focus will be on the engraving portraying the *Melancholic Temperament* (figure 12.1). This temperament is dominated by the planet Saturn, or Kronos, shown up in the clouds holding a scythe in one hand and devouring one of his children with the other. Saturn is accompanied by three signs of the zodiac, from upper left to right: Taurus, Virgo, and Capricorn. These signs of the zodiac do not correspond, as is often the case, to the appropriate season, but are simply arranged according to the traditional system of air, fire, earth, and water signs, and therefore are coupled with the element belonging to each temperament: earth, in the case of the melancholic. In the lower half of the picture, people of a melancholy disposition are depicted. Again, the engraving departs from traditional iconographic depictions for Saturn's children, whose interests are traditionally associated with agriculture and livestock or who are poor, ill, or imprisoned. Here, these have made way for geographers, cartographers, astrologers, and suicides.[7] The subscription by Hadrianus Junius, although not very flattering, confirms this: 'Surveyors and poets, and those who have not one ounce of common sense; it is they who are adopted by the scythe-bearing Saturn.'[8] These melancholics are not simply geometers and astrologers, or *typi geometriae* in Klibansky, Panofsky, and Saxl's sense (more on that later), but more precisely *mensores terrae*, surveyors or cartographers, readily identifiable by their respective instruments, depicted in curiously elaborate and accurate detail by Heemskerck.

Figure 12.1 Cartographical surveying under the sign of Saturn. *The Melancholic Temperament,* 1566, engraving by Herman Jansz. Muller after Maarten von Heemskerck, Print Cabinet, Collection Rijksmuseum, Amsterdam, Object no. RP-P-OB-2368. Photograph courtesy of Collection Rijksmuseum, Amsterdam.

In the immediate foreground of the lower right-hand corner, three Saturn adoptees huddle close together.[9] The melancholic on the far right is holding a quadrant. The plate of this instrument was engraved with a geometrical square as well as the marginal scale of degrees, and had sets of curved lines, clearly identifiable in this picture. The quadrant could determine the time of day and the sun's position in the zodiac by a plummet hanging off a silk thread. In addition to astronomical observation, the quadrant was also used for more mundane purposes such as geographical surveys, as it aided in measuring inaccessible heights and distances by the method of similar triangles. The middle figure, engaged in animated discussion with the melancholic on the left, is bent over a sphere and holds a compass in one hand and a square in the other. He appears to be measuring the sphere with latitudinal lines inscribed on it with these instruments, alluding to a vexing problem of projective geometry at the time, relevant to both cartography and perspective, namely, the projection and mapping of the spherical world, the longitudes and latitudes of the globe, onto a plane surface. Framing this first group, another set of three Saturn children in the middle background appears to be conducting a topographical survey. The two outer figures are both holding a primitive plane table, which was employed to triangulate the land. In triangulation, bearings from two vantage points are taken on a series of targets and then located in relation to each other and to the two stations. A single measured or known distance will give the scale to the map thus drawn. Alternatively, bearings taken from either end of a measured baseline can be used to locate an object at an unmeasured or immeasurable distance. By a series of such triangles, an entire map can be constructed without further linear measurement. The invention of the plane table allowed for greater precision in practical surveying and was first described as the holometer in 1551, by Abel Foullon, a member of the household of King Henry II of France and a student of mathematics. The important advance of the plane-table survey was that the position lines were ruled directly on a sheet of paper fastened to the table. In fact, in Heemskerck's engraving, a book, probably a notebook for recording measurements, lies at the feet of the figure on the left. In the earliest surviving plane tables, two sighting rods were attached to the edge of the instrument, one of them moving back and forth along a scale so that it could be set and used for sighting from the second vantage point at the end of the baseline (the imaginary line between the two surveyors handling the plane tables), which had been directly marked off to scale. That this group of melancholics is engaged in triangulating the land is further confirmed by the other instruments they are employing. The middle and left figures are holding a linked iron chain to measure the base line of the triangle. The surveyor to the far right is additionally holding a rod, which he, in his function as the front 'chain-man,' thrusts into the ground at the end of each chain length in order to mark his position for the rear chain-man. This array of surveying instruments is completed by the cross-staff or Jacob's staff lying at the feet of the figure on the left. The cross-staff was first described by the Provençal Jewish mathematician Levi ben Gerson in 1342 and was initially designed for the use of astronomers. But it, like the quadrant, could also be used for geometrical surveys, that is, for measuring terrestrial distances such as heights, the width of a river, or the dimensions of a building by the method of similar triangles. Historically, the Jacob's staff was a much cheaper instrument than the quadrant, served the same purpose, and was much easier to use.

With such an accurate and detailed depiction of geometrical and cartographical instruments of the time, Heemskerck's engraving documents the current state of cartographical and geographical knowledge and technology. Although the general principles had long been familiar to medieval scholars, there is no direct evidence of cartographical surveying or discussion of the appropriate instruments until the beginning of the sixteenth century, when geographical exploration and cartographical surveying developed rapidly.[10] In 1528 Sebastian Münster explained in a treatise, *Erklerung des newen Instruments der Sunnen nach allen seinen Sheyben und Circkeln* (Explanation of the New Instrument of the Sundial with all its Disks and Compasses), the principles of topographical surveying and illustrated them with a map of the surroundings of Heidelberg. Peter Apian's monumental work *Cosmographicus liber* (Cosmography), published in 1524, contained the geographical coordinates for 1417 places, which are, at least for locations in central Europe, astonishingly accurate. Just a decade later, the Dutch astronomer and geographer Gemma Frisius proposed a method to determine longitude, a problem which was to be solved only in the eighteenth century, and moreover provided the first complete description of cartographical triangulation. Later, Peter Apian's son Philipp conducted the first large-scale topographical survey by triangulation and published the results in 1568 as his *Bayerische Landtafeln* (Bavarian Maps). And finally, Christopher Saxton's *Atlas of England and Wales*, published in 1579, is the first comprehensive topographical survey of an entire national territory in Europe. These 'landmarks' suffice to sketch the historical context for the cartographical practices depicted in Heemskerck's engraving. My interest in this engraving, however, lies precisely in its confluence of melancholy and cartographical practices – practices that produce a new kind of space in the early modern period.

Melancholic Space

The practice of cartographical surveying depicted by Heemskerck as characteristic of a melancholic or saturnine disposition, historically forms part of the discipline of geometry. Klibansky, Panofsky, and Saxl were the first to highlight the geometrical symbolism in Albrecht Dürer's *Melencolia I* and other images of melancholy and to identify the *typus geometriae* as an iconographical subgroup of specifically early modern conceptions of melancholy.[11] According to their interpretation, the instruments of measure and geometrical bodies displayed in Dürer's famous print and many other images representing melancholy function as requisites or props of early modern subjectivity's melancholic disposition. Klibansky, Panofsky, and Saxl emphasize the abstraction and loftiness of geometry, and particularly of mathematics, as intrinsic to the melancholic temperament. Their reading seems to be confirmed by medieval authorities like Heinrich of Ghent and Raimundus Lullus, who claim that mathematicians in general are prone to melancholy. Yet, most instruments displayed in melancholic imagery following the *typus geometriae* belong to more applied forms of geometry. The sphere and compass depicted in Dürer's *Melencolia I* and in numerous other images of melancholy (cf. those of H.S. Beham and Lucas Cranach, to mention only the more famous ones) are requisites of projective geometry, central to optics and the art of perspective. Particularly the polyhedron in Dürer's *Melencolia I*, but also the sphere and other *corpora regularia*, the regular geometrical bodies deriving from Plato's *Timaeus*, so often found in melancholic imagery, denote the art or science of perspective. Similarly, the instruments in Heemskerck's engraving are used in terrestrial geometry, that is, geography and cartography. The quadrant in the same picture could – aside from surveying – be deployed for navigational purposes or used in astronomy and astrology, in other words, celestial geometry. As the personification of Geometry (figure 12.2) in Gregor Reisch's *Margarita philosophica* demonstrates, geometry as a spatial practice situates itself precisely at the intersection of lived and abstract spaces. Perspective and particularly cartography subject experiential space to geometrical procedures, resulting in spatial representations of increasing distance from lived everyday experience.[12]

Geometrical instruments as the requisites or props found in so many images representing a melancholic disposition suggest that the chthonic temperament of melancholy has more to do with the spatial practice of geometry and with the specific form of space produced by that practice than having a mere iconographic association. This set of melancholic props is of particular significance because the images that contain them are themselves commonly the products of geometrical practices using those instruments.[13] Furthermore, specifically in the case of the *corpora regularia* or regular geometrical bodies, projective geometry is

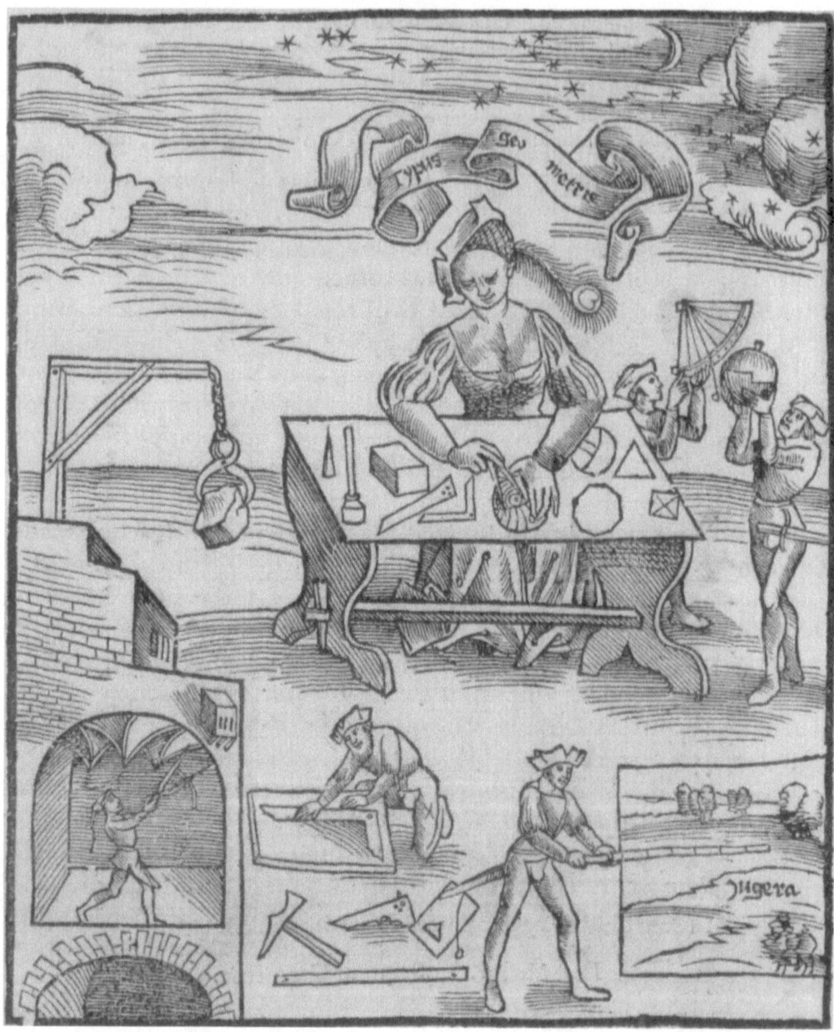

Figure 12.2 Geometry as lived spatial practice. *Geometry*, woodcut, Gregor Reisch, *Margarita philosophica* (Strassburg, 1504), Bayerische Staatsbibliothek, München, Shelfmark Res/4 Ph.u. 116 a, fol. 6v. Reproduced by permission of the Bayerische Staatsbibliothek, München.

Figure 12.3 Convergence of geometrical and melancholic gazes. Monogrammatist F.B., *Melancolia,* 1561, etching. © The Trustees of the British Museum [image AN82394001].

itself objectified and materialized because these bodies are not only constructed according to the mathematical rules of perspective but are also simultaneously representative of them. As such, these self-reflexive figures can be read as allegories of the geometrical gaze that produced them. In these images, which ostentatiously stage geometric artefacts, the geometrical gaze converges with the melancholic gaze as described by Benjamin. Both find themselves reflected in this world that is simultaneously the result of their own geometrical and melancholic construction. A particularly illustrative example of this convergence is a print from 1560 by the anonymous master F.B. (figure 12.3). It shows a personification of melancholy seated within a perspectival grid and surrounded by geometric bodies and instruments, intimating that the pictorial space itself has become a melancholic prop. Clearly, the world as the only adequate expression of the melancholic subject's inner feelings is radically geometricized.

If melancholy as it is traditionally represented has a particular affinity with geometrical spaces, what do we make then of its historical association with precisely the Other of space, namely, time and temporality? As the abundant pictorial material which Klibansky, Panofsky, and Saxl have assembled makes clear, images of melancholy, first and foremost Dürer's *Melencolia I,* contain numerous allusions to the passing of time. They abound with iconographical props such as hourglasses, sundials, death bells, skulls, ruins, and so forth. Above all, of course, Saturn, as the ruling planet of the melancholic temperament, has always been understood in his double figuration as Kronos (written with the Greek letter 'kappa'), the father of Zeus known for his cannibalistic appetites, and Chronos (written with the letter 'chi'), the god of time. The father who eats his children fuses with the arbiter of temporality, the *edax rerum*, making melancholy's relation to time one of suffering, attempted evasion, or repression and haunting.[14] Even the frequent pastoral moments in melancholic texts and images attest to such an evasion or repression of time. In that case, however, it takes the form of what Benjamin calls the 'restoration of the timelessness of paradise,' namely, a flight backwards out of time or before time.[15] What if time's repression and return in melancholy is also linked to the discovery of geometrical space? In *Origin of German Tragic Drama*, Benjamin explicates the spatio-temporal configuration in which objects of mourning appear under the melancholic gaze. According to him, 'here, as in other spheres of baroque life, what is vital is the transposition of the originally temporal data into a figurative spatial simultaneity.'[16] In the course of this 'transposition,' a 'chronological progression is expressed in spatial terms' and 'history merges into the scene of events.' Significantly, 'the transposition of the originally temporal data into a figurative spatial simultaneity' is, according to Benjamin, 'an expression of the same metaphysical tendency which simultaneously led, in the exact sciences, to the infinitesimal method. In both cases, chronological movement is grasped and analyzed in a spatial image.'[17] Because time can only ever enter geometrical space in spatial terms, its very temporality is eclipsed. In other words, the inscription of time into space results in the appearance of timelessness.[18] Instead of perceiving different 'points' in time in temporal succession and thus experiencing time's flow, we perceive them simultaneously, in one glance, as if timeless.

Not coincidentally, Benjamin describes the baroque concept of history as panoramic, precisely because time and history are explicitly described in spatial terms, and it is only a small step from a panoramic view to a cartographical view of space and time. As mutual metaphoric translations, time and space are irreducibly linked. Any attempt to isolate one from the other is doomed to fail, for, like all things repressed, the part cast aside will invariably return. The figurative transposition of time into space described by Benjamin comes at a cost. Everything entering the space enters it in altered, that is, petrified form; it must pass away. In other words, everything enters geometric space in the form of a ruin, a fragment, a relic, or a corpse, and thus as figures – quasi-allegorically – for spatialized time itself.

An explicit convergence between a ruinous cityscape and cartographical space is found in Leon Battista Alberti's map of Rome in his *Descriptio urbis Romae* (Delineation of the City of Rome). Alberti's map represents one of the earliest city plans obtained by both accurate measurement and topographic surveying, and it is no coincidence that its subject is Rome, the eternal city, full of ruins from the past.[19] These monuments to and of time's transience find their precise geographic coordinates in Alberti's map. In the simultaneity of the topographical space, time is figured as the presence of the past, as presence in a state of mortification. Thus, under the melancholic gaze, time enters space and reappears in the guise of its own ruin to haunt the melancholic subject.

In his sonnet 'On Abraham Ortelius's *Parergon*,' the German baroque poet Andreas Gryphius stages such a haunting while viewing one of the most popular cartographical publications of the early modern period, namely, Abraham Ortelius's *Parergon sive veteris geographiae aliquot tabulae* (Additional Ornament, or Several Images of Ancient Geography):

> XXXVIII. About Abraham Ortelius's *Parergon*
> The stage of the old world on which still remains
> What raging flames and hostile swords,
> Swift lightning and lengthy time turn over
> Is unlocked here by Ortelius's hand. Even if Athens itself disappears,
> Pergamon collapses; even if the swelling sea,
> Whipped up by proud winds, covers the lands;
> Even if the earth's maw swallows earth itself
> A free spirit cannot be bound by any power.
> It tears down all restraints in which flesh, misery,
> And dying hold us and overcomes pale death itself.
> It finds everything in itself and finds itself in everything.
> It sees what no longer is and what will come:
> It is comforted in the world's destruction and wretchedness,
> And can't fall even if the body, its abode, falls.[20]

Originally published as an addendum to Ortelius's famous *Theatrum orbis terrarum* (Theater of the World), the *Parergon* consists of historical maps that trace the journeys of famous men and peoples of the ancient world. As Walter Melion has shown, 'the maps devoted to sacred history constitute a subset characterized by their meditative format and function. They describe the *peregrinatio* of Old and New Testament figures who fulfilled their sacred vocation by undertaking arduous pilgrimages, upon whose nature and scope the maps and their corollary texts invite the viewers to reflect.'[21] The maps enable their viewers to participate as pilgrims in these voyages and transport them imaginatively into the past in order to make them eyewitnesses of these events. In the preface of his *Theatrum*, Ortelius explains: 'For we are greatly served when, having read in Scripture of the Israelites' journey out of Egypt through the Red Sea, we witness this deed as if we were ourselves present.'[22] Gryphius follows Ortelius's direction when he uses the map of the *Parergon* to visualize the represented lands and places. The medium of the cartographical map allows Gryphius's free spirit to tear down the spatio-temporal constraints that corporeality and mortality have placed upon it – literally permitting his spirit to transcend the bounds of space and time and travel into past (and future), as suggested by the word play on *durchreissen*, which literally means 'to tear down' but also echoes *durchreisen*, that is, 'to travel through.' While Gryphius's poetic self lets itself be transported into the past by Ortelius's maps, its viewing experience turns out to be very different. Whereas for Ortelius the medium of the map is able to bridge the chasm between the reader's present and the biblical past by transporting the former into the presence of the latter, Gryphius's viewing highlights the distance and difference between self and world, the present moment and ancient history. The presentation of the past foregrounds its pastness rather than overcoming it. In fact, the presence of the past seems to bring about almost inevitably the passing of the present. What this meditative – and maybe also melancholic – traveller finds is not a living, but a dead past; a past that is filled with the ruins of destruction which threaten to overpower the poetic self. Again, time and history are inscribed into cartographic space as transience or *Vergänglichkeit*.

The cartographic map does not only condemn the world to fall, but it also raises its observer up. The spiritual freedom of the subject appears as a variant of the imaginative freedom to travel through time and space afforded by a map. While the cartographic medium enables its viewers to enter the represented world, it clearly also allows them to detach and distance themselves from this very world. In fact, Gryphius seems to suggest that it actually frees the subject from the world. By viewing the world as a map, the subject can transcend it and view it from above – from the bird's-eye perspective or, more precisely, from the perspective of God.

This 'view from above,' as Pierre Hadot has termed it, is not an invention and achievement of early modern geography, but has a long tradition ultimately going back to the regime of spiritual exercises practised by Stoics (and to a lesser extent by Epicureans); and Andreas Gryphius, a student of Lipsius and early modern neo-Stoicism, was well acquainted with this spiritual practice.[23]

The view from above is intrinsically associated with mortality, since it can only be fully achieved with the soul's separation from the body in death. Adopting it in this life means pre-tasting death and thus experiencing one's mortality. Insofar as ancient philosophy always also conceived itself as a training to die in order to achieve an understanding of the world governed by the universality and objectivity of thought, not by our own particular desires and fears, the view from above, or from beyond the grave, was a quintessential philosophical practice; it shows the world and human existence in their true light. An aphorism from Marcus Aurelius's *Meditations* may stand in for numerous other passages from Stoic philosophers:

> Take a view from above – look at the thousands of flocks and herds, the thousands of human ceremonies, every sort of voyage in storm or calm, the range of creation, combination, and extinction. Consider too the lives once lived by others long before you, the lives that will be lived after you, the lives lived now among foreign tribes; and how many have never even heard your name, how many will very soon forget it, how many may praise you now but quickly turn to blame. Reflect that neither memory nor fame, nor anything else at all, has any importance worth thinking of.[24]

Again, the spatial overview gives way to a temporal overview in which not only the viewer's presence and lifespan come into sight but also past and future times and lives. 'By grasping the whole universe in your thought, contemplating the eternity of time, and reflecting on the rapid change of each thing in every part,' it is revealed to the viewer from above 'how brief the gap from birth to dissolution, how vast the gulf of time before your birth, and an equal infinity after your dissolution.'[25] Compared to the infinity of the universe and the eternity of time, one's own existence shrinks to almost nothing. Seen from an elevated vantage point, the material world and earthly life are radically relativized. This elevation, with which the self tears itself away from the world and its worries, puts it, as Seneca describes it in the *Naturales quaestiones*, 'in consortium Dei,' and lets it see the world the way God himself sees it.[26]

It is no coincidence that Gryphius would invoke the Stoic 'view from above' when viewing Ortelius's historical maps. The emblematic world map of 1587, the *Typus orbis terrarum* (Image of the World) (figure 12.4) that made Ortelius famous, is superscribed with a passage from Cicero's *Tusculan Disputations* (*Tusculanae disputationes*): 'For what can seem of moment in human occurrences to a man who keeps eternity before his eyes and knows the vastness of the universe?'[27] And it is circumscribed by four more citations from the Stoic canon: Seneca's *Ad Lucilium epistulae morales* (Moral Epistles to Lucilium) and *Naturales quaestiones* (Natural Questions) as well as Cicero's *De re publica* (On the Commonwealth) and *De natura deorum* (On the Nature of the Gods).[28] Thus, the view that the medium of the map enables – the bird's-eye view of the topographical map or the cosmographic view of the world map – is the material realization of the Stoic view from above and was, in Ortelius's and Gryphius's cases, conditioned by their neo-Stoic training.

But for the Christian self, reaching the point from which God himself sees the world is far from unproblematic. That Gryphius's viewer of Ortelius's maps indeed usurps God's vantage point is confirmed by another sonnet according to which God 'sees what is in the future as if it were present.'[29] Just like God, the cartographic subject not only observes the world from above, but can see past, present, and future in the simultaneity of cartographic space. Thus, the cartographical medium allows for the introjection of the divine perspective and gaze. With this *excessus mentis*, the cartographic subject realizes the movement that, according to Luther, Psalm 90 demands from its reader: 'And so Moses has us transport ourselves outside of time and has us look at our life with God's eyes.'[30] From this perspective, the span of our life shrinks to, as Luther puts it, a 'punctum mathematicum,' or geometrical point, which has no extension whatsoever.[31] The cartographical medium, thus, can literalize this condensation of time into a mathematical point, which hitherto could only be realized imaginatively. However, the cartographically induced introjection of the divine gaze comes at a high price for the human self. When it observes the world's ways *sub specie aeternitatis* (from the viewpoint of eternity), everything falls prey to the relentless working of time. Another mode of introjecting the divine gaze, which was very prominent in the early modern period, operates in a similar fashion. The topos of the *theatrum mundi*, in which the whole world is a stage, and life a play in which humans are the actors and God the spectator of it all, serves to unmask world and human existence as mere appearance and thus to invalidate their apparent substantiveness.[32] What therefore comes into view when the self views world and life with God's eyes are,

Figure 12.4 Cartography and the Stoic 'view from above.' Abraham Ortelius, *Typus orbis terrarum,* 1587, engraving, Bayerische Staatsbibliothek München, Shelfmark 2 Mapp. 255 c. Reproduced by permission from the Bayerische Staatsbibliothek München.

not surprisingly, their intrinsic fragility and inescapable fallenness. After all, it is this introjection of the divine gaze which the serpent promises Eve, if she eats from the tree of knowledge: 'On the day you eat of it your eyes will be opened and you will become as gods knowing good and evil' (Gen 3:5).[33] Commonly, the promise of becoming like God(s) is linked to knowing the difference between good and evil, but a closer look makes clear that both are a function of the opening of the eyes. Becoming godlike consists first and foremost in the transformation of vision; and this new mode of seeing reveals to the self its nakedness and mortality. Thus, the repression and haunting characterizing the melancholic temperament of cartographers and geometers is rooted in man's inescapable fallenness. The logic and economy of the Fall predicates that any attempt to deny or escape it inevitably repeats it and condemns the self more fully to its consequences. As the melancholic temperament of mathematical geography and cartography evidences, the advent of (early) modern science does little to change that – at least in the eyes of the painters and writers surveyed here. Of course, cosmographical mapping may open up the possibility of putting into practice the ironic suggestion of one of the interlocutors in Kleist's famous essay 'On the Marionette Theater': 'Paradise is bolted shut, and the cherub behind us. We have to make the journey around the world and see whether it isn't open somewhere in back again.'[34]

NOTES

1 I am using the somewhat problematical translation of John Osborne: Walter Benjamin, *The Origin of German Tragic Drama* (New York, 1998), 139. Where necessary, I have changed the translation. In parentheses, I will also be providing reference to the German original: Walter Benjamin, *Gesammelte Schriften* (Frankfurt am Main, 1991), vol. I.1:318.

2 Benjamin, *Origin,* 139 (I.1:318).

3 Ibid.

4 Raymond Klibansky, Erwin Panofsky, and Fritz Saxl, *Saturn and Melancholy: Studies in the History of Natural Philosophy, Religion, and Art* (London, 1964). The last section of the chapter 'Trauerspiel and Tragedy' mines the original German publication from 1923: Erwin Panofsky and Fritz Saxl, *Dürers 'Melencolia I.' Eine quellen- und typengeschichtliche Untersuchung* (Leipzig and Berlin, 1923).

5 Cf. Ilja M. Veldman, 'Seasons, Planets and Temperaments in the Work of Maarten van Heemskerck: Cosmo-Astrological Allegory in Sixteenth-Century

Netherlandish Prints,' *Simiolus: Netherlands Quarterly for the History of Art* 11 (1980), 169–73.

6 Muller had already engraved the plates for Heemskerck's *Seven Planets* but they would be published only several years later.

7 For the traditional children of Saturn, cf. Klibansky, Panofsky, and Saxl, *Saturn and Melancholy*, 178–95 and 204–7.

8 The original Latin inscription reads: 'Mensores terrae, vates Saturnus adoptat Falciger, et quibus est sana nulla uncia mentis.'

9 For much of the following, cf. Uta Lindgren, 'Land Surveys, Instruments, and Practitioners in the Renaissance,' in David Woodward, ed., *Cartography in the European Renaissance*, vol. 3 of *The History of Cartography*, ed. J.B. Harley and David Woodward (Chicago, 1987–2007), 477–508; all subsequent citations to this volume are indicated as Woodward, *Cartography in the European Renaissance.*

10 For the German lands, cf. Peter H. Meurer, 'Cartography in the German Lands, 1450–1650,' in Woodward, *Cartography in the European Renaissance,* 1172–1245; for the Low Countries, cf. Cornelis Koeman and Marco van Egmond, 'Surveying and Official Mapping in the Low Countries, 1500–ca.1670,' ibid., 1246–1295; for England, cf. Peter Barber, 'Mapmaking in England, 1470–1650,' ibid., 1589–1669.

11 Klibansky, Panofsky, and Saxl, *Saturn and Melancholy*, 327–45.

12 It is important to distinguish perspective and cartography in this respect. Whereas the former deploys geometrical procedures to construct a view of space that resembles 'normal' sensory experience, the latter produces a space radically different from what is accessible to the senses. For this, cf. Christine Buci-Glucksmann, *L'oeil cartographique de l'art* (Paris, 1996).

13 The woodcut from Gregor Reisch's *Margarita philosophica* (figure 12.2) is a notable example here, since it is not perspectivally constructed.

14 In this context, the susceptibility of melancholics to the visitation of ghosts and spirits comes to mind. The most famous and notable examples are surely Shakespeare's Hamlet and Robert Burton's 'digression of the nature of Spirits' in his *Anatomy of Melancholy*, ed. Floyd Dell and Paul-Jordan Smith (New York, 1938), 157–76. Cf. also Benjamin, *Origin*, 133–8 (I.1:312–16).

15 Benjamin, *Origin*, 92 (I.1:278).

16 Ibid., 81 (I.1:260).

17 Ibid., 92ff. (I.1:278ff.).

18 Cf. also Yves Bonnefoy, 'Time and the Timeless in Quattrocento Painting,' in Norman Bryson, ed., *Calligram: Essays in New Art History* (Cambridge and New York, 1988), 8–26, who argues that 'lived time disappears' in the rigorous perspectival art of Piero della Francesca (p. 23). Alexandre Koyré makes a similar point for the Cartesian universe: 'Thorough-going geometrization

– the original sin of Cartesian thought – leads to the intemporal: space is retained but time is eliminated. It dissolves the real entity into the geometrical. But reality has its revenge'; see Koyré, *Galileo Studies* (Atlantic Highlands, NJ, 1978), 91; cf. also 109 and 259f.

19 Leon Battista Alberti, *Descriptio urbis Romae*, ed. Martine Furno and Mario Carpo (Geneva, 1999). For a description of Alberti's technique and a reconstruction of the (lost) original accompanying map by Luigi Vagnetti, cf. Samuel Y. Edgerton, *The Renaissance Rediscovery of Linear Perspective* (New York, Evanston, San Francisco, and London, 1976), 115ff.

20 Andreas Gryphius, *Sonette*, Gesamtausgabe der deutschsprachigen Werke (Tübingen, 1963), 1:54:

> XXXVIII. Uber *Abraham Ortels Parergon*
> Den schaw = platz alter welt / in welchem noch zu finden
> Was harter flammen grim / undt rawer feinde schwerdt
> Was der geschwinde plitz / undt lange zeit verkehrt /
> Schleust Ortels Handt hier auff. Mus gleich *Athen*' verschwinden
> Bricht *Pergamus* schon ein; ob die von stoltzen Winden
> Hoch aufgeschwelte See / weit über länder fährt /
> Wirdt von der Erden schlundt die erden selbst verzehrt /
> Ist doch ein freyer sinn durch keine macht zu binden.
> Er reist die schrancken durch / in dehn fleisch und noth /
> Und sterben pochen will / und pocht den blassen todt.
> Findt alles in sich selbst / undt findt sich selbst in allen.
> Er siht was nicht mehr ist / und was noch kommen soll:
> Ihmb ist im untergang und weh der Erden wol.
> Undt kan ob gleich der leib / sein wohnhaus fält / nicht fallen.

Cf. also Peter Rusterholz, *Theatrum vitae humanae. Funktion und Bedeutungswandel eines poetischen Bildes. Studien zu den Dichtungen von Andreas Gryphius, Christian Hofmann von Hofmannswaldau und Daniel Casper von Lohenstein* (Berlin, 1971), 40–50.

21 Walter S. Melion, '*Ad ductum itineris et dispositionem mansionem ostendendam*: Meditation, Vocation, and Sacred History in Abraham Ortelius's *Parergon*,' *Journal of the Walters Art Gallery* 57 (1999), 49.

22 Quoted ibid., 51.

23 Pierre Hadot, *Philosophy as a Way of Life* (Oxford and New York, 1995), 238–50. Cf. also Michel Foucault, *The Hermeneutics of the Subject: Lectures at the Collège de France 1981–82* (New York, 2005), 275–85.

24 Marcus Aurelius, *Meditations* IX.30, trans. Martin Hammond (London, 2006).

25 Ibid., IX.32.

26 Seneca, *Natural Questions* I.6 (Cambridge, MA, and London, 1971).

27 Cicero, *Tusculan Disputations* IV.17.37 (Cambridge, MA, and London, 1945).

28 For the precise identification cf. Justus Müller Hofstede, 'Zur Interpretation von Pieter Bruegels Landschaft: Ästhetischer Landschaftsbegriff und Stoische Weltbetrachtung,' in Otto von Simson and Matthias Winner, eds, *Pieter Bruegel und seine Welt* (Berlin, 1979), 130–7. Cf. also Melion, *Ad ductum*, 52f.

29 Gryphius, *Sonette*, 105: 'Gott . . . Der was noch künfftig ist als gegenwärtig sieht.'

30 Martin Luther, *Works*, ed. J. Pelikan (St Louis, 1955–76), 13:100. The original reads: 'Monet igitur Moses, ut transferamus nos extra tempus et Dei oculis inspiciamus nostram vitam.' Cf. Martin Luther, *Werke: Kritische Gesamtausgabe*, vol. 40, pt. 3 (Weimar, 1883–1966), 525.

31 Luther, *Works*, 13:128: 'He wants us to reflect on what we are and to equate even a hundred years of this life with a mathematical point and the smallest fraction of a second.' For the original Latin passage, cf. Luther, *Werke*, vol. 40, pt. 3, 572. Already Seneca describes human existence as a punctum when viewed from above. Cf. his *Natural Questions* I.8 and 11.

32 It is no coincidence that Ortelius titled his opus magnum *Theatrum orbis terrarum* and thus parallelized map and stage, cartographical and theatrical viewing. Cf. Tom Conley, 'Pierre Boaistuau's Cosmographic Stage: Theater, Text, and Map,' in *Renaissance Drama*, n.s. 23 (1992), 59–86. Therefore, Gryphius was merely following Ortelius's lead when he refers to the maps of the latter's *Parergon* as the 'stage of the old world' (*schaw = platz alter welt*). Another famous early modern example of conjoining the medium of the map with the medium of the theatre is the 'Fool's Cap World Map' (ca. 1590), which figures the Ptolemaic projection of the globe on/instead of the face of a jester.

33 Robert Alter, *The Five Books of Moses: A Translation with Commentary* (New York, 2004).

34 Heinrich von Kleist, 'On the Marionette Theater,' trans. Carol Jacobs, *Connecticut Review* 44 (1997), 52.

chapter thirteen

Ingénieurs du Roy, Ingénieur du Moy: Self and Space in Montaigne and Descartes

TOM CONLEY

The guiding argument of the paragraphs that follow is that our appreciation of the 'self' in the early modern age, quite like the bee's wax that takes up much of Descartes's second *Méditation*, is pliable and of origins in the land and flora about and around it.[1] It is grounded in an emerging tradition of topographical investigation. A somewhat nascent science in the sixteenth century, topography is what locates and defines the self through the measure of space. It is inherently associated with ethnography, a discipline then equally nascent, given to the depiction of peoples and places in a world whose borders are extending but whose circumference and limits are being established. Between the topographer and what he or she observes, there develops an existential relation of curiosity, attraction, and admiration that mixes with astonishment and wonder. The welter of emotions in turn provokes fear and defensive or self-protective reaction that causes the self to become isolated, autonomous, and, paradoxically, both at home in and estranged from the milieu in which it finds itself.[2]

In sweeping terms it can be said that self-consciousness begins where space becomes felt. It occurs when a person gains the sensation of being located in an ambient milieu that can be at once welcoming, unsettling, and hostile. Such is what Descartes rehearses in his *Méditations*.[3] He finds himself in a locale that becomes identified by the warmth of the fire (that in the *Discours de la méthode* will be specified geographically as a *poêle*, a stove found in the northern climes of Europe), in which he contemplates the effects of hot and cold upon his body and the bee's wax he plies with his fingers. He progressively 'locates' himself in a northern European milieu, a place that he can provisionally call a site of security.

His reflections (in both the *Méditations* and the *Discours*) yield a sense of self that is defined spatially and, further, locally. In their expression they share much with the work of a topographer who takes account of a locale and its character as he develops the logistical and defence planning for a military campaign. At the time of the *Discours* and *Méditations,* a topographer had already long been associated with an engineer, the latter a specialist trained in the demarcation of national boundaries and the design of roads, fortresses, and modes of transport for purposes of protection and commerce.

In this essay I will argue that much of what Descartes makes of the 'cogito' and the 'self' in his French writings belongs to the world of the topographer and the 'king's engineer,' that is, to the strategic cartographer whose task is to map national boundaries and to design structures for the defence of country they surround. For the sake of this argument, I would like first to situate Descartes's identification with the topographer through his relation with Montaigne, the writer who brought the term forward in his famous essay (of 1580) 'Des cannibales' (On Cannibals). My contentions are (1) that the 'space' of the Cartesian ego is rooted in Montaigne's *Essais* and (2) that the figure of the topographer-engineer informs the concept of the cogito or thinking self. In other words, and perhaps more clearly put, the very being of the *moy* that haunts the author of the *Méthode* finds many of its pertinent traits in the activities of the king's engineer, who is the logistician, surveyor, artist, and cartographer of the nation. The space with which the *moy* is affiliated is defined topographically, but in topographies whose history is at once specific (in the documented labours of the *ingénieur du roy*) and, for the ends of the philosopher and writer, of a broader logical category (in the operation of 'thinking' and of discerning the space which reflection and ocular experience invent or cause to occur). Because the engineer surveys the accidental, uneven, and often vertiginous aspect of a landscape, he is also both a 'chorographer' and an 'orographer.' He is trained in trigonometry and triangulation so as to be able to determine distances between the summits of mountains and the depths of their valleys. As a surveyor of land and of the latitudes or climes of altitude, the engineer is at once a strategist (*stratège*) and a stratigrapher. He is a geographer and also an ethnographer, a person enquiring of physical and mental regions and their climates. The space of the Cartesian self is rooted in the world of the king's engineer.

The engineer and topographer are present in Montaigne's *Essais,* a work that bears strongly on the *Méditations* and the *Discours.* The topographers whom Montaigne seeks at the outset of 'Des cannibales' – 'il nous faudroit des topographes qui fissent narration particuliere des endroits où ils ont esté'[4] – are affiliated with individuals capable of furnishing reliable accounts of what they have seen in the places where they have been. Implied, first, is that they may be 'traders in commerce with natives,' Frenchmen who, having lived in 'Antarctic France' (the eastern regions of South America), have intimate knowledge of the newly discovered lands. By the end of the chapter, however, the topographers might be three native Americans (in most likelihood Tupinambas) whom the author reports having met and interviewed in Rouen in 1562. Yet, because of the freighted meaning of *topographe* in 1580, the context of the essay, allusion is also made to the artist-surveyors, employed under the aegis of Francis I, of Catherine de Medici, and, later, of Henry of Navarre, who would officially accede to the French throne in 1594. The tasks the engineers performed included the drafting and drawing of regional maps and, as their responsibilities expanded, the redesign of fortifications along the borders of the French kingdom.[5]

The topographers mentioned in 'Des cannibales' share much with the figure of the self-conscious writer seen in clearest definition at the moment when Montaigne's project of self-portraiture and the study of the *moy* are vertiginously close to those undertaken by the geographer in 'De l'exercitation' (Of Practice), the essay in which Montaigne recounts the story of a fall from a horse that left him unconscious and taken for dead before he painfully returned to life. Summing up his experience, he writes of the delights and the perils he faces when studying the tenuous movement of the mind. Having finished the account of his accident, he continues: 'Ce conte d'un évenement si legier est assez vain, n'estoit l'instruction que j'en ay tireé pour moy; car, à la verité, pour s'aprivoiser à la mort, je trouve qu'il n'y a que de s'en avoisiner. Or, comme dict Pline, chacun est à soy-mesme une très-bonne discipline, pourveu qu'il ait la suffisance de s'espier de près. Ce n'est pas ci ma doctrine, c'est mon estude; et n'est pas la leçon d'autruy, c'est la mienne.'[6]

A brush with death, an event of great gravity or force of attraction and repulsion, is far from 'legier.' It is anything but vain for being, in the shape of a printed book in a vernacular idiom, instructive for training in philosophy, the discipline said to teach the art of dying well. To 'domesticate' death (*s'y aprivoiser*), to bring it close to home – just as Montaigne's company carried his limp and bloodied body from the site of the accident to the confines of his chateau – happens to be in the neighbourhood of the very verb, *s'avoisiner*, that locates the subject close to death. The historical depth of the operation of self-study, felt in the distance between the here-and-now of the episode just recounted and the vague and distant whereabouts in a comparable example, found in the mass of Pliny's *Natural History*, is flattened when the name of the classical writer is folded into the very word that conveys the discipline of self-study: 'comme *dict Pline*, chascun est à soy-mesme une très-bonne *discipline*.'

The space the author invents for the project of self-study immediately is affiliated with or, better, folds into, *espionage*, an area then under the purview of the logistician and topographer. To 'spy on oneself from near' (*s'espier de près*) one must have compass enough to gain a focus on one-self. The writer – or better in this instance, the poet – chooses (or lets fall into the visual field of the text) words and letters that multiply or complicate the ostensible meaning. Double entendres, repetitions, contradictions, and unlikely figures cause the text to become a topographical form, indeed, a layered landscape in which transformations take place within and through the words and letters of the printed page. The text is of a complexity that allows it to be experienced differently over time and to be 'worked through' in the way that a landscape is encountered by the naked eye.[7] The sharp or even spiked quality of *s'espier de près*, in which the emblem of the cutting edge and tip of a sword (*espée*) is visible, carries on into a long addition (*alongeail*) in the Bordeaux copy in which, in one of the most moving observations of the *Essais*, Montaigne writes about the story he has just told:

> C'est une *espineuse entreprinse*, et plus qu'il ne semble, de suyvre une alleure si vagabonde que celle de nostre esprit; de penetrer les profondeurs opaques de ses replis internes; de choisir et arrester tant de menus airs de ses agitations. Et est un amusement nouveau et extraordinaire, qui nous retire des occupations communes du monde, ouy, et des plus recommandées. Il y a plusieurs années que je n'ay que moy pour visée à mes pensées, que je ne contrerolle et estudie que moy et, si j'estudie autre chose, c'est pour soudain le coucher sur moy, ou en moy, pour mieux dire.[8]

The 'thorny enterprise' that will 'follow an allure so vagabond as that of our mind' and that will 'penetrate the opaque depths of its inner folds' retains the sense of espionage, but also engages the artist-topographer who draws sketches of landscapes. At the same time, the 'thorny' operation, in which allusion to a dorsal column (*espine*) is folded into the adjective *espineuse*, recalls an anatomy lesson which proceeds from the head and shoulders to the viscera in the rib cage. The vitally vainglorious 'discipline' of which Montaigne writes is enveloped in *plis* that fold into the inner pleats and creases of the mind (*esprit*), seen taken in itself, as what is already refracted in the *espineuse* enterprise. The words that implicitly compare the art of introspection to espionage at once comprise and constitute the elements of a moving and even undulating field of words and images in which he finds himself. The reflections on the event become the elements of a landscape that both author and reader are invited to survey in the manner of a poetic topographer. The writer is an *ingénieur du moy* who uses the craft of observation, plotting, and drawing to establish the area of a region, its borders, its commerce, its vulnerable areas, and the high points where ordnance and defensive structures can be placed.

This is the milieu that Montaigne is getting at when, in 'Des cannibales,' he seeks the company of topographers who will offer, no matter how naive they may be, exact and 'particular' accounts of the places they have actually visited. They are, in other words, the contrary of cosmographers, those armchair geographers who represent the world through the filter of received information, who distort its image according to what they have seen in it, and who, 'pour donner credit à leur jugement et vous y attirer, prestent volontiers de ce costé là à la matiere, l'alongent et l'amplifient.'[9]

Before he names the topographer as such, Montaigne describes his attributes. First, 'il faut un homme tres-fidelle, ou si simple qu'il n'ait pas dequoy bastir et donner de la vray-semblance à des inventions fauces, et qui n'ait rien espousé.'[10] That the topographer has never *espousé* his subject – in its infinitive a verb translated in 1611 by Randle Cotgrave, in his *Dictionarie of the French and English Tongues*, as 'to espouse, wed, marrie; also to defend, imbrace, undertake, intertaine as his owne, take wholly upon him' – can be accredited to the optical distance between him and what he discerns. In the overall context, the passing remark that 'we need topographers,' astutely put forward to counter the cosmographer's distortions, folds into the landscape of the essay and returns at the end, when the author recalls the three cannibals whom he met in Rouen in 1562, during the city's visit by Charles IX. Their devastatingly direct answers to the questions posed by members of the royal entourage indicate that they are deceptively clever simpletons who see the world as it is.

By way of spatial contiguity with the essay on friendship, as well as through its praise of observation of local knowledge, Montaigne's chapter on the cannibals engages ingenuity and engineering. The natives whom he meets become a vital force of an alterity that he will later find in the folds of the self. They inhabit landscapes that can only be fathomed through those seen in the known world: 'Au demeurant, ils vivent en une contrée de païs très-plaisante et bien temperée; de façon qu'à ce que m'ont dit mes tesmoings, il est rare d'*y voir* un homme malade; et m'ont assuré n'en y avoir *veu* aucun tremblant, chassieux, edenté, ou courbé de vieillesse. Ils sont assis le long de la mer, et fermez du costé de la terre de grandes et hautes montaignes, ayant, entredeux, cent lieuës ou environ d'estendue en large.'[11]

Montaigne relies on his ocular witnesses who have *seen* in its moderate aspect a physical and moral region (*contrée*) far from what he had just described in the previous chapter, in his report of Cortez's encounter with Mexican natives.[12] In the delimited area where they are found, Montaigne's cannibals abut the sea and dwell at the foot of the mountains that separate them from the hinterland. They are possibly identical to us, unlike classical philosophers of times past who were, according to Montaigne, unable to discern, as we are now, 'par experience en ces nations-là,' what he calls 'une nayveté si pure et simple, comme nous la voyons par experience.'[13]

As the seemingly empirical description of the natives and their lands advances, images from travellers' accounts of 'Antarctic France' begin to accumulate. There follows a series of scenes drawn from depictions of North and South American continents on manuscript maps (possibly those of the Dieppe School) and from illustrations in books of cosmography (including André Thevet's *Cosmographie universelle* of 1575). The topographical inflection remains strong and true as the observation moves ahead. The ocular virtue the author associates with the topographer is found in the verbal details that render the content of common woodcut images and oral accounts of westward travel.

> Leurs bastimens sont fort longs, et capables de deux ou trois cents ames, estoffez d'escorse de grands arbres, tenans à terre par un bout et se soustenans et appuyans l'un contre l'autre par le feste, à la mode d'aucunes de noz granges, desquelles la couverture pend jusques à terre, et sert de flanq. Ils ont du bois si dur qu'ils en coupent, et en font leurs espées et des grils à cuire leur viande. Leurs lits sont d'un tissu de coton, suspenduz contre le toict, comme ceux de nos navires, à chacun le sien; car les femmes couchant à part des maris.[14]

Although mention is often made of ingenuity and tactical ruse, direct reference to cartographic material or to the tasks of a king's engineer is absent. Since the early editions of Pieter Apian's *Cosmographia*, topographers could be assumed to be those who describe specific places, 'toutes les choses, & a peu pres les moindres en iceulx contenues, comme sont villes, portz de mer, peuples, pays, cours des rivieres, & plusieurs autres choses, comme edifices, maisons, tours, & autres choses semblables.'[15] Under Francis I, the *ingénieur du roy* planned campaigns and devised strategies in the wars that led the French into Italy. Henri II employed them in his expedition that brought Calais and the Boulonnais back to France. One of them, Nicolas de Nicolay, a cartographer and a spy for whom Ronsard wrote lines of praise, drew faithful renderings both of the region and the coast of Scotland.[16] But it was during the Wars of Religion, the very context in which the *Essais* were written, that Henry of Navarre formalized the position.[17] *Ingénieurs du roy* were topographers who could be called practical artists, draftsmen who studied landscapes in view of military engagement.

Montaigne's topographer of 'Des cannibales' is of a similar character. He is given to careful observation and depiction, and he is both astute and clever in the art of 'bricole,' in other words, ruse and invention complementing the cartographer-engineer's mapping of lines of attack and defence along the peripheries of the kingdom. Montaigne's textual engineering uses the ploy of the detached observer or topographer to show obliquely that the barbarity of the conqueror exceeds that of his enemy; it fortifies the writing self. The topographer here is recalled through Pieter Apian's well-known similitude in the *Cosmographia*, which made the portrait of a human being relate to the depiction of the world in the same vein as a detail, such as an eye or an ear, would to a city-view. Where the cosmographer depicts things or persons in their entirety and situates them in a greater whole, the topographer attends only to detail. By extension, this attention to detail and perspective commands also the art of the engineer. In both the *Essais* and the *Discours de la méthode* the terms *ingénieur* and *topographe* acquire almost allegorical status.

Descartes unfolds and flattens the contours of Montaigne's descriptions. At the beginning of the second part of the *Discours*, a city-view, a remainder from the comparison of cosmography to topography, stands as one of the components of a metaphor in which architectural design is conflated with the design of the self.

> Ainsi voit-on que les bastimens qu'un seul architecte a entrepris et achevés ont coutume d'estre plus beaux et mieux ordonnés que ceux que plusieurs ont tasché de raccommoder, en faisant servir de vieilles murailles qui avaient esté basties à d'autres fins. Ainsi ces anciennes cités, qui, n'ayant été

au commencement que des bourgades, sont devenues, par succession de temps, de grandes villes, sont ordinairement si mal compassées, au prix de ces places régulières qu'un ingénieur trace à sa fantaisie dans une plaine, qu'encore que, considérant leurs edifices chacun à part, on y trouve souvent autant ou plus d'art qu'en ceux des autres; toutefois, à voir comme ils sont arrangés, ici un grand, là un petit, et comme ils rendent les rues courbées et inégales, on dirait que c'est plutôt la fortune, que la volonté de quelques hommes usant de raison, qui les a ainsi disposés.[18]

It cannot be doubted that the engineer to whom reference is made here is an *ingénieur du roi*, a designer of protective walls, battlements, and bulwarks to defend cities from siege and attack. His ultimate fantasy is one of drawing a plan, perhaps in the style of Claude Châtillon's *Topographie*, in which relief and contour are so reduced that the idea of the flat plain is equal to the paper, a two-dimensional surface, on which a carefully scaled drawing is penned. Yet in the verbal landscape, relief and contour are manifest in the multiple points of view brought forward to look over the land. Close attention is devoted to buildings whose scale, when seen near at hand, differs from what is far. A proximate monument is in detailed and precise perspective while others in the distance are less so, such that in the Latin drift of the French, in the geology of the image (in which, as in the *Essais*, one idiom is couched in another), clarity is gained when the viewer 'finds' or turns about – *trouve*, or *tourne autour* – a single point of interest. 'Here' and 'there' become sighting points in an implicit trigonometry in which the observing self accounts for the point whence it locates not only what it looks at but also where it is.[19]

When the uneven nature of a terrain is recognized as a topographical fact, the idea of imposing an orthogonal order upon a landscape becomes impractical. The zigzagged incline of roads on mountainsides serves as a metaphor for the dilemma resulting from the application of universal reason to local landscapes. The inherited imperfections of great political orders, like old buildings held together by the combination of real and historical weight, can be appreciated when they are figured as paths on hillsides, 'en même façon que les grands chemins, qui tournoient entre des montagnes, deviennent peu à peu si unis et si commodes, à force d'être fréquentés, qu'il est beaucoup meilleur de les suivre que d'entreprendre d'aller plus droit, en grimpant au-dessus des rochers, et descendant jusques au bas des précipices.'[20]

It appears that the altitude and the contour of the landscape are causing the author to imagine the existential nature of the self; landscapes must be encountered as they have been and as they are (in contrast to the fantasy of the drawing on a flat plane); as a result, the *moy* must follow the meanderings of roads that have been carved on mountainsides since time immemorial. 'Jamais mon dessein ne s'est étendu plus avant que de tâcher à reformer mes propres pensées, et de bâtir dans un fonds qui est tout à moi.'[21] What by *captatio* Descartes calls a simple design in comparison to better drawn designs (*des desseins plus relevés*) plays on the sketches an engineer makes of a terrain, represented in this instance as the itinerary drawn in a mountainous landscape as he prepares a plan of attack or defence.[22] The self that traces the lines of its identity through its passage affronts, as in the drawings of a Jean de Beins, a mountainous world in which paths are indirect, precipitous, and often dangerous.[23] The mental traveller who would follow the straight path of reason encounters one topographical obstacle after another. Those who leave the 'common road' will never hold to the path (*tenir le sentier*) that leads more directly to the goals and will remain lost for life (*égarés toute leur vie*).[24] Those who live among the Chinese and the Cannibals hear what in the same paragraph of the *Discours* is called a 'plurality of voices.' And individuals who walk in the shadows are those, in most likelihood, lost in the mountains. Having to walk slowly and with circumspection in all things (*circonspection en toutes choses*), Descartes keeps his footing on the slippery slope of his mind and refuses to be swayed by opinions 'qui s'étaient pu glisser autrefois en ma créance sans y avoir été introduites par la raison,'[25] which here, in the project to arrive at the knowledge of everything that his mind would be capable of, is associated with geometry.

The design and drawing of the 'method' that readers of the *Discours* know by heart (never take anything to be true unless it is shown clearly and distinctly in our mind; divide the difficulties we encounter into parcels, as if through a gridding; conduct our thoughts in order, from one degree to the next, from a simple echelon to more complex and higher rungs) is fraught with topographical language reaching back to a variety of manuals, including those of Oronce Fine, the author of local maps combining observation and Ptolemaic 'method.' Fine, author of *Le sphère du monde* (1549), chooses a site as a central point, and around and about that point he determines places by means of gridding that begins from the crossing of a vertical with a horizontal coordinate. The map is filled out by 'degrees,' first with latitudes and longitudes, then with cities and places as they are marked in Ptolemy, and then with the relief that allows the tracing of rivers. The groundwork is found in the gridding, and the elaboration of the greater picture is developed through the shading of relief. As in the work of early engineers, the experience of a landscape is at once tactile and ocular, and it is made manifest through mathesis in its equally local and general meanings. A point is established so that the 'self' or the observing subject can be located in respect to coordinate positions that are drawn about and around the site where it is located in the ambient world.[26]

The composition of the third part of the *Discours de la méthode* shares traits with this cartographic method. The chapter and its environs can be studied from at least three angles: first, as a topography in its own right, in which, as in Montaigne's 'Des cannibales,' locale (its context and relation with ambient chapters) is a measure of its meaning; second, as an abyssal structure in which the self is found at a vanishing point; and third, as a point or, as it were, a compass rose at which several vectors or rhumb lines converge and allow various ways of navigating the text of the *Discours* by way of the self.[27] As a local or 'regional' projection, the last sentences of the third chapter appear to use the metaphor of the 'tableau' announced in the incipit, to describe the drawing of the method, to align itself with the engineer's craft: 'Et enfin, comme ce n'est pas assez, avant de commencer à rebâtir le logis où on demeure, que de l'abattre, et de faire provision de matériaux et d'architectes, ou s'exercer soi même à l'architecture, et outre cela d'en avoir soigneusement tracé le dessin; . . . ainsi, afin que je ne demeurasse point irrésolu en mes actions pendant que la raison m'obligerait de l'être en mes jugements . . . , je me formai une morale par provision.'[28]

Descartes's mention of his *dessin* (translated as 'blueprint' or 'drawing') recalls the geometry of a project or *dessein* that marks the work as of the opening pages. And the physical sense of *provision*, meaning stone, mortar, and scaffolding, has the echo of provisions and supplies for military campaigns. Those responsible for providing materials and architects would be none other than engineers who had 'carefully drawn the blueprint' for a structure of defensive fortification.[29] The sentence itself seems to build and unbuild itself in the marked tension between a desire to reconstruct (*rebâtir*) and to demolish (*abattre*) the site whence the discourse begins. The resultant drawing could indeed be a sign of the chapter itself, the map on which the philosopher inscribes his three maxims (obey the laws and customs of one's country; be as firm and resolute as possible in deed and action; use thinking to obtain self-mastery), and in a broad sense it could be the very site where he 'finds himself' upon having followed 'la méthode que je m'étais prescrite.'[30] The architectural or spatial *dessin* folds into a broader plan recalling the design announced earlier, of a sort of itinerary, 'le *dessein* que j'avais de continuer à m'instruire.'[31]

The design is tantamount to an itinerary that guides the crossing of a territory. The abstract space of the *logis* (lodging) signalled at the outset is situated in a specific geographical location when the narrator avows, 'Et d'autant que j'esperérais en pouvoir mieux venir à bout, en conversant avec les hommes, qu'en demeurant plus longtemps renfermé dans le poêle où j'avais eu toutes ces pensées, l'hiver n'était pas encore bien achevé que je me remis à voyager.'[32] What he calls his nine years of errancy, indeed of living without spatial coordinates or a mental compass, were begun in northern climes (and possibly in a stale atmosphere). The geographical setting finds a complement in bookish points of reference. In admitting that 'je ne fis autre chose que rouler ça et là dans le monde, tâchant d'y être spectateur plutot qu'acteur en toutes les comédies qui s'y jouent,' he refers indirectly to the siteless world of Montaigne's 'Apologie de Raimond Sebond,' a work that demolishes all sense of lodging and human habitation before turning the impression of deracination into its contrary.[33]

Descartes has succeeded in uprooting, not himself as he has just described, but from his mind, like weeds, 'toutes les erreurs qui s'y étaient pu glisser auparavant,' implying that the *dessein* is a map that arrests movement and errancy or that he indeed *is* that map, a map, as history shows us, of dubious accuracy.[34] The borders of the chapter are drawn through the reiteration of its grounding metaphor of the lodging to which he returns to bivouac. It is a construction site where the material of the old building is refashioned to produce something new. Reference to the *poêle* and to the end of winter situates the author in a topographic context. Allusion is made to northern climes, making clear the contradiction between the place where he thinks and the anonymity of the mental space he has crafted for himself. That he is situated in the context of war makes especially clear the fact that his praise of logic is made in a lodge or a *logis*, and that the latter is the milieu of the cartographer and logistician. The reference to a specific place can point as much to a geographical location as to the textual topography before the reader's eyes, in which the implied strategist-engineer has the appearance of an *honnête homme*: 'Mais ayant le coeur assez bon pour ne vouloir point qu'on me prît pour autre que je n'étais . . . ce désir me fit résoudre à m'éloigner de tous les lieux où je pouvais avoir des connaissances, et à me retirer *ici*, en un pays où la guerre a fait établir de tels ordres, que . . .'[35] The 'here' indicates the abyssal character of the chapter at the cornerstone of its architecture. The reader is invited to look at the point as one of coextensive vanishing and origin of the self, as it is withdrawn from any specific place and yet located in a specific milieu. Descartes is at once in a throng of people under military protection, in a bustling city of the kind shown in Braun and Hogenburg's *Civitates orbis terrarum*, and in the most remote corner of the world, where he has been able to 'vivre aussi solitaire et retiré que dans les déserts les plus écartés.'[36] The author's name, refracted in the characters of the final sentence, just cited, underlines how much his name is given to signify a function of the flat plane. In this manner the tract that nowhere bears the signature of its author is ultimately named. The wilderness that would be off-map is paradoxically at its centre, and in its place is the name of the author that has uncanny cartographic resonance.[37]

If the wilderness or isolated places at the corners of the map, seen as the most remote areas (*les déserts les plus écartés*), happen to be at the virtual centre of the *Discours* at the end of the third chapter, halfway along its itinerary in six chapters or stages, or perhaps at a point of convergence in a virtual system of rhumb lines or in a perspectival plan, then the centre can be set in the context of a third reading: by which the chapter as *dessein* remains a plot-point of an itinerary that begins elsewhere, specifically in what the author notes, at the outset of the first chapter, as a desire to make visible (*faire voir*) 'en ce discours, quels sont les chemins que j'ai suivis, et d'y représenter ma vie comme en un tableau.'[38] The famous remark that would align Descartes with the tradition of Pieter Apian's distinction between topography and geography, in which the 'tableau' is also a portrait, could be interpreted as well in the manner of a 'table' or index of places and their spatial coordinates. The *Discours* would represent a picture of the self, but in its field of analogy it would also become a graph and a grid, what Cotgrave calls 'a table whereon things be painted, or written; a writing table; memorial, register.'

Seen in this way, the text would acquire an impression of depth – it would become an orography – yet at the same time it would be as flat as the name Des-Cartes, inscribed at the vanishing point: unique but collective, at a single location but everywhere, in suspension and on a ground, single but equally divisible into segments and units. It would be at the hinge between a world of illusory depth and one of the flatness of a ciphered table. The *Discours* would afford an itinerary not only in what it reports of the voyages of its author but also in its motion on and about the printed signs that compose the textual surface. It would be a work, like a piece of modern art according to Gilles Deleuze, in which 'la surface du tableau cessait d'être une fenêtre sur le monde pour devenir une table opaque d'information sur laquelle s'inscrit la ligne chiffrée.'[39] It would thus provide evidence of a shift – at least since the invention of perspective and its presence in the Ptolemaic tradition – where, 'au tableau-fenêtre se substitue la tabulation, la table où s'inscrivent des lignes, des nombres, des caractères changeants.'[40] The map now is a surface on which information is written. It is a creation far more folded and enveloped in itself than its beguiling clarity would lead us to believe.

From these three possible readings of the *Discours*, the 'self' can be seen as a creation engineered and, as a product of practical cartography, also invested in the new genre of the personal essay in which beginnings and endings are given rather than selected and imagined in the space that its language, its images, and its lines endlessly demarcate and coordinate. It begins where the student of the self is likened to a topographer who would be travelling to the New World or else to an engineer plotting elegant maps destined for defensive fortification of the borders – areas of continuous conflict and war – of a nation. The self is a function of the way that plotted space is constructed in order to situate it. Although it is a long-standing convention to read Descartes through the memory of Montaigne, comparison of their implicit textual topographies shows that the selves they fashion emerge from a broader context of conflict and war. Eminently visual, it is a context in which the self is shaped through various graphic strategies.

NOTES

1 The text of Descartes's meditation leads from one of the 'most common things,' a piece of wax, to a view of a city street from the commanding vantage point of a window on a building's upper floor. The shift from a fragment to a milieu in which his reflections are being 'essayed' serves to describe what he means by *res extensa*. 'Sumamus, exempli causa, hanc ceram' (Prenons pour exemple ce morceau de cire), he states, before examining its qualities and its transformations under the effect of heat and pressure, before he asks of the nature of ambient space: 'Quid extensum? Nunquid etiam ipsa ejus extensio est ignota?' (Qu'est-ce maintenant que cette extension? N'est-elle pas aussi inconnue?) He asks the question before wondering if the people

he sees in the street are humans or spectres wearing hats and coats; see René Descartes, *Méditations métaphysiques, objections et réponses suivies de quatre lettres*, ed. Jean-Marie and Michelle Beyssade (Paris, 1979), 89–95.

2 In his work on 'heterology' (what he calls the science of the 'other'), Michel de Certeau notes how encounters with alterity begin with a force of attraction that leads to repulsion; see Michel De Certeau, *L'écriture de l'histoire* (Paris, 1975), 3–4; and Michel de Certeau, Dominique Julia, and Jacques Revel, *Une politique de la langue: La révolution française et les patois* (Paris, 1975), 154–5.

3 De Certeau, *L'écriture de l'histoire*, 68–9. In the *Discours* Descartes locates the space in Germany: 'J'étais alors en Allemagne, où l'occasion des guerres qui n'y sont pas encore finies m'avait appelé; . . . le commencement de l'hiver m'arrêta en un quartier où, ne trouvant aucune conversation qui me divertît, et n'ayant d'ailleurs, aucuns soins ni passions qui me troublassent, je demeurais tout le jour enfermé seul dans un poêle, où j'avais tout loisir de m'entretenir de mes pensées.' See René Descartes, *Discours de la méthode*, ed. Geneviève Rodis-Lewis (Paris, 1966), 41. 'I was then in Germany, attracted thither by the wars in that country, which have not yet been brought to an end; . . . The setting in of winter arrested me in a locality where, as I found no society to interest me, and was besides undisturbed by any cares or passions, I remained the whole day in seclusion, in a stove-heated room, with full opportunity to occupy my attention with my own thoughts.'

4 'We need topographers who would provide a particular account of the places where they have been'; Montaigne, 'Des cannibales,' in *Oeuvres complètes*, ed. Albert Thibaudet and Maurice Rat (Paris, 1962). All subsequent citations of Montaigne's writings in French are to this edition.

5 See Monique Pelletier, 'Visions rapprochées du territoire,' in *De Ptolémée à La Guillotière (XVe–XVIe siècle): Des cartes pour la France pourquoi, comment?* CTHS Géographie 6 (Paris, 2009), 41–62, esp. 48 and 62.

6 Montaigne, 'De l'exercitation,' 357: 'This long story of so slight an accident would appear vain enough, were it not for the knowledge that I have gained by it for my own use; for I do really find, that to become acquainted with death, we need merely to approach it. Everyone, as Pliny says, is a good discipline to himself, provided he be capable of closely spying upon himself. Here, this is not my doctrine, it is my study; and is not the lesson of another but my own.'

7 Montaigne elsewhere uses the same formula in a broad and ironic mode, in discussing the pitfalls of memory, in 'De l'experience' (3.13): 'Si chacun espioit de près les effets et circonstances des passions qui le regentent, comme j'ay faict de celle à qui j'estois tombé en partage, il les verroit venir, et

ralanteroit un peu leur impetuosité et leur course' (If all people closely spied on the effects and circumstances of the passions that rule them, as I have done with the one that befell me, they would see them coming, and slow down a bit their impetuousness and their course).

This kind of writing is what Freud associated with topography. The founder of psychoanalysis develops the point throughout much of his work before summing up some of its features in 'Moses and Monotheism' (*The Standard Edition of the Complete Psychological Works of Sigmund Freud*, trans. James Strachey in collaboration with Anna Freud [London, 1964], 23:96–7). In these pages Freud calls his view of the mental apparatus 'topographical.' As Michel de Certeau has observed in a close reading of Freud's late essay, what is called the mental apparatus inheres in the shape and form of the writing; see De Certeau, *L'écriture de l'histoire*, 316–17 and note 2 above. In *L'inconscient graphique: Essai sur la lettre à la Renaissance* (Paris, 2000), I have called this dimension the 'graphic unconscious' of early modern printed writing.

8 'It's a thorny enterprise, and more than it seems, to follow an allure so vagabond as that of our mind; to penetrate the opaque depths of its inner folds; to choose and to arrest so many of the slight breaths of its agitations. And, yes, it is a new and extraordinary novelty that retracts us from the common occupations of the world, and the most recommended too. For several years now I have had only myself as the aim of my thoughts, I have reviewed and studied only myself, and if I were to study something else, it's been in order to suddenly place it upon myself or, better, in myself.' The French text is taken from Montaigne, 'De l'exercitation,' 358. The stresses are mine.

9 'to accredit their judgment and to seduce you, wilfully bring you on this side of the material, extending and amplifying it'; Montaigne, 'Des cannibales,' 202.

10 Ibid., 202: 'we need a very faithful man, or one so simple that he lacks what is needed to build and give likeness to false inventions, and who has espoused nothing.'

11 Ibid., 205, stress added: 'For they live in a very pleasant and temperate region of the country; such that according to what my witnesses said, rarely have they seen there a sick person; and they have assured me they've never seen a man feverish, bleary-eyed, toothless, or bent over with age. They are situated along the sea, isolated from the inland by large and lofty mountains, with a stretch between them of 100 leagues or so.'

12 Ibid., 199–200.

13 Ibid., 204: 'through experience in these nations . . . a state of nature so pure and simple as we see it.'

14 Ibid., 205: 'Their buildings are very long and can contain two or three hundred souls, furnished with the bark of great trees, holding to the ground at one end and supporting themselves and leaning one against the other by the roof, much as our own barns do, the covering of which hangs to the ground and serves as siding. They have wood so hard that they use it for cutting and fashioning their swords and grills for cooking their meat. Their beds are of a cotton fabric, suspended from the ceiling, like those of our boats, to each his own; for the women sleep apart from their husbands.'

15 Pieter Apian, *Cosmographie* (Paris, 1551), fol. aiv: 'all things, almost the slightest contained in them, as are cities, seaports, populations, countries, the courses of rivers, and several other things, such as buildings, houses, towers, and other similar things.' This edition is the most carefully executed and illustrated of the twenty-nine that appeared from 1529 up to the end of the sixteenth century. For an overview and bibliography of Apian's work see the entry in Robert Karrow, *Sixteenth-Century Mapmakers and Their Maps* (Chicago, 1993).

16 Monique Pelletier, 'L'enquête inachevée de Nicolas de Nicolay: Le Berry de 1567 et le Bourbonnais de 1569,' in *De Ptolémée à La Guillotière*, 35–9. See also Pierre de Ronsard, 'En faveur de N. Nicolai,' in Paul Laumonier, ed., *Pierre de Ronsard: Oeuvres complètes* (Paris, 1939), 10:124–5.

17 David Buisseret, 'French Cartography: The *ingénieurs du roi*, 1500–1600,' in David Woodward, ed., *Cartography in the European Renaissance*, vol. 3 of *The History of Cartography*, ed. J.B. Harley and David Woodward (Chicago, 1987–2007), 1504–21. See also Catherine Bousquet-Bressolier, 'Le territoire mis en perspective,' in Monique Pelletier, ed., *Couleurs de la terre: Des mappemondes médiévales aux images satellitaires* (Paris, 1998), 114–18.

18 Descartes, *Discours de la méthode*, 42: 'Thus we observe that the buildings which a single architect has undertaken and completed are customarily more elegant and commodious than those that a few have attempted to bring together by putting to use old walls that had been built for other ends. Those old cities, which in their beginnings were merely small villages and have, over the passage of time, become large cities, are ordinarily so poorly laid out – compared with the regularly constructed towns that an engineer draws according to his fancy on a plain – that yet, considering each of their edifices separately, as much or more art can be found than in those others; nonetheless, in seeing how they are arranged, here a large one and there one small, and how they cause streets to bend and become uneven, we might say that fortune, rather than the will of a few men using reason, is what has disposed them as they are.'

19 Or, as Montaigne had put it at the beginning of 'De l'institution des enfans' (1.26): 'Ce grand monde, que les uns multiplient encore comme especes soubs un genre, c'est le miroüer où il nous faut regarder pour nous connoistre de bon biais. Somme, je veux que ce soit le livre de mon escholier' (This great world, that some people even multiply as species of a genre, is the mirror at which we should look in order to know ourselves from a good angle. Altogether, I want it to be my student's book). When in the *Discours* Descartes avows that he abandoned his studies to read 'the book of the world,' the world to which he refers may indeed include this passage in the *Essais.*

20 Descartes, *Discours,* 44: 'in the same way that great roads that turn about between mountains slowly become so even and commodious by dint of being travelled that it is much better to follow them than to undertake a more direct route by climbing over outcroppings and descending into the depths of precipices.' In her gloss of the passage Rodis-Lewis recalls – who else – Montaigne, for whom, in 'De la vanité,' a political order must be recognized in all of its inherited complexity before any reformation can be made. Montaigne had written: 'Quand quelque piece se démanche, on peut l'estayer: on peut s'opposer à ce que l'alteration et corruption naturelle à toutes choses ne nous esloigne trop de nos commencemens et principes. Mais d'entreprendre à refondre une si grande masse et à changer les fondements d'un si grand bastiment, c'est à faire à ceux /c/ qui pour descrasser effacent, /b/ qui veulent amender les deffauts particuliers par une confusion universelle et guarir les maladies par la mort' (When a piece falls out of joint a strut can hold it in place; we can regret that the natural alteration of corruption in all things puts us at too great a remove from our beginnings and principles. But to undertake rebuilding such a great mass and changing the foundation of such a huge building is left to those who in order to wipe off their grime wipe themselves away, who wish to amend particular faults through a universal confusion and cure all maladies through death); Montaigne, *Essais,* 935.

21 Descartes, *Discours,* 44: 'Never has my design been extended further than to attempt to reform my own thoughts and to build on a ground that is entirely mine.'

22 Ibid.

23 See Pelletier, 'L'enquête inachevée de Nicolas de Nicolay,' 76–7, pl. 18 and 19; and Bousquet-Bressolier, 'Le territoire mis en perspective,' 104–9, and figs. 5 and 6.

24 Descartes, *Discours,* 44.

25 Ibid. 'that might have formerly slipped into my belief without having been introduced therein by reason.'

26 First in French in *Le sphère du monde: Proprement dicte Cosmographie*, 1549 (Harvard Houghton Library, MS Typ 57); soon printed (Paris, 1551). François de Dainville, SJ, describes the process by which a topographical map is made in 'How Did Oronce Fine Draw His Large Map of France?' *Imago mundi* 24 (1970), 49–55. I have studied Fine's map of the mountainous Dauphiné and environs from this point of view in *The Self-Made Map* (Minneapolis, 1996), 129–32.

27 In literary and art criticism, the term 'abyssal' designates a structure in which an abyss is found. Novelist and critic André Gide used the term *mise en abyme* to refer to a self-mirroring and self-enclosing structure in which the whole of a work finds itself reflected. Taken from early modern practice (specifically, in Rabelais), the term generally refers to a process of interior duplication. For years (until the company changed its label) the baseline 'example' of the *mise en abyme* had been the logo of 'Pet' seen on its cans of concentrated milk. The label displayed a label of a can of Pet Milk out of which a cow's head emerges. In that label is found the same image, and in that image, to a smaller degree, the same image, and so forth. Its use in a visual and cinematic context is taken up in my *Film Hieroglyphs* (Minneapolis, 2006), chap. 6, apropos of the fourth episode of *Paisan* (directed by Roberto Rossellini, 1947) in which – miracle of miracles – appears a can of Pet Milk.

28 Descartes, *Discours*, 51: 'And finally, since it is not enough, before beginning to rebuild the lodging where one lives, to knock it down, and to provide architects and materials, or train oneself in architecture, and furthermore to have carefully drawn its blueprint; . . . thus, so that I would not remain irresolute in my actions while reason would oblige me to be so in my judgments . . . , I shaped for myself a moral code through provision.'

29 As David Buisseret notes: 'The primary function of the engineers had originally been to design fortresses. In early modern armies, they had colleagues whose function was to attend to the soldiers on the line of march, making sure that they were properly supplied, and found suitable lodgings at the end of the day. In English these officers were called lodgings-masters, and in French *maîtres des logis*. The *maîtres des logis* in the time of Henri IV . . . produced more than two hundred manuscript maps designed to help them in their task.' *The Mapmaker's Quest: Depicting New Worlds in Renaissance Europe* (New York, 2003), 139.

30 Descartes, *Discours*, 54: 'the method I had prescribed for myself.'

31 Ibid.: 'the plan I had to continue to instruct myself.' As a genre, the road book informs the *Discours*. Descartes amplifies its philosophical implication by investing thought into displacement. The text begs us to reflect on how we 'think' when going from one site to another. The tradition of the road book is the subject of Catherine Delano-Smith, 'Milieus of Mobility: Itineraries, Route Maps and Road Maps,' in James Akerman, ed., *Cartographies of Travel and Navigation* (Chicago, 2006), 38–41.

32 Ibid., 55: 'And as I was hoping to be able to finish it [the project] better in conversing with people, than in living longer in the heated room where I had had all these thoughts, winter had not yet really ended when I started travelling again.' 'Heated room' translates *poêle*, a hot stove, which is a synecdoche if it also designates the greater space in which it is found. It is geographical in marking an orientation between northern and southern degrees or latitudes, on the one hand, while, on the other, it also refers to Montaigne's remarks about cultural differences in his essay on experience: 'Un Aleman me fit plaisir, à Auguste, de combatre l'incommodité de noz fouyers par ce mesme argument dequoy nous nous servons ordinairement à condamner leurs poyles . . . Car à la verité, cette chaleur croupie, et puis la senteur de cette matiere reschauffée dequoy ils sont composez, enteste la plus part de ceux qui n'y sont experimentez; à moy non. Mais au demeurant, etant cette challeur equiale, constante et universelle, sans lueur, sans fumee, sans le vent que l'ouverture de nos cheminées nous apporte, elle a bien par ailleurs dequoi se comparer à la nostre. Que n'imitons nous l'architecture Romaine?' (At Augsburg a German gave me the pleasure of fighting the inconvenience of our hearthsides by using this very argument we ordinarily use to condemn their heated rooms . . . For indeed this stale heat, and then the smell of this heated matter of which they are made, give headaches to those who aren't used to them; not at all for me. But as it is, given this even, constant and universal heat, without light, without smoke, without the wind that the opening of our chimneys brings us, it merits comparison to our own. Why not imitate Roman architecture?); Montaigne, 'De l'expérience,' 1058. On this passage see also Georges Van den Abbeele, *Travel as Metaphor: From Montaigne to Rousseau* (Minneapolis, 1992).

33 Descartes, *Discours*, 55: 'I did no more than to roll about the world, here and there, trying to be a spectator rather than an actor in all the comedies at play within it.' Montaigne writes: 'Finalement, il n'y a aucune constante existence, ny de nostre estre, ny de celuy des objects. Et nous, et nostre jugement, et toutes choses mortelles, vont coulant et roulant sans cesse' (In the end, there is no constant existence, neither of our being, nor of that of objects. And we, together with our judgment and all mortal things, are

endlessly flowing and rolling); Montaigne, 'Apologie de Raimond Sebond,' 586. The formula is reiterated elsewhere in the essay.

34 Descartes, *Discours*, 55: 'all the errors that might have formerly slipped within.'

35 Ibid., 57, stress added: 'But having courage enough not to wish that I would be taken for someone other than who I was . . . this desire brought the resolve to withdraw myself from all the places where I might have been known and to retire here, in a country where the war causes such orders to be established, that . . .'

36 Ibid., 57: 'live as alone and withdrawn as in the most remote deserts.'

37 The abyssal (but not the topographic) reading of the chapter is taken up in *The Self-Made Map*, 296.

38 Descartes, *Discours*, 35: 'in this discourse, what roads I have followed, and therein to represent my life as if in a picture.'

39 Gilles Deleuze, *Le pli: Leibniz et le baroque* (Paris, 1988), 38; in English, *The Fold: Leibniz and the Baroque* (Minneapolis, 1993): 'the surface of the painting was no longer a window on the world and became instead an opaque table of information on which the ciphered line is written.'

40 Deleuze, *The Fold*, 38: 'tabulation replaces the picture-window, the table on which lines, numbers, changing characters are drawn.'

PART III

NEW DIMENSIONS: INTERSTICES AND INTENSITIES

chapter fourteen

A Taste for the Interstitial (間): Translating Space from Beijing to London in the 1720s

ROBERT BATCHELOR

The cancellation of distance haunts the occupants of urban space.
Henri Lefebvre, *The Urban Revolution*[1]

A remarkable porcelain plate designed for Eldred and Isabella Lee of Coton Hall in Shropshire during the late 1720s or early 1730s can take the viewer to a core problem in thinking about spaces of the self in the early modern period (figure 14.1).[2] The plate is a particularly complex example of armorial ware, a style dating to the sixteenth century that expanded rapidly in the 1720s with the regularization of English East India Company trade at Guangzhou (Canton). This piece required assembling three different patterns – a copperplate engraving of London, a coloured drawing of the Lee crest presumably provided by the family, and a black-ink drawing of Guangzhou from a Chinese album. All of these ended up in the hands of enamel painters in south China, who worked in *encre-de-chine* (*mocai* 墨彩 or ink colour), a style designed to reproduce engravings, woodblock prints, and ink drawings. What seems at first glance to be a fantasy of continuity that places the owner of the plate within a homogeneous global trading space, on closer inspection reveals a series of discontinuities between competing media, aesthetic strategies, and symbolic codes that the artisans who made the plate and the Lees who ordered it seem to be attempting to confront. The Lee plate plays off the gaps among spatial and temporal representations, and in doing so it offers a different model of aesthetic judgment and cognition from the classical Cartesian or Lockean self. Yet those models, which also imply a certain conception of representational space, still hinder our understanding of emerging desires in the early eighteenth century not

Figure 14.1 Using a remarkable array of an English engraving, a Cantonese ink drawing, and a family crest, the cartouches on this plate from a much larger service dramatize the question of in-between spaces. Soup Plate, Lee Service, ca. 1733, The Reeves Center, Washington and Lee University, Lexington, Virginia [1975.1.1]. Photograph courtesy of The Reeves Center, Washington and Lee University, Lexington, Virginia.

only to possess objects like the Lee plate but also to define new spaces that could comprehend the translations embodied in them.

One thing that the Lee porcelains as objects indicate is a struggle over such translations. The general theme is a kind of doubling – two panoramas, two emblematic motifs – of contrasting yet related styles, which put the global processes of exchange that allow for the creation of such objects in relation to domestic space. This mixture of media and themes suggests a desire for distinction, perceptible even in the meritocratic family motto, *virtu vera est nobilitas* (true virtue is nobility). In putting above and below the coat of arms chrysanthemum motifs (*ju* 菊), a symbol of longevity and accomplishment in China, the painters showed that they were cognizant of this desire as well. Such broader echoes of Chinese meritocracy buttress the Lees' claims to nobility, fitting into the tendencies among the opposition to Robert Walpole in the 1720s and 1730s to understand commerce in terms of virtue and merit rather than the growth of the state and chartered corporations that could support public debt.[3] Paired panoramic images, of London with the Thames and the outer fortifications of Guangzhou with the Dutch 'folly fort' at Whampoa on the Pearl River, surround the interior crest, giving the whole a global urban and commercial frame.[4] Both city images suggest a kind of liminal or bounded relationship with the urban world: the fortresses and walls guarding the Pearl River Delta and the wall-like London Bridge simultaneously imply different modes of openness and closure. The junk-like ships on the Thames and the profusion of steeples with crosses, with which the Chinese artist seemed as fascinated as Europeans were with pagodas, almost appear to indicate a kind of return gaze, confirming the status of the Lees and their crest as a global sign and recognizing London's place as a global commercial centre.

Lee, a prominent member of the provincial gentry who owned about 5000 acres of land and assets such as East India stock, was certainly the kind of propertied person that John Locke admired, but he does not immediately seem to be the kind of travelling and trading 'global self' that early modern historians have begun to reconstruct from archives.[5] The plate setting, however, suggests that even in provincial Shropshire people were using the London market to put together a diverse range of images produced though various media. This active assembling says something about cognition in the early eighteenth century. Scholars have been discovering in Shakespeare's Globe and in the practices of early modern navigators the dynamic loops of environmental and action-oriented cognition.[6] Pieces like the Lee service suggest that even in domestic spaces in the countryside, early modern people appeared to be assembling, exploring, and testing new resources both for the way they embodied actions as simple as dinner and for their problem solving in terms of understanding highly extended networks of people and material things. In this case the 'cognitive artefact' produced through an extremely complex set of relations of production, exchange, and consumption was a set of dishes.[7] This kind of material production of new media (porcelains and modes of painting and engraving), along with the cognitive work and adjustments they required, fit in with broader contemporary processes. C.A. Bayly has called these 'the Great Domestication'; John Richards, an 'unprecedented intensity' of expansion of frontiers by various societies across the globe coupled with the development of the 'most efficient state and private organizations known since classical antiquity.'[8] Perhaps better than any text or printed image from the period, the plate articulates a process of globalization, one that conjoined precise urban localities like London and Guangzhou, as well as familial and corporate networks, and that entailed the cognitive processes of assembling different media in relation to one another.

That may seem to be a weighty interpretation for a fragile porcelain service to bear. In twentieth-century scholarship, porcelains of this kind have been classified as export ware or even chinoiserie, inauthentic and Westernized cultural representations that play to the fantasies of an urban European market.[9] To some eighteenth-century critics they represented distorted mirrors of the self, emblems of false representation and vanity. The latter often described the style as flat, lacking perspectival space as well as the psychological depth implied by chiaroscuro shading. Neither following the single-point techniques of Alberti, nor producing the kind of representational knowledge to which post-Baconian science aspired, a plate like that from the Lee service seemed a failure in terms of both form and content when judged by such classical standards.[10] As such it appeared superficial or even ephemeral, hardly the place to look for understandings of the process of globalization.

A different approach to the layers of spatial representation on the Lee plate unfolds through the concept 間 (*jian* in Mandarin), a word that can imply a state of betweenness in both time and space and, in noun form, an interstice or interval as well. It is an old word related to door or gate (*men* 門), which, since the nineteenth century, in both Japanese and Chinese, has formed part of the translations of Western concepts of space (*kong jian* 空間) and time (*shi jian* 時間). If one thinks in terms of philosophies using concepts of paths or 'ways' (*dao* 道), then *jian* is like an opening, not quite the Buddhist concept of emptiness (*kong* 空), but associated with it. As part of a representational strategy, *jian* works so that even though someone trained in single-point perspective might first be drawn to the plate's central crest, the surrounding images pull the gaze outward into a comparative sequence. The spatial and temporal intervals between images of Guangzhou and London and between the Lee crest and the far-flung juxtapositions of global trade do not directly undermine the aristocratic and rooted concept of self implied by the crest, but they suggest new openings, relations, and boundaries, new spaces of the self.

The concept of 間 has been particularly important for the architect Isozaki Arata, who sees today's world as surrounded by surface images, something he attributes to the 'superflat information surface' that mediates much of reality. For him, 'the dynamic is no longer situated at the interface between external and internal gaze, but rather in the relation between upper surface and the sediment below.'[11] Trying to access such phenomena, he calls attention to 間 (Japanese: *ma*), which does not imply the same kind of homogeneous space-time of Cartesian or Newtonian models, but rather emphasizes the 'undecidability that clings to [the process of] designing planes and surfaces' and the resulting imperfect and ongoing process of translation between representational spaces.[12]

When Isozaki began thinking conceptually about 間, he chose the 'Full Moon' (*Engetsukyo*) bridge (ca. 1670) in the Edo (Tokyo) garden Koishikawa Korakuen as a paradigmatic example.[13] Tokugawa Mitsukuni Mito (1628–1701), a wealthy scion of the second branch of the Tokugawa, had most of the garden built during the great period of urban expansion for Edo, a city of some one million people by the end of the seventeenth century. Zhu Shunshui (1600–82), a Ming scholar from Ningbo who had fled to Nagasaki after the Manchu conquest in 1644, helped with this particular bridge.[14] It makes a half-moon shape in the air mirrored in the surface of the water below, marking the interstitial in at least three ways – as a translation of an earlier Ming garden construction across space and time into Tokugawa Edo, as a conceptual relation of 'edges' and 'ends' that disjoin and connect, and finally as a garden device that performs these conceptual relations at an elemental level between water and earth as well as air and water. Relating surfaces was in this sense a technique for evoking 間.[15]

Such practices, however, were not confined to aesthetics and the built environment in the seventeenth century. In Japan and China, 間 raised complex philosophical and epistemological considerations. Distinct efforts to grapple with this issue appear in Ming and early Qing *kaozheng xue* (evidential scholarship), which used a kind of historical philology to debate the terms of the classics, and appeared in works by scholars and itinerant poets in Tokugawa Japan struggling with their relationship to both classical Chinese and Japanese.[16] For Matteo Ricci and Xu Guangxi, making the initial translation of Euclid into Mandarin in 1607, 間 also played a role. The Greek grammar in Euclid's definition of a line suggested two possible interpretations – either raising questions about the essential continuity of lines and points as 'the straight line lies in the same way as its points' or glossing those over as 'the straight line lies symmetrically through its points.' The subtle ambiguity disappeared in the Latin translation by Clavius, 'Recta linea est, quae ex aequo sua interiacet puncta' (The straight line exists by way of equally lying between its points), explained in terms of the concept of extension between the extreme points: 'quae aequaliter inter sua puncta extenditur' (where equally extended between its points).[17] Xu Guangxi and Ricci chose *jian* (間), a concept used in classical texts like the *Yijing* and *Zhuangzi*, to translate the verb *interiacere*, or 'lie between,' reopening ambiguities that the Latin had shut down. At the same time, they introduced new ones because the word had no bodily connotations, as opposed to *iaceo*, 'to lie down.' In their commentary, *jian* occurred again as 'between' in a translation of Archimedes's definition of a line – the shortest way between (*inter*) two points is a line. In this passage *jian* translated a concept of distance. But they did not use *jian* in a second reference to Plato's discussion about the division of 'the one' into parts from the *Parmenides*: 'And the straight, again, is that of which the middle is in the nearest line between the two extremes.'[18] Here they translated 'middle,' defined by Plato visually in terms of line of sight, with *zhong* (中), as in *zhongguo* (middle country, a traditional name for China), and they used the concept of 'covering' (*zhe* 遮), as in hiding with a screen, to bring in the notion of betweenness. In seventeenth-century Europe, dominated by the assumptions of linear perspective, such translation issues mattered less, but translating Euclid into Mandarin split the phenomenon of linearity into the centrally focused visual (*zhong* and *zhe*) and the interstitially spatial (*jian*). Thus, what appeared aesthetically in seventeenth-century Europe as a basic universal and unified approach to truth – linearity – in late Ming China only opened new questions about the much more complex problems of spatial depth raised by *jian*, *zhong*, and *zhe*.

The first translation of 間 that could have been read in England arrived in London in 1724 from the Qing capital, Beijing, by way of Matteo Ripa (1682–1746), a Vincentian (Lazarist) priest from Naples. While in London, with the help of his four disciples (ages twenty-two, eighteen, eleven, and ten) and their Chinese teacher, Ripa translated 間 into Italian as 'loco' or place in an inscription for one of the thirty-four engravings gathered into an album of the Kangxi emperor's new gardens, the Bishu Shanzhuang (避暑山庄, Mountain Resort for Escaping Summer Heat, their official name from 1703).[19] The scholarly debate about this album, a copy of which ended up in the library at Chiswick House in the London suburbs, has focused exclusively on representation and the

Figure 14.2 As suggested by the title, this particular view and garden location in the Bishu Shanzhuang is about the concept of *jian* 閒, which might be translated here as 'thinking space.' 濠濮閒想 (*Hao pu jian xiang*, aka 'Thirty-Six Views of the Imperial Summer Palace at Jehol),' ca. 1712, London, British Museum [1955,0212,0.1.8]. Photograph © The Trustees of the British Museum

influence of the image itself, whether it was 'seen,' and whether or not it confirmed Sir William Temple's translation of the supposedly Chinese word 'sharawadgi' as 'figures, where the beauty shall be great and strike the eye, but without any order or disposition of the parts, that shall be commonly or easily observed.'[20] Rudolf Wittkower's 1969 portmanteau-titled essay 'English Neo-Palladianism, the Landscape Garden, China and the Enlightenment' first made the strong case that the album Ripa brought fundamentally shaped ideas about landscape, design, and Enlightenment in England.[21] Wittkower began his article with one of the engravings from this album (figure 14.2). Of all the images in the album, this one perhaps most clearly made the visual link between the pavilions and bridges of Kangxi's new gardens and the chinoiserie pavilions and bridges that would later dot the English, and indeed, European countryside. But Wittkower cropped the Mandarin and Italian inscriptions out of the picture, and scholars since have generally avoided reading the album.

Yet, these inscriptions had been quite important at the time for understanding the images. Most likely after he had arrived in London, Ripa pasted a small slip with the Kangxi emperor's name for each image from the garden in the upper right corner of each engraving, in this case 濠濮間想 or *hao pu jian xiang*, romanized by Ripa as *hao po chien siang*. The literal translation is 'moat river thinking place.' Ripa's Italian translation was the 'loco [isolato] atto à pensare' ([isolated] place for thinking), with the brackets suggesting the difficulties in translating the idiomatic language.[22] The associated engraving depicts a pillared bridge going to a little grove on a small island, which itself could be a site of contemplation or could be used for viewing across a lake a nearby pavilion (亭 *ting*), nestled among two layers of hills and mountains but inaccessible from there. Kangxi had wanted this album in several versions that could appeal to the various groups under Qing sovereignty as well as to foreign powers like Russia, France, and Britain. He seems to have thought of his gardens and images of them not simply as a marker of imperial prestige but as a way of translating philosophical and spatial concepts like 間. Ripa seems to have felt that the images themselves were not enough in London, adding both the Kangxi emperor's place names and his own Italian translations.

Ripa came to Beijing in January 1711 on the cusp of two great changes in Qing court policy. Philosophically, Kangxi had, from the late seventeenth century, attempted to put together dynamic elements – from Ming neo-Confucianism and *kaozheng* scholarship in southern China, from Jesuit science and mathematics, and from Tibetan or Lama Buddhism – in an effort to develop new techniques of imperial administration as well as a broader rubric for cultural translations. He wanted to open up questions about boundaries and figures of space and time to better integrate the empire. After 1715, however, he would ban the public study of, and examination questions about, astronomical portents, musical harmony, or calculation methods, in order to keep speculative efforts about the future out of broader public discussions.[23]

A physical spatial shift at the Qing court followed these changes to court culture. After a period of suppressing Ming loyalist resistance between 1662 and 1684 in southern China and Taiwan, Kangxi worked to solidify his rule by going on six tours of the south (in 1684–5, 1689, 1699, 1703, 1705, and 1707) during which he visited the major Yangzi region cities of Suzhou, Nanjing, Yangzhou, and Hangzhou (in his first tour he avoided the latter two because of the fighting that occurred there during the Qing conquest). Certainly advanced age and the heat contributed to ending Kangxi's southern travels, but so also did his decision to shift from tours to architecture, developing a greater (extramural) Beijing that would symbolize a broader and more northerly empire than the Ming capital did.[24] Both as a symbol of this shift and a way of managing it, he built three new gardens, the Changchun Yuan (長春園, Eternal Spring Garden) and Yuanming Yuan (圓明園, Garden of Perfect Brightness, 1709), which were about three miles north-west of the Ming city wall, as well as the Bishu Shanzhuang, which Ripa would engrave.[25] Borrowing from the southern tradition of the urban and suburban scholar garden, the temple garden, and the Ming imperial gardens, these new gardens were also meant to tie urban commercial and scholarly tastes in garden design to broader territorial and religious ambitions in territories to the north and west of the old Ming Empire. Indeed, the basic strategy was to bring the power of territoriality to bear upon the urban elites of southern China and Beijing in ways that seemed syncretic and natural rather than linear and centralized like Ming Beijing, or the capitals of previous dynasties.[26]

Ripa himself was also a complex figure, who, at least judging from his memoirs, seemed open to what the philosopher Andy Clark calls 'ecological assembly,' a balanced use of highly heterogeneous resources pulled together on the spot for problem solving.[27] He was not a Jesuit with an accommodationist agenda but a Lazarist in the service of the Congregatio Missionis (est. 1632), having no formal education in either painting and draftsmanship or mathematics. He studied moral theology, not at a Jesuit institution, but at the Collegio Urbano di Propaganda Fide in Rome under the sway of Clement XI, who in 1704 would actually ban the Chinese Rites. Even his engagement with moral theology was largely self-driven and centred on a certain kind of sensual and spatial spiritual practice that differed greatly from the more intellectual Jesuit training. He claimed in his autobiography to have had a life-changing auditory vision commanding him to go 'to Rome,' during which 'in an instant, it represented to my mind a confused multitude of things, not in bodily imaginations or through fantasy, but in another intellectual mode that I cannot express.'[28] This synaesthetic approach to the intellect and cross-sensory language justified flexibility on issues relating to the visual arts and accommodation. He coupled this with a very practical rather than intellectual sense of Catholic theology. His birth at Eboli where, as the saying goes, Christ and Christian orthodoxy stopped (*Cristo si è fermato a Eboli*), his initial work as a priest in Capradosso, and his early pilgrimages in Italy all emphasized the very local difficulties that the Church encountered in translating its message, even in Italy.[29] His subsequent founding of the Collegio dei Cinesi (1732) in Naples under the sponsorship of Clement XII with the five Chinese he had first brought to London suggests a strategy quite at odds with that of the Jesuits. Rather than exporting Catholicism through confraternal orders, a challenging problem even in Eboli let alone Beijing, the Church was to embed Chinese language study within Europe. The Jesuits had always produced printed works in Europe to define and convey their experiences in the Ming and Qing empires. Ripa brought Qing productions of spatial representations and a permanent contingent of Mandarin teachers to Europe.

Arriving in Macao in 1710, Ripa was bitterly disappointed to learn that he would most likely be serving the Kangxi emperor as a painter rather than acting as a missionary to the common people. At Guangzhou, the governor tested his talents in painting and his beliefs about religious accommodation. Ripa refused to copy a conventional picture from Sima Qian's dynastic history, the *Shiji*, of Kong Fuzi (Confucius) kneeling before Laozi and asking him about funeral rites, mistaking its depiction of central figures from Confucianism and Daoism as a form of idol worship. He did, however, agree to perform the 'northern' (*settentrione*) or Manchu ceremonies as opposed to the more elaborate Ming 'southern' (*mezzogiorno*) rites, arguing that the former were 'per lo politico' ('for the political') while the latter, which were more intricate, belonged to a 'culto divino.' When he finally got to Beijing and was introduced to the room of the oil painters in the palace, he worried that lacking a talent for 'invenzione' he could only produce 'mediocre copia.' He found a solution in landscapes with Chinese houses, 'paesi, coll'accordo di alcune case Cinesi,' which the emperor enjoyed and which did not require an ability to reproduce the corporeality or the spiritual dimensions of the human figure (*figura*).[30] This approach to missionary work involved no serious commitment of either body or mind, the poles of Cartesian epistemology and representation. It not only worked well in negotiations over ritual in a relatively tolerant (multi-ritualist) society, but also prepared Ripa for translating Qing projects into a broadly acceptable idiom that could play simultaneously at court in Beijing, in the urban worlds of southern China, and in Protestant and Catholic Europe.

When Ripa arrived in Beijing, most of the Jesuits were working outside of the gardens on a mapping project that would include not only the old Ming territories but also Tibetan, Mongol, and Korean areas. They had begun in 1709, and because of the extensive fieldwork required, the map would not be finished until January of 1717. The Chinese 'trigonometric' (*sanjiao xue*, 三角學) surveying technique employed for the map used a baseline in which a chain was stretched from a latitudinal location determined by stellar measurements and then a third point was triangulated to determine longitude.[31] After recruiting Ripa's companion, the mathematician and French Augustinian Father Guillaume Bonjour-Fabri (d. 1710), for this expensive and long-term project which would also involve surveys of cities, Kangxi asked whether Ripa and his fellow Lazarist, the musician Teodorico Pedrini, had anything else to contribute.[32] Ripa announced that he had seen engraving practised but had never done it himself. He then made a simple copperplate engraving with lampblack and aquafortis (nitric acid). Kangxi was evidently pleased with the quality of the reproduction of Chinese landscape-painting techniques, which sparked both the garden and map-engraving projects.[33] Having produced a xylographic edition of the map in 1717 and a subsequent manuscript revision of the same, Ripa made a copperplate edition in 1719, which Kangxi sent to Peter the Great in March 1721, by means of a Russian embassy returning to St Petersburg. A further xylographic edition followed that same year.[34] Ripa considered not the album but the map his greatest accomplishment, as it demonstrated an empire-wide effect of the Catholic mission and showed his own work supplementing and making visible the work of the Jesuits.

In London, a decade before Ripa's 1724 return, the Royal Society, which knew about the map project but not the garden engravings, alerted readers to the project by reprinting a letter about it from the *Lettres édifiantes*, in the 1713 edition of the *Philosophical Transactions*.[35] Ripa brought with him to London a large copy of the map of the Qing Empire with coloured-ink annotations in Italian, one of which read, 'Jehol – villa imperiale dove il Imperatore desento Kanghi ogni anno andana a diporto' (Jehol – imperial villa where every year the emperor goes for recreation). This map ended up in the royal family's collection.[36] Unlike the French and the Russians, the British Hanoverians had little desire to explore this graphic representation of territorial empire, and the map attracted hardly any attention. But in Paris it was anxiously awaited, and – like the translations of Confucius in the 1680s – it somewhat paradoxically served to confirm the power of French knowledge production. The map would be re-engraved there in the early 1730s from a 1721 edition and then printed in 1735 and 1737.[37]

The album, Ripa's original vehicle for developing his technical printing abilities, had a greater impact in Britain than the map. In making the album, Ripa had not only to essentially reinvent the chemical techniques of engraving and printing, having only seen them once, but also to work with Chinese printers to design an appropriate press. Disastrous early efforts caused great amusement at court, but the experiment actually done in the gardens themselves eventually paid off. In tandem with painters, woodcutters, and officials, a truly synthetic album emerged, juxtaposing layers of different techniques. The hills and mountains are the easiest place to see this contrast in the engraving. A 1712 prototype album of paintings showed the interest of court artists like Wang Yuanqi (1642–1715) in the 'dragon veins' (*longmai* 龍 脈) technique for making mountains, a style taken from Ming woodcut engravings. In early woodcut efforts, from 1712, after paintings by Shen Yu, the nearby hills were done in *longmai*, but the outlines of the distant mountains were left for Ripa to fill in with single-point techniques of shading.[38] Likewise, a synthetic scheme of shadowing, engraved with the help of Zhu Gui and Mei Yufeng, mixed chiaroscuro with conventions derived from the ink washes of Chinese *wangliang hua* (shadow or penumbra painting, 罔两畫), a spare technique with few lines and light ink wash used for shadows and reflections. Unlike chiaroscuro, which was derived from drawing and translated particularly effectively into etchings, Chinese popular woodcuts traditionally looked to a technique used in narrative paintings and calligraphy, the *baimiao* (白描), linear and in monochrome ink with no colour or wash. Anita Chung has noted that this shift – exemplified by the painter and Chinese bannerman Shen Yu – was called *jiehua* (boundary painting, 界畫).[39] *Jiehua* unquestionably involved 'foreign' techniques, but it also allowed for certain aspects of 間 in the depiction of visual space to be carried over into these images that had in many ways been designed for global circulation. In this case, like the Lee plate, it layered a series of techniques derived from fundamentally different traditions.

A leaf from the British Museum album that was separated from the original set refers to the engravings as 'views' or 'scenes' (*jing* 景). The implied contrast here between the inner world of sentiment (*qing* 情) and the outer world of scene (*jing*) comes from Chinese painting. Before

1200, the Southern Song artists included few figures in their landscape paintings, in part because the paintings themselves were meant to literally transport the viewer into the space of the landscape. A classic example is Master Li's 'Dream Journey over Xiao Xiang' (瀟湘臥遊図巻, 1170), produced for the hermit Yungu Yuanzhou, who was too old to travel to Xiao and Xiang rivers. In the late eighteenth century, the Qianlong emperor wrote a title, 李公麟瀟湘臥遊圖 (*Li Gong Xiao Xiang woyou tu*, Master Li's Xiao Xiang Lying Journey Map), on the silk frontispiece of this painting. Here *woyou* is short for *woyi youzhi* or 'roaming the mountains while lying down.'[40] The kind of self-transport that the play between *qing* and *jing* implies is quite distinct from looking or watching within the garden, for which the more visual concept of *guan* (觀) is used elsewhere in the album in relation to watching fish. Like Master Li's painting, the garden views are not about representing a place but about simulating the experience of contact with nature that travelling to the physical space would achieve. Albums of *qing* were tools for making far space into near space.[41]

For a short time in England, through gardens, these kinds of intervals of contemplation provoked through looking at Chinese images of the interstitial spaces designed to evoke them seemed less foreign. On the eve of Ripa's arrival on 12 August 1723, Alexander Pope wrote to Robert Digby explicitly about 'Sharawaggis of China' (changing Temple's spelling) that are 'both very great and very wild,' in other words radically foreign, as they had been in 1685 for Temple.[42] But ideas of radical foreignness began to temper with the increasingly regular East India Company trade at Guangzhou in the 1720s and then with Ripa's arrival. Ripa went on tours of London and attended various dinners, including one where he convinced those present that Guangzhou was twice as big as London, which he estimated at 800,000 people, and that Beijing was larger still at over two million.[43] An East India Company merchant at that dinner was reluctant to acknowledge this initially, but then confirmed Ripa's observations to the astonished group of gentlemen. Ripa and his students drew public attention to widespread but rarely openly articulated knowledge about networks of relations with the Qing Empire, an increasingly important trading partner for London's prosperity and overall financial stability. In this context, the album and map were comparative and differential rather than inscrutable and radically foreign, evocative like the Lee plate of the gaps in layered and juxtaposed space.

Over the course of the next decade, first in Britain then in the rest of Europe, the Chinese garden came to be an acceptable international style. Robert Castell wrote about such gardens in his *Villas of the Ancients Illustrated* (1728), which claimed to reconstruct the villa of Pliny the Younger.[44] According to Castell, Greek and Roman gardening design was largely accidental until the application of geometry to aesthetics, after which were produced 'Plantations of Gardens by the Rule and Line . . . by an Art that was visible in every Part of the Design.' A post-geometric way subsequently developed in urbanized China: 'By the Accounts we have of the present Manner of Designing in *China*, it seems as if from the two former Manners a Third had been formed, whose Beauty consisted in a close Imitation of Nature; where, tho' the Parts are disposed with the greatest Art, the Irregularity is still preserved; so that their Manner may not improperly said to be an artful Confusion, where there is no Appearance of that Skill which is made use of, their *Rocks*, *Cascades*, and *Trees*, bearing their natural Forms.'[45] 'Present manner' is vague, but the writing does mark a shift. Castell highlights intentional and non-geometric disguising ('artful Confusion') of the strict boundary between practical plantation and geometric design, wild and domestic. His writing suggests that the concept of difference as exotic was shifting towards differential techniques for comprehending both nature and the relationship between urban space and countryside.

Such techniques were historical as well as cognitive. Thirty years after the album arrived in England during the height of a chinoiserie craze, the Chiswick album was re-engraved with English titles. The chinoiserie in the new images of this 1753 album, by reintroducing figures and placing sharp conventional shadows into the landscape to indicate distance, resists the process of evoking *qing*, or sentiment, which characterized the version brought from China and translated in the 1720s. The new publication claimed it was representing the totality of the emperor's gardens rather than giving a series of disconnected views designed to evoke contemplation through intervals of looking. Instead of experiencing a virtual version of Kangxi's gardens, the viewer faced a representation of exotic Chinese figures contemplating a stylized version of 'their' landscapes (figure 14.3). The new caption (and first English translation) reads, 'The Place for Thinking: A Pleasure House in View of a very pretty little Island.' In this translation from the Italian, Chinese cognition and English cognition are distinctly separated.

Henri Lefebvre once argued that planetary urbanization should be described as a 'virtual object,' a horizon with potential, an abstraction derived from temporary assemblages across surfaces – paper, porcelains, and now digital screens – that ultimately disguised a series of gaps. Before the cognitive philosophers of the last two decades made their

Figure 14.3 In this *chinoiserie* reingraving of figure 14.2, despite many additions to fill out the space, the concept of a thinking place is retained. 'The Place for Thinking – A Pleasure House in View of a very pretty little Island,' *The Emperor of China's Palace at Pekin, and his Principal Gardens, as well in Tartary, as at Pekin, Gehol and the Adjacent Countries with the Temples, Pleasure-Houses, Artificial Mountains, Rocks, Lakes &c. as disposed in different parts of those Royal Gardens, printed and sold by Robert Sayer, Henry Overton, Thomas Bowles, and John Bowles and Son* (London, 1753), 9. Reproduced by permission of Research Library, The Getty Research Institute, Los Angeles [92-B26685].

broader claims about mind, he made the more limited assertion that social space in the context of such urbanization ceases to be distinguishable from mental and physical space. Part of this is an abstraction into the virtual through mediating surfaces, the screens that now surround us and make our world superflat.[46] The various versions of the Kangxi album suggest that such abstraction is never complete, since even the 1753 album still contained elements of the negotiated layers of technique that had emerged from Kangxi's court. Out of the new urban, that 'Great Domestication' of the seventeenth and eighteenth century, came not alterity or absolute otherness but differential space-times, highlighting the problem of surfaces in a world of 間. To borrow a phrase from a much older text, the chapter of the *Zhuangzi* entitled 人間世 (The Person amidst the World): 'Gaze at that opening – the void of the room lives through its brightness.'[47] The above reflections offer a broader metaphor for translation and perhaps cognition itself. They also suggest an alternative paradigm to Greek representation that may be more helpful in understanding increasingly urban and mediated lives – a passing of energy through an opening, which creates shadows and redefines surfaces in the room it enters.

NOTES

1 Henri Lefebvre, *The Urban Revolution,* trans. Robert Bononno (Minneapolis, 2003), 39.

2 Ten pieces of this set are in the Reeves Center Collection at Washington and Lee University, including 1975.1.1. On this see Thomas Litzenburg and Ann Bailey, *Chinese Export Porcelain in the Reeves Center Collection at Washington and Lee University* (London, 2003), 95. One plate is owned by Geoffrey Godden of Britain's *Antiques Roadshow.* My thanks to Mr Godden for his correspondence on the plate in question, which is reproduced in Godden, *Oriental Export Market Porcelain and Its Influence on European Wares* (London, 1979), frontispiece and 15–17. See also David Howard, *Chinese Armorial Porcelain* (London, 1974), 323–9; David Howard and John Ayers, *Masterpieces of Chinese Export Porcelain* (London, 1980), 44–5; Clare Le Corbeiller, *China Trade Porcelain: Patterns of Exchange* (New York, 1974), 96, no. 39; William R. Sargent and Patrick Conner, *Views of the Pearl River Delta: Macau, Canton, and Hong Kong* (Hong Kong, 1996), 114–15; and Howard and Richard Ashton, *A Tale of Three Cities* (London, 1997). An innovative portrait of the family made in 1736 by Joseph Highmore, two years after Eldred's death, is at the Wolverhampton Art Gallery, http://www.wolverhamptonart.org.uk/learning/craft/family. Since this was probably commissioned by Isabella, it is possible that the porcelain set was as well.

3 Juvenal, *Satires* 8.20 : 'nobilitas sola est atque unica virtus.' The motto is very close to Trinity College, Cambridge's 'virtus vera nobilitas.' On the question

of merit and China see Robert Batchelor, 'Concealing the Bounds: Imagining the British Nation through China,' in Felicity Nussbaum, ed., *The Global Eighteenth Century* (Baltimore, 2003), 81–92. See also J.G.A. Pocock, *Virtue, Commerce and History* (Cambridge, 1985), 68–9. Another branch of the Lees of Shropshire had this coat of arms recognized in 1641, although their motto is *Ne incautus futuri* (Not careless for the future), from the description of the ant in Horace, *Satires* 1.1.35.

4 The Thames panorama is possibly derived from that of Joseph Smith, 'View of the City of London' (London, 1710), 2 sheets, Guildhall La.Pr. V gp. 3; but see also Johnannes Kip, 'La Ville de Londres / Prospectus Londinens' (London, ca. 1720); James Walker, 'View of the City of London' (London, 1710), Guildhall Art Gallery Store 258; George Seutter, 'Prospect der Königl. Haupt und Residentz Stadt London' (Augsburg, ca. 1710), Guildhall La.Pr. V gp. 3; Friedrich Werner, 'London' (Augsburg, ca. 1710), Guildhall La.OS V gp. 3; Johann Haffner (artist) and Marc Ruprecht (engraver), 'Londinum Londen' (ca. 1730), Guildhall La.Pr. V gp. 3; anon., 'The South Prospect of the City of London,' ca. 1710,Guildhall Art Gallery Store 255; and anon., 'The South Prospect of the City of London,' ca. 1720, Guildhall La.Pr.V gp.3. Panoramas of London were extremely popular in the early eighteenth century, and many of these appeared in other editions. Augsburg artists in particular emphasized the steeples of London, thereby giving their London views a dense and 'Gothic' appearance. For the source of the Canton drawings see the album 'Views of Canton' at the Chinese Pavilion, Castle of Drottningholm, produced by Chinese artists in Guangzhou, possibly at the request of the Qing. The piece could have been ordered through the Swedish East India Company (est. 1731), or more likely a copy of this album was used in Guangzhou by enamellers. For the use of Chinese painted and woodcut albums for porcelain designs by the Swedish Company see Bo Gyllensvard, 'Catalogue of Far Eastern Objets d'Art,' in Ake Setterwall et al., *The Chinese Pavilion at Drottningholm* (Malmö, 1974), 199–203, 206, 322; and Sven T. Kjellberg, *Svenska Ostindiska Compagnierna, 1731–1813* (Malmö, 1974).

5 See for example Linda Colley, *The Ordeal of Elizabeth Marsh: A Woman in World History* (New York, 2007); Miles Ogborn, *Global Lives: Britain and the World, 1550–1800* (Cambridge, 2008). Ogborn's discussion, on pages 6–9, of the tendency of global histories to be written in terms of a singular system or economy is particularly useful.

6 Evelyn Tribble, 'The Dark Backward and Abysm of Time: The Tempest and Memory,' *College Literature* 33, 1 (Winter 2006), 151–68; 'Distributing Cognition in the Globe,' *Shakespeare Quarterly* 56, 2 (Summer 2005), 135–55; Edwin Hutchins, *Cognition in the Wild* (Cambridge, MA, 1995).

7 On the cognitive artefact see Andy Clark, *Supersizing the Mind: Embodiment, Action and Cognitive Extension* (Oxford, 2008), 39–42; R.A. Wilson, *Boundaries of the Mind* (Cambridge, 2004), 176–7; Francisco Varela, Evan Thompson, and E. Rosch, *The Embodied Mind* (Cambridge, 1991). On the broader context of porcelain, see Batchelor, 'On the Movement of Porcelains: Rethinking the Birth of Consumer Society as Interactions of Exchange Networks, 1600–1750,' in John Brewer and Frank Trentmann, eds, *Consuming Cultures, Global Perspectives: Historical Trajectories, Transnational Exchanges* (Oxford, 2006), 95–122.

8 C.A. Bayly, *The Birth of the Modern World, 1780–1914* (Oxford, 2004), 49; John Richards, *The Unending Frontier: An Environmental History of the Early Modern World* (Berkeley, 2003), 1. Bayly relies on the work of Richards among others for his thesis. Within an English context Michael McKeon has described this as a devolution of absolutism; see his *Secret History of Domesticity: Public, Private and the Division of Knowledge* (Baltimore, 2005), xxiv, 48. For a more economic argument see Jan de Vries, *The Industrious Revolution: Consumer Behavior and the Household Economy, 1650 to the Present* (Cambridge, 2008).

9 For the classic definition see Hugh Honour, *Chinoiserie: The Vision of Cathay* (London, 1961).

10 See Francis Bacon, *The Advancement of Learning* (London, 1605), 1.4.8. For the 'classical' (usually defined in terms of Descartes) theory of representation as constitutive of knowledge see Michel Foucault, *Les mots et les choses* (Paris, 1976); Richard Rorty, *Philosophy and the Mirror of Nature* (Princeton, 1979), 3–11. Ola Söderström, 'Representation,' in David Atkinson et al., eds, *Cultural Geography* (London, 2005), 11–15, links Cartesian epistemology with Alberti's linear perspective.

11 Isozaki Arata, 'Fall and Mimicry: A Case Study of the Year 1942 in Japan,' in *Japan-ness in Architecture*, trans. Sabu Kohso (London, 2006), 103.

12 Isozaki, 'Fall and Mimicry,' 103. See also Isozaki's 1981 publication 'Ma-Space/Time in Japan' (1981) in Ken Tadashi Oshima, ed., *Arata Isozaki* (London, 2009), 156–61.

13 See Hans Hollein, *MAN transFORMS: Aspects of Design for the Opening of the Smithsonian Institution's National Museum of Design* (1976); Isozaki Arata, '*Ma* (Interstice) and Rubble,' in *Japan-ness*, 93. The point of this exercise related to a series of meditations on images of Japanese cities bombed in 1945, including of course Nagasaki, out of which Isozaki 'believed [he] might be able to construct a point of view with which to confront world history' (ibid., 99). For the problem of hybrid concepts that emerged in Japanese in the late nineteenth century – especially the self and landscape – see Karatani Kojin, *Origins of Modern Japanese Literature*, ed. Brett de Bary (Durham, 1993), 11–75.

14 On Zhu Shunshui see Minamoto Ryoen, 'Confucianism and Nativism in Tokugawa Japan,' in Wing-tsit Chan and William de Bary, eds, Meeting of Minds: Intellectual and Religious Interaction in East Asian Traditions of Thought (New York, 1996), 238–77, and *Kinsei shoki jitsugaku shiso no kenkyu* (Tokyo, 1980); also Yuxin Lu, 'Confucius, Zhu Shunshi, and the Origins of Japanese State Building in the Tokugawa Era, 1650–1700,' MA thesis, St Johns University, 1998; 'Zhu Shunshui,' in *Routledge Curzon Encyclopedia of Confucianism* (London, 2003), 845–6.

15 A standard critique formulated by Japanese modernist literature in the nostalgic mode is that the West fails to attend to surfaces – porcelain, paper, lacquerware, etc. See Jun'ichiro Tanizaki, *In Praise of Shadows* [*In'ei raisan,* 1933–4], trans. Thomas Harper and Edward Seidensticker (Sedgwick, 1977).

16 Susan Naquin and Evelyn Rawski, *Chinese Society in the Eighteenth Century* (New Haven, 1989), 65–6; Benjamin Elman, *From Philosophy to Philology: Intellectual and Social Aspects of Change in Late Imperial China* (Cambridge, 1984).

17 For the Greek translations see T.L. Heath, *The Thirteen Books of Euclid's Elements* (New York, 1956), 1:166–7. The Latin is Christophoro Clavio [Clavius], *Euclidis elementorum libri XV* (Rome, 1574), 2v. The Chinese translated from Clavio is Matteo Ricci and Xu Guangxi, *Jihe yuanben* 几何原本 (Beijing, 1607). See Peter Engelfriet, *Euclid in China: The Genesis of the First Chinese Translation of Euclid's Elements Books 1–VI (Jihe yuanben; Beijing, 1607) and Its Reception up to 1723* (Leiden, 1998), 157–8. For readings of Euclid in the late Ming and early Qing see J.C. Martzloff, 'La compréhension chinoise des méthodes démonstratives euclidiennes au cours du XVIIe siècle et au début du XVIIIe,' *Actes du IIe Colloque international de sinologie: Les rapports entre la Chine et l'Europe au temps des Lumières* (Paris, 1980).

18 The concept of 'between' (*inter*) is from the Latin translation of Archimedes's first 'assumption' in 'On the Sphere and the Cylinder' by way of Proclus's commentary. It does not appear in the Greek [See T.L. Heath, *The Works of Archimedes* (Cambridge, 1897), 3]. The Latin 'middle' (*medius*) goes back to the Greek of Plato (μέσον), 'Καί μὴν εὐθὺ γε, οὗ ἂν τὸ μέσον ἀμφοῖῖν τοῖν ἐσχάτοιν ἐπίπροσθεν ᾖ'; see Plato, 'Parmenides,' in *Plato in Twelve Volumes,* trans. Harold N. Fowler (Cambridge, MA, 1925), 9:137e. The Ricci and Xu translation of Plato reads '直線之中點能遮兩界' (*zhi xian zhi zhong dian neng zhe liang jie*).

19 The first name was the 熱河上營 (*Rehe shangying* or Upper Camp on the Rehe River). After making the gardens his summer capital, the Emperor Qianlong (ruled 1735–96) changed their name to Chengde. They are referred to by various groups at times as Rehe, Zehe, or Jehol. On the Bishu Shanzhuang see James Millward, *New Qing Imperial History: The Making of the*

Inner Asian Empire at Qing Chengde (London, 2004); and Philippe Forêt, *Mapping Chengde: The Qing Landscape Enterprise* (Honolulu, 2000).

20 Sir William Temple, 'Upon the Gardens of Epicurus: or, Of Gardening, in the year 1685,' *Miscellanea*, pt. 2 (London, 1690), 58. For the remarkably contested debate over the status of *sharawadgi* as an actual translation (variously attributed to Mandarin, Japanese, and Persian) see Qian Zhongshu, 'China in the English Literature of the Seventeenth Century,' *Quarterly Bulletin of Chinese Bibliography* 1 (1940), 351–84; Ciaran Murray, '*Sharawadgi* Resolved,' *Garden History* 26, 2 (1998), 208–13; Michael Sullivan, 'Chinese Art and Its Impact on the West,' in Paul Ropp, ed., *Heritage of China* (Berkeley, 1990), 285.

21 The album in question, catalogued as British Museum 1955,0212,0.1.1–34, labelled 'Emper. Of China's Pal-laces' on the spine, has a bookplate from the Chiswick library of the dukes of Devonshire, heirs to the famous 'gardening earl,' Lord Burlington. The eighteenth-century binding only contained thirty-four engravings (the full set is thirty-six), but the two missing leaves were acquired in 1968, and are catalogued as British Museum 1968,0212,0.27 and 28. The former leaf (no. 27) is titled 熱河第三十三景雙湖夾鏡 (*re he di san shi san jing shuang hu jia jin*, Thirty-Three Views of the Imperial Summer Palace at Rehe) and seems to have been a title page that was separated from the other engravings at some point before the Latinate transliterations and Italian translations were added. Most of the fifteen surviving copies of the album, such as Bodleian Arch. B d.16, have no Mandarin or Italian descriptions. The presence of this album in Lord Burlington's library was first noted by Basil Gray, 'Lord Burlington and Father Ripa's Chinese Engravings,' *British Museum Quarterly* 22 (1960), which inspired Rudolf Wittkower, 'English Neo-Palladianism, the Landscape Garden, China and the Enlightenment,' *L'Arte* 6 (1969), 18–35. Patrick Conner dismissed any such connections in 'China and the English Landscape Garden: Reports, Engravings and Misconceptions,' *Art History* 2 (1979), 429–40 and in *Oriental Architecture in the West* (London, 1979), as did David Jacques, 'On the Supposed Chineseness of the English Landscape Garden,' *Garden History* 18, 2 (Autumn, 1990), 180–91. There is a vast literature, but by and large it does not engage with Ripa's autobiography (especially the Italian version) or the album and map themselves. See for example the recent piece that follows Conner's argument by Richard Strassberg, 'War and Peace: Four Intercultural Landscapes,' in Marcia Reed and Paola Demattè, eds, *China on Paper: European and Chinese Works from the Late Sixteenth to the Early Nineteenth Century* (Los Angeles, 2007), 121–32; and the Wittkoweresque argument of Yu Liu in *Seeds of a Different Eden* (Columbia, SC, 2008), 24–7. Liu reproduces the

print 濠 濮 閒 想 from the New York Public Library copy of the album that was owned by George McCartney, which only has the Chinese titles. Originally the NYPL copy (acquired in the 1950s) had an accompanying letter from Ripa dated 26 August 1714 to his superior, Alesandro Bussi. My thanks to David Helliwell of the Bodleian Library for helping me track down all fifteen surviving copies of the Ripa album.

22 British Museum, 1955,0212,0.1.8. The bracketed 'isolato' here suggests confusion about the translation of 濮 (*pu*, the name of a river) with the character 漠 (*mo*, desert or unconcerned), circumstantial evidence that the translations were not made in Beijing. Evidence from the other fourteen surviving copies, which do not have the Latin transliterations and Italian translations (and are often without Mandarin titles), confirm this. The Dumbarton Oaks copy of the album (acquired 1955 by Mildred Bliss) has an Italian MS insert, 'La villa Imperiale detta Geho King, dove l'Imperatore della Cina tiene le sue Delizie e specialmente della Caccia e Pesca, &c,' but no other writing. The same would hold true for the large map with its unique manuscript additions in Italian, formerly in the Hanoverian royal collection and now in the British Library.

23 Elman, *From Philosophy to Philology*, 79–80; Elman, *A Cultural History of Civil Examinations in Late Imperial China* (Berkeley, 2000), 484–5. On the question of music see Joyce Lindorff, 'Missionaries, Keyboards and Musical Exchange in the Ming and Qing Courts,' *Early Music* 32, 3 (August 2004), 403–14.

24 On the spatial relations of intramural Beijing in this period see Susan Naquin, *Peking: Temples and City Life, 1400–1900* (Berkeley, 2001).

25 On Changchun Yuan and the Yuanming Yuan see Young-Tsu Wong, *Paradise Lost: The Imperial Garden Yuanming Yuan (Honolulu, 2000); and Che Bing Chu and Gilles Baud-Berthier, Le Yuanming yuan: Le jardin de la clarté parfaite* (Paris, 2000).

26 In this the Qing strategy was not unique, as similar claims have been made about Mughal gardens in relation to cities; cf. James Wescoat, 'Picturing an Early Mughal Garden,' *Asian Art* 2, 4 (1989), 76.

27 Clark, *Supersizing*, 13.

28 Matteo Ripa, *Matteo Ripa, Storia della fondazione della congregazione e del Collegio de'Cinesi*, 3 vols. (Naples, 1832), 1:16: 'In una istante mi si rappresentò alla mente una moltitudine confuse di cose, non con immagini corporali, o fantastiche, ma con altro modo intellectual, che non so esprimerle.'

29 This is important in relation to the new historical work that emphasizes the spread of the dynamic confraternity model put forward by the Jesuits among Chinese Christians, which was less authority-driven but similar in its isolation from church governance to the parish churches on the fringes of

ecclesiastical authority in rural Naples familiar to Ripa; see Liam Matthew Brockey, *Journey to the East: The Jesuit Mission to China* (Cambridge, 2007), esp. 329–31. The Lazarists replaced the Jesuits as the official missionary presence at Beijing in 1785.

30 Ripa, *Storia*, 1:345–7, 387.

31 The method is described in Benjamin Elman, 'Ming-Qing Border Defense, the Inward Turn of Chinese Cartography and Qing Expansion in Central Asia in the Eighteenth Century,' in Diana Lary, ed., The Chinese State at the Borders (Vancouver, 2007), 47–8; and Sun Jili, *Kang-yong-Qian shiqi yutu cehui yu jiangyu xingcheng yanjiu* (Beijing, 2003). See also Laura Hostetler, 'Contending Cartographic Claims? The Qing Empire in Manchu, Chinese, and European Maps,' in James Ackerman, ed., *The Imperial Map* (Chicago, 2009), 93–133, 324; Joseph Needham, *Science and Civilisation in China* (Cambridge, 1959–), 3:569–79; and Walter Fuchs, *Der Jesuiten-Atlas der Kanghsi-Zeit* (Beijing, 1943). On the development of geography in early Qing China and its relation to the Jesuits and imperial expansion, see Benjamin Elman, *On Their Own Terms: Science in China, 1550–1900* (Cambridge, 2005), 195–6 and passim; Laura Hostetler, *Qing Colonial Enterprise: Ethnography and Cartography in Early Modern China* (Chicago, 2001); James Millward, 'Coming Onto the Map: Western Regions' Geography and Cartographic Nomenclature in the Making of the Chinese Empire in Xinjiang,' *Late Imperial China* 20, 2 (1999), 61–98.

32 On Pedrini see Peter Allsop and Joyce Lindorff, 'Teodorico Pedrini: The Music and Letters of an Eighteenth-Century Missionary in China,' *Vincentian Heritage Journal* 27, 2 (2007), 43–59.

33 Ripa, *Storia*, 1:411–40, esp. 421.

34 Fuchs, *Der Jesuiten-Atlas der Kanghsi-Zeit*, 43; Hostetler, 'Contending,' 323n. See also the two different 1721 editions in the British Library: Maps C.11.d.15 and *Fenfu zhongguo quantu* 15271.a.20.

35 Pierre Jartoux, 'The Description of a Tartarian Plant, Call'd Gin-Seng; with an Account of Its Virtues in a Letter from Father Jartoux, to the Procurator General of the Missions of India and China. Taken from the Tenth Volume of Letters to the Missionary Jesuits, Printed at Paris in Octavo, 1713,' *Philosophical Transactions* 28 (1713), 237–47. It begins: 'The Map of Tartary, which we made by order of the Emperor of China, gave us an Opportunity of seeing the famous Plant Gin-Seng, so much esteem'd in China, and so little known in Europe' (237).

36 British Library, Maps K.Top.116.15. The map is in three separate parts now, the other two being K.Top.116.15a and b. See also Ripa's Italian chart of the Chinese coast, K.Top.116.18. Place names are printed in Manchu north of

the Great Wall and in Mandarin south of the great wall, with red, green, and yellow ink manuscript transliterations and translations in Italian.

37 Du Halde obtained the map in the mid-1720s. This map only circulated in Europe widely when it was re-engraved by Jean Baptiste d'Anville in 1735 and subsequently appeared in Du Halde, *Description de la Chine* (Paris, 1735) and the *Atlas de la Chine* (Hague, 1737). There was some effort to promote an English version of this map (along with a Persian one) by a correspondent with the new 'Society for the Encouragement of Learning' in July of 1736; British Library, Add 6190, f. 11. The French (Anville) edition of Ripa's map was also in the royal collection as K.Top.116.5 in forty-two sheets. Some of this material in the royal collection may have been assembled later in the eighteenth century in preparation for the McCartney embassy.

38 A set of woodcut album leaves with no inscriptions, without any shading marks, and using different conventions survives, as well as copies of Ripa's engravings with Kangxi's poems and the title of the locations in Mandarin on a separate page but without Italian translation or manuscript Mandarin inscriptions. Both seem to have been entirely produced in China. See 'Han-I araha Alin-i tokso de halton be jailaha gi bithe,' MSO Mandchou 111–12; and Estampes et Photographie, Réserve Hd-90, both Bibliothèque nationale de France. Leaves from both are in Nathalie Monnet, *Chine, l'empire du trait: Calligraphies et dessins du Ve au XIXe siècle* (Paris, 2004). Online, see http://expositions.bnf.fr/chine/index.htm. The entire album with Kangxi's poetry has been reprinted as *Tongban Bishu Shanzhuang sanshiliu jing shi tu* (Beijing, 2002). See for comparison Wang Yuanqi, 'Wangchuan Villa' (1711), Metropolitan Museum of Art, Dillon Collection, 1977.80.

39 Valérie Malenfer Ortiz, *Dreaming the Southern Song Landscape* (Leiden, 1999), 145; Anita Chung, *Drawing Boundaries* (Honolulu, 2004), 6, 49–50.

40 Valérie Malenfer Ortiz, 'The Poetic Structure of a Twelfth-Century Chinese Pictorial Dream Journey,' *The Art Bulletin* 76, 2 (June 1994), 257–78. The painting is now in the Tokyo National Museum and images of both the painting and inscriptions can be found at http://www.tnm.go.jp.

41 Ibid., 262. On the cognitive dimensions of this, see A. Berti and F. Frassinetti, 'When Far Becomes Near: Re-Mapping of Space by Tool Use,' *Journal of Cognitive Neuroscience* 12 (2000), 415.

42 See Joseph Addison, *Spectator*, no. 411 (21 June 1712), no. 412 (23 June 1712), no. 413 (24 June 1712), no. 414 (26 June 1712); Alexander Pope, *Guardian*, no.173 (1713); Alexander Pope, 'Preface,' in *The Iliad* (London, 1715). Addison's pieces do not mention Temple or *sharawadgi*, but are clearly derived from that essay.

43 Ripa, *Storia,* 1:339, and 2:192–6. Ripa suggests that the larger population is due not only to less warfare and the absence of contagious diseases, but also to the fact that there are far fewer monks, nuns, and priests who remain celibate. London's population in the 1720s was closer to 600,000, and Guangzhou and Beijing were probably nearer to 800,000 and 1,000,000 respectively, although the estimates for London are based on more extensive data. Ripa composed his journal, the primary source about his life, between 1743 and 1745.

44 Despite its dedication to Lord Burlington, the expensive edition with its elaborate engravings apparently left Castell financially ruined. He could only find a total of 116 subscribers and died in debtor's prison of smallpox in 1729: *Journal of the House of Commons,* xxi, 277.

45 Robert Castell, *Villas of the Ancients Illustrated* (London, 1728), 32. This tripartite division of gardens may derive from Timothy Nourse's essay 'Of a Country House' (1700). Nourse argues that 'this Third Region or Wilderness be Natural-Artificial; that is, let all things be dispos'd with that cunning as to deceive us into a belief of a real Wilderness or Thicket, and yet to be furnished with all the Varieties of nature,' in *Campania Foelix* (London, 1700), 321–2. Nourse clearly draws upon the seventeenth-century tradition of 'irregular nature' in this passage.

46 Henri Lefebvre, *Urban Revolution,* 17. Abstraction is the critical launching point for Lefebvre in *La production de l'espace* (Paris, 1974). I have consulted the English version, *The Production of Space,* trans. Donald Nicholson-Smith (Oxford, 1991), 5–6, 48–51. For Lefebvre, projects like Derrida's on writing, Foucault's on power/knowledge, Kristeva's on the body, and Barthes's on the sign attempt to address this but without attending to the material conditions of their own productions of theoretical space. One might add to this list Habermas on the public and communication. Claude Lévi-Strauss, conversely, recognizes that all theoretical spaces are embedded in exchange, which involves mediation and conflation of the mental and social.

47 '瞻彼闋者，室生白' [*Zhuangzi,* IV, pt. 1, sec. 4 ('人間世,' The Person amidst the World), 2.], cf. Chinese Text Project, *Zhuangzi,* http://chinese.dsturgeon.net/text.pl?node=2740&if=en; original edited version *Zhuangzi yi zhu* (Beijing, 2002).

chapter fifteen

Sculpted by Dead Marbles: Winckelmann's 'Outer Selves' and the Body without Organs

JEAN-PHILIPPE ANTOINE

> For the thinking ones, the supreme subject of Art is Man, or rather his outer surface, and this surface is as hard to explore for the artist, as his inner side is for the philosopher.
>
> Johann-Joachim Winckelmann, *Erinnerung über die Betrachtung der Werke der Kunst*[1]

Ever since their publication in 1764, in his *Geschichte der Kunst des Altertums* (*History of Ancient Art*), Winckelmann's descriptions of the most famous statuary of classical antiquity have been, in the recent words of Élisabeth Décultot, 'anthology pieces that no man of letters, in Germany or Europe, could afford to ignore.'[2] Indeed, the descriptions' detailed accuracy outdid any previous writings in the field. But the open display of a subjective investment in the statues seems to have been the deciding factor in this quick and lasting popularity, an investment that the reader was invited to replicate through his/her (mostly his) own sympathetic reading.

In a famous remark of his 1765 *Salon*, Diderot, comparing Winckelmann's 'fanatical' efforts to Jean-Jacques Rousseau's, emphasized both writers' emotional density:

> I love fanatics . . . Those are pleasant, they amuse me, sometimes they astonish me. When by chance they have met with truth, their energy in exhibiting it breaks and overthrows everything. Paradoxically accumulating image over image, calling to help all the powers of eloquence, figured expressions, bold comparisons, turns, movements, addressing themselves to sentiment, to imagination, assaulting soul and sensitivity through all sorts of places, the

> spectacle of their efforts still has beauty . . . Such is Winckelmann, when he compares the productions of ancient artists with those of modern artists.[3]

To his audiences, Winckelmann's way of investing ancient statues as a subject, and his ability to communicate this process through writing, became the main engine driving the descriptions and provided them with their superior ability to move.[4] 'What doesn't he see in this trunk of a man we call the Torso?' asks Diderot further, praising Winckelmann's imagination while simultaneously condemning the pre-eminence given by the German author to antiquity as a model for the contemporary production of art.

To investigate the nature of this subjective investment, I would like to walk a different path from those taken by my predecessors in the field. Yes, the power of Winckelmann's descriptions does lie with his investment in the monumental sculptural forms he endeavoured to describe. But, I will contend, this does not happen through the projection of an 'inner self' onto these forms, nor through the reader's empathy supposedly prompted by this gesture – as suggested, on the heels of Diderot, by nineteenth-century art history, and by more recent literature. Rather, this power originates in the very original and new construct of the body provided in Winckelmann's description of the statues.

This construct entails operating on the self, but it does not require the building of a human inner self – even though the self may indeed possess, as we shall see, innermost recesses. I would rather speak, if I may, of 'outer selves,' as I will explain shortly. My argument will concentrate on the literary and critical exercise most prized by Winckelmann's readers, the descriptions of the Belvedere Torso, the most significant, or most 'sublime,' antique sculpture according to him. I will also dwell on his Belvedere Apollo and Laocoon.

Winckelmann's descriptions combine different methods or patterns, either alternately used or blended together. All of them are governed by a constant balancing between what the author termed 'an ideal and poetical idea' and 'a description according to all the lights that art may lend.'[5] To 'description' proper belong the physical description of the artefact, its comparison with other works (both artistic and historical), and finally the identification of its iconography. To the 'poetical idea' belong the multiple encomiums bestowed by the writer on his objects and the description of the effects induced in the viewer by the contemplated piece. These fundamental polarities entail two different concepts of space and surface, both of them at work in the text. But their functions are not quite symmetrical.

The first concept – the material of the artful descriptions – may be called 'extensive space': it is linked to the possibility of measuring extension, of establishing stable outlines and proportions – a series of tasks which, by the way, provides a valid definition of the sculptor's trade, at least in the periods here considered. The surfaces thus obtained will be proportioned, and seen from a distance. Their shape will provide a formal identity for the figure, while guaranteeing the possibility, given a knowledge of context, of recognizing its iconography or *historia.* Just as well, the beauty of its surface will precipitate words of praise, addressed to its formal determinations and to the figuring of the passions they embody.

The use of this extensive concept of space does not stop at the description of the most shapely sculptures, such as the Belvedere Apollo. It also informs Winckelmann's remarks on the 'shapeless' Torso, when, in order to restore its original integrity, he imaginatively replaces the missing parts in the statue: 'The divine character and perfection shine through the form as well as through the sweetness of the powerful muscles of the deified hero. Whoever possesses a concept of the greatness of Greek artists will easily replace in his thoughts the missing parts.'[6] The outline and proportions of this 'ruined' fragment allow for a '*virtual* perception' of the missing limbs, according to a principle of imaginative restoration, which depends for a good part on a knowledge of proportions; that is, on a relationship between extensive parts. But Winckelmann's repeated condemnation of integrations and unacknowledged restorations, his refusal of modern geometrical report techniques in the sculptor's trade, and the meagre role eventually allowed in his description to the extensive consideration of space, all point towards an alternate polarity in his writing, and in his gaze: the consideration of *intensive* spaces and surfaces.[7]

'Intensive space,' or 'place' – *spatium* as opposed to *extensio,* to borrow from Leibniz – may be defined as a field of coexistence involving multiple, heterogeneous entities. Their distribution in that field escapes measurement through rational numbers, and thus cannot be displayed in separate, divided extensions. Entities in intensive space do distinguish themselves from one another by their difference, which allows their ordering.[8] But this ordering never resolves itself in a distribution point by point across extended space. Nor will it ever become mere juxtaposition.

On the contrary, it will dwell, in time, as difference, and thus contrast with immediate, extensive space.

Winckelmann's descriptions progressively shy away from extensive space, somewhat paradoxically given the immediately extensive nature of sculpture.[9] We first spot this movement towards a consideration of the intensive in the *History of Ancient Art*, when, in his description of the statue Laocoon, he associates the superficial play of muscles and skin with inner movements, thoughts, and affects:

> And while pain swells the muscles, the strongly armed mind manifests itself in the distended brow. The chest rises upwards as the breathing is stifled and the outpouring of feeling suppressed so the pain is contained and locked up within. The alarmed sigh, which he draws into himself with his breath, drains the abdomen, hollowing out its sides, at the same time exposing to our view the movement of his entrails . . . Beneath the brow the battle between pain and resistance is fashioned with great wisdom, as if it were brought together at one point: for while pain drives the eyebrows upwards, the flesh on the eyelids is thrust downwards in the struggle against this pain, pressing upon the upper eyelid, so that the latter is almost completely covered by the flesh pushing over it.[10]

The detailed scanning of the priest's figure here describes the play of internal forces which shape its surface. The famous 'noble simplicity and still grandeur' of the works of antiquity once praised in the *Thoughts on Imitation* – and there already indexed to the Laocoon – is thus revealed as a surface effect: the superficial display, frozen in artificial immediacy, of furious forces at work. Strikingly, this description does not revolve around the sense organs of the face: eyes, mouth, nose, ears. Rather, it produces an interplay of invisible forces that fold and unfold the skin, and give the face its peculiar expression, with its irrational mix of pain and melancholy. The fact that pain provides the main engine in this process confirms its intensive nature. Pain cannot be quantified by numbers along an extensive scale. Its only measure is felt intensity, or its mimicry.

While it brings us into intensive territory, this description of the Laocoon remains partly anchored in the organic, functional body. The folds and accidents in the figure's surface expose the workings of internal organs: lungs, entrails – as if pain (along with its counter-movement, the mind's resistance to pain) made the body's surface semi-transparent, allowing us a view of its inner workings. The descriptions of the Torso and Apollo, however, proceed quite differently. Their effort to animate antique sculpted figures blurs their actual shapes. It precipitates the birth of a 'monstrous,' un-organic body, whose characteristics I shall attempt to spell out.

The second published description of the Torso provides a good starting point for this task.[11] After praising the balanced play of muscles in the statue, and the strength it exemplifies, Winckelmann weaves a new analogy:

> Just as in a surging movement of the sea the formerly still surface grows with playful waves, in a gently changing swell, where one will be swallowed by another, and then again rolled out by the same; just so, here a muscle, in soft swelling and tender tension, flows into another, and a third one, which rises in-between them and seems to reinforce their movement, loses itself in them, and our gaze is similarly swallowed in it.[12]

The movement here described – as opposed to the actual stillness of the sculpture – does not belong to the outlines of the human figure displayed by the statue. It animates an impersonal, boundless entity. The illimitable surface of the ocean weaves together a multiplicity of continuous movements, impossible to embrace separately because of their variable speeds, durations, and lengths. Transmogrified into a tumultuous surface, changing and unstable, the sculpture loses definition. It is no longer embraceable by a unified activity of the gaze. The endlessness of its configuration holds perception in check, and ends up swallowing it entirely. Blurring the boundaries that separate who sees from what is seen, writing the sculpture undoes its existence as a 'good image' of an external object.[13]

This un-definition is not an abstraction, nor does it result from a process of abstraction. As such, it differs from the indetermination – *Unbezeichnung* – which Winckelmann elsewhere assigned to ideal beauty as its most essential character.[14] Rather, it signals a resistance, within the sculpted body, to becoming absorbed into mere visibility.

Whereas the proportioned, outlined plastic surface prompted the recognition of formal (and iconographical) identities and favoured imitation through projection at a distance, the new, 'oceanic' surface summoned by writing suppresses any distance between the object and the viewer, and threatens to annihilate the latter's gaze. It engineers a proliferation of transient details, whose divergent intensities and tactility attach an unseen lining to the surface, and never come to roost in an accomplished, static synthesis.[15]

A similar strategy informs the second comparison used by Winckelmann, this time to describe the back of the Torso: that of a landscape of valleys and hills seen from higher up.[16] The change of scale, the serpentine lines of concave and convex shapes, the importance of height and depth, all undo the recognizable outline of the sculpture; they compose instead an impersonal, multiple-scaled, boundless entity. Even contour, an unavoidable feature of stable shapes, now comes through as a meandering line being traced – with no end in sight, and no predictable resolution in a fixed, controlled image.

As inorganic surfaces and aggregates of forces moving at slow, varying speeds, ocean and landscape imply a concept of the body quite different from the one demanded by imitation and by its set of extensive prescriptions. This concept is further characterized in another remark about the Torso: 'No mortal foods and gross morsels feed his living body: what maintains him is the food of gods, and he seems only to enjoy, and not to take; to be full, without being filled out.'[17] Without head, shoulders, breast, arms, or legs (not to mention sex or voice), the Torso is but a ruined, literally dismembered fragment; that is, from an extensive point of view. But this parcelled-out body does not eat or drink, aside from the virtual food provided by the gods. It does not absorb anything external or linked to death. As a consequence, its positive, autonomous mass reveals itself as a 'glorious body.'

This quality becomes especially relevant in the Torso, because of its strikingly fragmented nature, but it also informs Winckelmann's description of the Belvedere Apollo: 'This state of calm, and equally this *enjoyment of self* in which *the senses are gathered inwards and withdrawn from any external object*, permeate the whole stance of this noble figure.'[18] Here too, what the description brings forward is the autonomy of a living body whose invaginated senses have ceased to exchange with the outside world. No longer fed by flows of external information, it is now entirely turned inwards.

It would be tempting to associate once and for all the beautiful surfaces of the Apollo to the enjoyment of self it supposedly embodies and, in a way, actually does embody, but this would require shying away from the uncanny structural resemblance between the calm self-enjoyment displayed in the statue and the painfully extreme tension exhibited by Laocoon's bodily features. In both cases, the superficial animation of outlines becomes but the expressive border of numerous small inner movements, whose composition builds a quiet, balanced core. This core is devoid of any assignable passions: it accommodates Apollo's self-enjoyment just as well as Laocoon's pain and desperation. In his

Thoughts on Imitation, right before the Laocoon's description, Winckelmann stated: 'Just as the depth of the sea remains calm in all circumstances, as wild as the surface may be, so does the expression of the figures of the Greek show, in the midst of all passions, a great and balanced soul.'[19] Is this 'great and balanced soul' to be identified with the conscious individual self? Or does it embrace murkier depths – the very ones explored through the oceanic analogy which runs through nearly all of Winckelmann's description?

While it may sound paradoxical, given the highly defined character of these sculptures, I would like to suggest that the set of practices conceptualized by Gilles Deleuze and Félix Guattari as the 'Body without Organs' provides interesting instruments to explore what is at stake in the reconstructed bodies – especially in that of the Torso – that Winckelmann's descriptions set out to invent. In his *Logic of Sense*, Deleuze, while discussing schizophrenia, had contrasted a 'split,' 'parceled-out,' 'riddled body' with a 'glorious body' which, borrowing from Antonin Artaud, he styled the Body without Organs.[20] Artaud had publicly coined the expression in his famous 1947 radio program 'To Have Done with the Judgement of God,' where he lashed out, in controlled delirium, against the 'Americanization' of bodies and the upcoming reign of ersatz products.[21] There he contrasted the body to an organism that the combined logics of industrial production and war subject to a rigid hierarchy.

Actually, Artaud's Body without Organs does not necessarily lack organs. Rather, it refuses to organize them into a functional whole.[22] Its 'true organs, which must be composed and positioned' resist 'the organic organization of the organs.'[23] Artaud's refusal to 'submit to the Judgement of God' becomes then synonymous with the refusal to obey a mandatory organization of bodies entirely geared towards (re)production by the development of modern capitalism. The Body without Organs is the agent of this protest. Producing it is a complex task, which entails recomposing and relocating organic hierarchies along new, unpredictable intensive lines.[24]

Indeed, organized by the many forces which criss-cross its *spatium* without ever coalescing into stable shapes and point-by-point locations, the Body without Organs may be described as a field of individuation, and its best model is the egg. An egg possesses a surface without salient parts, and in contrast with the omnidirectionality and global symmetry of the sphere, its overall continuity begets inner directions.[25] A surface without holes or breaks, inside which no empty areas are to be found, the egg, busy distributing in its *spatium* the topological differences which will later become organic differences and transform it into a developed animal, feeds upon itself and does not engage in any exchange with the outside world.[26]

Winckelmann's statues possess all the characteristics of the Body without Organs – none of them more so than the Torso. In this lump of stone, the visual shapelessness induced by all the missing parts – shoulders, arms, legs, head, sex – to which one should add the scratches that mar its surface, stands in stark contrast to the dynamic fullness and shining glory nonetheless attributed to the figure by the writer.[27]

Perhaps the very disappearance of the signifiers of a functional, healthy, working body allows for the surge, in its stead, of a new, impersonal and intensive experience of the body, freed from the shackles of functionality and (re)production, and inscribed by writing upon the sculpture's surface for viewers to see it anew. For despite its lack of members this body is filled out and whole. And this wholeness is achieved without the mediation of terrestrial foods; that is, without producing excrements – another staple of the Body without Organs according to Artaud, who contrasts it with an organism not only condemned to dirty exchanges with the world outside, but shamefully eager to enter into them.[28]

Though it exchanges a definite, stable outline for an illimitable, variable surface, this transformed body does not become a mere undifferentiated space but rather a world/egg, whose criss-crossing dynamics, axes, and directions account for its singularity. This development is especially salient in the Laocoon's description already quoted above. There, the forces and counter-forces associated with pain, not satisfied with shaping its manifold surface, sculpt its inner depth. Their interplay reassembles the internal organs. And identifying pain or its contrary remains quite subsidiary here, since the same effects are elsewhere attributed to passions with other names. Indeed, from the divine self-enjoyment of the Apollo to the fear of death (*Todesfurcht*) displayed in Niobe's Daughters, the same unassignable forces are at work, creating variegated mixes of stillness and movement. A flurried surface hovers upon limitless depth and its still recesses, as in the muscles of the Hercules.[29] Or an arrested superficial movement expresses the violent but balanced play of forces which agitate the figure, as in the muscles of the Laocoon. In each case, what matters most is the new body construct now at work: impossible to assign to any specific, extensive locality, it pervades nevertheless the entire set of descriptions.

I would like to suggest that both the independence from any coherent theory of passions manifest in the laying out of this new body construct and its ability to resurface in totally different narratives point towards the dissolution of the self into a heterogeneous and transient set of entities. Because they resist completion into an organic, functional living whole, these entities do not coalesce into a self, just as they do not constitute a space, properly speaking.

After describing the Body without Organs as a 'field of individuation,' Deleuze and Guattari declare: 'The BwO is not space, nor is it in space; it is matter that occupies space to a given degree – to the degree corresponding to the intensities produced . . . [It is] as the full egg before the extension of the organism and the organization of the organs, before the formation of the strata.'[30] Winckelmann's descriptions of the most famous statues of antiquity entail just the same type of regression to an inorganic or preorganic body construct. The undoing of the visual surface and contours in the descriptions thus marks the unmaking of the determinate selves possibly allegorized in the features of the characters represented. Indeed, given the exquisitely detailed contours of the actual sculptures, Winckelmann's endeavour entails both an aggressive and a regressive dimension: *aggressive*, for the transformation of the beautiful outlines of human bodies into impersonal shapeless lumps, oceanic swellings or geological folds, through its reliance on *expression*, undoes the very categories of imitation and beauty which openly inform the project; *regressive*, for this transformation attempts to return the dead white marbles and their ruined surfaces to the once alive beautiful bodies they mimic. And this endeavour entails not so much the imitative craft of statuary as an attempt to replicate the very processes of individuation that inform the living (through their prime engine, desire) and their re-creation in memory.

'The BwO,' write Deleuze and Guattari, 'is the field of immanence of desire, the plane of consistency specific to desire (with desire defined as a process of production without reference to any exterior agency, whether it be a lack that hollows it out or a pleasure that fills it).'[31] Writing marks the place wherein occurs this invasion of plastic imitation by the living forces of a desire now detached from its functional associations with (re) production. Simultaneously reinvented as dead ruins and glorious bodies by the dual tasks of history and memory, the sculptures stop acting as ideally mimetic visual projections of productive, functional bodies. They now offer themselves as a new locus of investigation, demanding to be ceaselessly undone and rebuilt by writing. For this process alone will remake them into an image of the intensive life their viewers long to forge: into a Body without Organs.

As soon as it was published, Winckelmann's work was praised for associating Art with Freedom. Its French reception especially, both before and during the Revolutionary years, was chiefly based on the idea that republican culture, along with temperate climate conditions and a good health regimen, had been the main ingredient in the development of Greek art in classical Athens. We may now recognize a different link between art and freedom. It depends less on the picture of Greek culture provided by the *History* and more on the peculiarities of its 'enthusiastic' descriptions.

This dimension was acknowledged by at least some of Winckelmann's immediate contemporaries, as once more attested by Diderot. Following on the rhetorical question quoted at the beginning of this essay – 'What doesn't he see in this trunk of a man we call the Torso?' – the French author anthologizes the very characteristics, impersonal and un-human, isolated above:

> The muscles which swell on the breast, are nothing less than the undulations of the sea; his large, curved shoulders, a great, concave canopy, which cannot be broken, and instead is fortified by the burdens it is loaded with; and compared to its nerves, the ropes of ancient ballistas, which threw chunks of rock at a great distance, are but spiderweb threads.[32]

What does Diderot see in the description of 'this trunk of a man,' if not the very elements which declare Winckelmann's fanatical new body construct and impersonal outer selves: the floating intensities and unheard-of balance of a Body without Organs?

Indeed, fascinated by an all-pervasive reference to ancient Greece, we may have neglected to assess the ways in which Winckelmann's writing allegorically speaks of the present. Yes, the Torso, the Laocoon, the Apollo, or Niobe function as traces of a destroyed, irretrievable past. But the remaking of their anatomy in the guise of impersonal ocean currents or wavy hills also embodies the resistance to an emerging political and social constraint: the imperative consideration of bodies as functional organisms and individual selves, so as to better enlist them in the specialized tasks of production, reproduction, war, and consumption.

Out of Winckelmann's many readers, it will be left to Schiller to systematically contrast, in his *Letters on the Aesthetic Education of Man* (1795), the whole bodies of the ancient Greeks described by his predecessor with the shrunken and partial individuals begotten by the modern division of labour:

> [The Greek mind] did indeed divide human nature into its several aspects, and project these in magnified form into the divinities of its glorious pantheon; but not by tearing it to pieces; rather by combining its aspects in different proportions, for in no single one of their deities was humanity in its entirety ever lacking. How different with us Moderns! With us too the image of the human species is projected in magnified form into separate individuals – but as fragments, not in different combinations, with the result that one has to go the rounds from one individual to another in order to be able to piece together a complete image of the species. With us, one might almost be tempted to assert, the various faculties appear as separate in practice as they are merely distinguished by the psychologist in theory, and we see not merely individuals, but whole classes of men, developing but one part of their potentialities, while of the rest, as in stunted growths, only vestigial traces remain.[33]

Schiller's contrast between the glorious bodies of the ancient Greeks and the fragmented, shrunk individuals that characterize modern societies leaves the restricted terrain of art in which Winckelmann still dwelled for that of an 'Art of Living' (*Lebenskunst*) where the relationships between beauty, freedom, and politics are now made explicit.[34] But we may already hear, voiced in the descriptions of Winckelmann's *Thoughts* or, later on, of his *History*, and embedded in the impersonal outer selves that writing wrings from the ruined monuments of ancient statuary, a faltering protest against the demands that modernity is about to make on the living bodies of human beings.

NOTES

1 Johann-Joachim Winckelmann, 'Erinnerung über die Betrachtung der Werke der Kunst,' in *Kleine Schriften. Vorreden. Entwürfe*, ed. Walter Rehm (Berlin, 1968), 151: 'Der höchste Vorwurf der Kunst für denkende Menschen ist der Mensch, oder nur dessen äussere Fläche, und diese ist für den Künstler so schwer auszuforschen, wie von den Weisen das Inneredesselben'; my translation.

2 See Élisabeth Décultot, 'Winckelmann et l'art de la description,' intro. to Johann-Joachim Winckelmann, *De la description*, trans. Élisabeth Décultot (Paris, 2006), 6.

3 Diderot, 'Sculpture,' in *Salon de 1765*, ed. Else-Marie Bukdahl and Annette Lorenceau (Paris, 1984), 277: 'J'aime les fanatiques, . . . Ils sont plaisants

ceux-ci, ils m'amusent, ils m'étonnent quelquefois. Quand par hasard ils ont rencontré la vérité, ils l'exposent avec une énergie qui brise et renverse tout. Dans le paradoxe, accumulant images sur images, appelant à leur secours toutes les puissances de l'éloquence, les expressions figurées, les comparaisons hardies, les tours, les mouvements, s'adressant au sentiment, à l'imagination, attaquant l'âme et sa sensibilité par toutes sortes d'endroits, le spectacle de leurs efforts est encore beau . . . Tel est Winckelman [*sic*] lorsqu'il compare les productions des artistes anciens et celles des artistes modernes'; my translation.

4 These first publications did not feature any image of the statues described in writing. Only some rare details pertaining to technical discussions were engraved in the volumes.

5 Letter to G.L. Bianconi (in French), 25 September 1756, quoted in Décultot, 'Winckelmann,' 17: 'Je donne de chacune [des statues du Belvédère]: / 1. Une idée idéale et poétique dans un stile [*sic*] élevé. / II. Une description selon tout ce que l'art peut preter [*sic*] de lumières.'

6 Winckelmann, 'Entwürfe zur Beschreibung des Torso im Belvedere im Florentiner Manuskript,' in *Kleine Schriften*, 281: 'Die Gottheit und Vollkommenheit erscheinet so wohl durch die Form als Zärtlichkeit der mächtigen Muskeln des vergötterten Helden. Derjenige so einen Begrif von der Grossheit der Griechischen Künstler hat, wird in seinen Gedanken leicht die verlohrnen Theile ersetzen.'

7 See Winckelmann, 'Gedanken über die Nachahmung der Griechischen Werke in der Malerey und Bildhauerkunst' (1755), in *Kleine Schriften*, 48. See also 'On the Imitation of the Painting and Sculpture of the Greeks,' in *Winckelmann: Writings on Art*, ed. David Irwin (London, New York, 1972), 61–85.

8 'Spatium est ordo coexistendi' (Place is the order of coexistence), writes Leibniz in his *Nouveaux essais sur l'entendement humain* (Paris, 1966 [1765]), bk. 2, chap. 23, 189.

9 A comparison between the different manuscripts and published versions provides significant information in that regard. See Winckelmann, *Description*, 169–73, and *Kleine Schriften*, 267–85. The greater proportion shifts in time from 'extensive' to 'intensive' remarks.

10 Winckelmann, 'Geschichte der Kunst des Altertums' (1764), 348–9, quoted in Alex Potts, *Flesh and the Ideal: Winckelmann and the Origins of Art History* (New Haven, 1994), 137, 142: 'Und indem sein Leiden die Muskeln aufschwellet, und die Nerven anziehet, tritt der mit Stärke bewaffnete Geist in der aufgetriebenen Stirne hervor, und die Brust erhebet sich durch den

beklemmten Othem, und durch Zurückhaltung des Ausbruchs der Empfindung, um den Schmerz in sich zu fassen und zu verschliessen. Das bange Seufzen, welches er in sich, und den Othem an sich zieht, erschöpfet den Unterleib, und machet die Seiten hohl, welches uns gleichsam von der Bewegung seiner Eingeweide urtheilen lässt . . . Unter der Stirn ist der Streit zwischen Schmerz und Widerstand, wie in einem Punkte vereiniget, mit grosser Weisheit gebildet: denn indem der Schmerz die Augenbrauen in die Höhe treibet, so drücket das Sträuben wider denselben das obere Augenfleisch niederwerts, und gegen das obere Augenlied zu, so dass dasselbe durch das übergetretene Fleisch beynahe ganz bedeckt wird.'

11 It was published in 1759 in the 'critical review' *Bibliothek der schönen Wissenschaften und der freyen Künste.* See also Winckelmann, 'Beschreibung des Torso im Belvedere zu Rom,' in *Kleine Schriften*, 169–73.

12 Ibid., 171: 'So wie in einer anhebenden Bewegung des Meers die zuvor stille Fläche in einer lieblichen Unruhe mit spielenden Wellen anwächset, wo eine von der andern verschlungen, und aus derselben wiederum hervorgewälzet wird: eben so sanft aufgeschwellet und schwebend gezogen, fliesset hier eine Muskel in die andre, und eine dritte, die sich zwischen ihnen erhebet, und ihre Bewegung zu verstärken scheinet, verlieret sich in jene, und unser Blick wird gleichsam mit verschlungen.'

13 Ibid.: 'Hier möchte ich stille stehen, um unsern Betrachtungen Raum zu geben, der Vorstellung ein immerwährendes Bild von dieser Seite einzudrücken: allein die hohen Schönheiten sind hier ohne Grenzen, und in einer unzertrennlichen Mittheilung' (I would like to hold still, in order to give space to our contemplations, and impress upon an ever present image of this side; but these high beauties are here without limits, and in an indestructible communication); my translation.

14 Winckelmann writes: 'From unity derives another characteristic of high beauty, its lack of definition [*Unbezeichnung*], that is, it cannot describe either forms or points, except those alone that constitute beauty; consequently, it is an image that is peculiar neither to this nor that particular person, nor expressive of any state of mind or movement or feeling, for this would mix alien traits with beauty and disturb its unity' [Aus der Einheit folget eine andere Eigenschaft der hohen Schönheit, die Unbezeichnung derselben, das ist, deren Formen weder durch Puncte, noch durch Linien, beschrieben werden, als die allein Schönheit bilden; folglich eine Gestalt, die weder dieser oder jener bestimmten Person eigen sey, noch irgend einen Zustand des Gemüths oder eine Empfindung der Leidenschaft ausdrücke, als welche fremde Züge in die Schönheit mischen, und die Einheit

unterbrechen]; Winckelmann, *Geschichte,* 150, quoted in Potts, *Flesh,* 170. Indetermination (*Unbezeichnung*) here becomes the paradoxical existence of form, once stripped of any individual *extensive* determination.

15 On the tactile nature of this approach, see Apollo's description in the *History of Ancient Art*: his muscles are 'more apparent to Touch than to Sight' [und werden mehr dem Gefühle, als dem Gesichte, offenbar], in Winckelmann, *Geschichte,* 164. The relationship between these two modes of apprehension – visual/distant and tactile/close – as well as their relationship to unity is declared in another passage from the *History*: 'A beautiful youthful figure is fashioned from forms like the uniform expanse of the sea, which from a distance appears flat and still, like a mirror, though it is constantly in motion and rolls in waves' [Ein schönes jugendliches Gewächs aus solchen Formen gebildet ist, wie die einheit der Fläche des Meers, welche in einiger Weite eben und stille, wie ein Spiegel, erscheinet, ob es gleich allezeit in Bewegung ist, und Wogen wälzet]; *Geschichte,* 152–3, quoted in Potts, *Flesh,* 170.

16 Winckelmann's description of the Laocoon in the *History* also employs the same image: 'and they [Laocoon's muscles]lie like hills which grasp one another, so as to express the supreme effort of forces in pain and resistance' [und sie liegen wie Hügel, welche sich in einander schliessen, und die höchste Anstrengung der Kräfte im Leiden und Widerstreben auszudrücken]; *Geschichte,* 163, partially quoted in Potts, *Flesh,* 171.

17 Winckelmann, 'Beschreibung,' 173.

18 Winckelmann, *Geschichte,* 409, quoted in Potts, *Flesh,* 150, italics mine: 'In dieser Ruhe, und gleichsam *in dem Genusse seiner* selbst, mit gesammelten und von allen äussern Vorwürfen zurückgerufenen Sinnen, ist der ganze Stand dieser edlen Figur gesetzet.'

19 Winckelmann, 'Gedanken,' 43: 'So wie die Tiefe des Meers allezeit ruhig bleibt, die Oberfläche mag noch so wüten, eben so zeiget der Ausdruck in den Figuren der Griechen bei allen Leidenschaften eine grosse und gesetzte Seele.'

20 Gilles Deleuze, *The Logic of Sense* (London, 2004), 101.

21 See Antonin Artaud, 'To Have Done with the Judgement of God,' in *Selected Writings,* ed. Susan Sontag (Berkeley, 1988). A streaming audio recording of the original radio program is available on UbuWeb, at http://www.ubu.com/sound/artaud.html.

22 See Gilles Deleuze and Félix Guattari, 'November 28, 1947: How Do You Make Yourself a Body without Organs?' in *A Thousand Plateaus,* trans. Brian Massumi (London, 2004), 182: 'It is not at all a question of a fragmented, splintered body, of organs without the body (OwB). The BwO is exactly the opposite. There are not organs in the sense of fragments in relation to a lost

unity, nor is there a return to the undifferentiated in relation to a differentiable totality. There is a distribution of intensive principles of organs, with their positive indefinite articles, within a collectivity or multiplicity, inside an assemblage, and according to machinic connections operating on a BwO.'

23 Ibid., 176, my italics.

24 Ibid., 182: 'The organs distribute themselves on the BwO, but they distribute themselves independently of the form of the organism; forms become contingent, organs are no longer anything more than intensities that are produced, flows, thresholds, and gradients.'

25 In *Erinnerung über die Betrachtung der Werke der Kunst*, Winckelmann privileges elliptical against spherical shapes. He writes that 'the line which describes beauty is elliptical, and it is in itself the Simple, and a perpetual change; for it cannot be described by any circle and its direction changes at every point' [Die Linie, die das Schöne beschreibet, ist elliptisch, und in derselben ist das Einfache und eine beständige Veränderung: denn sie kann mit keinem Zirkel beschrieben werden and verändert in allen Puncten ihre Richtung]. Winckelmann, 'Erinnerung,' 152.

26 Deleuze and Guattari, 'November 28, 1947,' 181–2: 'The BwO is the egg. But the egg is not regressive; on the contrary, it is perfectly contemporary, you always carry it with you as your own milieu of experimentation, your associated milieu. The egg is the milieu of pure intensity, spatium not extensio. Zero intensity as principle of production. There is a fundamental convergence between science and myth, embryology and mythology, the biological egg and the psychic or cosmic egg: the egg always designates this intensive reality, which is not undifferentiated, but is where things and organs are distinguished solely by gradients, migrations, zones of proximity. The egg is the BwO. The BwO is not "before" the organism; it is adjacent to it and is continually in the process of constructing itself.'

27 See Artaud's statement of his project: 'No mouth No tongue No teeth No larynx No esophagus No stomach No belly No anus I will reconstruct the man I am.' The quotation is from Artaud, *84, 1948*, in Deleuze, *Logic*, 108.

28 Artaud, 'To Have Done with the Judgement of God,' pt. 5, 'The Pursuit of Fecality,' in *Selected Writings*: 'Là où ça sent la merde, ça sent l'être. L'homme aurait très bien pu ne pas chier, ne pas ouvrir la poche anale, mais il a choisi de chier comme il aurait choisi de vivre au lieu de consentir à vivre mort' (There where it smells of shit, it smells of being. Man could just as well not have shat, not have opened the anal pouch, but he chose to shit as he would have chosen to live instead of consenting to live dead).

29 Winckelmann, *Geschichte*, 163–4: 'In dem Rumpfe des vergötterten Hercules ist in eben diesen Muskeln eine hohe idealische Form und Schönheit; aber

sie sind wie das Wallen des ruhigen Meeres, fliessend erhaben, und in einer sanften abwechselnden Schwebung. Im Apollo, dem Bilde der schönsten Gottheit, sind diese Muskeln gelinde, und wie ein geschmolzen Glas in kaum sichtbare Wellen geblasen, und werden mehr dem Gefühle als dem Gesichte offenbar' (In the trunk of the deified Hercules, there is in these very muscles a highly ideal form and beauty; but they are like the swaying of the calm sea, flowing majestically, in a gentle alternating beat. In Apollo, the image of the most beautiful godhead, the muscles are soft, like molten glass blown in barely visible waves, and more apparent to touch than to sight).

30 Deleuze and Guattari, 'November 28, 1947,' 169–70.

31 For undoing an image requires a specific image, or type of images. See Gilles Deleuze, *Difference and Repetition*, trans. Paul Patton (New York, 1994), 240: 'Difference pursues its subterranean life while its image reflected on the surface is scattered. Moreover, it is in the nature of that image, but only that image, to be scattered, just as it is in the nature of the surface to cancel difference, but only on the surface.'

32 Diderot, *Salon*, 277–8.

33 Friedrich Schiller, *On the Aesthetic Education of Man: In a Series of Letters*, ed. and trans. E.M. Wilkinson and L.A. Willoughby (Oxford, 1982), Letter 6, pp. 31–3. The German original text is: '[Die Griesche Vernunft] zerlegte zwar die menschliche Natur und warf sie in ihrem herrlichen Götterkreis vergrössert auseinander, aber nicht dadurch, dass sie in Stücken riss, sondern dadurch, dass sie verschiendentlich mischte, denn die ganze Menschheit fehlte in keinem einzelnen Gott. Wie ganz anders bei uns Neuern! Auch bei uns ist das Bild der Gattung in den Individuen vergrössert auseinander geworfen – aber in Bruchstücken, nicht in veränderten Mischungen, dass man von Individuum zu Individuum herumfragen muss, um die Totalität der Gattung zusammenzulesen. Bei uns, möchte man fast versucht werden zu behaupten, äussern sich die Gemütskräfte auch in der Erfahrung so getrennt, wie der Psychologe sie in der Vorstellung scheidet, und wir sehen nicht bloss einzelne Subjekte, sondern ganze Klassen von Menschen nur einen Teil ihrer Anlagen entfalten, während dass die übrigen, wie bei verkrüppelten Gewächsen, kaum mit matter Spur angedeutet sind.'

34 Ibid., Letter 15, 108–9.

Contributors

Gadi Algazi, Professor of History at the Department of History, Tel Aviv University, is also the senior editor of *History and Memory* and a member of the editorial board of *Past and Present.* His fields of interest are historical anthropology, social and cultural history of late medieval western Europe, and history and theory of the social sciences. His current research project deals with the making of scholars' habitus in the fifteenth and sixteenth centuries and the shaping of their family households. He is currently preparing a book manuscript, provisionally entitled 'Nowhere Men: Shaping a Scholarly Way of Life, 1450–1630.' Recent publications include *Negotiating the Gift: Pre-Modern Figurations of Exchange,* co-edited with Valentin Groebner and Bernhard Jussen (Göttingen, 2003); 'Scholars in Households: Refiguring the Learned Habitus, 1480–1550,' *Science in Context* 16 (2003), 9–42; and 'Norbert Elias's Motion Pictures: History, Cinema and Gestures in the Process of Civilization,' *Studies in History and Philosophy of Science* 39 (2008), 444–58.

Jean-Philippe Antoine is Professor of Contemporary Art History and Theory at Université Paris VIII. His recent book publications include *La traversée du XXe siècle: Joseph Beuys, image et souvenir* (forthcoming, 2011) and *Marcel Broodthaers: Moule, Muse, Méduse* (Dijon, 2006). The turn taken by the relationship between memory, words, and images in and after modernity has led him to investigate its prehistory in late eighteenth- and early nineteenth-century art and thought. He is currently researching Samuel F.B. Morse's multiple careers as a painter, art theoretician, photographer, and inventor of the Morse code and electric telegraph.

Andreas Bähr is Private Lecturer [Privatdozent] at the Department of History and Cultural Studies, Freie Universität Berlin. He has published *Der Richter im Ich. Die Semantik der Selbsttötung in der Aufklärung* (Göttingen, 2002); 'Furcht, divinatorischer Traum und autobiographisches Schreiben in der Frühen Neuzeit,' in *Zeitschrift für Historische Forschung* 34 (2007), 1–32; and 'Die Furcht der Frühen Neuzeit: Paradigmen, Hintergründe und Perspektiven einer Kontroverse,' *Historische Anthropologie* 16 (2008), 291–309; and has edited a theme issue in *WerkstattGeschichte* 49 (2008). His current book, *Fear and Fearlessness: Divine Violence and Self-Constitution in the 17th Century*, is expected to be published in Spring 2012.

Robert Batchelor studies interactions between East Asia and Europe in the early modern period, with a particular focus on media of exchange and the history of translation. He has published several articles and book chapters and currently has a book manuscript under review, entitled 'London: The Making of a Global City, 1549–1687.' He is Associate Professor of History at Georgia Southern University.

Déborah Blocker, born in New York and educated in France, was a fellow at the École Normale Supérieure and earned her PhD in French literature and civilization from the University of Paris III (Sorbonne Nouvelle). Currently Associate Professor of French at the University of California, Berkeley, she specializes in the social and political history of literary practices in early modern Europe, with a particular interest in theatre and in aesthetics. Her book *Instituer un 'art': Politiques de la littérature dans la France du premier XVIIe siècle* (Paris, 2009) tracks the social mechanisms of instituting early modern French theatre as an art (1630–60). This project led to a broader interest in discourses on poetry and the arts in early modern Europe (1500–1800). As the 2010–11 Florence J. Gould Fellow at the Villa I Tatti, the Harvard University Center for Italian Renaissance Studies, she researched the social and political circumstances in which new conceptions of 'art' emerged in Renaissance Florence, through an archival study of the Accademia degli Alterati (ca. 1570–1620).

Tom Conley, Abbott Lawrence Lowell Professor of French at Harvard University, recently published *An Errant Eye: Poetry and Topography in Early Modern France* (Minneapolis, 2010), a sequel to *The Self-Made Map: Cartographic Writing in Early Modern France*, re-ed. (Minneapolis, 2010). He is author of *L'inconscient graphique: Essai sur la lettre à la Renaissance* (2000) and translator of works by Marc Augé, Michel de Certeau, Christian Jacob, Gilles Deleuze, and others. His work in film studies includes *Film Hieroglyphs*, re-ed. with a new intro. (Minneapolis, 2006) and *Cartographic Cinema* (Minneapolis, 2007).

Robert Dimit is Associate Director of the John W. Draper Program at New York University's Graduate School of Arts and Science, where he teaches courses on European literature and philosophy. He has published articles on rhetoric and the passions in early modern Europe and is preparing a book manuscript entitled 'The Natural Language of the Passions: Rhetoric and Affect in French and English Theater, 1660–1690.'

Frédéric Gabriel is a researcher at the CNRS (French National Center for Scientific Research, Historical Institute of Early Modern Thought, Lyon). He works on the history of theological texts in the sixteenth and seventeenth centuries and is currently coordinating a complete edition of the works of Gabriel Naudé, to be published by Éditions Classiques Garnier. His recent publications include 'Roi mineur et naissance de la majesté dans les discours auliques: Une raison d'État encomiastique,' *Revue de Synthèse* 130, 2 (2009), 233–65; 'Periegesis and Scepticism: La Peyrère Geographer,' in J.R. Maia Neto, G. Paganini, and J. Ch. Laursen, eds, *Skepticism in the Modern Age: Building on the Work of Richard Popkin* (Leiden, 2009), 159–70. He may be contacted at http://www.fredericgabriel.ovh.org.

Erec R. Koch is Head and Professor of French, Department of Modern Foreign Languages and Literatures, University of Tennessee-Knoxville. A specialist in French literature and culture of the seventeenth century, Professor Koch's most recent book is entitled *The Aesthetic Body: Passion, Sensibility, and Corporeality in Seventeenth-Century France* (Newark, DE, 2008). He has also published extensively on Pascal, Nicole, Racinian and Cornelian tragedy, polemics of rhetoric and painting, subjectivities, Cartesian ethics, and political theory. He is currently preparing a study focusing on theories of taste and art before the development of modern aesthetics.

David Packwood is Lecturer in Art History and Art Theory at Warwick University, UK. He has published various reviews and articles including 'Poussin and the Archaeology of Knowledge' (2003), 'Caravaggio: A

Brush with Death' (2005), and 'Rembrandt: Art and Money' (2008). He has a chapter, 'Dream Perspectives,' on Damisch, psychoanalysis, and Renaissance art, in press for a reader in French visual theory. He recently participated in a symposium entitled 'Baroque Anatomy' in Los Angeles, and is currently developing articles from that on anatomical drawing and self-reflexivity in Pietro da Cortona. He is also working on a book, 'Poussin's Testament: Painting and Inheritance Strategies in Seventeenth-Century Rome.'

David Warren Sabean is Henry J. Bruman Professor of German History at the University of California, Los Angeles. A graduate of the University of Wisconsin, where he studied under George Mosse, Sabean has taught at the University of East Anglia, University of Pittsburgh, and Cornell University, and has been a fellow at the Max Planck Institut für Geschichte in Göttingen, the Maison des Sciences de l'Homme, the Wissenschaftskolleg zu Berlin, the American Academy in Berlin, the National Humanities Center, and the International Research Center for Cultural Studies in Vienna. He received an Alexander von Humboldt Foundation Research Prize and is a fellow of the American Academy of Arts and Sciences. His publications include *Power in the Blood: Popular Culture and Village Discourse in Early Modern Germany* (Cambridge, 1984); *Property, Production, and Family in Neckarhausen, 1700–1870* (Cambridge, 1990); and *Kinship in Neckarhausen, 1700–1870* (Cambridge, 1998). He is co-editor with Simon Teuscher and Jon Mathieu of *Kinship in Europe: Approaches to Long-Term Development (1300–1900)* (New York and Oxford, 2007). Currently, he is engaged in an extensive study on the history of incest and other fields of European cultural history.

David S. Shields is McClintock Professor of Southern Letters in the English and History Departments at the University of South Carolina. From 1999 to 2008 he edited the journal *Early American Literature.* Recent titles include *Material Culture in Anglo-America* (Columbia, SC, 2009) and *Pioneering American Wine* (Athens, GA, 2009). He edited the landmark Library of American anthology *American Poetry: The Seventeenth and Eighteenth Centuries* (New York, 2007) and has published extensively about sociability and the institutions of literary production, including *Civil Tongues and Polite Letters in British America* (Chapel Hill, NC, 1997) and the portrait of eighteenth-century literary culture contained in volume 1 of *A History of the Book in America.* Forthcoming works include a history of photography and American silent cinema, and one of nineteenth-century

American cuisine considered from the viewpoint of the changing practices of agriculture.

Malina Stefanovska is Professor and Chair of the Department of French and Francophone Studies at the University of California, Los Angeles. She has published *La politique du cardinal de Retz: Factions et passions* (Rennes, 2008), and *Saint-Simon, un historien dans les marges* (Paris, 1998), as well as articles on French seventeenth-century memoirs, conspiracy tragedies, historiography, and non-fictional prose genres. Her recent publications include 'Cardinal De Retz's *Memoirs*: Encountering Fortune and Taking Timely Steps,' in John Lyons and Kathleen Wine, eds, *Chance, Literature, and Culture in Early Modern France* (London, 2009) and 'Exemplary or Singular? The Anecdote in Historical Narrative,' *Sub/Stance* 38, 1 (2009). She is currently working on *Fictions of Factions: Writing the Social Bond in Early Modern French Memoirs.*

Michael Taormina is Assistant Professor of French in the Department of Romance Languages at Hunter College of the City University of New York. His research focuses on the intersection of eloquence and lyric poetry and examines the socio-political role played by poets as members of noble patronage networks in early seventeenth-century France. He has published articles on Malherbe, Théophile de Viau, and Voiture and is currently writing his first book, 'The Dangerous Art of Rhyme: Virtue and Ethos in Early Seventeenth-Century Lyric Poetry.' He is also the translator of Deleuze's posthumously collected essays and interviews, *Desert Islands and Other Texts: 1953–1974.*

Anne C. Vila is Professor of French at the University of Wisconsin-Madison. She is the author of *Enlightenment and Pathology: Sensibility in the Literature and Medicine of Eighteenth-Century France* (Baltimore, MD, 1998) and is currently completing a book entitled 'Singular Beings: Passions and Pathologies of the Scholar in France, 1700–1840.' She is also co-editing (with Alexandre Wenger) a re-edition of Samuel-Auguste Tissot, *Oeuvres*, for Éditions Classiques Garnier. Her research interests revolve largely around the interrelations of literature and medicine, the history of the body, and the literature and culture of eighteenth- and early nineteenth-century France.

Lee Palmer Wandel is Professor of History, Religious Studies, and Visual Culture at the University of Wisconsin, Madison. She is the author of

Always among Us: Images of the Poor in Zwingli's Zurich (Cambridge and New York, 1990); *Voracious Idols and Violent Hands: Iconoclasm in Reformation Zurich, Strasbourg, and Basel* (Cambridge and New York, 1995); and *The Eucharist in the Reformation: Incarnation and Liturgy* (Cambridge and New York, 2006). Currently she has completed *The Reformation: Towards a New History*, forthcoming in 2011 (Cambridge) and is working on 'Catechisms and the Construction of Religion in the Reformation.'

Christopher Wild is Associate Professor of Germanic Studies as well as Theater and Performance Studies at the University of Chicago. He is the author of *Theater der Keuschheit – Keuschheit des Theaters. Eine Geschichte der (Anti-)Theatralität von Gryphius bis Kleist* [Theatre of Chastity – Chastity of Theatre. A History of (Anti-)Theatricality from Gryphius to Kleist] (2003), and numerous articles on early modern theatrical culture. Currently, he is pursuing two book projects: one, co-authored with Juliane Vogel, on entrances and exits in European theatre; and another that asks the seemingly simple question why Descartes's founding text of modern philosophy was titled *Meditations on First Philosophy*, in order to take its generic affiliation seriously. In 2009–10 he co-organized (with Ulrike Strasser) the core program of the Center for Seventeenth- and Eighteenth-Century Studies at UCLA entitled 'Cultures of Communication, Theologies of Media in Early Modern Europe and Beyond.'

Index

www.ingramcontent.com/pod-product-compliance
Lightning Source LLC
LaVergne TN
LVHW040153080826
844660LV00014B/943/J

* 9 7 8 1 4 4 2 6 4 3 9 4 9 *